'In this trenchant analysis of Europe's recent economic experience, Hans-Werner Sinn conducts a post-mortem for the Euro as an ambitious political gambit that has failed to overcome bad incentives and missing institutions. His forensic investigation uncovers staggering fiscal commitments that have been made through the conduct of monetary policy and without the explicit recognition or approval of those on whom the burdens will fall. Sinn issues a call to action, making a compelling case that the most important obstacle on the path to European stability and prosperity is a system that is illogical and unsustainable. This excellent book virtually compels a response from those who would substitute hope for facts in their defense of the Euro and its prospects.'

Alan J. Auerbach, Professor of Economics and Law, University of California, Berkeley

'Hans-Werner Sinn has written an exceptional book on the euro crisis—rich in substance and yet understandable for the layman. It is to be hoped that it not only will be read, but taken to heart by politicians.'

Ernst Baltensperger, Professor Emeritus of Macroeconomics, University of Bern

'Hans-Werner Sinn offers an outstandingly clear overview of the perils posed by excessive sovereign debt and by the divergence in competitiveness across the EU. The steep increase in the credit that the southern countries have received from the ECB and the corresponding risk brought upon the assets of the stable members are rightly emphasised.'

Peter Bernholz, Professor Emeritus of Public Finance, University of Basel

'Hans-Werner Sinn has emerged as the most prolific and profound economist in Germany, writing on the euro and indeed much else. This book is a tour de force.'

Jagdish N. Bhagwati, Professor of Economics, Law and International Affairs, Columbia University, and author of *In Defense of Globalization*

'I was riveted. With this book, Sinn has finally written his masterpiece. It is so well written that even non-economists can easily understand it. It jolts you up without ever veering into hyperbole.'

Friedrich Breyer, Professor of Economics and Public Policy, University of Konstanz

'Professor Sinn has again enlightened and provoked us, and offered strong policy medicine. In his view, the southern tier should temporarily exit the Eurozone, devalue, and establish fiscal order with clear financial and public balance sheets, hence regaining competitiveness. A 'new' EU—restructured as a federal state with a US-type financial system, tight fiscal constraints on the states, a new 'target balance' settlement system, and interregionally-neutral monetary policy—would then welcome them back on new terms. This model is contrasted with Sinn's view of existing policy—forced huge north-to-south capital transfers ('debt mutualization') and a printing-press central *bank—which he believes has resulted in recurrent bubbles, the acceptance of southern tier non-competitiveness, and a history of 'stumbling from crisis to crisis'. Sinn lays out all of the relevant issues, and in the process teaches us how Europe got into this pickle. Complex puzzles are solved, myths exposed, and the arcane explained in non-technical terms. While others will surely disagree with this analytical and historical perspective, they must now deal with Sinn's clear delineation of the relevant issues and explain how they weight and interpret these issues differently. All readers will gain perspective and learn much from Sinn's timely effort. The book is a 'must-read' for all who are interested in thinking through the web of difficult questions now facing Europe; I highly recommend it.'*

Robert Haveman, Professor Emeritus of Economics and Public Affairs, University of Wisconsin-Madison

'Hans-Werner Sinn is a master at presenting research findings understandably and yet accurately to a wider readership. An important book!'

Stefan Homburg, Professor of Public Finance, University of Hannover

'In his masterly analysis Hans-Werner Sinn unravels the tangled tale of the Euro crisis with remarkable patience, wisdom and clarity. His painstaking analysis makes it clear that the Eurosystem is unsustainable without major reforms, and his bold recommendations for how to carry out those reforms deserve to be taken seriously by everyone.'

Peter W. Howitt, Professor Emeritus of Social Sciences, Brown University

'Hans-Werner Sinn once again brilliantly manages to explain complex interactions in easily understandable terms to deliver an important message.'

Otmar Issing, Professor of Economics, Money and International Economic Relations, University of Frankfurt, and former ECB Chief Economist

'Sinn offers a sobering look back combined with a realistic list of options going forward. A 'must-read' for anyone who wants to know where Europe is headed and what it would take to save the euro.'

Anil K. Kashyap, Professor of Economics and Finance, University of Chicago

'Sinn's forthright acceptance that those who opposed Germany's adoption of the Euro were right after all, sets the tough-minded and honest tone of this provocative book, which offers penetrating analysis of what went wrong—and right—with the system as well as how—and how not—it might be repaired. It is required reading for all who worry about Europe's future.'

David Laidler, Professor Emeritus of Economics, University of Western Ontario

The Euro Trap

THE EURO TRAP

ON BURSTING BUBBLES, BUDGETS, AND BELIEFS

HANS-WERNER SINN

OXFORD
UNIVERSITY PRESS

OXFORD

UNIVERSITY PRESS

Great Clarendon Street, Oxford, ox2 6DP,
United Kingdom

Oxford University Press is a department of the University of Oxford.
It furthers the University's objective of excellence in research, scholarship,
and education by publishing worldwide. Oxford is a registered trade mark of
Oxford University Press in the UK and in certain other countries

Published in the United States of America by Oxford University Press
198 Madison Avenue, New York, NY 10016, United States of America

British Library Cataloguing in Publication Data

Data available

Library of Congress Cataloging in Publication Data

Data available

ISBN 978–0–19–870213–9 (Hbk.)
ISBN 978–0–19–879144–7 (Pbk.)

For
Meinhard Knoche

ACKNOWLEDGEMENTS

This book began as a translation by Julio Saavedra of my German book *Die Target-Falle*, which was published in 2012 by Carl Hanser Verlag, Munich. While the translation of the original German text was excellent, my reworking of the English manuscript changed the structure of the book entirely. So a new book emerged. The English text has also been updated to include new policy topics that have come up since the German original went to press and addresses a wider audience with different interests. After the refereeing processes, the book's figures were updated a second time, most of them including now the full year 2013.

I received skilled technical support from various people, above all Wolfgang Meister who helped with the statistics, Christoph Zeiner who constructed the graphs, and Julio Saavedra who edited the manuscript. Anja Rohwer, Jakob Eberl, and Christopher Weber helped me to research the literature and performed various technical tasks. Lisa Giani Contini, Paul Kremmel, Heidi Sherman, and Justin Tumlinson helped check my English. Jennifer Hinchliffe converted the manuscript into OUP's format. I am very grateful for their careful assistance.

Jürgen Stark, Christoph Trebesch, and Timo Wollmershäuser read the entire manuscript and gave useful comments. I also received helpful remarks on parts of the book by Philippine Cour-Thimann, Anil Kashyap, Harold James, David Laidler, and Frank Westermann. I thank them all, as well many others who allowed me to draw from their wisdom, including Giuseppe Bertola, Beat Blankart, Michael Burda, Kai Carstensen, Giancarlo Corsetti, Paul De Grauwe, John Driffill, Achim Dübel, Klaus Engelen, Udo di Fabio, Martin Feldstein, Carl-Ludwig Holtfrerich, Otmar Issing, Wilhelm Kohler, Kai Konrad, William Levine, Georg Milbradt, Dietrich Murswiek, Manfred J. M. Neumann, Bernd Rudolph, Jan Scheithauer, Helmut Schlesinger, Gerlinde Sinn, Jan-Egbert Sturm, Jens Ulbrich, Akos Valentinyi, Xavier Vives, and Andreas Worms. Finally, I would like to thank three anonymous referees consulted by the publisher for their useful comments and those who, after reading the book, gave OUP the right to publish their endorsements.

Munich, February 2014

CONTENTS

LIST OF FIGURES

LIST OF TABLES

The Euro Crisis

The European Union has freed Europeans from the yoke of nationalism and greatly contributed to freedom and prosperity in the continent. Its stability lies in the voluntary, mutually advantageous cohesion of its peoples. This stability, however, is being threatened by the euro crisis, which has given rise to a great deal of contention and resentment between these peoples and has resurrected many old ghosts that had long since been presumed dead and buried. As great as the beneficial effect of the European Union is, just as destructive has been the impact of the common currency on the cohesion of Europe.

Twenty years ago Europe was brimming with euro enthusiasts, and I was one of them, unable to understand, or unwilling to hear, the warning voices of older and more experienced economists. Back then Europe seemed to have arrived at a stage in its history where a common currency was a logical step towards preserving peace and promoting greater prosperity on the Old Continent. Sadly, those high hopes have been brutally dashed. Today the Eurozone is a shambles, staggering from one crisis to the next. Whilst southern Europe is caught in a relentless trap of ruined competitiveness, the northern countries find themselves caught in an unprecedented spiral of rising public debt and liabilities. Only a masochist could continue to welcome the decision to introduce the euro, writes Martin Wolf, of the *Financial Times*.[1] The Dutch ex-EU commissioner Frits Bolkestein, one of the architects of the EU, has argued that the euro project is doomed and that his country should exit the European Monetary Union.[2]

---

[1] See M. Wolf, 'Why the Euro Crisis Is Not Yet Over', *Financial Times*, 19 February 2013, available at: <http://www.ft.com/intl/cms/s/0/74acaf5c-79f2-11e2-9dad-00144feabdc0.html#axzz2QE1xDy8K>.

[2] See 'VVD'er Bolkestein will parallelle munt naast euro', (Bolkestein wants a parallel currency besides the euro) *Algemeen Dagblad online*, 11 April 2013, available at: <http://www.ad.nl/ad/nl/1012/Nederland/article/detail/3423694/2013/04/11/VVD-er-Bolkestein-wil-parallelle-munt-naast-euro.dhtml>.

Jean-Claude Juncker, ex-President of the Eurogroup, even compared the complacency of the year 2013 with 1913 when, as he said, no one could have imagined that a year later a war would break out.[3] Although this comparison is largely overblown, it is certainly true that post-war Europe is currently experiencing an unprecedented period of aggravation and animosity amongst its peoples, who feel caught between a rock and a hard place.

The crisis spilled over from US banks to European sovereigns and banks in 2007/2008, triggering the world's most severe post-war recession to date. This recession, which was temporarily contained by extensive rescue operations, is now crushing the real economies of southern European countries. Unemployment rates in Spain and Greece are edging towards 30%, a level last seen in the world during the Great Depression of the 1930s. Youth unemployment rates, meanwhile, have soared to about 60% in these countries. Even Italy's has exceeded 40%. Industrial production in Spain, Italy, and Greece was devastated by a double-dip recession, if not depression, whilst France and Portugal are doing extremely poorly. Even the Netherlands is suffering from a bursting property bubble.

True, there are signs of relief. The world economy has recovered, and capital markets have calmed down since 2012. The general impression conveyed by the media is that the worst of the crisis is behind us. However, the smouldering fire of a severe structural crisis in southern European countries is still creeping underfoot. The recovery is extremely fragile, as it rests largely on the assurances and guarantees given by the European Central Bank (ECB) and fiscal rescue programmes rather than on an improvement in the fundamentals. With its assurances, in particular the Outright Monetary Transactions programme (OMT), which promises unlimited purchases of government bonds issued by distressed countries, the ECB has provided free-of-charge insurance to investors buying government bonds of over-indebted states. This has been a game changer for markets, bringing calm by shifting the risk of bankruptcy from clever investors to gullible taxpayers and welfare recipients of the Eurozone's still-solvent countries. This mirage of a solution may evaporate as soon as the potential losers understand the nature of the risk-shifting game. Long-lasting political instability and mistrust in EU institutions may be the cost of stabilising markets in the short run.

The shifting of risk from investors to taxpayers may also prove legally unsustainable: the German Constitutional Court declared in February 2014 that the OMT violates EU primary law and that the ECB Council has overstepped its mandate. While the Court has not yet issued a final ruling and has asked the European Court of Justice for its opinion on a potential modification of the OMT

---

[3] See 'Jean-Claude Juncker Interview, 'The Demons Haven't Been Banished', *Spiegel Online International*, 11 March 2013, available at: <http://www.spiegel.de/international/europe/spiegel-interview-with-luxembourg-prime-minister-juncker-a-888021.html>.

programme, it seems very unlikely that the ECB will be able to keep investment risks in check with its assurances.

The societies of southern Europe are also becoming increasingly brittle. While international rescue programmes, including those of the ECB, have kept people from starving and open political turmoil under control, Europe is seething with unrest. Separatist movements in Spain have gained new strength, and trade unions in Greece have organized increasingly violent strikes. In 2011 Italian Prime Minister Silvio Berlusconi initiated secret international negotiations about an Italian exit from the euro, because Italy had entered the second phase of its catastrophic double-dip recesssion, which still has it in its grip as of this writing.[4] Now, two-and-a-half years and three prime ministers later, the situation in Italy is worse than ever. The new Prime Minister Matteo Renzi has announced revolutionary changes in Italian politics. It remains to be seen whether he can turn Italy around.

The internal tensions have led politicians and voters to look for scapegoats abroad. In Italy, Berlusconi's party Forza Italia blames Germany for its problems. Demonstrations have increasingly turned against German calls for austerity in Greece, Portugal, and Cyprus, where Germany is held responsible for the lamentable state of their public finances and mass unemployment. When Chancellor Angela Merkel visited Athens in October 2012, the city had to be put in security lockdown to prevent violence. The euro has turned out to be anything but a peace project.

The tensions have funnelled voters towards Eurosceptic parties. In Germany, the alleged euro winner, economics professor Bernd Lucke founded a surprisingly successful anti-euro party called Alternative for Germany (AfD). In Greece, a colleague of his from the University of Piraeus, Theodorus Katsanevas, founded the party Drachme Five Stars on a similar platform, trying to imitate the success of Italy's Beppe Grillo, whose anti-euro and anti-establishment party, Five Stars, came third in the 2013 election, garnering a quarter of the votes. The French National Front, led by Marine Le Pen, and the Dutch Freedom Party, led by Geert Wilders, both of which are leading the polls, have formed an international coalition against the euro. In Greece the socialist party Syriza, led by Alexis Tsipras, now the party with the strongest support in Greece, has declared that it will no longer obey any of the austerity measures imposed by the Troika, made up of the International Monetary Fund (IMF), the ECB, and the European Union (EU). Should it come to power, its stance might result in Greece exiting the euro.

---

[4] See L. Bini-Smaghi, *Morire di austeritá: Democrazie europee con le spalle al muro*, Il Mulino, Bologna 2013, especially chapter 3, *Indietro no si torna*; Translation: *Austerity: European Democracies against the Wall*, Centre for European Policy Studies (CEPS), Brussels 2013, especially chapter 3: *No Turning Back*, p. 29.

Austerity, however, has not been imposed by policymakers, but by the capital markets, which have become increasingly nervous about southern Europe's ability to sustain its levels of public and private debt. Without the lifeline provided by the northern states through the ECB and the intergovernmental rescue operations, public and private debtors in southern Europe would have had to pay much higher interest rates, and in all likelihood some of them would have already gone bankrupt. And yet the South's anger is directed towards the still-solvent countries of the North, because the public help they provide is considered insufficient. The northern countries, in turn, are proving increasingly reluctant to accept further bail-out operations and take on more of the South's debt, if only because some are significantly less wealthy than their southern counterparts, as shown by a recent ECB study.[5] Growing tensions between southern austerity fatigue and northern rescue fatigue are endangering the future of the European project.

From a Keynesian perspective, southern Europe is just undergoing a recession that could be overcome by more deficit spending. After all, the greater the unemployment in the economy, the higher the multipliers. Such a policy would be plausible if the economies of southern Europe were structurally sound and only suffering from a temporary shortfall in demand. However, as credit at market conditions is now too expensive for the crisis-hit countries, the Keynesian policies would have to be carried out with credit provided or guaranteed by other states.

What is more, the crisis-hit countries are suffering from a serious competitiveness problem that would only be exacerbated by further demand stimuli. The southern countries became too expensive under the inflationary credit bubble ushered in by the euro. They substantially increased their wages and prices relative to the northern Eurozone countries just as a number of eastern European countries joined the EU and became fierce low-wage competitors, attracting private direct investment and selling conveniently priced goods to European markets. Spanish and Greek manufacturing wages are more than three times and more than twice as high as those in Poland, respectively, while Polish workers and craftsmen are renowned for their skill and diligence. This handicap can only be overcome over a long period of time, and Keynesian deficit spending will not be the right tool for the task. To regain competitiveness, the southern countries will have to become substantially cheaper by inflating less than their Eurozone competitors, or even by *de*flating. A depreciation of the euro would also be useful. However, both require *less* rather than more public demand stimulus by way of Keynesian deficit spending.

Demand- and liquidity-creating rescue operations have several side effects: they buy time for financial investors who want to cut and run, they put

---

[5] See European Central Bank, 'The Eurosystem Household Finance and Consumption Survey: Results from the First Wave', *Statistics Paper Series*, No. 2, April 2013, available at: <http://www.ecb.int/pub/pdf/other/ecbsp2en.pdf>.

at risk the money of northern European taxpayers who are taken hostage in their stead, and they reduce the pressure on southern European governments to implement the painful reforms that could bring about the wage and price adjustments needed to restore competitiveness. Such operations are mere pain-killers that postpone the administration of the real medicine.

It is true that financial markets can theoretically have multiple equilibria, and that public debt guarantees under certain conditions might be able to achieve a better equilibrium that ensures low interest rates and debt sustainability, without such guarantees ever having to be honoured. I call this the money-in-the-display-window theory. According to this theory, the money needs only lie in the display window to elicit a reassuring effect, without it ever having to be actually drawn.

However, there are two reasons why this theory does not seem to apply in the European case. Firstly, the countries of southern Europe built up huge current account deficits *before* the crisis, even when interest rates were low, and the structural component of those deficits has not yet disappeared. Their difficulties therefore do not stem from the financial crisis, but have deeper roots.

Secondly, the money in the display window has actually been taken. By the end of 2013, € 339 billion in rescue funds had been provided by way of intergovernmental, EU and IMF credit. In addition, the ECB provided a huge volume of rescue credit that the public knows little or nothing about. The ECB has not only purchased massive amounts of the crisis-hit countries' government bonds, announcing that it will continue buying such bonds in unlimited amounts if necessary; it has also helped the crisis-hit countries and their foreign creditors by allowing their national central banks (NCBs) to solve national financing problems with the printing press, enabling citizens and companies to pay for imports of goods and redeem their foreign private debt. This help took the form of so-called Target credit. Target (Trans-European Automated Real-time Gross settlement Express Transfer system) is an acronym for the Eurosystem's internal payment settlement system. As will be shown in this book, the combination of that system with the NCBs' local refinancing operations has become the distressed countries' main rescue facility, outgunning any of the rescue operations controlled by the parliaments of Europe. At the end of 2013, the Target credit provided to southern European countries and Ireland stood at € 613 billion, nearly twice the sum of the combined intergovernmental, EU, and IMF rescue credits. The volume of Target credit has been coming down of late and will likely decline further as fiscal credit by intergovernmental rescue funds replaces it.

By offering Target credit, the ECB has turned into an institution that carries out regional fiscal policies within the currency union, rendering the financing of particular countries and states largely independent of the capital market. As will be shown, neither the unlimited Target credit line nor the OMT programme have counterparts in the policies of the US Federal Reserve System. In the US, the printing presses cannot be used to provide particular states or regions with credit at below-market interest rates.

The overriding theme of this book is that, before and during the crisis, the Eurosystem experienced soft budget constraints. Before the outbreak of the crisis, too much private capital flowed from North to South, creating the inflationary bubble that deprived the South of its competitiveness. The excessive capital flows resulted primarily from the implicit protection that the common currency represented for investors, who could not imagine any risk of bank or state insolvencies in countries that had access to the liquidity of the Eurosystem, being able to print the money needed to redeem the debt if necessary. It also resulted from the encouragement that investors received from the EU's banking and insurance regulation system. This system contradicted the no-bail-out clause of the Maastricht Treaty which, had it been taken seriously, should have given investors pause and reduced the capital flows.

After the outbreak of the crisis, public capital was made available via the ECB to compensate for the dearth of private flows. In 2008, in the aftermath of the Lehman crisis, this was defensible given the need to avert an immediate collapse of the European economy. However, rather than attempting to return to the tight public budget constraints demanded by a market economy, the ECB and the community of euro states continued their policy of soft budget constraints by providing a growing amount of public credit at below-market interest rates, bailing out both the debtors and their creditors in the process. This destroyed one of the basic pillars of the Maastricht Treaty.

The French, German, and British banking systems, in that order, were heavily exposed to the crisis countries. They benefited from the bail-out policy insofar as without it, they might not have been able to recoup their money; but they also suffered inasmuch as they were unable to earn risk-commensurate interest rates, since the policy of financial repression forced them to compete with credit from the local money-printing presses and from public rescue funds aimed at helping the banks and governments of the debtor countries.

The Hungarian economist János Kornai predicted in 1980 that soft budget constraints would lead to the demise of the communist economic system.[6] The Eurozone currently runs the risk of sharing this fate. While soft budget constraints help in the short run and reduce the probability of a collapse of the system, they remove the incentives to tackle the structural reforms that would cure the disease. By preserving asset prices and balance sheets, the governments and the ECB rescue fragile financial institutions in uncompetitive countries, but at the price of keeping the rates of return on real capital below the level necessary to trigger new investment, which is the prerequisite for supply-driven growth. The result of such rescue operations will be Japanese-style secular stagnation

---

[6] J. Kornai, '"Hard" and "Soft" Budget Constraint', *Acta Oeconomica* 25, 1980, pp. 231–246.

rather than recovery. The economy is not exactly rescued, but merely shielded from potentially beneficial creative destruction.

It is also doubtful whether Europeans will continue to live in harmony if the public bail-out policy persists, for such a policy raises creditor–debtor relationships from the private to the public sphere, where there is no civil law to settle the disputes, and fuels heated public debates that stir up animosity and strife. History is full of examples of the problematic relationship between creditors and debtors, and one such example, during the early years of the United States of America, will be discussed in the last chapter of this book. The range of ills that could be triggered by public creditor–debtor relationships is truly chilling, even if the horrors alluded to by Jean-Claude Juncker never materialize.

The situation is now fairly stuck, and there is a very limited choice of policies that might preserve the euro without turning Europe into an economy with a centrally-planned capital market. Still, it is worth trying to prevent the implosion of the Eurosystem and to uphold the idea of the euro as a European peace project. To achieve this, however, far more radical reforms are required than those currently envisaged by politicians.

This book tries to sort through the mess that the euro has created in Europe. It analyses the factors that led to the crisis, describes the southern countries' loss of competitiveness, documents the rescue operations undertaken to date by the ECB and the community of states, and discusses the few policy options that still remain open.

Over the course of the book I will explain why I think that the Eurozone cannot survive in its current form. I will also argue that it would be in the interest of some euro countries to temporarily exit the euro and devalue their new currencies in order to regain their competitiveness. This would not only be easier for them: it also represents the only chance of stabilizing the Eurosystem. In fact, I am convinced that for Europeans to succeed in creating a common state they will have to go through a phase of a 'breathing euro,' i.e. a more flexible currency union that lies somewhere between the dollar and a fixed-exchange-rate system like the Bretton Woods system that prevailed in the post-war period. In my opinion, a big debt conference should also be held to clean up the afflicted private and public balance sheets and relieve the unbearable burden currently borne by some of the debtor countries. The earlier this conference is held, the quicker a recovery will be. Such a conference could also reduce the burden imposed on Europe's taxpayers, as well as magnify the disciplinary effect for the future, a factor that is crucial for the functioning of a capitalist market economy.

Despite my fundamental scepticism regarding the functioning of the Eurosystem in its present form, I refuse to give up my hope for the euro, and much less my hope for a united Europe. In view of the horrifying events of the twentieth century, for which my home country bears the greatest responsibility, I see no alternative to deepening European integration. Indeed, I would go as far as advocating the creation of a United States of Europe. A common European state would constitute the binding insurance contract without which it may prove impossible to achieve a fiscal union and a steadfast mutual risk sharing between successful and faltering regions to ensure the equality of living standards. I attempt to outline what a common European state entails, and what it does not, in the latter part of the book, praising the Swiss Confederation as a useful example to follow. Whilst I harbour no illusions about the likelihood of this project being achieved in my lifetime, I find it worthwhile to have a goal that gives hope and direction to the peoples of Europe.

I am not convinced, however, that there is only one way towards deeper European integration, and therefore welcome the debate triggered by British Prime Minister David Cameron when he announced a referendum on EU membership for Britain.[7] It is high time to critically review developments in the EU over the last twenty years, as the original goals of European integration drift ever further out of sight. Our leaders continue to argue that the route laid out by them is the correct path to follow, and that we should simply accelerate our pace along that path in order to reach our goals. However, the current mess, and the crushingly high unemployment rates in many European countries in particular, raise doubts over whether this is the right way to proceed. It may be better to return to the last fork in the road and try another route. I deplore the politicians and scholars who offer no other response to this opinion than to label those who voice it as 'anti-European'. Clinging to the status quo is no longer a politically or economically viable option for Europe. Alternative paths forward must be found if Europe is to prosper in the future. This calls for courage and vision, not simply more of the same.

Munich, February 2014
Hans-Werner Sinn

---

[7] See 'David Cameron's EU Speech—Full Text', *The Guardian*, 23 January 2013, available at: <http://www.guardian.co.uk/politics/2013/jan/23/david-cameron-eu- speech-referendum>.

CHAPTER I

Wish and Reality

*Euro Dynamics—The Euro and Peace—Advantages of the Euro for Trade
and Capital Flows—The Path to a Currency Union—The Price of German
Reunification?—Transfer and Debt Union—The European Central Bank*

Euro Dynamics

When attempting to judge the effects of the euro, it is worth recalling what
Europe's politicians expected from it and what was announced to the public.
Particularly high expectations were raised regarding the European economy.
Nothing portrays this better than the final declaration of the Lisbon Strategy,
also called the Lisbon Agenda, of March 2000:[1]

> The Union has today set itself a new strategic goal for the next decade: to
> become the most competitive and dynamic knowledge-based economy in the
> world, capable of sustainable economic growth with more and better jobs and
> greater social cohesion.

The Lisbon Strategy was a large-scale programme to foster innovation and
economic growth, conceived as a complement to the euro and whose effects
should unfold concurrently with the new common currency. The big starting
shot was intended to kindle a new spirit of optimism in Europe and usher in a
new Golden Age for the Old World. The euro had been introduced the previous year as a transaction unit for banks; its physical introduction was slated for
2002. The Lisbon Agenda and the euro seemed to signal a period of growth and
prosperity.

---

[1] See European Parliament, *Lisbon European Council 23 and 24 March 2000, Presidency
Conclusions*, available at: <http://www.europarl.europa.eu/summits/lis1_en.htm>.

The optimism was also fuelled by the economic boom that Europe and the world were enjoying. The countries that now make up the European Union had grown by 3.9% in the year 2000, a rate considerably higher than the average for the previous decade. Unemployment, in turn, was decreasing. There was every reason to believe that even better days were coming. The brave new world of a common currency would impart an impetus to the Old World that it had not experienced since the post-war period. 'The euro will rejuvenate Europe', said McKinsey chief Herbert Henzler.[2] Bank economists like Kim Schoenholtz (Salomon Smith Barney) predicted 'the euro zone is going to enjoy a golden childhood' while officials from the European institutions praised the euro as a 'true accelerator of economic growth' (Christian Noyer, Vice-President of the ECB).[3] There were many such expressions, and the author must admit that he shared them.[4]

Reality ended up being quite different. The boom turned out to be no more than an Internet bubble that burst as early as 2001, and over the decade envisioned by the Agenda Europe did not become the world's most dynamic region, but rather the world's lamest laggard. Figure 1.1 shows this very clearly. From 2000 to 2010, the world economy grew by 43%, while the EU, with barely 17%, exhibited the weakest growth among the large regions, a bit lower than the US, and that only thanks to the fact that the rapidly growing eastern European countries were included, which had a lot of catching up to do. Taken by itself, eastern Europe, including the formerly Communist countries in central Europe, clocked up a remarkable 45%. The current members of the Eurozone, in contrast, grew by barely 12% and, except for Japan, were by far the world's worst performers,

[2] See H. Henzler, 'Zunehmender Druck', *Wirtschaftswoche*, No. 26, 20 June 2002, p. 24.

[3] See A. Friedman, 'Without Structural Changes, Experts Cautious on Economic Growth', *The New York Times*, 2 May 1998, available at: <http://www.nytimes.com/1998/05/02/news/02iht-simpact.t.html?pagewanted=all>; C. Noyer, 'The Euro: Accelerator of Economic Growth in Europe', *Speech delivered at the lunch-meeting of Cercle d'Union Interalliée in Paris*, 23 June 1999, available at: <http://www.ecb.europa.eu/press/key/date/1999/html/sp990623_1.en.html>. Furthermore, a panel of economists chaired by Michael Emerson, then the European Commission's chief economist, estimated that the elimination of currency transaction costs alone would boost gross domestic product by between 0.5% and 1%. See also P. Gumpel, 'Is the Euro Good for Europe?', *TIME Magazine*, 26 September 2004, available at: <http://www.time.com/time/magazine/article/0,9171,702088-1,00.html>.

[4] H.-W. Sinn and R. Koll, 'The Euro, Interest Rates and European Economic Growth', *CESifo Forum* 1, No. 3, October 2000, pp. 30–31, available at: <http://www.cesifo-group.de/DocDL/Forum300-sl1.pdf>.

relegated to the very bottom of the scale. China topped the league, with 171%, and even Sub-Saharan Africa grew by 74%; Latin America managed 39%. Seldom has the gulf between wish and reality been so great as in Europe under the euro.

And worse was to come. A financial crisis hit the US first in 2006/2007, spilling over to Europe as early as summer 2007. A year later all Eurozone countries slumped during the Great Recession that ensued, which eventually had the whole world in its grip, and many of them slipped into serious trouble. As of this writing, these countries still have not managed to return to their pre-crisis Gross Domestic Product (GDP) levels.[5]

A deep funding crisis, unprecedented in recent history, befell Greece, Ireland, Portugal, Spain, Italy, and Cyprus (grouped here under the acronym GIPSIC), triggering huge international rescue operations by the European Central Bank (ECB), the International Monetary Fund (IMF),

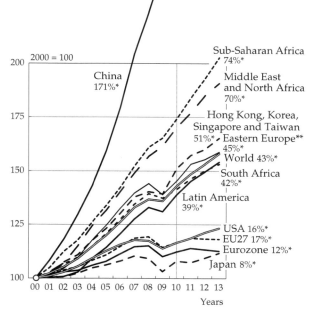

Figure 1.1 Growth in selected countries and regions (2000–2013)
* GDP growth 2000–2010.
** Including the formerly Communist areas in central Europe.
Source: International Monetary Fund, *World Economic Outlook*, October 2013.
Note: GDP growth rates according to chain-linked volumes at 2005 prices.

[5] See B. Eichengreen, 'The Great Recession and the Great Depression: Reflections and Lessons', *Journal Economía Chilena* 13, 2010, pp. 5–10.

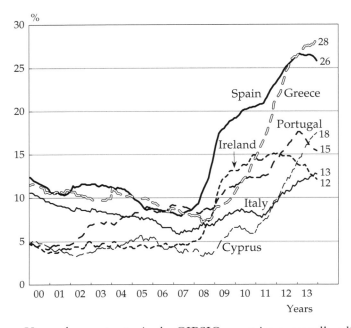

Figure 1.2 Unemployment rates in the GIPSIC countries, seasonally adjusted

Source: Eurostat, Database, *Population and Social Conditions*, Labour Market, Employment and Unemployment.

the European Union (EU), and the euro member states.[6] The rescue efforts, however, acted as mere painkillers, without visibly improving the underlying structural and competitiveness problems. As Figure 1.2 shows, 28% of Greeks were unemployed in November 2013. In Spain the unemployment peaked at 27% in February 2013, declining slightly to 26% by December 2013. Though significantly lower, the unemployment rates in Ireland (12%), Italy (13%), Portugal (15%) and Cyprus (18%) are also alarmingly high. While Portugal and Ireland show clear signs of a genuine trend reversal, the rise of unemployment in Italy, Greece and Cyprus continues unabated. In Spain, the slight reduction in unemployment seems to have resulted entirely from rapidly rising emigration of the unemployed.

Youth unemployment is even more alarming. The high level of protection afforded to workers under permanent contracts keep younger job-seekers

---

[6] Italy does not belong to the group of countries receiving help from the formal rescue funds, but it has received extensive support from the ECB's government bond purchase programme (Securities Markets Programme, SMP). See Figure 8.1 in Chapter 8.

Figure 1.3 Youth unemployment (< 25 years of age) in the GIPSIC countries, seasonally adjusted

Source: Eurostat, Database, *Population and Social Conditions*, Labour Market, Employment and Unemployment.

outside the factory gates. As Figure 1.3 shows, by the end of 2013, youth unemployment for the under-25s stood at 59% in Greece and 54% in Spain. Since these are seasonally adjusted data, they understate the unadjusted rate of youth unemployment in winter months, which in Greece stood at 61.4% in November 2013. Youth unemployment in Italy and Portugal, with rates of 42% and 36% respectively, is less catastrophic, yet alarming enough (see Figure 1.3 below). Both are about five times as high as Germany's (7.4%), whose vocational training scheme helps to make it an exception among the Eurozone countries. At first glance, it might be assumed that youth unemployment rates are so high because many young people are still in education. Sadly, this is not the case: neither the numerator nor the denominator of the youth unemployment rate includes young people in education. The figure only refers to the people under twenty-five years of age registered in the labour force. This desperate state of affairs in southern Europe is a veritable catastrophe. It could give rise to violence and other uncontrollable developments that may jeopardize the European project.

In some countries, the economy has been in free fall. In 2011, 2012, and 2013 the Greek economy contracted by 7.1%, 6.4%, and 4.0% respectively. Italy,

Portugal and France are shaking in their boots. Many euro countries are in recession, and some even in depression. In 2011, the Eurozone's GDP, excluding Germany, the Netherlands and Austria, rose by a meagre 1.0%, to contract by 0.8% in 2012 and by 0.5% in 2013. Even France is having a hard time getting its unemployment rate under control. At 10.8%, its rate is more than twice as high as Germany's (see Chapter 3, Figure 3.8). Youth unemployment in France, at a rate of 25.6%, is more than three times as high as Germany's.

Southern Europe's increasing economic difficulties prompted investors to flee in droves. Some € 640 billion in liquid assets fled Italy and Spain alone between mid-2011 and mid-2012, as will be discussed in Chapter 7. Capital flight came to a halt in September 2012, when the German Constitutional Court rejected the appeals against Germany's participation in the permanent rescue programme ESM (European Stability Mechanism; see Chapter 8) and the ECB announced its Outright Monetary Transactions programme (OMT), which provided a guarantee for investors buying government bonds of the Eurozone's troubled countries. These measures have stabilized the financial markets, but they have not been able to stabilize the real economies, as the unemployment and growth figures show. It is only a matter of time until the next bout of financial turmoil starts. The Cyprus crisis in the first quarter of 2013 will not be the last to challenge Europe.

European policymakers stumble from one crisis to the next. When a problem appears, they take some action to solve or contain it, but after only a few months of seeming tranquillity a new crisis crops up somewhere else, and again some measures are taken, without anyone foreseeing where the process will lead in the end. Greece, Ireland, Portugal, Spain, and Cyprus have been thrown a lifeline by intergovernmental rescue programmes, and they, as well as Italy, have received massive support from the ECB (see Chapter 8 for an overview). None of these countries currently borrows at market conditions. They all live on funds provided or guaranteed by other Eurozone countries, which mitigate, with their taxpayers' money, the austerity demanded by markets. The crisis rumbles on and is far from being resolved. It's all a far cry from the Lisbon Agenda's wish-list. Something has definitely gone wrong in Europe.

The Euro and Peace

The euro was not solely about economics.[7] The political goals were even more important. In 1990, Helmut Kohl and François Mitterrand declared that it was

---

[7] For a comprehensive analysis of Europe's process of monetary cooperation and unification, in particular from a historical and political perspective, see H. James, *Making the European Monetary Union*, Harvard University Press, Cambridge 2012; see also H.-W. Sinn, 'Die Europäische Fiskalunion', *Perspektiven der Wirtschaftspolitik* 13, 2012, pp. 137–178.

their concern 'to transform the relations between the member countries into a genuine political union'.[8] Moreover, former French Finance and Prime Minister Pierre Bérégovoy stated in May 1992 at the French National Assembly, after signing the Maastricht Treaty:[9]

> Yes, I believe in Europe because I passionately desire peace. Peace on the continent itself.

German Chancellor Helmut Kohl justified the introduction of the euro before the Bundestag on 23 April 1998 by saying:[10]

> The euro strengthens the European Union as a guarantor of peace and freedom.... Today's decision—and this is no hyperbole—will largely determine whether future generations in Germany and the rest of Europe will be able to live in peace and freedom, with social stability and prosperity.

He added that he was 'quite certain...that those who today say No to the euro in a few years will deny that they ever voiced such an opinion'. Other European politicians, such as Jean-Claude Juncker,[11] also stressed the fact that the euro was a project for European peace, while Germany's current chancellor, Angela Merkel, now proclaims very similar views when defending the rescue packages.[12]

But also in this respect did the euro fail to fulfill its promise. The economic problems of the stricken countries and the scepticism of the capital markets are fraying nerves and beginning to undermine harmony in the Eurozone. With every passing summit, the animosity among the member countries has become a bit more acrimonious. Some feel that they are being pushed against a wall, in particular some large members like Spain and Italy that had expected to weather

---

[8] Letter from H. Kohl and F. Mitterrand to the Irish President C. J. Haughey, Agence Europe, 20 April 1990.

[9] See P. Bérégovoy, 'Adapter la Constitution à Maastricht', *Speech at the French National Assembly*, 5 May 1992, Paris, available at: <http://www.beregovoy.org/Discours%20PB/sur_maastricht.htm>.

[10] See H. Kohl, *Speech at the German Bundestag during the Debate on the Resolution of the German Federal Government Regarding the Definition of the Participants in the Third Stage of the European Economic and Monetary Union*, 23 April 1998, Berlin, available at: <http://helmut-kohl.kas.de/index.php?menu_sel=17&menu_sel2=&menu_sel3=&menu_sel4=&msg=1764> (translated by the author).

[11] See J.-C. Juncker, *The Euro is a New Instrument to Achieve Peace and Stability*, Brussels Economic Forum 2008, available at: <http://ec.europa.eu/economy_finance/emu10/quotes_juncker_en.htm>.

[12] See A. Merkel, 'Der Euro—weit mehr als Währung', Interview by K. Dunz, *Deutsche Presseagentur*, 9 November 2011, available at: <http://www.bundesregierung.de/ContentArchiv/DE/Archiv17/Interview/2011/11/2011-11-09-merkel-dpa.html >.

Figure 1.4 Protesting against austerity

Sources: 'Protesting against austerity', © REUTERS/Hugo Correia (top left), © REUTERS/Yannis Behrakis (top right), © REUTERS/Yannis Behrakis (bottom left), © REUTERS/Yannis Behrakis (bottom right). Reprinted with permission.

the crisis more or less unscathed. Others fear deep haircuts on bonds they issued and intend to avoid a financial fiasco through a mutualization of debt. Italy's then Prime Minister Mario Monti believed that the tension 'already bears the marks of a psychological dissolution of Europe', and feared that the euro could become 'a factor in this drifting apart'.[13] And as mentioned in the introduction, Jean-Claude Juncker recently even compared the year 2013 with the complacency of 1913, when only few people would have thought it possible that a year later war would break out.

The high rates of unemployment naturally breed social unrest. Over the past four years, Europe-wide protests against spending cuts and unemployment have brought people onto the streets in many countries. Some pictures are shown in Figure 1.4. In Spain, around fifty cities saw major demonstrations that started in May 2011 under the heading '¡Democracia real ya!' (True democracy

---

[13] See M. Monti, 'Spiegel-Gespräch mit Premier Mario Monti', Interview by F. Ehlers and H. Hoyng, *Der Spiegel*, No. 32, 2012, pp. 44–47.

now!). In Barcelona alone, a demonstration gathered 80,000 people. Much of the protest was directed against the eviction of homeowners unable to repay their mortgages; some homeowners have committed suicide. In September 2012, about one million people participated in demonstrations in Portugal under the slogan 'To the devil with the Troika', the Troika being the delegation of the International Monetary Fund, the European Central Bank, and the European Commission that reviews compliance with austerity commitments in the crisis-stricken countries benefiting from public rescue funds. In Greece, demonstrations are a daily occurrence; they have already claimed a number of fatalities. In 2011 alone, the unions organized four nationwide strikes against austerity. Often during demonstrations, public transportation stands still, public offices remain closed and hospitals reduce their service to emergency cases. In Italy, 100,000 people demonstrated in October 2012 against the Monti government reforms, with the press taking an increasingly aggressive stance against austerity; a general revolt, however, has not yet taken place. Tensions reached their first climax during the 'Day of Action and Solidarity' against austerity measures in 23 countries on 14 November 2012.

The tensions have also changed the political landscape in Europe. In Italy a euro-sceptic party lead by Beppe Grillo received 26% of the popular vote off the cuff,[14] while in Germany a similarly euro-sceptic party founded by economist Bernd Lucke hopes to repeat Grillo's success, although the views of the two parties are diametrically opposed. In Greece the coalition of the moderate parties Nea Dimokratia, Panellinio Sosialistiko Kinima, and Dimokratiki Aristera, with a share of 48% of the popular vote in June 2012, garnered only a slight majority over the Syriza-EKM and other parties that advocate a much more aggressive rejection of austerity.[15] In France, the National Front under Marine Le Pen, which wants to exit the euro, is rapidly gaining support and might well become the strongest party overall. In Portugal and Germany, the respective constitutional courts have established themselves as important players in the political arena. The Portuguese Constitutional Court rejected a measure to scrap summer holiday bonuses for public sector workers and pensioners, as well as cuts to unemployment and sickness benefits, forcing the government to scramble to devise alternative budget cuts.[16] The German Constitutional Court, in turn, forced the government to demand an addendum to the treaty on the establishment of the European Stability Mechanism

---

[14] See Ministero dell'Interno, *Elezioni 2013 Politiche e Regionali del 24 e 25 Febbraio*, available at: <http://elezioni.interno.it/camera/scrutini/20130224/C000000000.htm>.

[15] See A. Dabilis, 'New Coalition Government Fails to Calm Greek Worries', *Southeast European Times*, 21 June 2012, available at: <http://www.setimes.com/cocoon/setimes/xhtml/en_GB/features/setimes/features/2012/06/21/feature-01>.

[16] See 'Portugal Constitutional Court Rejects Budget Articles', *BBC News Europe*, 6 April 2013, available at: <http://www.bbc.co.uk/news/world-europe-22048169>.

(see Chapter 8) that reduced the participating states' joint and several liability to proportional liability.[17] Pending appeals may also mean that the Court will limit the Bundesbank's ability to participate in certain policy actions or force the German government to renegotiate the Maastricht Treaty.

As the pictures above show, the tensions have a strong international dimension, as austerity fatigue and rescue fatigue clash ever more often. The governments of the South rail against the constraints that the Troika imposes on them. Germany in particular has become the target of demonstrations. The governments of the South attack Germany, the main provider of the rescue funds, for having pushed through a Fiscal Compact that imposes austerity, which is perceived as causing the unemployment that affects them. And the governments of the North complain about the South's wastefulness and lack of fiscal discipline; they fear that their aid is flowing into a bottomless pit.

The animosity Germany faces in western Europe is stronger than anything the country has experienced since World War II. Swastikas are being pointed at Germany in Greece, while the Italian daily *Il Giornale* sees signs of Germany trying to establish a Fourth Reich.[18] Monti prophesied Italian demonstrations against Germany should the country fail to help Italy lower the premia on its sovereign debt.[19] The British left-wing weekly magazine *New Statesman* said German Chancellor Angela Merkel is 'the most dangerous German leader since Hitler'.[20]

The influential American speculator George Soros, who once brought the Bank of England to its knees, accused Germany of taking on imperial airs and prophesied the hate of the masses against it[21] if it does not acquiesce to further rescue operations. In September 2012 he asked Germany to 'lead or leave',[22]

---

[17] See Federal Constitutional Court, *2 BvR 987/102, BvR 1485/102, BvR 1099/10*, press release, No. 55/2011, 7 September 2011, available at: <https://www.bundesverfassungsgericht.de/en/press/bvg11-055en.html>.

[18] See 'Quarto Reich', *Il Giornale*, 3 August 2012, title page.

[19] See R. Alexander, 'Mario Monti wehrt sich gegen Italien-Misstrauen', *Welt Online*, 11 January 2012, available at: <http://www.welt.de/politik/ausland/article13810405/Mario-Monti-wehrt-sich-gegen-Italien-Misstrauen.html>.

[20] See M. Hasan, 'Angela Merkel's Mania for Austerity is Destroying Europe'. The issue's cover title is 'Europe's most Dangerous Leader' (Cover story), *New Statesman*, 20 June 2012.

[21] See G. Soros, 'Star-Investor prophezeit Hass auf Deutschland', Interview by M. Müller von Blumencron, S. Kaiser and G. P. Schmitz, *Der Spiegel*, 26 June 2012, available at: <http://www.spiegel.de/wirtschaft/interview-mit-george-soros-zu-deutschland-und-zur-euro-krise-a-841021.html>.

[22] See G. Soros, 'Why Germany Should Lead or Leave', *Project Syndicate*, 8 September 2012, available at: <http://www.project-syndicate.org/commentary/why-

and in April 2013 he urged it to accept Eurobonds or leave.[23] Eurobonds ought to be issued and guaranteed jointly by the euro countries and used to replace the outstanding government bonds, thus resulting in debt mutualization. Anatole Kaletsky, an award-winning British journalist, chairman of the board of the Institute for New Economic Thinking, financed by George Soros, struck the same note when he said Germany started World War I and World War II, and now once again poses a great danger for Europe. Isn't it time for Europe 'to stand up to Germany'? he asks his readers.[24]

These statements and the objections to austerity show that Europe has become stuck in a fundamental distributional dispute about unresolved debt issues. Since debtors over-borrowed and now cannot repay, their creditors, fearing write-off losses, are looking for someone else to foot the bill. From the perspective of international investors the situation is crystal clear. They lent their money to Greece, Spain, and other now-troubled countries because they are part of the Eurozone. If those countries now cannot pay back their debts, other Eurozone members must stand in for them. Europe is large and strong enough to solve its own problems. Europe's strong economies must shoulder their responsibility. It is unfair of them to try to shirk their duty.

However, the investors overlooked the rules of the Maastricht Treaty. After all, one of the pillars of this treaty is the no-bailout clause (article 125 of the Treaty on

germany-should-lead-or-leave-by-george-soros>; also G. Soros, *Financial Turmoil in Europe and the United States*, Public Affairs, New York 2012, and G. Soros, 'How to Save the European Union from the Euro Crisis', remarks delivered at the Center for Financial Studies, Goethe University in Frankfurt, 9 April 2013. For the reply of the author, see H.-W. Sinn, 'Spiel mit dem Feuer', *Handelsblatt*, 25 April 2013, p. 64, and for a debate between both, see also G. Soros and H.-W. Sinn, 'Saving the European Union. Are Eurobonds the Answer? A Debate between George Soros and Hans-Werner Sinn', *CESifo Forum* 14, No. 2, June 2013, pp. 41–48, available at: <http://www.cesifo-group.de/DocDL/forum2-13-special2.pdf>.

[23] See G. Soros, 'Germany's Choice', *Project Syndicate*, 9 April 2013, available at: <http://www.project-syndicate.org/commentary/a-simple-solution-to-the-euro-crisis-by-george-soros>; also H.-W. Sinn, 'Should Germany Exit the Euro?', *Project Syndicate*, 23 April 2013, available at: <http://www.project-syndicate.org/commentary/should-germany- exit-the-euro-by-hans-werner-sinn>; G. Soros and H.-W. Sinn, 'Soros versus Sinn: The German Question', *Project Syndicate*, 6 May 2013, available at: <http://www.project-syndicate.org/commentary/soros-versus-sinn--the-german-question>.

[24] See A. Kaletsky, 'Can the Rest of Europe Stand up to Germany?', *Reuters*, 20 June 2012, available at: <http://blogs.reuters.com/anatole-kaletsky/2012/06/20/can-the-rest-of-europe- stand-up-to-germany>.

the Functioning of the European Union), which states that no Eurozone member state shall be liable for, or assume the commitments of, another member state:[25]

> The Union shall not be liable for or assume the commitments of central governments, regional, local or other public authorities, other bodies governed by public law, or public undertakings of any Member State.... A Member State shall not be liable for or assume the commitments of central governments, regional, local or other public authorities, other bodies governed by public law, or public undertakings of another Member State....

The no-bailout clause makes it clear that the euro has not been designed as a mutual insurance or debt mutualization system. On the contrary, such support has been explicitly ruled out.

From the outset, some European countries have feared that the euro project could turn out to be a debt mutualization scheme, and therefore they insisted that the no-bailout clause be included in the Treaty. Germany, in particular, had made this a condition for giving up the deutschmark.[26] And France, in turn, objected to Germany's idea of creating political structures that would serve as the basis for a federal European State.

Given that at the time of the Maastricht Treaty a vast majority of the German population objected to the idea of replacing the deutschmark with the euro,[27] the Kohl government emphasized again and again that the introduction of the new common currency would not imply debt mutualization or transfer schemes among the members of the Eurozone. In his great speech on the introduction of the euro, Kohl asked his audience to pause for a moment and pay close attention to what he was going to say. He then intoned, twice in a row to lend it gravitas:[28]

---

[25] See EU, 'Treaty on the Functioning of the European Union (TFEU)', *Official Journal of the European Union* C 115/47, 9 May 2008, available at: <http://eur-lex.europa. eu/LexUriServ/LexUriServ.do?uri=OJ:C:2008:115:0058:0199:en:PDF>.

[26] See M. Sauga, S. Simons, and K. Wiegrefe, 'You Get Unification, We Get the Euro', *Presseurop*, 1 October 2010, available at: <http://www.presseurop.eu/en/content/article/ 351531-you-get-unification-we-get-euro>.

[27] According to polls conducted by the institutes Emnid and Ipsos, rejection of the euro in 1996 to 1998 ranged from 49% to 70%, while acceptance reached barely 44% and 26%, respectively; see 'Ohne D-Mark, ohne Kohl?', *Der Spiegel*, No. 2, 5 January 1998, pp. 22–25, available at: <http://www.spiegel.de/spiegel/print/d-7809473.html>; and Bankenverband—Bundesverband Deutscher Banken, *Zehn Jahre Europäische Wirtschafts- und Währungsunion (EWWU), Ergebnisse einer repräsentativen Meinungsumfrage im Auftrag des Bankenverbands*, March 2008, available at: <http://bankenverband.de/down-loads/meinungsumfrage/08-05-05_10%20Jahre%20EWWU-Anlage-mit.pdf> (accessed 7 February 2014).

[28] See H. Kohl, *Speech at the German Bundestag*, 23 April 1998, Berlin (translated by the author).

> According to the treaty rules, the euro community shall not be liable for the com-
> mitments of its member states and there will be no additional financial transfers.

This rigour and determination is the main reason why the German government today is so reluctant to acquiesce to extensive rescue operations and debt mutualization schemes.

That said, the actual rescue operations that have already been undertaken by the community of states and the ECB, which mitigate the austerity that markets impose on debtor countries, are huge by any standards. As will be shown later in this book (see in particular Chapter 8), at the peak of the crisis in August 2012 the community of states and the ECB provided a total of € 1.339 trillion to the six crisis-stricken countries (GIPSIC), which amounted to € 10,000 per capita on average. This is obviously no small contribution. It is one of the ironies of Europe's crisis that those who shoulder the rescue programmes and mitigate the markets' austerity are not perceived as rescuers, but as oppressors who impose austerity and withhold some of the rescue sums to which the recipients of the resources feel entitled. Should the euro break up and the GIPSIC countries default on their debts, Germany alone would bear a loss of about € 450 billion, or € 5,500 per capita, as will be shown in Chapter 8 (Table 8.2). The Dutch and the Finns would even bear a loss of € 6,900 per capita. These three countries currently contribute much to mitigating austerity among the struggling Eurozone countries.

Kohl's confidence that the no-bailout clause would be respected was clearly betrayed during the crisis. Christine Lagarde, a former French finance minister and now Managing Director of the IMF, bluntly admitted that the rescue programmes were illegal:[29]

> We violated all the rules because we wanted to close ranks and really rescue
> the euro zone.

In view of the fact that the credit granted by French banks to the stricken states was twice as large as a proportion of its GDP than the equivalent lent by German banks, this position is understandable,[30] but it reveals the willingness, when it seems expedient, to disregard European laws and treaties written precisely in

---

[29] See B. Carney and A. Jolis, 'Toward a United States of Europe', *The Wall Street Journal*, 17 December 2010, available at: <http://online.wsj.com/article/SB100014240527 4870403480457602568108734202.html>.

[30] See Bank for International Settlements, *BIS Quarterly Review*, September 2010, p. 16. According to the BIS, French banks' exposure to the public sectors of Greece, Ireland, Portugal, and Spain was $ 103.0 billion at the end of March 2010, while that of German banks amounted to $ 66.4 billion. As a share of 2009 GDP, French claims were 95% larger than those of German banks. See also Chapter 7, section on France.

order to free decision-makers from the pressures of the practical necessities of the day.[31]

At the time the Maastricht Treaty was being discussed, there were more than enough voices warning against placing too much naïve faith in mere protection clauses built into the treaty, in the hope that they would be respected in crunch times. Among those who issued such warnings were former Bundesbank President Hans Tietmeyer,[32] Nobel Prize winner Milton Friedman,[33] the previous head of the US Council of Economic Advisors, Martin Feldstein,[34] and the former president of the London School of Economics, Ralph Dahrendorf, who found particularly clear words about the euro's future:[35]

> The currency union is a great error, a risky, reckless and mistaken goal that will not unite Europe, but divide it.

No less than 155 German economists signed a public appeal in 1998 against what they considered a premature introduction of the euro.[36] Scientific honesty demands an acknowledgement that they, unfortunately, were right.

Advantages of the Euro for Trade and Capital Flows

All this does not mean that the Eurozone should simply give up the euro, since what happened, happened. You can bake a cake from many ingredients, but once you have baked it, you cannot get the ingredients out of the cake, at least

[31] Some lawyers see this as a destruction of one of the constitutional principles of the Maastricht Treaty. See D. Murswiek, 'Verfassungsrechtliche Probleme der Euro-Rettung', lecture given at *Munich Seminar*, CESifo and Süddeutsche Zeitung, 30 January 2012.

[32] See 'Die Allianz der Skeptiker', *Der Spiegel*, No. 37, 8 September 1997, pp. 22–24.

[33] See M. Friedman, 'Why Europe Can't Afford the Euro—The Danger of a Common Currency', *The Times*, 19 November 1997.

[34] See M. Feldstein, 'The Political Economy of the European Economic and Monetary Union: Political Sources of an Economic Liability', *Journal of Economic Perspectives* 11, 1997, pp. 23–42.

[35] R. Dahrendorf, 'Alle Eier in einen Korb', interviewed by T. Darnstädt and R. Leick, *Der Spiegel*, No. 50/1995, 11 December 1995, pp. 27–33 (translated by the author); also R. Richter, 'Europäische Währungsunion: Mehr Kosten als Nutzen, Altar der Einheit', *Wirtschaftswoche*, No. 49, 29 November 1991, p. 97; M. J. M. Neumann, 'Die Mark ist ein Wohlstandsfaktor', *Zeit Online*, 16 October 1992, available at: <http://www.zeit.de/1992/43/die-mark-ist-ein-wohlstandsfaktor>; J. Starbatty, cited by 'Vier gegen den Euro', *Der Spiegel*, No. 3, 12 January 1998.

[36] See manifest of German economics professors against a premature introduction of the euro, 'Der Euro kommt zu früh', *Frankfurter Allgemeine Zeitung*, No. 33, 9 February 1998.

not easily. The Eurozone's financial systems are so strongly interconnected that a conversion of debts and liabilities into old currencies is anything but unproblematic. In addition, the euro has such great symbolic power for the continent's further political integration that it can only be hoped that it will be possible to keep it under reasonable conditions. While Angela Merkel's pronouncement that 'If the euro fails, Europe fails' is exaggerated, it does contain a grain of truth. From an economic perspective, the euro is nothing but a clearing system for the exchange of goods and services. But from a political perspective it represents a bold phase in the historical integration of Europe, one that, it is to be hoped, will find a good end.

Reforms and an adjustment of the Eurozone's size, concentrating on the countries that function well within the core Eurozone, could be necessary, despite all the difficulties that such a course would entail. Why this is so and what such a reform could look like, a reform that could be particularly attractive for countries leaving the Eurozone temporarily, will be discussed in Chapters 4 and 9.

This process should not be aimed at setting the euro up for disposal, however, but at saving it. The euro offers a range of advantages from which all members benefit. In that light, its fathers were right, and this book will not call into question the northern countries' permanence in the Eurozone, however unsparing its appraisal of the monetary union may be. The criticism voiced here is intended as a basis for reform proposals to strengthen the European idea, not to undermine it.

A manifestly positive effect of the euro is the lowering of currency transaction costs, which every tourist perceives immediately as advantageous. In the past, for every 1,000 francs in foreign trade, 15 francs were lost to transaction costs. Business travellers used to have several wallets for the different notes and coins left over from their trips, in order to use them next time around, and tourists remember well all that foreign cash they struggled to make sense of. The euro did away with this hindrance.

Even more important is the disappearance of exchange rate uncertainty. The continuous oscillations of the exchange rates were a significant obstacle to intra-European trade. When goods were bought for future delivery, the contract parties often had no idea what price they had actually agreed. If the currency of the seller was used, the buyer faced a kind of lottery; if the currency of the buyer was adopted, the seller didn't know how much he would eventually receive. Both could, of course, buy insurance against such exchange risk, but that was expensive and posed a burden to trade.

The euro protected the Eurozone's businesses and finances against the turbulences of flexible exchange rates, which had been a huge problem in the decades before the new currency was introduced, in particular around 1992 when the nominally fixed exchange rate was suddenly realigned. However, it also prevented inflation-prone countries from maintaining their competitiveness by performing regular devaluations. From the time the Bretton Woods system collapsed (1973) to the virtual introduction of the euro (1999), the lira devalued against the deutschmark by 80%, the peseta by 76% and the French franc by 52%.[37] In the EMS period (13 March 1979 to 31 December 1998), Italy devalued thirteen times and revalued once, France devalued six times and Spain (after accession in 1989), four times.[38] France, however, ended the process of regular devaluations in 1993, when Central Bank President Jean-Claude Trichet introduced a 'franc fort' policy; 'franc fort' means 'strong franc', but it was evidently a play on Frankfurt, the seat of Germany's Bundesbank. The franc-fort policy was proclaimed as a competitive dis-inflation policy aimed at avoiding a depreciation of the French franc against the deutschmark.[39] It is still open to debate how strong the exchange-rate-uncertainty argument is and whether the devaluations were primarily a burden or a blessing.

The fact that the shares of exports of the large economies that go to the rest of the Eurozone have been declining, as shown in Figure 1.5, is often cited in this regard. In 1999, almost 44% of German exports of goods and services went to the Eurozone; nowadays, the Eurozone accounts for only around 36%. The other large countries show a similar downward trend, albeit at a higher level. Thus, after the introduction of the euro, a *relative* decoupling from the Eurozone has clearly taken place.

The explanation for this phenomenon is not that the euro countries mutually lost interest in their partners' goods. The downward trend depicted in the chart is explained by the dynamic development of other large regions in the world, as shown in Figure 1.1 above. Since European exports are widely spread around the world, the Eurozone countries benefited hugely from world dynamism, and so the exports destined for faster-growing regions inevitably grew faster than exports to the more sluggish Eurozone.

In addition, it is an open question how intra-European trade would have developed without the euro. Drawing hasty conclusions is therefore unadvisable. Even without the euro, the EU's internal market itself would have provided a strong impulse to intra-European trade. Free trade is the real motor

[37] See Deutsche Bundesbank, Statistics, Time Series Databases, *Macroeconomic Time Series*, Time Series BBK01.WT5006: Devisenkurse der Frankfurter Börse/100 ESP = ...DM / Spanien, BBK01; WT5007: Devisenkurse der Frankfurter Börse/1000 ITL = ...DM / Italien, BBK01; WT5012: Devisenkurse der Frankfurter Börse/100 FRF = ...DM / ab 1960/Frankreich.

[38] See Deutsche Bundesbank, *Statistisches Beiheft 5 zum Monatsbericht Devisenkursstatistik*, January 2000, pp. 45–47.

[39] See M. Par Faure, 'Jean-Claude Trichet, chevalier du franc fort' (Jean-Claude Trichet, knight of the franc fort), *L'Express*, 16 September 1993, available at: <http://www.lexpress.fr/informations/jean-claude-trichet-chevalier-du-franc-fort_595798.html>.

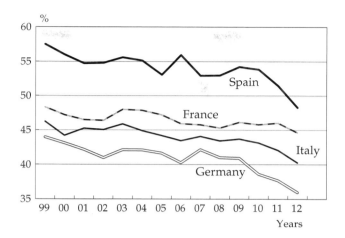

Figure 1.5 Share of exports going to the Eurozone (1999–2012)

Source: Eurostat, Database, *Economy and Finance*, National Accounts, Annual National Accounts, Exports and Imports by Member States of the EU/third Countries.

for integration and the division of labour in Europe. How much the protection against exchange rate variations actually contributed is unclear.

Exchange rate turbulence does much more than hinder trade, however. It disrupts the free movement of capital, since credit contracts, given the long maturities involved and their low margins relative to the transaction volume, are particularly vulnerable to exchange rate fluctuations. If the creditor provided a loan in his home currency, the risk upon maturity lay with the borrower. Many borrowers in eastern Europe who took on credit denominated in euros or Swiss francs are burdened now by the relative depreciation of their local currencies, making it very hard for them to continue servicing their debts at all. This was exactly the situation among western European countries before the currency union. If, on the other hand, credit was granted in the currency of the borrower, the lender couldn't know what he was getting into. Either way, international credit relations were disrupted.

The elimination of this type of uncertainty, as will be explained in detail in Chapter 2, exerted a much stronger influence on events in the Eurozone than the removal of uncertainty in trade, since it led to a dramatic convergence of interest rates on credit taken in the respective domestic currencies. Before the euro, foreign investors demanded premia that reflected the risk of depreciation of the currency in question until maturity. Soon after the euro was announced these premia disappeared, ushering in a divergence in economic development across the Eurozone that largely explains the crisis we are experiencing today.

To some degree, this interest rate convergence was beneficial for Europe as a whole, since it triggered a useful capital flow from north to south. Presumably there were investment opportunities with much higher yields to be found in southern than in northern Europe that investors had previously not dared to grab because of the exchange rate uncertainty. Thus, growth-enhancing capital flows were naturally to be expected from the introduction of the euro. To some observers, including the author, this was the biggest advantage of the common currency.[40] Unfortunately, however, this process gained too much momentum and went out of control, with accelerating price and wage expectations as the interest convergence went too far, because investors disregarded the bankruptcy risks that had replaced some of the former exchange rate risks. How reality failed to live up to the original beliefs will be discussed extensively in Chapters 2 and 4.

The Path to a Currency Union

Europe's political establishment had long set its sights on an exchange rate union. Following the Werner Plan of 1970, Europe's governments in 1972 agreed to coordinate their exchange rates by intervening so as to make them move like a 'snake in a tunnel'. A binding exchange rate relative to a central exchange rate that floated in relation to the dollar was set for each currency, and a limiting band was set around it. The corresponding central banks were obliged to intervene in the currency markets by buying or selling currency in order to keep their exchange rate within this band. The currency snake was not very successful. Most countries abandoned it, and in the end only a few currencies around the deutschmark remained. In 1979 a new attempt to keep the exchange rates under control was made with the European Exchange Rate Mechanism (ERM) proposed by French president Valéry Giscard d'Estaing and German chancellor Helmut Schmidt. With a varying number of members, it lasted until the euro was introduced. However, in 1992 it could not withstand the strain imposed on currency markets by German reunification. Quite a number of countries devalued their currency relative to the deutschmark in proportions much higher than foreseen. In addition to intervening in the currency markets, the central banks of the countries threatened with devaluation had tried to maintain the exchange rates by raising interest rates, with Sweden even bringing its own central bank refinancing rate temporarily up to an annualized rate of 500%. However, the speculation of financial investors put such large amounts of money in motion

---

[40] This view was expressed at the time the euro was introduced by H.-W. Sinn and R. Koll, 'The Euro, Interest Rates and Economic Growth', October 2000. For a hindsight criticism of this view see H.-W. Sinn, *Rescuing Europe, CESifo Forum* 11, Special Issue, August 2010, available at: <http://www.cesifo-group.de/DocDL/Forum-Sonderheft-Aug-2010_0.pdf>.

that the central banks were plainly powerless to stem the tide. The British pound lost 14% against the deutschmark in 1992, the lira 17%, the peseta 10%, the Swedish krona 16%, and the Finnish markka 16%.[41] Italy then left the ERM temporarily, and the UK permanently.

The turbulences stoked the wish, in particular in France, to do away with national currencies, leading in 1989 to the so-called Delors Plan, commissioned the year before by the European Council.[42]

The Delors Plan envisioned achieving a currency union in three stages. During the first stage (starting in January 1990), all barriers to the free movement of capital among the member states should be removed. In the second stage (starting in January 1994), the participating countries were to consolidate their budgets and thus lay the foundation for a stable common currency. The third stage included fixing the exchange rates and then introducing the euro as the common currency. The idea was to create a system whose solidly credible exchange rate would put an end to currency speculation, and the euro appeared to be the way to accomplish it.

Germany dithered in putting the Delors Plan into practice, because as the EU's largest economy, it did not want to subject its monetary policy to the influence of other countries. It favoured the 'crowning theory', according to which Europe would first need to attain a high level of fiscal integration before the common currency, as the crowning element, should be introduced. There were also misgivings regarding the other nations' commitment to stability as well as the fear of becoming infected with the southern countries' inflation bug.

Even Helmut Kohl, who ultimately pushed for the introduction of the euro in its present form, warned:[43]

> It cannot be said often enough: the political union is the indispensable counterpart to the economic and monetary union. Recent history…teaches us that the notion that it would be possible to sustain an economic and monetary union without political union is absurd.

Conversely, the other countries felt constrained by the Bundesbank's dominance over their decisions. They were forced to adhere to the Bundesbank's interest-rate policy, but given that the Bundesbank crafted its policy to suit its own economic

---

[41] See Deutsche Bundesbank, *Currency Statistics*, January 2000, pp. 6 f.

[42] See Committee for the Study of Economic and Monetary Union, *Report on Economic and Monetary Union in the European Community*, 1989, available at: <http://ec.europa.eu/economy_finance/publications/publication6161_en.pdf>.

[43] See H. Kohl, 'Regierungserklärung zum Gipfeltreffen der Staats- und Regierungschefs der NATO in Rom sowie zur EG-Konferenz in Maastricht', German Bundestag, *Plenarprotokoll* 12, No. 53, 1991 (translated by the author); O. Issing, who later became the ECB chief economist, agreed to this; see 'Gut für Deutschland', *Der Spiegel*, No. 3, 15 January 1996, p. 84.

jurisdiction, it did not sit well with other economies. There were times, for instance, when higher rates for refinancing credit from the Bundesbank were necessary in order to put a check on inflation, while in neighbouring countries an economic slump called for lower rates, and vice versa. The Bundesbank's interest rate policy always managed to hold sway on account of the sheer size of the deutschmark economic area. The other countries saw themselves forced to adjust their interest rates to those of the Bundesbank in order to avert capital flight. It is easy to see why countries strove to change this state of affairs. For this reason, the French President considered the crowning theory to be nothing more than a delaying tactic of the Germans. 'The harmonisation of economic policy will follow by itself', he replied later to the question of whether it was possible to have the euro without economic policy coordination.[44]

The Price of German Reunification?

The standoff between Germany and its neighbouring countries was not solved until German reunification was imminent. On the one hand, many Europeans pleaded for a stronger political binding of a Germany that was expected to become stronger through reunification. On the other, Germany itself was ready to compromise in order to make reunification a reality without undue political resistance. After all, Germany was still not a sovereign country and needed the formal consent of the World War II's victorious powers to proceed with reunification. To be sure, no European country could have realistically hindered German reunification, since the USA and Russia had already signalled their consent. US President George H. W. Bush had become a particularly strong advocate of reunification, and Russian President Mikhail Gorbachev had agreed to German reunification, given that he could not keep the Soviet Union together anyway. A French blockade, however, would have jeopardized the French-German axis and, with it, European integration, which has been one of Germany's paramount goals since the end of World War II.

On 4 January 1990, a Franco-German governmental summit decided in favour of going ahead with the implementation of the Delors Plan, which two

---

[44] J. Chirac, 'Nur der Euro bringt Fortschritt', Interview by H. Nathe, H. Oschwald, and M. Weber-Lamberdière, *Focus*, No. 38, 15 September 1997, available at: <http://www.focus.de/politik/ausland/ausland-nur-der-euro-bringt-fortschritt-und150-1-ar-chivdokument-2-teile_aid_168401.html>. For an early criticism of trying to have a fiscal union without a common currency see H. Uhlig, 'One Money, but many Fiscal Policies in Europe: What Are the Consequences?', in M. Buti (ed.), *Monetary and Fiscal Policies in the EMU*, Cambridge University Press, Cambridge 2003, pp. 29–56.

years later, in July 1992, would lead to the Maastricht Treaty.[45] With this treaty, the EU member countries agreed to introduce the euro after a number of convergence criteria were fulfilled, but no later than 1 January 1999.[46]

France pushed strongly for the euro, since its central bank had seen itself forced to follow the monetary policy decisions of the Bundesbank, without being in a position to exert any influence over such decisions. Mitterrand had at first actively opposed German reunification, but seemed to have acquiesced in exchange for Germany's agreement on introducing the euro. While this deal has always been denied officially and certainly has no legal standing, given that it is mentioned in none of the official documents, its implicit nature is all too obvious.[47] The agreement to the 2+4 negotiations, and the European Summit planned in Maastricht, which would lay a cornerstone for the Economic and Monetary Union, were announced jointly by Mitterrand and Kohl after their summit.[48]

The significance accorded by France to the power of the Bundesbank can be gleaned from the fact that President Mitterrand dubbed the Deutschmark 'Germany's force de frappe', i.e. its atomic bomb,[49] and from his comment to his countrymen that the Maastricht Treaty was even better for France than the Treaty of Versailles—indeed, a 'Super-Versailles'.[50] The influential newspaper *Le Figaro* crowed 'Elle paie aujourd'hui'[51] (Today she, Germany, must pay), using the slogan 'Le Boche paiera tout' (The Jerries will pay it all) directed against Germany when it was forced to sign the Treaty of Versailles, which brought up the ire of Rudolf Augstein, then chief editor of *Der Spiegel*, Germany's most influential weekly.[52] It can hardly be presumed that *Le Figaro* divined at the time that Germany would one day have to pay for the EU bailout packages. Still, embedding Germany in

---

[45] See EU, 'Treaty on European Union', *Official Journal* C 191, 29 July 1992, available at: <http://eur-lex.europa.eu/en/treaties/dat/11992M/htm/11992M.html>.

[46] EU, 'Treaty on European Union', 29 July 1992, article 109 littera j paragraph 4.

[47] See M. Sauga, S. Simons, and K. Wiegrefe, 'Der Preis der Einheit', *Der Spiegel*, No. 39, 27 September 2010, pp. 34–38.

[48] See 'Gespräch des Bundeskanzlers Kohl mit Staatspräsident Mitterrand, in Latché, 4 January 1990', *Dokumente zur Deutschlandpolitik* 1998, p. 582 ff.

[49] See W. Proissl, 'Why Germany Fell out of Love with Europe', *Bruegel Essay and Lecture Series*, 1 July 2010, available at: <http://www.bruegel.org/publications/publication-detail/publication/417-why-germany-fell-out-of-love-with-europe>.

[50] As testified by Hubertus Dessloch, former Head of the Representation of the Free State of Bavaria to the European Union, in a letter to the author dated 27 May 2010.

[51] See F.-O. Giesbert, 'De Versailles à Maastricht' (From Versailles to Maastricht), *Le Figaro*, 18 September 1992, p. 1.

[52] See R. Augstein, 'Neues vom Turmbau zu Babel', *Der Spiegel*, No. 42, 18 October 1993, p. 29.

a common currency system was expected by some of the euro advocates in Latin Europe to lead, one way or another, to a convergence in living standards and, perhaps, the mutual assumption of debts.

In exchange for giving up the deutschmark, Kohl tried to steer Europe towards a political union, but Mitterrand did not agree. Political union found no consensus in France. President Chirac even said, when the euro was introduced:[53]

> I will not accept Europe to become a super state or that its institutions be fashioned after those of the United States.

Thus, Kohl had to be content with the introduction of the euro without any political concessions from the other euro countries that could have been construed as leading to deeper political integration.

Transfer and Debt Union

While France and Germany regarded the decision to introduce the euro as a central step in the process of reconciliation, some of the southern European countries were compelled by another motivation. They hoped to gain access to lower interest rates for their sovereign debt, and they regarded the euro as a vehicle to reach the levels of prosperity enjoyed by the northern European countries.

Among the southern countries' populations the expectations of advantages offered by the euro were even simpler and clearer. As Greek singer Costa Cordalis colourfully put it,[54]

> The Greek were salivating for the euro. They wanted for once in their life to own a sleek German car.

That calls to mind some feelings surrounding German reunification: the call 'either the D-mark comes to us, or we come to the D-mark' made by the German Democratic Republic citizenry before reunification showed just as starkly the symbolic aspect of the currency. Many politicians saw the euro as a peace project, while most economists saw it as a technical means to facilitate transactions, but the true reason why the southern European countries pushed for it was probably that it was a symbol of new wealth and prosperity.

---

[53] See J. Chirac on 6 March 2002 according to W. Vogel, 'Frankreichs Europapolitik nach der Wahl', Deutsch-Französisches Institut, *Aktuelle Frankreichanalysen*, No. 18, 2002 (translated by the author).

[54] See C. Cordalis in TV talk show *Menschen bei Maischberger* of 28 February 2012, Topic: 'The Last Sirtaki: Greece Bankrupt, Germans Pay Nonetheless?' (translated by the author).

Some analysts and policy advisers even gave this interpretation a more concrete meaning by mulling over a transfer union, an equalization transfer system between regions similar to the one operating in Germany.[55]

The German government and the Bundesbank naturally inferred as much. They wanted to exclude the southern European countries, because they were afraid of the high level of public debt of such countries. The Bundesbank was not as certain as Helmut Kohl had said in his 1998 speech cited above that there would be no transfer union. That was the reason behind its insistence in incorporating into the Maastricht Treaty the condition that, to accede to the euro, public debt was not to exceed 60% of GDP. In 1991, the year for which data were known when the Maastricht Treaty was agreed, the debt-to-GDP ratios of Italy (102%), Greece (92%), Belgium (128%), Ireland (95%), and the Netherlands (79%) were so far above the 60% limit that it appeared unfeasible for them to meet this criterion. And indeed they did not manage to fulfil the accession criterion, just as most of the euro member countries did not. In the control year 1997, only Finland (56%), France (58%), Luxembourg (7%), and Great Britain (54%) were below the 60% limit. Seen in this light, legally the euro project should not have started at that time.

But even then it was clear that Europe's politicians were inventive when it came to formulating treaty texts. The Maastricht Treaty contained a fuzzy remark that the 60% limit could be set aside when at least the deficit ratio was diminishing and approaching the 3% benchmark, or when it exceeded this value

[55] The role of fiscal transfers had already been addressed by the Werner Plan (European Commission, *Report to the Council and the Commission on the Realization by Stages of Economic and Monetary Union in the Community*, 1970); see also T. Mayer, *Europe's Unfinished Currency*, Anthem Press, London 2012, especially chapter 1. In the MacDougall Report (European Commission, *MacDougall-Report, Vol I: The Role of Public Finance in European Integration*, and *MacDougall-Report, Vol II: Individual Contributions and Working Papers*, 1970) a budget of between five and seven percent of GDP was suggested for transfers between the member countries. It was argued in a number of places that a redistribution mechanism for the Eurozone was desirable. See T. Courchene, C. Goodhart, A. Majocchi, W. Moesen, R. Prud'homme, F. Schneider, S. Smith, B. Spahn, and C. Walsh, 'Stable Money—Sound Finances', *European Economy* 53, 1993; P. Van Rompuy, F. Abraham, and D. Heremans, 'Economic Federalism and the EMU', *European Economy,* Special Edition, 1, 1991; M. Obstfeld and G. Peri, 'Regional Nonadjustment and Fiscal Policy: Lessons for EMU', *NBER Working Paper*, No. 6431, June 1999; 'Maastricht Follies—Fiscal Policy Should Not Be Constrained Under a Single Currency', *The Economist*, 9 April 1998, available at: <http://www.economist.com/node/159467>; D. Fuceri, 'Does the EMU Need a Fiscal Transfer Mechanism?', *Vierteljahreshefte zur Wirtschaftsforschung* 73, 2004, pp. 418–428.

as an exception and only temporarily.[56] Thus, everything was possible after all, and the southern countries that wanted to join the euro despite their high indebtedness saw the door opening up. The euro itself was already a firm project. Paramount was now to be counted among the countries that would adopt it as a currency. The southern countries and France, which naturally had large interests in the Mediterranean region, exerted pressure until the Kohl government relented and accepted an enlarged Eurozone. With hindsight, this planted the seed for the debt problems affecting Europe today.

There are, however, indications that Kohl himself wanted to leave aside the 60% limit in order to bring Italy in, waving away the concerns of the Bundesbank and its experts.[57] Faced with a choice between exhausting his energy in a tussle with France and Italy on the one hand, and realizing his dream of going into history as the father of a united Europe on the other, the decision for him was not so difficult after all.

It appears that Finance Minister Theo Waigel tried until the last moment to avert this.[58] His position was weakened, however, because the EU had forced Germany to include the Treuhand obligations in the government debt.[59] This led to a jump in Germany's debt-to-GDP ratio by eight percentage points, bringing it to 58%, just a little below the 60% limit, from 1994 to 1995. In 1996, the ratio reached 60.4%, just surpassing the limit, and in the reference year 1997, Germany's ratio was clearly too high, at 61.3%, which would have left the country out of the euro if the Maastricht criteria for accession had been

[56] See EU, 'Treaty on European Union', 29 July 1992, article 104 littera c.

[57] The Kohl government was well aware of the enormous risks posed by taking in Italy, with its high indebtedness, as can be seen from the files released upon request of the weekly *Der Spiegel*. In January 1998, Kohl's foreign policy adviser Joachim Bitterlich and the state secretary of the Federal Ministry of Finance, Jürgen Stark, pointed out that Italy's lower deficit was due primarily to exceptional effects, such as the disproportionate drop in market interest rates, which provided no guarantee for the permanence of sound finances. Kohl overruled these concerns. See 'Kohl kannte Risiken', *MMNews*, 6 May 2012, available at: <http://www.mmnews.de/index.php/wirtschaft/9996-kohl-kannte-e uro-risiken>.

[58] 'Theo hat alles gegeben', *Der Spiegel*, No. 51, 16 December 1996, available at: <http://www.spiegel.de/spiegel/print/d-9133850.html>; 'Kreative Buchführung', *Der Spiegel*, No. 41, 7 October 1996, available at: <http://www.spiegel.de/spiegel/ print/d-9102323.html>; M. Reimon, 'Eurokrise (nicht nur) für Dummies—Teil 1', *Der Standard,* 2 November 2011, available at: <http://derstandard.at/1319181752075/ Eurokrise-nicht-nur-fuer-Dummies—Teil-1>; I. Zöttle, 'Gewaltige Sprengsätze', *Focus*, No. 13, 23 March 1998, available at: <http://www.focus.de/politik/deutschland/ waehrungsunion-gewaltige-sprengsaetze_aid_170413.html>.

[59] Treuhand was East Germany's trust fund for ex-communist firms and its privatiza- tion agency.

applied. However, the whole point of introducing the euro was to deprive the Bundesbank of its power to set the interest rates in Europe or, to put it differently, to liberate the countries of western Europe from the Bundesbank's diktat. Thus, since the euro without Germany would have been pointless, the entry criterion was waived. And this, in turn, opened the gates to new entrants. The overly indebted southern candidate countries and Belgium used the argument that Germany had been accepted as a euro member to demand access as well.

German Finance Minister Waigel tried to forestall this by begging the Bundesbank to revalue part of its undervalued gold reserves in order to receive higher transfers of Bundesbank profits, which could have helped Germany to avoid exceeding the debt limit. But the Bundesbank remained stubborn as a matter of principle.

The European Central Bank

Thus, a new currency was introduced for a large number of European countries, and the European Central Bank (ECB) became the continent's most powerful political institution. The ECB turned out to be the only institution able to protect the Eurozone against the shock waves created by the financial crisis. But, as will be shown, in doing so it heavily interfered with the allocation of resources, a course of action that may have long-lasting implications on the distribution of wealth and economic activity among regions.

While the idea of making the ECB a centralized institution like the Bank of England had been discussed, the local preferences of the existing national central banks (NCBs) put a stop to such aspirations and a much more decentralized structure was created instead. The local NCBs continued to exist as institutions owned by their respective sovereigns, with their assets and debts not being socialized, and they basically retained their economic functions in terms of carrying out the monetary operations. However, they do have to follow the rules and conditions set by the ECB Governing Council in Frankfurt, as well as share their income from monetary policy operations in accordance with their respective shares in the ECB's subscribed capital. Thus, the system of central banks issuing euros is called 'Eurosystem'. In this book the terms ECB and Eurosystem will often be used as synonyms, unless clarity requires a distinction.

The national central banks of the EU countries (not only those of the euro countries) had to contribute to the ECB's original subscribed capital of € 5.76 billion, capital that was increased to € 10.76 billion at the end of 2010. Adding the profits resulting from the revaluation of assets such as gold reserves, the ECB's equity capital as of December 2013 amounted to € 21.0 billion.[60] The capital

---

[60] See European Central Bank, *Annual Accounts 2013*, p. 4.

allocation key was set according to the relative size of the EU member countries, calculated as the average of their GDP and population figures.[61] Leaving out the capital contributions of the non-euro EU countries, the adjusted capital key for Germany in 2013 was 27.0%, for France 20.3%, and for Italy 17.9%, while for Greece it was 2.8%, and for Malta, 0.1%, for example. These adjusted capital keys play a role in many important calculations, such as those for the distribution of profits and losses that accrue from monetary policy.

The Eurosystem is directed by a Governing Council which delegates everyday businesses to an Executive Board consisting of six members, including the ECB president, currently Mario Draghi of Italy. In 2013, the Council itself consisted of the seventeen presidents of the member NCBs, plus the six members of the Executive Board. At the beginning of 2014 Latvia joined as the eighteenth member, being granted an additional Council seat. If the number of euro member countries exceeds 18, as could soon be the case when Lithuania joins, a rotation system will apply for membership in the Governing Council so as to limit the number of its active members.

The NCB presidents are elected for a period of at least five years, the members of the Executive Board for a period of eight years, and the ECB President for eight years. While the NCB mandates are renewable, the ECB mandates are not.

Although the NCB presidents are chosen through domestic political processes, they are not assumed to act as country representatives, being expected to make their decisions as pure technocrats for the common good, independent of political influence. When the Maastricht Treaty was agreed, political independence was considered one of the fundamental requirements for a well-functioning monetary system, one that would prevent opportunistic behaviour geared at serving particular interests.

In this spirit, the voting rights of all NCB presidents were made identical, regardless of the size of their respective home countries and the share of the liability their countries assumed. This structure deviated strongly from the way private corporations are run, and even from the IMF, where countries' voting rights are proportional to their paid-in capital and liability. At the ECB, the representative of Malta has the same voting right as that of France, Germany, or

---

[61] All EU countries, even those not introducing the euro as a currency, became shareholders. Thus, for example, even the United Kingdom and Denmark, which are the only EU countries that have 'opt-out' clauses in the Treaty exempting them from participation, contributed their shares to the capital stock. However, the countries that have not yet introduced the euro do not vote on monetary policy, are not bound to carry out the ECB's monetary policy, and do not participate in the distribution of the Eurosystem income from money creation. Share ownership is thus primarily notional for the non-euro area EU countries, without real importance.

Italy, even though Malta has barely $1/156^{th}$, $1/195^{th}$ or $1/142^{th}$ of the respective populations.

If one considers that the members of the Executive Board, including the ECB President, also have voting rights, and given that each of the three countries above (France, Germany, and Italy) traditionally has one representative on the Board, their respective shares in the voting rights would amount to 8.7%, still much less than their respective liability shares. In fact, Malta has a per capita voting right that is seventy-eight times larger than that of France, ninety-eight times larger than that of Germany, or seventy-one times larger than that of Italy. Figure 1.6 gives an overview of the relevant figures for all euro countries.

Treating all countries as equal regardless of their size was also justified inasmuch as the ECB's only goal according to the Maastricht Treaty is to maintain price stability. In fact, referring to the European System of Central Banks (ESCB), article 105 of the Treaty of the European Union states:

> The primary objective of the ESCB shall be to maintain price stability.

As all countries presumably fully share this goal, conflicts of interest were not foreseen, and it seemed reasonable to treat the NCB presidents as technocrats devoid of a political agenda.

However, as this book will argue, the ECB is, to a large extent, carrying out local rescue operations to the benefit of troubled countries and their creditors, becoming the principal bailout institution in the process. By preventing sovereign and bank bankruptcies, it helps private investors to escape the consequences of their failed investment decisions. It grants credit to troubled banks at conditions that are better than those offered by markets and buys government bonds of troubled countries to stabilize their market prices, acting as a lender of last resort. All of this has dramatic implications for the distribution of wealth among the euro countries and for the geographical allocation of capital investments. Thus, the interpretation of the ECB Council as a mere technocratic body that limits itself to monetary decisions seems questionable.[62]

---

[62] Nitsch and Badinger show that the ECB's decisions to set interest rates depending on inflation and the gap between actual and potential output, according to the so-called Taylor rule, can best be explained by weighting the national inflation and unemployment data with the respective nationalities' share in the ECB personnel rather than using the actual statistical averages. See H. Badinger and V. Nitsch, 'National Representation in Multinational Institutions: The Case of the European Central Bank', *CESifo Working Paper* No. 3573, September 2011, available at: <http://www.cesifo-group.de/DocDL/cesifo1_wp3573.pdf>.

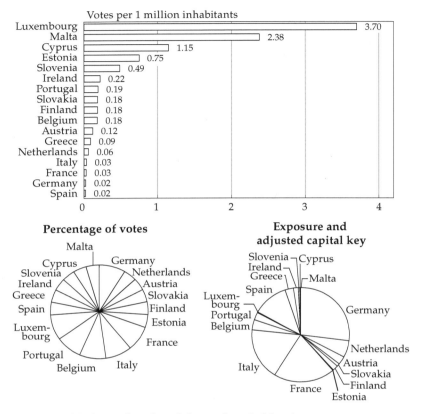

Figure 1.6 ECB Council voting rights and capital key/exposure 2013

Sources: European Central Bank, *Organisation*, Decision-making Bodies, ECB Council and Capital Key; European Commission, Economic and Financial Affairs, *Economic Databases and Indicators*, AMECO–the annual macro-economic database.

Note: The adjusted capital key (equity share) is the capital key divided by the sum of the capital keys of those central banks that participate in the Eurosystem and share in the profits and losses from monetary operations. The Bank of England, for example, owns an equity share in the ECB, but does not participate in the pooling of profits and losses. The adjusted capital key gives a country's liability and profit share. The capital keys, in turn, are determined by the mean of a country's population and GDP share.

Potential gains and losses from direct redistribution effects are not limited to the ECB's equity capital, as one may think. The equity capital of all national central banks of the Eurozone, including the ECB's € 21 billion on 31 December 2013, was € 353 billion (including revaluation reserves).[63] The true volume of resources potentially subject to redistribution among countries is much bigger, as it includes the seignorage income central banks earn through money creation, that is, by lending out self-created money to commercial banks against interest. The present value of this seignorage income, which we could label 'seignorage capital', under static conditions is the stock of central bank money (Mo) itself. In December 2013, the Eurosystem's static seignorage capital was € 1.262 trillion, or 13% of the Eurozone's 2013 GDP. Adding the nominal equity capital of € 353 billion gives a total of € 1.615 trillion, or 17% of Eurozone GDP.

If account is taken of the fact that the stock of money balances will grow apace with the economy and the price level, the seignorage capital attains an even bigger value.[64] According to a Citigroup study, the sum of notional equity and seignorage capital might even amount to € 3.4 trillion, or 36% of Eurozone GDP.[65] The largest chunk of this sum, about € 2.9 trillion, is seignorage capital. Managing this capital through the policies of the ECB is not a trivial matter and cannot simply be subsumed under the innocuous term 'monetary policy'. A later chapter in this book will explain in detail, in the context of the so-called Target balances, why the ECB's policies have induced massive shifts in the seignorage capital between the Eurozone's countries, potentially exerting distributional effects that go far beyond the realm of monetary policy.

[63] See European Central Bank, *Weekly Financial Statements*, Consolidated Financial Statement of the Eurosystem as at 31 December 2013, press release, 8 January 2014.

[64] Let M be the monetary base (stock of central bank money), i the (constant) nominal rate of interest and r the (constant) annual nominal growth rate of the economy, then the present value of the seignorage revenue of the Eurosystem is $M\,i\,/(i-r)$. In the case of non-constant growth rates and interest rates, a somewhat more sophisticated formal expression results.

[65] See W. Buiter and E. Rahbari, 'Looking into the Deep Pockets of the ECB', Citi Economics, *Global Economics View*, 27 February 2012, available at: <http://blogs.r.ftdata.co.uk/money-supply/files/2012/02/citi-Looking-into-the-Deep-Pockets-of-the-ECB.pdf>.

CHAPTER 2

Bubbles in the Periphery

Importing Capital—The Disappearance of Interest Rate Spreads—The Timing Problem—Relief for Government Budgets—The Lack of Fiscal Discipline—Italy's Missed Opportunity—The Foreign Debt Problem—Bubbles—Property Prices— Private Wealth—Market or Government Failure?

Importing Capital

As mentioned at the beginning of Chapter 1, when the euro was introduced there was the widespread belief that the new currency would stimulate growth and prosperity in Europe. After all, the euro would create a true common capital market by levelling the playing field and providing cheaper credit to countries that hitherto had had to pay high interest rates, thereby triggering productive capital flows from the northern to the southern countries that would enhance European growth by replacing low-yield with high-yield investments.[1] While the growth expectations turned out to be overly optimistic, as Figure 1.1 showed, a large-scale reallocation of capital in favour of the now-distressed GIPSIC countries (Greece, Ireland, Portugal, Spain, Italy, Cyprus) did indeed take place. This chapter

---

[1] See H.-W. Sinn and R. Koll, 'Der Euro, die Zinsen und das europäische Wirtschaftswachstum', *ifo Schnelldienst* 53, No. 32, 2000, pp. 46–47, available at: <http://www.cesifo-group.de/DocDL/ifosd_2000_33_8.pdf>; Translation: 'The Euro, Interest Rates and European Economic Growth', *CESifo Forum* 1, No. 3, October 2000, pp. 30–31, available at: <http://www.cesifo-group.de/DocDL/Forum300-sl1.pdf>; additionally, see H.-W. Sinn, *Rescuing Europe, CESifo Forum* 11, Special Issue, August 2010, available at: <http://www.cesifo-group.de/DocDL/Forum-Sonderheft-Aug-2010_0.pdf>; and O. Blanchard, 'Current Account Deficits in Rich Countries', *IMF Staff Papers* 54, 2007, pp. 191–219; F. Giavazzi and L. Spaventa, 'Why the Current Account May Matter in a Monetary Union: Lessons from the Financial Crisis in the Euro Area', *CEPR Discussion Paper* No. 8008, September 2010.

looks at the reallocation process from the viewpoint of the recipient countries. The next chapter will focus on the capital-exporting countries, and on Germany in particular.

The GIPSIC countries were all huge capital importers in the years preceding the outbreak of the crisis, as shown in Figure 2.1. While their aggregate capital import (contoured line near the centre) was small until the year 2000, it exploded after 2002 and peaked, at about 6% of their combined GDP, in 2008, the year of the Lehman Brothers collapse. Subsequently, during the crisis, it was still substantial, but shrank year by year and eventually turned into a capital export in 2013. Only Cyprus and Greece kept up capital imports, while Ireland turned into a capital exporter as early as 2010. As will be shown in Chapter 7, the capital imports during the first years of the crisis were largely explained by various sorts of public international credit provided to the crisis-hit countries rather than private capital flows.

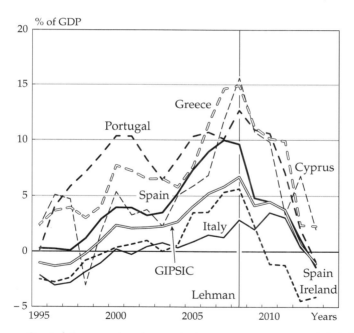

Figure 2.1 Capital imports (or the equivalent current account deficits) of the GIPSIC countries as a share of GDP (1995–2013)

Source: Eurostat, Database, *Economy and Finance*, Balance of Payments—International Transactions, Balance of Payments Statistics by Country; European Commission, Economic and Financial Affairs, *European Economic Forecast*, Autumn 2013; Ifo Institute calculations.

Note: Disregarding net errors and omissions in the balance of payments, capital imports are identical in size to the current account deficits (see also Chapter 6). 2013 European Commission forecast, Autumn 2013.

The largest capital importers in relative terms were Greece, Portugal and Cyprus. At the time the Lehman Brothers crisis broke out, capital imports amounted to more than 12% of GDP, an extremely high level from a historical perspective. Among the bigger countries, Spain stands out with a peak capital import of 10% of GDP in 2007. As will be discussed below, Spain was by far the largest capital importer in absolute terms.

It follows from the definition of the balance of payments that the capital import of a country is identical to its current account deficit, i.e. basically the excess of imports and net interest payments to foreigners over exports. Thus, the curves depicted in Figure 2.1 can be interpreted in two different ways. Capital flows and current account balances are two sides of the same coin. They are numerically identical and mutually dependent.[2] During a business cycle, exports and imports of goods go up and down depending on the relative speed of the domestic economy and that of its external trading partners, leaving in their wake a capital flow as a residual. This is the usual way of seeing the issue, since business-cycle phenomena attract by far the most public attention. However, with upheavals causing investors to rebalance their wealth portfolios, the causality is reversed. Desired portfolio reallocations become the driving force, and real economic activity adjusts so as to generate current account imbalances that make possible the desired portfolio reallocations, which show up as capital flows. The introduction of the euro induced such a desired portfolio adjustment, since countries that had hitherto appeared risky in terms of investment now seemed attractive to international financial and real investors.

---

[2] This is a relationship that every student of economics learns in the initial courses. The goods (including services) measured in the gross domestic product (GDP) are used for consumption, domestic real investment and net exports. Since GDP minus depreciation is the sum of all income earned in a country, GDP minus depreciation minus consumption is the savings of that country. These savings are also equal to domestic net investment plus net exports. Since the part of savings that is not used for domestic investment flows abroad, net exports of goods equal net capital exports. A more precise analysis shows that, strictly speaking, it is the current account surplus that is equal to net capital exports. The current account surplus is equal to net exports of goods plus net capital income received from abroad minus transfers sent abroad (current donations made to people in other countries, such as guest worker remittances or development aid). The current account surplus is by definition equal to the net capital export of a country up to the very last cent, just as the left column total of a company's balance sheet shows the same figure as the right column total, although the type of items that are booked in the columns are different.

The Disappearance of Interest Rate Spreads[3]

The driving force that caused investors to seek a portfolio restructuring in favour of the GIPSIC countries was the removal of uncertainty. For one thing, the exchange-rate uncertainty disappeared with the introduction of the currency union, and for another the union seemed to signal sufficient stability and mutual protection to make bankruptcies of states and banks appear more unlikely.

The extent to which investors perceived the euro as reducing investment uncertainty in southern Europe and Ireland can most clearly be seen in the retrenchment of interest rates for these countries. Figure 2.2 illustrates the yields for the ten-year government bonds of the various euro countries. What the figure shows must also have applied to the interest rates on private credit, for which no corresponding dataset is available: high spreads in earlier years, a dramatic convergence of rates as the euro approached, a nearly decade-long phase of identical rates for most countries, and then a new phase of large spreads during the current crisis.

Interest spreads always result from the fear of investors that they might lose their money. Investors charge a premium above the interest rate that would be demanded for a presumably safe investment to compensate for the risk that the debt may not be fully repaid. When they reckon with the possibility of losing all the money invested because of bankruptcy, or if they fear that they will be repaid with a devalued currency, the rule of thumb is that they calculate the effective annual rate of interest as the nominal rate agreed in the borrowing contract minus the annual bankruptcy probability and minus the expected rate of annual currency devaluation. Thus, for the effective rates of interest to be equal and for investors to be indifferent between alternative portfolio options, the nominal rates of interest have to differ by the expected default risk and the expected rate of currency devaluation. This makes interest rates that look equal actually different, and rates that look different actually equal, and it ensures that interest rate differentials (i.e. spreads) reflect the investors' risk assessment. Interest rate differentials that reflect investment risks are necessary for the 'law of one price', one of the fundamental efficiency requirements of a market economy, to hold.

Over the period covered by the chart, the German interest rate was the lowest of all, the other rates differing according to the idiosyncratic risks involved, which kept the GIPSIC countries all on the higher side. On the left part of the chart the spreads presumably resulted primarily from the risk of inflation and subsequent devaluation, while on the right-hand side they resulted primarily from the risk of default. Other risks may have been present, but presumably to a

---

[3] For this and the following sections, see also H.-W. Sinn, *Rescuing Europe*, August 2010.

lesser extent. Only for the intermediate period of a decade or so investors seemed to have believed that they would get their money back after lending to the GIPSIC countries and really earn the rate of interest stipulated in the debt contract.

Before it was clear that the euro would come, private and public debtors in the southern countries, as well as in Ireland, had to offer very high yields to their foreign creditors to compensate for potential exchange rate depreciations, most of the debtors' currencies having depreciated repeatedly during the previous decades. In the five-year period between 1991 and late 1995, when the euro was announced at the Madrid Summit, the ten-year government bond yields of Italy, Spain, and Portugal were 4.8 percentage points higher on average than those of Germany. The Greek interest rate hovered above 20%, at least 15 percentage points above the German one.

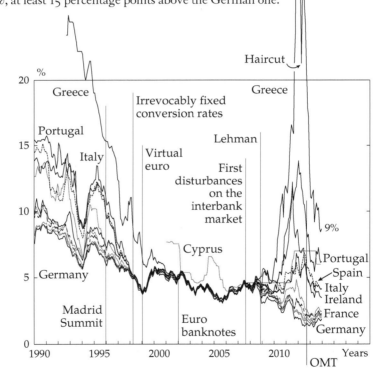

Figure 2.2 Ten-year government bond yields (1990–2013)

Source: Thomson Reuters Datastream, Data Category: *Interest Rates, Benchmark Bonds*.

Note: The interest rates correspond to average yields for government bonds with ten-year maturity (so-called Benchmark Bonds). Reuters calculates the yield of a fictitious ten-year bond issued on a given date, applying the theory of expectations for interest rates to the observed yields of various instruments with different maturities at that particular date.

The interest burden for private and public debtors was huge. In some countries, over 10% of GDP was devoted to servicing the interest burden stemming from the public debt alone. That was the main reason why the southern countries wanted the euro so badly. The new currency, they thought, would bring about a lasting reduction in exchange-risk-motivated spreads, bringing significant relief to the debtor parties.

To be sure, flexible exchange rates always offered the possibility of reducing the debt burden through inflation and depreciation. Still, the hope was that the euro would generate more confidence among investors and that the interest burden would be correspondingly lighter. The money spared thanks to lower interest payments was to be applied to reducing the principal on the debt and to steering a course towards credible, long-term stable growth. The vicious circle of ever higher interest rates and, as a result, ever more financial distress, ever higher indebtedness and higher interest payments that had plagued these countries for decades, would be broken once and for all.

The lurking long-term risk of giving up the depreciation option by adopting the euro was deemed smaller than the immediate advantage of calmer financial markets and the resulting lowering of the interest burden.

Everything appeared to work just fine initially. Exchange rate uncertainty disappeared and interest rates converged within just two years of the Madrid Summit of December 1995, which set the timetable for the introduction of the euro, and it became clear which countries would participate. Convergence was completed by May 1998, when the exchange rates of the 11 participating countries in the first round[4] were irrevocably fixed. The formal introduction of the euro as legal tender between banks due to start on 1 January 1999, as well as the physical introduction of the currency in January and February 2002, no longer played any role, because the capital markets had already priced in these developments. After that point in May 1998, the interest spreads were so low that they can hardly be made out in the chart. Typically, countries like Italy or Spain had to offer an interest premium of only 20 basis points, i.e. 0.2%, above the German benchmark to convince investors to buy their government bonds.

Greek yields sank as well, although somewhat later, as the figure shows, since Greece's reference year for fulfilling the accession criteria was 1999. Greece sneaked into the currency union, as was later shown, by doctoring its budget deficit figures,[5] joining the Eurosystem in 2001, just in time for the physical introduction of euro

[4] These countries were: Austria, Belgium, Finland, France, Germany, Ireland, Italy, Luxembourg, Netherlands, Portugal, and Spain. Greece (2001), Slovenia (2007), Cyprus (2008), Malta (2008), Slovakia (2009) and Estonia (2011) joined later.

[5] See Eurostat, *Report on the Revision of the Greek Government Deficit and Debt Figures*, 22 November 2004.

notes and coins. The Greek spreads fell to 35 basis points (0.35%) and below, which was insignificant compared to the spreads prevalent before its adoption of the euro.[6]

Cyprus did not join the Eurozone until 2008, much later than the other countries, but its accession had been decided on 10 July 2007, and it had been anticipated even earlier. Its spreads over the German benchmark fell from 2.5 percentage points at the beginning of 2005 to barely 30 basis points, on average, during the period August–December 2007.

The phase of nearly identical interest rates ended in summer 2007, about a decade after the convergence began and five years after the physical introduction of the euro, when the US subprime crisis spilled over to Europe and led to the collapse of the interbank market.[7] It all began with the declaration of German Industriekreditbank IKB on 30 July 2007 that it had come into a dangerous situation because of pending write-off losses on assets involving claims in the US subprime market. A few days later, in early August, BNP Paribas, the biggest French bank and the second-biggest of the Eurozone, declared that its hedge funds were having difficulties because of their involvement in the US subprime market and that it would stop funding them. These announcements sent shock waves through the financial markets that led to the first crisis of the interbank market in August 2007. Banks ceased to trust one another and froze interbank lending. The ECB managed to keep the crisis from spreading by helping with generous liquidity injections that went largely unnoticed by the general public. But the seed of scepticism was by then deeply lodged among investors. In September, Northern Rock, a British bank, faced serious difficulties, followed a month later by Sachsen LB Europe, a Dublin

---

[6] For the smaller debt markets like those of Greece, the reduction in spreads can also reflect a liquidity effect, the creation of the Eurozone triggering new demand for the respective government bonds from investors who seek to match the Eurozone composition in their portfolio holdings.

[7] See R. J. Shiller, *The Subprime Solution: How Today's Global Financial Crisis Happened, and What to Do About It*, Princeton University Press, Princeton 2008; W. Münchau, *Kernschmelze im Finanzsystem*, Hanser, Munich 2008, translation: *The Meltdown Years: The Unfolding of the Global Economic Crisis*, Mcgraw-Hill Professional, New York 2009; G. A. Akerlof and R. J. Shiller, *Animal Spirits: How Human Psychology Drives the Economy and Why It Matters for Global Capitalism*, Princeton University Press, Princeton 2009; C. Reinhart, and K. S. Rogoff, *This Time is Different: Eight Centuries of Financial Folly*, Princeton University Press, Princeton 2009; H.-W. Sinn, *Kasino-Kapitalismus. Wie es zur Finanzkrise kam, und was jetzt zu tun ist*, Econ, Berlin 2009. Translation: *Casino Capitalism. How the Financial Crisis Came About and What Needs to Be Done Now*, Oxford University Press, Oxford 2010; H.-W. Sinn, *Die Target-Falle, Gefahren für unser Geld und unsere Kinder*, Hanser, Munich 2012; A. Admati and M. Hellwig, *Bankers' New Clothes: What's Wrong with Banking and What to Do About it*, Princeton University Press, Princeton 2013.

conduit of a German state bank, and in January 2008 US investment bank Bear Stearns began to tumble, leading to its being taken over by JPMorgan Chase in the period March to May 2008.

With some delay, the banking crisis spread to the government sector when investors began to fear that banks and countries might not be able to service their maturing debts. Initially spreads grew only minimally, but when the US investment bank Lehman Brothers collapsed one year later, in September 2008, the dam burst. The crisis escalated and, with it, the spreads over the German benchmark for those countries deemed unsafe. A number of rescue operations and the occasional positive business climate news temporarily halted the growth of spreads, but in general terms they kept on growing until the summer of 2012.

The Greek interest rate for ten-year government bonds shot up over this period to a peak of 39%, the Portuguese to 14%, the Irish to 12%, and the Spanish to 7%. The euro seemed to be close to collapsing at that stage.

But then came a further turnaround in the summer of 2012. For one thing, the ECB announced its Outright Monetary Transactions programme (OMT) on 6 September 2012, with which it basically promised to buy unlimited amounts of the crisis stricken countries' government bonds if necessary, putting potential write-off losses in its books in the process and, in effect, bailing out the investors.[8] This public insurance promise, which the President of the ECB announced with the words that the ECB will do 'whatever it takes', understandably calmed the markets and reduced the spreads on government bonds.[9] For another, the permanent rescue mechanism ESM finally reached the necessary quorum of 90% of its capital when the Bundestag ratified it on 29 June 2012 and the German Constitutional Court on 12 September of that year turned down appeals to stop it.[10]

Figure 2.3 shows how the crisis and the calming news of the summer of 2012 have affected the prices of outstanding government bonds. The figure is another way of presenting the information contained in Figure 2.2 for yields,

---

[8] See European Central Bank, *Technical Features of Outright Monetary Transactions*, press release, 6 September 2012, available at: <http://www.ecb.europa.eu/press/pr/date/2012/html/pr120906_1.en.html>.

[9] See Introductory Statement to the Press Conference (with Q&A) by Mario Draghi, President of the ECB, and Vítor Constâncio, Vice-President of the ECB, 6 September 2012, available at: <http://www.ecb.europa.eu/press/pressconf/2012/html/is120906.en.html>. Draghi had made a similar statement, though without alluding to the OMT already in July 2012. For an explicit discussion of the OMT see Chapter 8.

[10] See Federal Constitutional Court, *2 BvR 1390/12, 2 BvR 1421/12, 2 BvR 1438/12, 2 BvR 1439/12, 2 BvR 1440/12, 2 BvE 6/12*, 12 September 2012, available at: <http://www.bverfg.de/entscheidungen/rs20120912_2bvr139012en.html>. Germany's President gave the final signature on 27 September 2012.

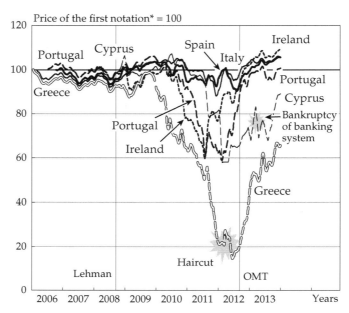

Figure 2.3 Prices of ten-year government bonds

Source: Thomson Reuters Datastream, *Bonds & Convertibles*.

Note: The chart shows the market value of ten-year government bonds issued in 2006 (Ireland 2007). After the Greek haircut in 2012, it shows the market value of the bonds investors received in exchange for the bonds defaulting relative to the value of the original papers issued in 2006.

with a focus on the crisis-stricken countries. The rising spreads that made the outstanding government bond prices plummet had caused huge wealth losses to the respective bondholders. By the same token, the interventions of the ECB have brought about windfall gains, in particular for hedge funds that snapped up the bonds held by many who had lost hope in the meantime. The recovery of Irish bonds was a source of huge profits. The ups and downs of asset prices is the true reason why the financial industry has such a strong interest in the continuation of the ECB's rescue policies, and why such policies have huge redistributive implications for European taxpayers and international investors.

The chart shows a discontinuity in the Greek curve in March 2012. That was the time when a so-called voluntary haircut was imposed on Greek government bonds, shaving off € 105 billion from private investors' nominal claims. The curve shows the market value of an initial investment in Greek government bonds. Interestingly enough, while the expected haircut had caused the decline in the value of Greek bonds, the actual haircut in itself did not reduce the market value of investors' wealth, since it only acknowledged the discount that the markets were already applying to such bonds. In fact, since the haircut cleared the air and reduced the probability of further haircuts in the near future, it more than doubled the value of the new Greek government bonds in a short period of time.

After Greece, Cyprus' banking sector ran into difficulties, culminating in the default of Laiki Bank in early 2013 and a near default of the Cypriot state, requiring the freezing of bank accounts and international capital controls lasting until this writing. Nevertheless, the various rescue operations taken by the ECB and the community of states have calmed the situation in financial markets. Politicians are reassuring the public that everything is under control. Perhaps they are right, perhaps not. But the fact is that they definitely do not have the real crisis in southern Europe under control, as Chapter 4 will demonstrate. It continues to smoulder. This is why interest spreads are still sizeable. There is still a great deal of political uncertainty in the air, despite many wishful declarations.

Before the euro was announced, investors used to worry that the funds they had lent in southern Europe would not be repaid in full, and today they are fretting again. While the reasons may be different—back then the risk of inflation and devaluation, now the danger of default—the issue is basically the same. Risk-commensurate yields are always charged to compensate investors for expected losses. Seen in this light, the euro only managed to concern the creditworthiness problems of some countries for a number of years, but did not contribute towards a real solution to the problem. Just like the rust under an old car's paint, the problems surfaced again after a while, and have in fact been exacerbated in the meantime by the enormous build-up of foreign debt.

The Timing Problem

While the convergence of interest rates is an obvious indicator of the forces that induced the capital flows, it may seem a bit puzzling that the timing of interest convergence shown in Figure 2.2 does not exactly coincide with the development and growth of current account deficits shown in Figure 2.1. After the main convergence of interest rates was completed in early 1998, it took another two or three years for sizeable capital imports to emerge in the GIPSIC countries. How can the interest convergence result from desired portfolio shifts if these portfolio shifts have not yet taken place? What is the causal relationship between the portfolio rebalancing that the euro introduced, the convergence of interest rates, and the emergence of current account deficits?

As mentioned above, a capital import is by definition equal to a current account deficit. Current account balances, however, are subject to much inertia, reacting only sluggishly to economic incentives. After all, a change in the balance may involve a change in production structures, trade infrastructure and even the emergence or disappearance of industries. Thus, the reactions of the current account limit the capital flows that actually can take place in net terms, when investors want to rebalance their international asset portfolios. The desire to rebalance portfolios changes market prices of assets and interest rates immediately, but it cannot be fulfilled unless the real economies involved react in a way that generates complementary changes in the demand for foreign credit and the supply of savings by foreigners, but this usually comes along with expansions and contractions of the real economies as well as substitution effects which take time to materialize. This has been thoroughly analysed for the case of flexible exchange rates,[11] but with fixed exchange rates or within a currency union things are very similar.

Of course, any limited group of investors can always change their portfolio structure if they find another group that does the countertrade. If, however, investors want to bring their capital in net terms to a particular country (without any public institutions effecting the countertrade), that country's current account will have to react by going into deficit. This is because otherwise investors will not find households, firms and public institutions that are willing to borrow the funds offered to purchase goods in other countries.

In a currency union, such a deficit may be caused by an internal real investment boom (e.g. in real estate) resulting from improved credit conditions that creates jobs and increases incomes, which in turn increase imports. The reaction of the current account is reinforced by a decline in exports resulting from the wage increases that the boom brings about and that undermine the competitiveness of export industries. For several reasons, however, it may take a few years until the current account shows a noticeable reaction. For one thing, the emergence of such an investment boom takes time, and, for another, exports start to decline only when export prices increase, which requires a transmission of wage increases from the investment industries to the export industries. Furthermore, even when export prices increase, it is possible that, as is known from the case of flexible exchange rates, the value of exports initially rises because prices increase faster and earlier than quantities decline.

[11]   See A. Marshall, *Money, Credit and Commerce*, Macmillan, London 1932; A. P. Lerner, *The Economics of Control*, Macmillan, London 1962; St. P. Magee, 'Currency Contracts, Pass-through and Devaluation', *Brookings Papers on Economic Activity* 1, 1973, pp. 303–325; R. Dornbusch, 'Expectations and Exchange Rate Dynamics', *Journal of Political Economy* 84, 1976, pp. 1161–1176; R. Dornbusch and S. Fischer, 'Exchange Rates and the Current Account', *American Economic Review* 70, 1980, pp. 960–971; D. W. Henderson, 'The Dynamic Effects of Exchange Market Intervention Policy: Two Extreme Views and a Synthesis', *Kredit und Kapital* 6, 1981, pp. 156–209; H.-W. Sinn, 'International Capital Movements, Flexible Exchange Rates and the IS-LM Model. A Comparison Between the Portfolio Balance and the Flow Hypotheses', *Weltwirtschaftliches Archiv* 119, 1983, pp. 36–63; R. Dornbusch, 'Exchange Rates and Prices', *American Economic Review* 77, 1987, pp. 93–106.

Interestingly enough, while the current account starts reacting to a capital import only with a certain delay, the reverse reaction can be very sudden, for if a country cannot borrow abroad to finance an import surplus, the goods will simply not be delivered from abroad.[12] Thus, it is as if the current account deficit hinges on a string of portfolio investment decisions. By pulling the string, it is possible to close it immediately, but when the string is loosened, the opening process depends on voluntary decisions within the country that take much longer to be made and are less certain. Thus, when investors pulled the string in 2007 and the period of equal interest rates ended, the trend increase of the GIPSIC current account deficits reversed. If there is anything astonishing about the current account reductions during the present crisis, after the capital markets refused in 2007/2008 to continue financing current account deficits, it is not how abruptly the deficit trends have reversed, but how slowly the deficits have been disappearing. As Figure 2.1 showed, by the end of 2012, fully five years after the interbank market first broke down, the current account deficit of the GIPSIC countries had not yet fully disappeared. It only disappeared and turned into a slight surplus in 2013. Later chapters in this book will show that the sluggishness in the downward reaction of the current account was due to the provision of public credit by the ECB and the community of states, which covered these countries' financial gaps and financed a substantial portion of their current account deficits and in some cases outright capital flight.

Relief for Government Budgets

Let us go back to the 'good' years of the euro. For many acceding countries, the decision to adopt the euro had primarily to do with a wish to lower their interest rate burden, and that is what actually occurred. All highly indebted euro members benefited massively from this relief.

Consider Italy. Before the Madrid Summit, the Italian interest burden on its public debt had become a problem eliciting growing concern. Relative to GDP, the country's interest burden had increased from 8.4% in 1985 to 11.5% in 1995, putting substantial strain on the government budget.[13] The chief reason was the rapidly growing volume of Italy's debt, which had jumped from 82% of GDP in 1985 to 125% in 1994. Investors had become increasingly nervous about Italy's ability to repay its debt.

---

[12] See G. A. Calvo, 'Capital Flows and Capital-Market Crises: The Simple Economics of Sudden Stops', *Journal of Applied Economics* 1, 1998, pp. 35–54.

[13] See Eurostat, Database, *Economy and Finance*, Annual National Accounts; and Government Finance Statistics.

The announcement of the euro at the Madrid Summit in 1995 greatly calmed investors' fears, bringing down the interest rate the government had to pay on its bond issuance by 6 percentage points in only two and a half years, as shown in Figure 2.2. This allowed Italy to roll over its debt at much more favourable conditions, reducing the interest burden for the government. Five years after the Madrid Summit, in 2000, Italy no longer had to devote 11.5% of GDP, but only 6.3%, to service its interest payments; ten years later, in 2010, the burden had sunk to 4.5%. The relative interest burden fell because of rate convergence, but also due to Italy's inflation rate, which was still high and inflated nominal GDP. Figure 2.4 illustrates this advantage.

The situation in Greece was quite similar, as the chart shows. The Greek curve overlaps with Italy's over long stretches, revealing a stunning parallelism

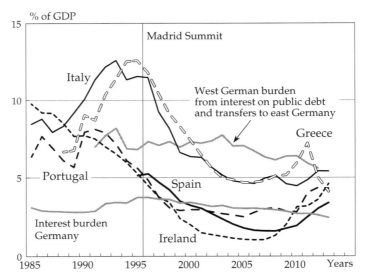

Figure 2.4 The interest burden of public debt as a percentage of GDP (1985–2012/2013)

Sources: Eurostat, Database, *Economy and Finance*, Annual National Accounts; and Government Finance Statistics, Annual Government Finance Statistics, Government Revenues, Government Expenditures, and Main Aggregates; European Commission, Economic and Financial Affairs, *European Economic Forecast*, Autumn 2013; Organisation for Economic Co-operation and Development, *iLibrary*, National Accounts, Main Aggregates; and M. Kloß, R. Lehmann, J. Ragnitz, and G. Untiedt, 'Auswirkungen veränderter Transferzahlungen auf die wirtschaftliche Leistungsfähigkeit der ostdeutschen Länder', *ifo Dresden Studien* 63, Munich 2012, p. 35.

Note: West Germany comprises the states of the former Federal Republic of Germany (without Berlin). 2013 European Commission forecast, Autumn 2013.

until 2008. As in Italy, the state greatly benefited from the falling interest rates brought by the euro. After the outbreak of the crisis, the Greek interest burden increased sharply, peaking in 2011 to then fall to lower levels. The likely explanation is the replacement of expensive market credit with cheap public rescue credit, as will be documented in Chapters 7 and 8, and the Greek default of early 2012, which reduced the Greek government debt by € 105 billion, or 54% of its GDP.

Unlike Greece, the other crisis countries experienced rising interest burdens for their government debt during the crisis. That has led many to complain. A frequently heard argument is that current interest rates are unbearable. Eurobonds are needed to tap credit jointly and reduce the interest rates. Indeed, the mutual liability offered by the issuing countries would likely bring yields back down to tolerable levels. Germany, however, refuses to yield to this pressure to introduce Eurobonds because it fears that it could end up paying the sovereign debts of the southern countries, which may well grow even larger if they continue to be shielded from market sanctions.

The degree to which the complaints are justifiable is open to debate. Firstly, the current rates are certainly not the rates that markets if left by themselves would have charged, but rates that have artificially been reduced through various kinds of intervention of the ECB and the community of states, providing assurance to investors that they would get their money back. Secondly, the yields that these countries now deem intolerable were once the norm, even for Germany, which has always been a low-interest country. Thirdly, as shown in Figure 2.2, the market rates the countries have paid during the crisis were typically much lower than before the euro was announced. In fact, as Figure 2.4 shows, their interest burden relative to GDP was in all cases lower than before the announcement of the euro, even though the debt-to-GDP levels rose sharply.

To be sure, at that time inflation was generally higher, making it possible for a country to grow out of its debts. GDP expanded through inflation, while debts were set at nominal values, thus gradually decreasing in size relative to GDP, provided no new debt was taken on. The yields had a built-in inflation component, which the investors in government bonds demanded as compensation for the depreciation their capital would suffer. Still the inflation component in interest rates had to be included in the budget, even though it was possible to fund it by borrowing without increasing the debt-to-GDP ratio. The aspiration to join the euro had also to do with a wish to avoid this inflation component.

A comparison with West Germany's burden after reunification can be a useful indicator for assessing whether or not the burdens involved were tolerable. The respective (grey) curve in Figure 2.4 shows that the sum of the burden of the interest on sovereign debt and the West–East transfers that West Germany had to shoulder hovered at around 6% of GDP, while the interest burden of Italy and Spain in 2013 lay at only 5.4% and 3.4% of GDP, respectively. Thus, contrary to what these governments now claim, the present situation is not one of exorbitant interest burdens resulting from their debt.

In 2012, despite the yawning spreads of 2011 and 2012, the advantage of the lower interest rates that Italy enjoyed thanks to the euro, relative to a reference period from 1991 to 1995, was € 96 billion. This was more than the entire value-added tax revenue of that year, which was € 93 billion.

Italy received kudos for bringing its deficit, against all expectations, down to the Eurozone accession criterion so quickly. In 1995, its budget deficit was still 7.7% of GDP, but in 1997, the reference year, it had fallen to 2.7%, comfortably below the 3% cap, making Italy qualify for adopting the euro. However, almost half (2.3 percentage points) of the 5.0 points in deficit reduction over this period was brought about by the savings in interest payments. In this sense, the euro itself largely fulfilled the conditions for Italy's accession.

The Lack of Fiscal Discipline

The falling interest rates did not just represent a direct cost advantage for the debtors. They also changed their behaviour, inducing them to relax their efforts at saving and to take on more debt instead.

To some extent this development had been foreseen when the euro was set up. This is the reason why at the 1995 Summit in Madrid a stability pact was envisaged that would put a ceiling on the member countries' budget deficits. The December 1996 Summit in Dublin drew up this pact, which was subsequently ratified, but not before France watered down some of its rules and changed its name to the Stability and Growth Pact. The member countries committed to setting up medium-term goals for righting their public finances and promised that their structural budget deficit, i.e. the deficit adjusted for changes in the business cycle and temporary measures, would not exceed 1% of GDP.[14] A level of up to 3% for the actual deficit was permitted in the exceptional case of an economic slump, and more than 3% was allowed to stimulate the economy only if a country found itself in a recession in which its real GDP dropped by at least 2% within a year. The member countries committed to adopting corrective budgetary measures if there were signs of deviation from the budget goals, as well

[14] See Council of the European Union, 'Council Regulation (EC) No. 1466/97 of 7 July 1997 on the Strengthening of the Surveillance of Budgetary Positions and the Surveillance and Coordination of Economic Policies', *Official Journal* L 209, 1997, p. 1, available at: <http://eur-lex.europa.eu/LexUriServ/LexUriServ.do?uri=CELEX:31997R 1466:EN:HTML>, in particular article 2 littera a.

as a prompt elimination of budget deficits.[15] If the 3% budget deficit limit was exceeded, the rules stipulated the levying of sanctions.[16]

But as in the case of the Maastricht Treaty itself, the rules were not obeyed, not even those that in 2005 had been watered down by limiting the possibility of imposing sanctions, after Germany and France violated them. By 2013, the 3% deficit ceiling had been breached on 148 occasions. [17] Figure 2.5 gives an overview of the paths that the deficit ratios of the Eurozone's biggest debtors have followed over time. As can be seen, the deficit was more often above rather than below the 3% maximum that the Stability and Growth Pact allowed.

Only in 51 of the 148 cases exceeding the 3% limit would have been allowed on account of a deep-enough recession. In other words, sanctions should have been levied in 97 cases. According to the original rules that prevailed before 2005, 117 cases should have actually merited sanctions. As it happened, not a single sanction was ever levied, because the body that was to decide on their application was the ECOFIN Council, comprised of the economics and finance ministers of the EU member states, who basically were the perpetrators themselves. All the holy covenants to exercise discipline turned out to be just so much hot air.

The countries with the weakest fiscal discipline were Greece and Portugal. Neither country was ever below the 3% budget deficit mark over the period considered, although initially both, and Greece even until the onset of the financial crisis, enjoyed exorbitant growth rates and could definitely not claim exceptionally bad circumstances. The new credit was used in Greece and Portugal mainly to pay higher salaries to public employees, and less to improve the infrastructure. From 2000 to 2008, salaries increased by 80% (nominal) in Greece and 30% in Portugal. By contrast, over the same period they rose in Germany by only 10%, less than consumer price inflation (which was 15% in cumulative terms over the

---

[15] See European Council, 'Resolution of the European Council on the Stability and Growth Pact, Amsterdam, 17 June 1997', *Official Journal* C 236, 1997, available at: <http://eur-lex.europa.eu/LexUriServ/LexUriServ.do?uri=CELEX:31997Y0802(01): EN:HTML>, p. 1, IV, The Member States, 5. It reads: 'This correction should be completed no later than the year following the identification of the excessive deficit, unless there are special circumstances'.

[16] See Council of the European Union, 'Council Regulation (EC) No. 1467/97 of 7 July 1997 on Speeding Up and Clarifying the Implementation of the Excessive Deficit Procedure', *Official Journal* L 209, 1997, p. 6, available at: <http://eur-lex.europa.eu/ LexUriServ/LexUriServ.do?uri=CELEX:31997R1467:EN:HTML>, in particular articles 11–13.

[17] H.-W. Sinn, 'Die Europäische Fiskalunion', *Perspektiven der Wirtschaftspolitik* 13, 2012, pp. 137–178. Updated on the basis of data from Eurostat, Database, *Economy and Finance*, Annual National Accounts; Eurostat, Government Finance Statistics; and European Commission, Economic and Financial Affairs, *European Economic Forecast*, Autumn 2013.

period).[18] The number of public employees increased as well, by 6% in Portugal and 16% in Greece; in Germany, it decreased by 7% between 2000 and 2008.[19]

In Portugal and Greece excessive public borrowing also led to a consumption boom. The aggregate of private and public consumption reached 106% and 103% of the countries' net national income in 2007, respectively, and rose further to 111% and 117% during the crisis. While there were other countries that consumed large fractions of their incomes—in particular Italy, which lately has been consuming all of its income—Greece and Portugal were the obvious outliers, as Figure 2.6 shows. Both of these countries used the euro to live beyond their means.

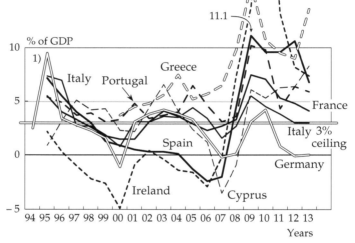

Figure 2.5 Public deficits of selected euro countries

1) Including the assumption of Treuhand debts derived from German reunification.
2) Including the assumption of commercial bank debts.

Source: Eurostat, Database, *Economy and Finance*, Government Finance Statistics, Government Deficit and Debt; European Commission, Economic and Financial Affairs, European Economic Forecast, Autumn 2013; German Federal Statistical Office, *Fachserie 18*, Reihe 1.4; Ifo Institute, *Ifo Economic Forecast 2012/2013: Increased Uncertainty Continues to Curb German Economy*, 28 June 2012.

Note: 2013 European Commission forecast, Autumn 2013.

[18] For Greece and Portugal, calculated on the basis of Organisation for Economic Co-operation and Development, *iLibrary*, OECD Economic Outlook: Statistics and Projections, Economic Outlook No. 86; for Germany: German Federal Statistical Office, *Fachserie 18*, Volkswirtschaftliche Gesamtrechnungen, Reihe 1.4, 2012, Status: September 2013; and German Federal Statistical Office, *Fachserie 17*, Preise, Reihe 7, September 2013.
[19] See Eurostat, Database, *Economy and Finance*, Annual National Accounts, National Accounts Detailed Breakdowns, National Accounts Aggregates and Employment by Branch.

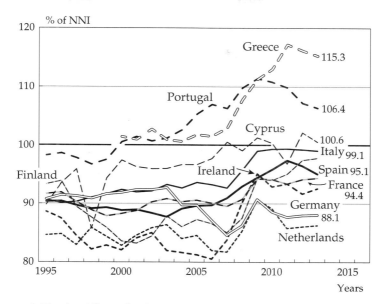

Figure 2.6 Total public and private consumption of selected euro countries as a share of net national income (1995–2013)

Source: Eurostat, Database, *Economy and Finance*, National Accounts (including GDP), GDP and Main Components—Current Prices, Final Consumption Expenditures; and Income, Saving and Net Lending/ Borrowing, Gross National Income at Market Prices; European Commission, Economic and Financial Affairs, Economic Databases and Indicators, AMECO – the annual macro-economic database; Ifo Institute calculations.

Note: 2013 European Commission forecast, Autumn 2013.

While Greece and Portugal were the great outliers among the euro countries, nearly all of them increased their sovereign debt faster than their GDP. The lure of low interest rates spread out wide and far. Many countries, including some that are not shown in Figure 2.5, failed to comply with the deficit ceiling. Figure 2.7 shows how the debt-to-GDP ratios of the countries currently (in 2013) in the Eurozone evolved from 1995 to 2013. In most countries, debt-to-GDP ratios at present hover much farther above the 60% ceiling allowed by the Maastricht Treaty than they did in 1995. Commendable exceptions are Belgium and the Netherlands. The Belgian success is particularly remarkable when compared with Italy's performance. While Belgium started with a ratio of 130% and now stands at 100%, Italy started at 121% and now stands at 130%.

On average, the debt-to-GDP ratio of the euro countries rose by more than 20 percentage points, from 72% to 96%. In this light, the Eurozone itself shouldn't have been allowed into the currency union.

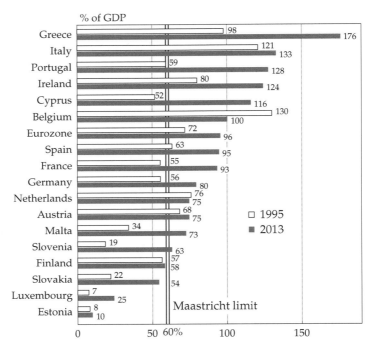

Figure 2.7 Public debt of the euro countries, 1995 and 2013

Source: Eurostat, Database, *Economy and Finance*, Government Finance Statistics, Government Deficit and Debt; European Commission, Economic and Financial Affairs, *Economic Databases and Indicators*, AMECO – the annual macro-economic database.

Note: 2013 European Commission forecast, Autumn 2013.

Among the early transgressors was Germany, since its budget deficit, as Figure 2.5 shows, exceeded the 3% ceiling in the years 2002 through 2005, without the country being in recession, the only circumstance that would have provided a justification. In 1995 Germany's deficit, at 9.5%, had already been extremely high, but that was due to the inclusion in the budget of the Treuhand debts that had arisen in earlier years through reunification, a one-time effect.[20] Excluding this one-time effect, the deficit would have been 3.1%. The real problem was with the years 2002 through 2005.

At the time, Chancellor Gerhard Schröder exerted massive pressure to soften the strictures of the Stability and Growth Pact so that Germany would not have

---

[20] See Eurostat, Database, *Economy and Finance,* and Government Finance Statistics, Government Deficit and Debt.

to pay sanctions. Given that France had also breached the deficit ceiling in 2003 and 2004, both countries practically scuttled the Pact.[21] Germany had its difficulties with the deficit criterion at the time because its revenues had plunged in the wake of its own euro crisis, as will be discussed in the next chapter, and the government hesitated over imposing upon the people budget cuts on top of the painful Agenda 2010 social reforms. However, this does not detract from the fact that Germany's breaching of the pact contributed to the deterioration of debt temperance among the rest of the Eurozone's members.

Germany's debt jumped, moreover, by 8.0 percentage points, or € 287 billion, in 2010 because the country created a bad bank for the toxic assets, primarily of US origin, accumulated by its Landesbanks and Hypo Real Estate, a spin-off from Hypovereinsbank that had run into difficulties because of risky international investment and the absorption of large parts of Hypovereinsbank's real-estate portfolio. The creditors of those state-owned banks had a direct claim on the government (guarantor liability or *Gewährträgerhaftung*).[22] In 1995, Germany's debt-to-GDP ratio was 56%; by 2013 it had climbed to 80%.

The French debt-to-GDP ratio jumped from 56% in 1995 to 93% in 2013, as a result of years of excessive deficits, low growth during the crisis, and various bank rescue operations, in particular in the context of Dexia, a banking group that defaulted in 2008.

Amidst all the widespread moral hazard, a commendably Spartan stance regarding budget deficits was shown by Ireland and Spain, presently two of the more notorious crisis victims: during the time when the euro appeared to be functioning well they did not exceed the ceilings stipulated in the Stability and Growth Pact, if only because the credit-driven boom they enjoyed boosted nominal GDP and tax revenues faster than their debt could grow. Spain's deficit had exceeded 3% only at the very beginning, until 1998, to drop steadily in the years thereafter until it turned into a surplus in 2005. By 2007, its surplus amounted to 2.0% of GDP. Ireland did even better, posting a deficit only in 1995 and 1996; after that, the Irish paid back their debt in almost every single year until 2007.

The problems for these two countries came when the crisis broke out. Both developed huge budget deficits and debts, particularly because of the large bailout operations in favour of their banking systems, but also as the economy and tax revenue shrank. In 2010 Ireland posted an astronomical deficit, of 30.6% of GDP, because the government had assumed huge amounts of debt from the private sector. It also gave guarantees that amounted to 245% of

[21] See C. Reiermann and K. Wiegrefe, 'Herr und Helfer', *Der Spiegel*, No. 29, 16 July 2012, pp. 32–34.

[22] See H.-W. Sinn, *The German State Banks. Global Players in the International Financial Markets*, Edward Elgar, Aldershot 1999.

its GDP.[23] The Anglo Irish Bank alone accounted for 16 percentage points of the Irish deficit in that year. (According to the somewhat mysterious rules of Eurostat, the assumption of that bank's debt was counted as a public deficit, whereas the assumption of the debt of the German Landesbanks and Hypo Real Estate, which increased the German debt-to-GDP ratio by 8 percentage points, was not.) In Spain, the debt increased during the crisis primarily as a result of capital injections into several commercial banks.[24]

Italy's Missed Opportunity

The largest among the countries now in trouble is Italy. Following its conduct under the euro is illuminating, as it helps us to understand the incentives brought about by the euro. Italy's history is a story of missed opportunities.

As Figure 2.5 showed, the Italian deficit decreased until the year 2000, but rose slightly above the 3% threshold over the 2001-2006 period, falling temporarily below it in 2007 and 2008, to once again exceed it thereafter.

This development is disappointing, because Italy has been one of the biggest beneficiaries of interest rate convergence. If Italy had kept its primary surplus, i.e. the surplus of revenue over expenditures that are not related to servicing its debt, at a constant 4%, the level it achieved in 1995, the interest savings that the euro made possible would have given the country a budget deficit of 0.5% to 1% of GDP in the years 2003 to 2011. As it turned out, Italy posted a deficit of 1.6% to 5.5% instead. Thus, evidently, the interest advantage brought by the euro was not used to redeem debt, but was consumed by the various governments.

At the beginning all was good intentions. Prime Minister Lamberto Dini, who had negotiated Italy's accession, tried to keep his promises, managing initially to save the interest advantage and, in addition, to increase the primary surplus of the government budget. As a result, the primary surplus rose from 4.1% to 5.4% between 1995 and 2000. Italy, at that time, applied its entire interest-rate relief to

---

[23] Those guarantees are contingent liabilities that do not appear in the public deficit or debt statistics. See H.-W. Sinn, *Casino Capitalism*, 2010, chapter 9: *Rescue Attempts*, p. 193.

[24] Banco Financiero y de Ahorros (BFA) of € 18.9 billion, Catalunya Banc € 11.3 billion, NCG Banco € 7.6 billion, Banco de Valencia € 5.5 billion, Unnim Banc € 1.0 billion; see Eurostat Statistics, *Government Finance Statistics*, Supplementary Tables for the Financial Crisis. These figures refer to 2012, the most recent data available at this writing, and they probably do not yet include the funds set aside for the Spanish bad banks FROB and SAREB, which received voluminous funds at the turn of 2012/2013. SAREB alone is said to have received € 2.5 billion.

repaying its debt, and even saved part of its normal budget. A serious effort was made towards achieving a lasting budget consolidation.

But the good intentions did not last long. By 2001, just five years and four prime ministers after Dini, the primary surplus had fallen to 3.1%, and in 2008, the year before the slump triggered by the financial crisis, it was a paltry 2.5%. In 2010 it disappeared altogether (0.1%). The primary surplus then rose to 1.1%, 2.5% and 2.3% respectively in 2011, 2012 and 2013, but remained always below the 1995 level of 4.1%.[25] Thus, since 2001 Italy has squandered considerable parts of the interest advantage the euro brought it rather than using it for debt redemption. Small wonder then that Italy's debt-to-GDP ratio today is even higher than it was in 1995.

This is apparently the problem with democracy. A government commits to agreements and sticks to its promise of fulfilling them, but its successor dumps the commitments in favour of pandering to the current needs of voters, instead of doing something for future generations, perhaps even secretly speculating on its neighbours' eventually accepting joint liability for its debts. As long as the hope held that the ECB would keep interest rates low, taking on debt was always a more comfortable way to top up the government budget.

If Italy had continued to save the interest it was spared from paying, it would have wiped out most of its sovereign debt by now. The following calculation sheds some light on what could have happened if the government had not squandered the interest advantage brought about by the euro.

Let us assume that Italy's budget, in the period after 1996, had set aside every year the same proportion of GDP for interest payments on, and amortization of, its sovereign debt as it needed in 1995 for interest payments alone (i.e., 11.5%). In other words, assume Italy would have paid the interest on its outstanding debt and applied the spared outlays resulting from interest rate convergence to repaying the debt itself. Under the same conditions, in particular with the same evolution of its economy, Italy's debt-to-GDP ratio would have fallen in each and every year, as depicted in Figure 2.8 by the curve labelled 'Hypothetical (nominal)'. At the end of 2013, its sovereign debt would have amounted to only 8% of GDP, or € 117 billion, instead of 133%, or € 2.1 trillion.[26] As it turned out, however, the savings in interest payments were essentially squandered and were merely used to increase the government's expenditure.

[25] See Eurostat, Database, *Economy and Finance*, Government Statistics, Government Deficit and Debt; and European Commission, Economic and Financial Affairs, *European Economic Forecast*, Autumn 2013, Table 38.

[26] See Eurostat, Database, *Economy and Finance*, Government Statistics, Government Deficit and Debt; and European Commission, Economic and Financial Affairs, *Economic Databases and Indicators*, AMECO – The annual macro-economic database.

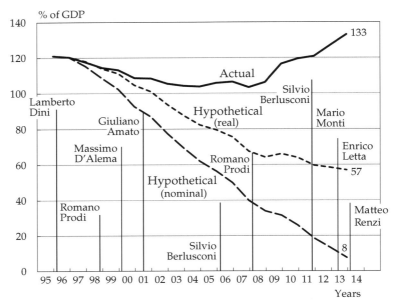

Figure 2.8 Hypothetical and actual evolution of Italy's public debt (1995–2013)

Source: Eurostat, Database, *Economy and Finance*, Annual National Accounts; and Government Finance Statistics, Annual Government Finance Statistics; and Government Deficit and Debt; European Commission, Economic and Financial Affairs, *Economic Databases and Indicators*, AMECO – the annual macro-economic database; Ifo Institute calculations; Governo Italiano, *Presidenza del Consiglio dei Ministri*, 7. August 2012, available at:<http://www.governo.it/Governo/Governi/governi.html>.

Note: 2013 European Commission forecast, Autumn 2013, and Ifo Institute calculations.

Admittedly, this calculation does not take into account the reduction in the inflation rate that occurred under the euro. Italy's high inflation had always facilitated servicing its debt. While the nominal interest burden was high, the inflationary growth of GDP had kept the debt-to-GDP ratio in check and had implied that part of the state's interest payments could be covered with new debt rather than taxes, without increasing the debt-to-GDP ratio. Adjusting the interest saving that could have been used for debt redemption for the decline in the inflation rate relative to the base year (1995), yields the dashed curve in Figure 2.8 labelled 'Hypothetical (real)'. It obviously implies a less rapid reduction in the hypothetical Italian debt-to-GDP ratio. Still, Italy's debt-to-GDP ratio would have halved relative to 1995, standing at only 57% by the end of 2013, and Italy would have had no difficulty whatsoever convincing the market to lend it money at the German interest rate.

Similar calculations could also be made for other countries that are in distress today. They would typically show that, rather than using the interest saved to redeem their debt, they kept borrowing to finance their budgets, in some cases borrowing even more than before. The reduction of interest rates that the euro brought about both provided the possibility to save and increased the incentive to borrow, but the latter nearly always proved to be more preponderant. Thus, in view of today's crisis, the euro did not help the over-indebted countries to escape their debt traps, but let them sink even further.

The Foreign Debt Problem

Most Eurozone countries were pushed into higher sovereign debt levels as a result of the crisis. However, sovereign debt is not necessarily foreign debt, since domestic investors may have bought government bonds, and foreign debt is not necessarily sovereign debt, since private households and institutions may also have borrowed abroad. Thus, the thesis that countries slid into crisis because they had issued too much public debt is not generally correct: while it does apply to Greece and Portugal, it does not apply to Ireland and Spain.

Despite their prudent public debt policies, these two latter countries suffer from a high foreign debt burden, as Figure 2.9 below shows. The figures next to the bars show the net foreign asset positions in the year 2012 of the countries then in the Eurozone.[27] A negative number shows a net foreign debt position, and a positive one a net foreign asset position. By the end of 2012, Ireland had a net foreign debt of 112%, Greece one of 109% and Spain one of 91% of GDP, all truly alarming levels. They were surpassed only by the debt level of Portugal (115%). This qualifies the frequent assertion that the GIPSIC countries are suffering from a sovereign debt crisis. Obviously, the countries' private economies also borrowed abroad, and in some cases this was the dominant factor. The GIPSIC countries are suffering primarily from a foreign debt crisis rather than a mere sovereign debt crisis.

The net foreign asset position of a country (sometimes also called net international investment position) is defined as the sum of all financial claims held by nationals against foreigners minus the claims that foreigners hold against residents of the country in question, including real assets and shares of stocks. If it is negative, one speaks of a net foreign debt position. A net foreign asset position builds up over time through the accumulation of current account surpluses; its value is subject to adjustments due to changes in the market value of the underlying assets.[28] Similarly, a net

---

[27] Data that would have allowed the construction of this graph for 2013 were not yet published as of this writing (February 2014).

[28] Revaluation effects occur when, for instance, the market value of assets or securities changes. Interestingly, the statistics also keep track of the changes on the value of the

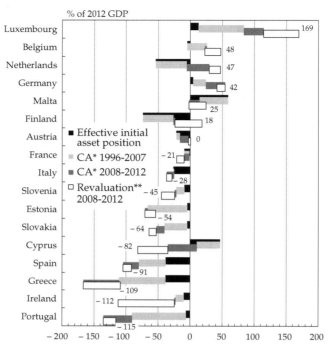

% of 2012 GDP

Luxembourg — 169
Belgium — 48
Netherlands — 47
Germany — 42
Malta — 25
Finland — 18
Austria — 0
France — −21
Italy — −28
Slovenia — −45
Estonia — −54
Slovakia — −64
Cyprus — −82
Spain — −91
Greece — −109
Ireland — −112
Portugal — −115

■ Effective initial
   asset position
▨ CA* 1996-2007
▬ CA* 2008-2012
□ Revaluation**
   2008-2012

−200 −150 −100 −50 0 50 100 150 200

Figure 2.9 Net foreign asset position and its components (2012)

* CA = cumulative current account balance.

** Change in market value of foreign claims and liabilities for each country.

Sources: Eurostat, Database, *Economy and Finance*, Annual National Accounts and Balance of Payments—International Transactions, Balance-of-Payments Statistics by Country; and International Investment Positions; Banca d'Italia, *Base Informativa Pubblica*, Balance of Payments and International Investment Position; Ifo Institute calculations.

Note: The figures show the Eurozone countries' net foreign asset positions as a share of GDP at the end of 2012. They are depicted by the overall length of the country bars. The black areas show the estimated effective net foreign asset position in 1995, the light grey area the current account imbalances accumulated from 1996 to 2007, the dark grey areas the current account imbalances accumulated during the crisis (2008–2012), and the bordered white areas the revaluation effects due to changes in the market value of both assets and debts between 2008 and 2012. (The revaluation effects between 1996 and 2007 are compounded with the initial net foreign asset position of 1995 to form what is called the *effective* initial position.) Bars to the right measure an increase in assets (or reduction in debts), bars to the left an increase in debts (or reduction in assets). All bars are expressed as percentages of the countries' GDP in the year 2012.

foreign debt position results from previous current account deficits and its value is also affected by revaluation effects.

An interesting question concerning the net foreign asset positions concerns the time when they emerged. Did they build up before the euro was announced, or during the subsequent period when the interest rates had already converged, or did they result from the crisis itself? Answering this question is important insofar as it would shed some light on the debate about whether the interest-rate relief given to debtor countries would reduce their debt burden through an income effect, because they could repay their debts more easily, or instead increase it due to a moral hazard effect, given that lower interest rates provide an incentive to borrow more (and thus accumulate current account deficits).

Figure 2.9 gives an answer to this question, providing information on a country's initial foreign debt or asset position in 1995 before the beginning of interest rate convergence, and on the accumulation of foreign debt or assets since then, broken down into the period before and after the outbreak of the crisis. It decomposes the net foreign asset and debt positions of the euro countries in 2012 into four components:

1. An effective initial net foreign asset position baselined on the year of the Madrid Summit, 1995, covering the actual initial book value of foreign assets and a subsequent statistical revaluation of these assets due to a decline in the market rate of interest for new debt.[29]
2. Current account deficits and surpluses as the bubbles built up, from 1996 to 2007, depicted by the light-grey areas.
3. Current account deficits and surpluses during the crisis, from 2008 to 2012, illustrated by the dark grey areas.
4. Revaluation effects on account of a decrease in the market value of long-maturity debts and claims during the crisis, from 2008 to 2012, illustrated by the contoured white areas.

The components are indicated by horizontal bars, which add up to the value of the net foreign asset position of the respective country in 2012. Each component

debt itself. Thus, the net foreign debt of Greece and Portugal decreased on account of a decline in the market value of their bonds held by foreigners, although the obligation to pay in full still stood (i.e. even before the Greek haircut of 2012).

[29] The effective initial net foreign asset position is calculated by subtracting the accumulated current account surpluses in the period 1996 to 2007 from the known 2007 value of the asset positions. It may include revaluation effects during that period which, as the text explains, resulted from the high rates of interest on the initial debt and thus constitute a hidden, implicit part of the initial debt. As the Eurostat statistics only disentangle these two effects for a few countries, they are lumped together here under the item of an 'effective' initial net foreign asset position.

is expressed in units of the country's 2012 GDP (not in terms of the GDP of the respective period). If the sum of the effects is negative (to the left of the zero line), the country had a net foreign debt by the end of 2012; if it is positive (to the right of the zero line), it held net foreign assets. The sum of the light- and dark-grey areas is basically the same as that shown underneath the capital import curves in Figure 2.1.

To give an example of how to read the graph, consider Spain, whose *effective* initial net foreign debt in 1995 amounted to € 390 billion (or 38% of its 2012 GDP), depicted by the black bar. A cumulative current account deficit of € 433 billion in the period from 1996 to 2007 (light-grey bar) augmented this debt in the 'good' years of the euro. During the crisis, from 2008 to 2012, Spain accumulated a further € 253 billion of net foreign debt through additional current account deficits (dark-grey bar). Over the same period, the decline in market value of Spanish debt securities reduced the country's net foreign debt by € 135 billion, a so-called revaluation effect. Thus, Spain's ultimate net foreign debt by the end of 2012 was € 941 billion (= € 390 billion + € 433 billion + € 253 billion − € 135 billion), or 91% of the country's 2012 GDP.

The example of Spain shows that the net foreign debt essentially built up not during the crisis, but between 1996 and 2007, when the interest rates had already converged. The decline in interest rates brought about by the euro had three effects on net foreign debt. The first was a positive revaluation effect: the decline in interest rates increased the market value of the initial stock of government bonds, which still bore the high pre-summit interest rates. This effect contributed to pushing the *effective* initial net foreign debt position upwards.[30] The second effect of the decline in interest rates was in the opposite direction: it reduced the debt service burden for Spanish debtors, enabling them to roll over and pay back their external debt much more easily. Sadly, they squandered this opportunity. The third effect came to dominate the evolution of net foreign debt: the lure to borrow at low interest rates. During the fat years of the euro, from 1996 to 2007, Spaniards borrowed even more than in the preceding years, increasing their external debt via current account deficits by € 433 billion.

This qualifies the view that Spain as a whole practiced debt restraint. Only the Spanish government sector was parsimonious; the Spanish economy as such was not. In fact, as will be shown in the next section, the gigantic size of the

---

[30] The effective initial debt in 1995 itself consisted of two components, for which data are available in the case of Spain. The first component was the notional value of Spain's net foreign debt in 1995, i.e. at the time of the Madrid Summit, which was € 99 billion. The second component was a huge revaluation effect, amounting to € 291 billion, that materialized thereafter as the interest rates for new debt came down. In a sense, this effect simply revealed the part of the initial debt that was hidden behind the high interest rates. The sum of both components results in its effective initial debt of € 390 billion (the black bar).

Spanish net foreign debt is now by far the Eurozone's biggest unresolved financial problem.

Figure 2.9 shows that Greece, Portugal, and Ireland were in a similar situation to Spain. They all accumulated sizeable foreign debts in relation to their GDP after the Madrid Summit and before the crisis (light-grey bars), even though they already had a substantial effective net foreign debt to start with and thus benefited significantly from the decline in interest rates. The lower interest rates were an opportunity to repay at least some of their debt without making undue sacrifices, but they preferred instead to borrow even more.

In addition to the accumulation of foreign debt before the crisis, Portugal and Greece also accumulated even more foreign debt through current account deficits during the crisis (dark-grey bars), which exacerbated their debt problem.

Among the GIPSIC countries only Ireland did not add to its debt by borrowing more in net terms during the crisis. However, despite its high net foreign debt, Ireland experienced a huge debt revaluation effect when the interest rates went up, because Irish financial institutions had specialized in maturity transformation by borrowing short-term and lending out long-term. These institutions suffered from write-off losses on long-term foreign assets they held, without being able to benefit from countervailing write-off gains on their short-term foreign debt.

Spanish, Greek and Portuguese institutions, by contrast, benefited from the revaluation effects, since the market value of their long-term net foreign debt declined. In the case of Greece, which came close to a default, the outright debt relief in spring 2012, of € 105 billion, worked in the same direction.

By the end of 2012 Greece still had a net foreign debt amounting to 109% of its GDP, Portugal to 115%, Ireland to 112%, and Spain to 91% of their respective GDP. Without the debt relief and revaluation effects, the net foreign debt positions of Greece, Portugal and Spain would have been 221%, 135% and 105% respectively. If only the formal Greek debt relief had been subtracted, but no revaluation effects, the Greek net foreign debt position would have been 167% of GDP.

Cyprus differed from the other crisis countries inasmuch as it did not start off with net foreign debt, but with sizeable net foreign assets. Cyprus also grabbed the opportunity to borrow abroad in net terms both before and during the crisis. In addition, it suffered from a similar revaluation effect as Ireland, presumably also because of maturity transformation of debt instruments. The Cypriot net foreign debt position by the end of 2012 was 82%, about the size of Spain's.

Among the other net debtors, the eastern European members Slovenia, Estonia and Slovakia stand out. They had all borrowed substantially before the crisis, but less so during the crisis. Estonia, in particular, borrowed very little after 2007, and it profited from the devaluation of its debt. Slovenia, in turn, suffered from a devaluation of its assets, presumably for the same reason as Ireland.

By the end of 2012, Slovenia's net foreign debt position amounted to 45% of GDP, Estonia's to 54%, and Slovakia's to 64%.

Among the crisis countries, Italy is a noteworthy exception inasmuch as it has a rather small net foreign debt relative to its GDP. This is surprising, given that the Italian state did squander the advantage of lower interest rates, as shown above. Unlike the other countries, Italy did not worsen its net foreign debt position during the good years from 1996 to 2007, when the interest rates were low, by borrowing from other countries, and actually lent a small amount instead (€18 billion). Only during the crisis did Italy's current account turn negative, making its net foreign debt position worsen by about as much as it had improved due to the devaluation of its outstanding debt (contoured white area). By the end of 2012, Italy's negative net foreign asset position amounted to only 28% of GDP, between a third and a quarter of that of the other members of the GIPSIC group. This was just a bit more than one fifth of Italy's government debt-to-GDP ratio. The main explanation for this remarkable fact is that Italy's foreign debt is largely private, not public, and that Italian government bonds are typically held by Italians rather than foreigners. Italians seem to be prudent private and imprudent public borrowers.

Luxembourg is the champion among those countries whose net foreign asset position is positive, with net holdings amounting to 169% of GDP. Belgium holds the second position with net foreign assets of 48% of GDP. Belgium had significant current account surpluses before the crisis, and during the crisis it benefited even more because its long-run foreign debt was devalued. In view of its huge public debt, of about 100% of GDP, this wealth is truly surprising, and reminiscent of the above characterization of Italians, the only difference being that private Belgians are not even net foreign borrowers.

Other countries with sizeable net foreign asset positions are Finland and the Netherlands. Both exported substantial amounts of capital before and after the outbreak of the crisis. However, they had negative effective net foreign assets to start with, and their external debt did not lose value during the crisis. Thus, they rank behind Belgium in terms of their final relative net foreign asset position.

Germany's net foreign asset position is somewhat smaller in relative terms than that of the Netherlands and Belgium, but since Germany's economy is much bigger than Belgium's, it is by far the biggest in absolute terms. Germany accumulated net foreign assets before and during the crisis, but it suffered from a substantial devaluation of its claims during the crisis, of some 13% of GDP or € 336 billion, as long-term assets held by Germans, such as foreign government bonds and other securities issued by the crisis countries and the US, suffered substantial losses in market value. Despite these losses, by the end of 2012 German net foreign wealth amounted to 42% of GDP, or € 1,107 billion. Without the revaluation effects, the German net foreign asset position would have been 54% of GDP, ahead of the Belgian position, which, without the revaluation effects, would have amounted to 23% of GDP.

Bubbles

Regardless of whether foreign debt was amassed by the public or the private sector, in all these countries the euro gave rise to an inflationary boom that deprived them of their competitiveness, an issue whose implications for the future of the Eurozone will be examined in depth in Chapter 4. The boom resulted from two effects.

For one thing, the savings in interest payments of private and public debtors translated into an increase in real disposable income, which stimulated consumption and stoked inflation. Private debtors were able to consume more, while the governments had more money available to hire more employees and raise the salaries of those already on their payrolls, which also stimulated consumption.

For another, the lower interest rates encouraged more borrowing, which again had inflationary demand effects. This temptation did not befall only the governments; private debtors were equally affected. Indeed, in Spain private debt was clearly dominant, as shown above.

Before the euro was introduced, Spain had not had long-maturity mortgages at fixed interest rates, as was the norm in Germany.[31] Furthermore, interest rates for construction were extremely high, higher even than the yield on government debt. For instance, in 1991 the initial interest rate was 17%,[32] which led to little construction activity. This all changed as soon as the euro was announced in the Madrid Summit of December 1995. Now that the Spanish banks could borrow at far lower interest rates in the European interbank market, they gradually offered builders much more convenient terms[33]—but certainly not before profiting themselves mightily from the fat margins. The Spaniards didn't hesitate to grab the chance. They took the credit on offer, bought houses and refurbished them, or built new ones, triggering a colossal construction boom that pulled the entire economy in its wake.

[31] See European Mortgage Federation, 'Study on Interest Rate Variability in Europe', 2006, pp. 1–29, available at: <http://www.hypo.org/content/default.asp?PageID=203#INTEREST%20RATE%20VARIABILITY>; and European Mortgage Federation, 'Hypostat 2010. A Review of Europe's Mortgage and Housing Markets', 2010, pp. 1–98, in particular p. 8, available at: <http://www.hypo.org/Content/Default.asp?PageID=524>.

[32] See Banco de España, 'Official Mortgage Market Reference Rates', *Boletín Estadístico* 2013, available at: <http://www.bde.es/webbde/es/estadis/infoest/series/be1901.csv>.

[33] Mortgage interest sank in Spain between 1995 and 2001 by 5.44 percentage points, whereas in Germany it fell by only 1.75 percentage points. See European Central Bank, *Structural Factors in the EU Housing Market*, 2003, pp. 1–55, in particular p. 22, available at: <http://www.ecb.int/pub/pdf/other/euhousingmarketsen.pdf>. For the 1991–2001 period, the retreat of mortgage interest amounted to more than 10 percentage points. See Banco de España, 'Official Mortgage Market Reference Rates', 2013.

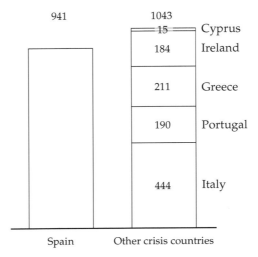

Figure 2.10 Spanish net foreign debt in comparison (2012, € billion)

Source: Eurostat, Database, *Economy and Finance*, Balance of Payments—International Transactions, Balance of Payments Statistics and International Investment Positions; Banca d'Italia, *Base Informativa Pubblica*, Balance of Payments and International Investment Position.

The external debt that Spain accumulated on account of having the euro represents the Eurozone's greatest debt problem at present, simply because Spain is a big country, with correspondingly large debts. As Figure 2.10 shows, its debts, at € 941 billion, are only a bit smaller than the net external debt of all the other stricken countries combined (€ 1,043 billion). Coincidentally, this volume is nearly as large as Germany's total net foreign assets, which amount to € 1,107 billion.

The banks and other lenders could have reined in this process, but they also got carried away by the fever and relaxed their usual due-diligence guidelines. In mortgage lending terms, the same thing occurred in Spain as in the US. The banks showered customers with lending offers, pronounced themselves satisfied with little collateral, and financed a much higher portion of the property price than is common in other countries, for instance in Germany, where a maximum of 60% is customary for private mortgages. It was not unusual for banks to lend up to 130% of the property's value in order for their customers to splash out on a sports-utility vehicle with the surplus, as a Barcelona banker once told the author.

By the end of 2013 the debts of the banks of the six crisis-stricken countries, including € 3.6 trillion in deposits from their clients, added up to € 8.2 trillion, or

263% of these countries' combined GDP.[34] They arose largely from the granting of dodgy loans to the private economy and to property developers and buyers, which came to grief during the crisis. The collective rescue operations undertaken by the Eurozone countries, which as per the EU summit of July 2012 are to make vast sums also available for rescuing the banks, will try to contain the spillover effects of write-off losses to other sectors. Chapter 8 will discuss this in more detail.

The Spanish construction boom had an effect on immigration as well. Labour was sought after, wages were on the rise, and the number of jobs on offer kept rising steadily. In the ten years from 1999 to 2008, when the construction boom came to an abrupt end with the collapse of Lehman Brothers, 6 million immigrants came to take on Spain, mostly to jobs in construction and in the rest of the economy. Some 2.3 million of them came from EU countries—primarily from Romania, which accounted for more than 770,000—and the rest mostly from North Africa and Latin America.[35] That amounted to a gross immigration equivalent to 15% of the original population, which is an extremely high proportion for a single decade. The construction workers now had the money to spend on other goods, which led to further people finding gainful employment in the production of such goods. Real GDP in Spain grew by 55% from 1995 to 2007, while the German economy only managed 21% (see also Figure 3.2 in the following chapter).

The picture in Ireland was quite similar. The real-estate boom was even more pronounced than in Spain, and massive immigration was one of the results. Over the same decade, immigration amounted to 20% of the original population in gross terms and 10% in net terms, i.e. accounting for emigration.[36] Ireland grew even faster than Spain and topped the league in the whole of Europe, with 129% growth from 1995 to the onset of the crisis in 2007. Its economic output, in other words, more than doubled. These developments occurred without government participation, unlike in the Greek and Portuguese cases.

But at the end of the day it was irrelevant whether the cheap credit that fuelled the boom reached the economy through the private or the public sector, since one sector profited automatically from the other sector. In Portugal and Greece the state employees bought and built houses from their credit-financed

---

[34] See Deutsche Bundesbank, Time Series Database, *Time Series MFI (Monetary Financial Institutions),* Bestandsangaben; and European Commission, Economic and Financial Affairs, *Economic Databases and Indicators*, AMECO – The annual macro-economic database.

[35] See Eurostat, Database, *Population and Social Conditions*, International Migration and Asylum.

[36] See Eurostat, Database, *Population and Social Conditions*, International Migration and Asylum.

wage increases, while in Ireland and Spain the construction workers, developers and homeowners paid taxes out of their credit-financed incomes. This boosted the economy and eventually turned into what is known as a bubble: a boom fuelled by exaggerated optimism that must burst sometime because the country's fundamentals no longer correspond to the nominal asset values, sparking fears among creditors for the safety of their investments.

The economic boom was exactly what one had expected from the euro. It led to real convergence within the Eurozone, that is, to a catch-up process among the hitherto poor countries. The boom, however, took on too much momentum and boosted wages, goods prices and property prices beyond a level sustainable in the long-term. In making their investment decisions, people projected the observed trend into an arbitrarily far future, shooting too often far beyond the mark.

Property Prices

This is particularly true of property prices. When property prices start to go up, an increasing number of people become more optimistic and believe that they can still get in on the ground floor in order to profit from the price hike. Prices then really pick up as a result, and even more people become infected. A process of self-reinforcing expectations takes hold, with ever higher prices, ever more real construction projects, a strongly booming domestic economy and steadily rising wages, which comes to an end when the first construction project finds no takers, doubts begin to spread, buyers become rare and excess supply in the real-estate market becomes evident. Prices begin to plummet, new projects are stopped, construction workers are sacked, demand slumps, and a general economic crisis sets in that unleashes massive unemployment.

Figure 2.11 shows how quickly property prices rose—and subsequently fell—in different European countries. Particularly strong price fluctuations were evident in Ireland and Spain, where the real-estate boom started. From the Madrid Summit to Lehman Brothers, i.e. in only 13 years, Irish property prices quadrupled and Spanish prices tripled. Even the Greek and French property prices were two-and-a-half times higher at the outbreak of the crisis than at the time the euro was announced.

It is noteworthy that Germany did not partake of the rise and fall in property prices. Since it was mired in its own euro crisis, property prices fell continuously until the onset of the worldwide crisis and started to rise only thereafter, thanks to a new construction boom paradoxically resulting from this very same crisis. This will be explained in more detail in the next chapter.

The bubble in the crisis-stricken countries was not only in rising property prices. The general upward trend of goods prices and real income fuelled by the cheap euro credit also fostered the belief among both public and private debtors

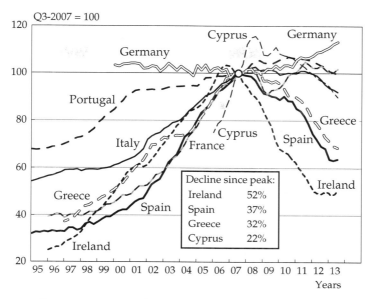

Figure 2.11 Property prices in the Eurozone

Sources: European Central Bank, Statistical Data Warehouse, *Economic Concepts—* Prices, Output, Demand and Labour—Prices—Residential Property Price Indicator, Residential Property Price Index Statistics; German Federal Statistical Office, *Genesis Database*, Themen, Preise—Agrarpreise, Preise gewerbl. Produkte, Baupreise— Häuserpreisindex, Preisindex für bestehende Wohngebäude; Central Bank of Cyprus, Media & Publications—Publications—Surveys—*Residential Property Price Indices*, Data Series; Central Bank of Greece, Statistics—*Real Estate Market Analysis*—Index of Prices of Dwellings (Historical Series).

Note: For Ireland, quarterly data until Q3 2010; thereafter only monthly data were available. For Germany data from the German Federal Statistical Office were used for the period until Q3 2011. Later data for this country stem from the ECB.

that it was safe to take on more debt. The notion was widespread that it was possible to grow out of the debts, making leveraging appear fairly risk-free. This is not as irrational as it seems, since most of the countries now affected by the crisis grew at blistering rates for an entire decade. The error was to think that this process would continue indefinitely.

Every stormy growth process must come to an end at some point in time; a sudden end, when the perception takes hold that the increases in goods prices and wages resulting from the boom are actually robbing companies of their competitiveness. By the time doubts about the continuation of the growth trend set in, it is usually too late. Once goods prices and wages have drifted too far from their sustainable competitiveness level, it is very difficult to bring them back down again. Only property prices move freely in both directions.

By now, nearly all the prices that had exploded in the 'good' years of the euro have come down again, more hesitantly than they increased, but still at a dramatic pace. The price decline in Ireland was particularly fast. Irish property prices have fallen by more than 50% since 2006. By contrast, French property prices have yet to come down. In the first wave of the crisis they declined by about 10%, but then they stabilized and continued to increase beyond the level they had at the outset of the crisis. Should the French prices remain as high as they are despite their explosive rise after the introduction of the euro, this would be a truly astonishing event in history.

Private Wealth

The boost to economic activity given by the credit inflows that the euro encouraged not only created jobs and raised income in the southern countries, but also gave rise to considerable wealth, making these countries richer than the rest of the Eurozone. This is shown in Figure 2.12, which summarizes the result

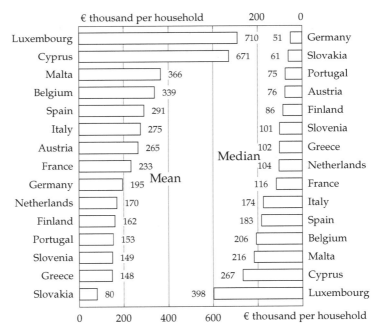

Figure 2.12 Household wealth (2010)

Source: European Central Bank, 'The Eurosystem Household Finance and Consumption Survey: Results from the First Wave', *Statistics Paper Series*, No. 2, April 2013, p. 76.

of a survey of household wealth conducted by the ECB between late 2008 and mid-2011, with 2010 as the reference year for most of the countries surveyed. The left-hand bars show the average wealth per household, the right-hand columns the median wealth, i.e. the level of wealth that divides the population into two halves. Surprisingly, the crisis-stricken countries perform rather well. On average, Spanish households are 49%, and Italian households 41%, richer than German ones, for example, and even Greek and Portuguese households lag behind by not more than 24% and 22%, respectively. Cypriot households, with an average wealth of € 671,000, are a whopping 3.4 times as wealthy as German ones, and 2.9 times as wealthy as French ones. Unfortunately, Ireland refused to participate in the survey. It would have been interesting to compare it with Cyprus, given that both economies show some similarities in terms of the role of the banking sector. On average, household wealth in Greece, Italy, Portugal, Spain and Cyprus exceeds household wealth in the rest of the Eurozone by 23%.

The differences are even bigger when median wealth is considered. Median wealth lies everywhere below average wealth, since income distribution is skewed, with long tails to the right that affect means more than medians. As the chart shows, even Greek and Portuguese median wealth levels are much higher than the German one, exceeding it by 98% and 46%, respectively. Spanish median wealth exceeds the German one by 255%, Italian median wealth does so by 238%, while Cypriot median wealth dwarfs the German one by 419%.

There have been doubts as to the accuracy of the ECB study, given that the good performance of the southern countries relative to northern ones, Germany and Finland in particular, did not seem to conform to prior expectations. For example, it has been argued that the differences can be explained by differences in household size.[37] However, even if this effect is taken into account, both Italians and Spaniards on average are still 14% wealthier than Germans, 42% wealthier than Dutchmen and 40% wealthier than Finns.[38]

There are two explanations for the high wealth of southern households shown in the ECB survey. For one thing, the increase in government debt meant

[37] See G. D'Alessio, R. Gambacorta and G. Ilardi, 'Are Germans Poorer than other Europeans? The Principal Eurozone Differences in Wealth and Income', *VoxEU*, 24 May 2013, available at: <http://www.voxeu.org/article/are-germans-poorer-ot her-europeans-principal-eurozone-differences-wealth-and-income>.

[38] See European Central Bank, 'The Eurosystem Household Finance and Consumption Survey: Results from the First Wave', *Statistics Paper Series*, No. 2, April 2013, p. 76. Average household size is 2.53 in Italy, 2.68 in Spain, 2.04 in Germany, 2.22 in the Netherlands and 2.08 in Finland. See European Central Bank, *The Eurosystem Household Finance and Consumption Survey*, 2013, p. 12. Net wealth per capita amounts thus to € 108,800 in Italy, € 108,700 in Spain, € 95,700 in Germany, € 76,700 in the Netherlands and € 77,600 in Finland.

that the citizens of southern countries did not pay enough taxes to balance the budget, which enabled them to accumulate private wealth. To some extent, the enormous private wealth in the south simply mirrors public impecuniousness, while in the north private poverty reflects the sounder public finances. To put it another way: in both the northern and southern countries governments took money from their citizens to finance their expenditure, but while the northern governments took this money in the form of taxes, the southern governments issued government bonds in exchange, which then became part of private wealth.

For another thing, the inflow of credit from abroad led to the building boom in the south described above, which boosted the value of real-estate property beyond the liabilities built up by borrowing abroad. Credit created additional private wealth, or at least the illusion of it.

Market or Government Failure?

In view of the horrors that the bursting of bubbles brought to the western and southern European countries, which is now threatening the EU's cohesion and the very existence of the euro, the question is: how could this happen? How was it possible for investors to dump their caution overboard for a whole decade and invest, for a mere risk premium of 30 basis points, in assets that in the end turned out to be junk, such as Greek government bonds (see Figure 2.3)? How could they disregard the bankruptcy risk for a full decade, although the Maastricht Treaty had made it utterly clear (article 125 TFEU) that there would be no bail-out once a country goes bust and that the creditors in that case would have to bear the losses?

There are two potential answers to this. The first is that market agents often have wrong expectations about the future and therefore make wrong decisions in the present. After all, there have been credit bubbles in many places around the world and throughout history.[39] Investors at times neglect their caution, get carried away, and infect each another expecting eternal growth, driving up asset prices until the bubble bursts; then, all of a sudden, their mood changes. Animal spirits fuel irrational expectations, and irrational fear erupts in panic.[40]

Some say this is a market failure, but in fact it is the lack of a complete set of futures markets on which plans can be coordinated through binding inter-temporal contracts on the delivery of goods and credit.[41] The incompleteness of

---

[39] See C. Reinhart and K. S. Rogoff, *This Time is Different*, 2009.

[40] See P. De Grauwe, 'Animal Spirits and Monetary Policy', *Economic Theory* 47, 2011, pp. 423–457; G. A. Akerlof and R. J. Shiller, *Animal Spirits*, 2009.

[41] See R. J. Shiller, *The New Financial Order: Risk in the 21st Century*, Princeton University Press, Princeton 2003; also O. Hart, 'On the Optimality of Equilibrium

futures markets substitutes expectations of future market prices and incomes for known market parameters, but these expectations often turn out to be wrong because the intuitive or objective models of the world on which agents base their decisions are wrong. Unfortunately, this problem cannot be easily resolved due to the cost of creating such markets and enforcing long-term contracts, and just adding a few future markets without having a complete set of them may actually make things worse.[42] Still, it is a bit too simplistic to speak of a market failure if the incompleteness of markets is what is causing the problem.

The other answer is that policymakers themselves contributed to causing the problems. For example, they distorted expectations, creating excessive optimism in the phase of bubble-building, because their expectations were based on even worse models of the economy than those of market agents, or because they deliberately wanted markets to deviate from an efficient allocation of capital across the countries of the Eurozone to benefit their own constituencies.

In fact, the EU sent many signals that made investors believe that in case of trouble other governments would bail out the bankrupt countries and their creditors at the expense of their taxpayers, despite the no-bailout clause of the Maastricht Treaty. The EU undermined the Maastricht Treaty by encouraging investors to disregard risks and put their money in places they would normally stay away from. The whole institutional apparatus was directed so much towards this goal, given that it was the driving force for the euro project in the first place, that a mere treaty clause, especially one on which only a minority of countries had insisted, was not taken seriously by market agents.

Had the no-bailout clause been taken seriously, the Eurozone countries would have had to implement directives and procedures for the case of state insolvencies, specifying what would happen in such a case, in particular the sequence in which creditors would be affected by haircuts and debt-rescheduling operations. In addition, rules for orderly exits from the Eurozone would have had to be specified. This would not only have provided clear guidelines for the rescue operations for Greece that started in May 2010 and avoided the confusion at the time of the Greek debt rescheduling of March 2012. It would also have sent a signal to investors that the no-bailout clause was to be taken seriously and that

---

when the Market Structure is Incomplete', *Journal of Economic Theory* 11, 1975, pp. 418–443; and the contributions by K. Arrow, P. Diamond, J. Drèze, P. Dubey, D. Duffie, J. Geanakoplos, S. J. Grossman, A. Mas-Colell, O. Hart, R. Radner, and M. Santos, in M. Magill and M. Quinzii (eds), *Incomplete Markets*, Edward Elgar, Northampton 2008.

[42] See O. Hart, 'On the Optimality of Equilibrium when the Market Structure is Incomplete', 1975; as well as M. C. Kemp and H.-W. Sinn, 'A Simple Model of Privately Profitable but Socially Useless Speculation', *Japanese Economic Review* 51, 2000, pp. 85–95.

they do actually bear a sizeable risk by lending to over-indebted and uncompetitive countries.

The bubbles in Greece and Portugal would have hardly been possible under such circumstances, because markets would have demanded risk premia early on, spoiling the debtor states' appetite for ever more foreign credit. Indirectly, such measures would also have reined in the forces inflating the private property bubbles in Spain and Ireland, because they would have reduced the chances of banks being bailed out by their governments, as eventually happened. As will be explained in Chapter 8, the EU is currently preparing rules for bank resolution, but exits and state bankruptcies remain taboo so as not to spook investors.

One of the most important policy decisions of the EU that reflected the neglect of the no-bailout clause was to allow commercial banks, regardless of the regulatory model they chose, to buy government bonds of all EU countries without having to hold capital against such bonds. Small wonder then that the banks dumped caution overboard and loaded their balance sheets with government bonds, which later turned out to be toxic.[43]

According to the Basel Accords on banking regulation, banks had to hold a certain proportion of their risk-weighted assets as equity capital (Tier 1 capital), the risk weights being determined exogenously by a standard approach or endogenously by a coherent internal risk model that the banks had to submit to their supervising agencies. While the Basel Accords allowed the risk weights of government bonds to be set at zero, when banks used the standard approach, the more attractive internal risk models forced the banks to assign non-zero weights to government bonds. The EU changed this rule in 2006, allowing the banks to combine the advantage of being able to use their own risk models with a zero risk weight for government bonds.[44] Thus, banks didn't have to set aside any

---

[43] See H.-W. Sinn, *Casino Capitalism*, 2010, chapter 4: *Why Wall Street Became a Gambling Casino*, p. 92.

[44] See *Regulation Governing the Capital Adequacy of Institutions, Groups of Institutions and Financial Holding Groups*, paragraph 26 number 2 littera b in connection with paragraph 70 section 1 littera c; *Directive 2006/48/EC of the European Parliament and of the Council of 14 June 2006 Relating to the Taking Up and Pursuit of the Business of Credit Institutions (Recast)*, paragraph 80 number 1 in connection with paragraph 89 number 1 littera d. As far as is known, all euro countries implemented these rules in their national legislation. For the example of Germany, see *Verordnung über die angemessene Eigenmittelausstattung von Instituten, Institutsgruppen und Finanzholding-Gruppen*, paragraph 26 number 2 littera b in connection with paragraph 70 number 1 littera c; *Richtlinie 2006/48/EG des Europäischen Parlaments und des Rates vom 14. Juni 2006 über die Aufnahme und Ausübung der Tätigkeit der Kreditinstitute (Neufassung)*, paragraph 80 number 1 in connection with paragraph 89 number 1 littera d.

While the Basel Accord stipulates risk weights for government bonds, which, depending on a formal rating or the classification of an export insurance agency, could be set at

capital against government bonds, and unless rating agencies withdrew a country's investment-grade rating, no distinction was made among more or less creditworthy countries. This practice was not implied by the Basel Accords, which governs the way many banks worldwide are regulated, but by a special provision that the EU governments added, belatedly and deliberately and without public notice, to the Basel Accords.

Small and undifferentiated risk weights were also allowed for if banks were lending to other banks in the Eurozone. Regardless of differences in creditworthiness, a uniform risk weight of only 0.2 was required for claims on other banks, much less than for lending to even well-run firms, which required differentiated risk weights of 0.5 and more, often even 1. This provision artificially heated up the European interbank market, by directing credit flows to banks with low creditworthiness that would otherwise have found borrowing more difficult. It induced northern European banks to lend excessively to the banks in southern Europe and Ireland, encouraging them, in turn, to lend excessively to local firms, households, and governments. This, too, contributed to the exorbitant boost in investment and consumption that inflated the bubbles. Much of this credit translated into higher wages for government employees and construction workers, increasing the general living standard and boosting imports, but making the economies dependent on the cheap-credit drug.

A mere political decision by bureaucrats far below the Treaty level, unnoticed by the public, reduced the effective equity requirements of lending banks and pronounced all borrowing governments and banks in the Eurozone as equally safe, although they weren't. This undermined the fundamental role of the capital markets in assessing risks and charging well-differentiated risk premia. The representatives of countries that considered themselves discriminated against before the introduction of the euro because they did not understand or respect the risk assessments conducted by markets now formed a majority in the corresponding EU bodies, thus managing to secure access to cheap credit to the detriment of safer investment opportunities and in blatant disregard for the Maastricht Treaty's stipulations.

The reckless decisions of bureaucrats were a major reason why the banks in Europe were so willing to lend to each other and to governments, with such disregard for the underlying risk of default. These decisions explain why the banks of

---

zero, they are only meant for the case where a bank keeps to the standardized approach to risk assessment. Furthermore, the standardized approach considers the option that claims on the bank's own sovereign can be accorded a low risk weight. If the banks, however, prefer the option of resorting to their own risk-assessment model (Internal Ratings Based Approach, IRBA), the risk weights for government bonds are to be assigned endogenously. Thus, the EU policy was bending and stretching the Basel rules substantially. See also H.-W. Sinn, *Casino Capitalism*, 2010, chapter 7: *Policy Failure*.

the north gobbled up the southern countries' government bonds and were lending such gigantic volumes of funds to the banks of the countries now in crisis. They also explain the problematic linkage between southern European banks and their sovereigns that the EU currently so deplores. The regulatory mistakes created a huge distortion in international capital flows that made the southern countries drug-addicted, destroyed their export industries, and built up retail economies that concentrated on the delivery of imported goods. It also caused the painful withdrawal symptoms when the drug supply was interrupted and market-dictated austerity set in.

In the meantime, the Basel Committee on Banking Supervision has set up a new regulatory system, Basel III, which is to become effective during a transition period from 2013 to 2019 and be implemented by Europe's national parliaments before 2019. Unfortunately, that system perpetuates the old mistakes. The risk weights that the EU had introduced are now even part of the formal Basel Accords, granting the misallocation of capital an even more solid base.[45]

This is also true of the new regulation of insurance companies, Solvency II, agreed to by the European Parliament and the Council of the European Union.[46] The solvency regulation hitherto imposed on insurance companies only specified equity holdings in relation to the premium revenue. In the future, insurance companies in principle will also have to hold equity in proportion to their investment. However, like banks, they do not need to hold equity against government bonds of EU countries as well as Norway, Liechtenstein, and Iceland. Again, the system fails to discriminate between good and bad borrowers, inducing insurance companies to turn a blind eye when lending out their funds.

To be sure, the banks and insurance companies could have charged differentiated risk premia and decided to voluntarily set aside more buffer capital. But they didn't do that, because they knew that they would lose any additional precautionary capital if the worst came to the worst. The strategy of operating with a minimum of capital is widespread around the world and is the core of the business model of thousands of financial institutions. In normal times, if all goes well, the profits are distributed to the shareholders; if a crisis hits and the institution defaults, the only loss the shareholders have to bear is the bit of

[45] See Basel Committee on Banking Supervision, *Basel III: A Global Regulatory Framework for more Resilient Banks and Banking Systems*, December 2010 (revised June 2011), available at: <http://www.bis.org/publ/bcbs189.pdf>; and Basel Committee on Banking Supervision, *Basel III: The Liquidity Coverage Ratio and Liquidity Risk Monitoring Tools*, January 2013, available at: <http://www.bis.org/publ/bcbs238.pdf>.

[46] See EIOPA, *EIOPA Report on the Fifth Quantitative Impact Study (QIS5) for Solvency II*, 2011, available at: <https://eiopa.europa.eu/fileadmin/tx_dam/files/publications/reports/QIS5_Report_Final.pdf>.

capital they injected. Gambling with limited liability is the basic principle of casino capitalism.[47]

The effects of overly lax and distortionary regulation were exacerbated by the implicit promise of protection that, in the eyes of the capital markets, the Eurozone countries had been given through the mere fact of their forming a currency union. The conviction among investors that the stronger countries would be bound to rescue the weaker ones in case of an impending sovereign default or a collapse of their banking system, or that the weaker ones would have enough political power to draw the necessary resources out of the common monetary system, was built into the Eurosystem, since the ECB was seen as a lender of last resort, available to provide cheap refinancing credit if necessary. Even if other countries had not come to the rescue with fiscal funds, which in the end they did, the local printing presses still available to the euro states that enabled them to print euros instead of drachmas, liras or pesetas made it unlikely that a borrowing country and its banking system would run out of money. True, these printing presses could not be activated without obeying the rules of the ECB, but for one thing these rules were flexible, including emergency drawing rights (Emergency Liquidity Assistance, ELA; see Chapter 5) at a country's own discretion, and for another, the over-indebted and potentially imperilled countries commanded substantial voting rights and political influence in the ECB's decision-making bodies. The ECB was seen as an institution with unlimited firepower that could put massive sums of money on display to avert liquidity crises and protect against insolvency.

In view of the negative experiences the European economies had had under the European Exchange Rate Mechanism (ERM) set up in 1979, the ECB's unlimited firepower seemed to be the ultimate solution to the foreign exchange problem. As explained in Chapter 1, the ERM collapsed when the German reunification shock required exchange rate adjustments that the central banks

---

[47] See H.-W. Sinn, *Casino Capitalism*, 2010, chapter 4: *Why Wall Street Became a Gambling Casino*. The author once called the incentives to gamble because of limited capital the BLOOS Rule, alluding to the term 'You cannot get blood out of a stone' and he analysed this formally in his dissertation; and H.-W. Sinn, *Ökonomische Entscheidungen bei Ungewißheit*, Mohr Siebeck, Tübingen 1980, English edition: *Economic Decisions under Uncertainty*, North-Holland, Amsterdam 1983, chapters III B and V C , available at: <www.cesifo-group.de>. Others have spoken of a Gamble for Resurrection to characterize this same phenomenon; see M. Dewatripont and J. Tirole, 'Efficient Governance Structure: Implications for Banking Regulation', in C. Mayer and X. Vives (eds), *Capital Markets and Financial Intermediation*, Cambridge University Press, Cambridge 1993, pp. 12–35; and M. Dewatripont and J. Tirole, *Prudential Regulation of Banks*, MIT Press, Cambridge, Mass. 1994, pp. 97 and 113; see moreover, H.-W. Sinn, *Risk-Taking, Limited Liability, and the Banking Crisis*, Selected Reprints, Ifo Institute, Munich 2008, available at: <www.ifo.de/de/w/43e7rkviz>.

of Europe were ill-equipped to cope with, lacking enough funds to counteract the speculative attacks.[48] The Bundesbank, for instance, had set aside a total of 92 billion deutschmarks in September 1992 to buy ailing foreign currencies,[49] of which 60 billion deutschmarks were used to prop up the French franc,[50] but these sums were evidently not enough. The thinking was that with a currency union, as opposed to a mere monetary system, no investor could expect depreciation and hence the interest rates had to converge, providing the desired relief to both private and public debtors, enabling the economies of Europe to settle to a better equilibrium.[51] But it was exactly this unlimited firepower that created the bubble and all the catastrophic events derived from it. By virtue of its mere existence, the Eurosystem helped generate ten years of calm and a convergence of interest rates across the currency area. For ten years, the display of money in the shop window sufficed. But the unwarranted confidence this engendered led to the emergence of inflationary bubbles that eventually burst, prompting the affected countries to take the money on display after all.

This illustrates the dilemma in putting together the Eurozone. On the one hand, exchange rate stability is a must, which speaks for giving the ECB unlimited firepower. On the other hand, tight control of budgets and avoidance of debt excesses by all participating countries is also mandatory, which calls for tight budget constraints and interest premia commensurate with each debtor's credit-worthiness. The Eurozone evidently failed in its attempt to perform a balancing act between these divergent aims, placing all the emphasis on the first goal and disregarding the second. The budget brakes kicked in far too late, when some rapidly accelerating economies had already derailed.

Most European politicians did not recognize this problem at all and were ostensibly blindfolded by the short-term benefits of soft budget constraints to their own countries, while those who did realize that there was a problem consoled themselves with the belief that the Stability and Growth Pact would apply the brakes in time. This belief proved delusory, since for one thing the

---

[48] See H. Geiger, *Das Währungsrecht im Binnenmarkt der Europäischen Union*, Verlag Versicherungswirtschaft, Karlsruhe 1996, p. 40.

[49] See H. Hesse and B. Braasch, 'Zum optimalen Instrumentarium der Europäischen Zentralbank', in B. Gahlen, H. Hesse, and H. J. Ramser (eds), *Europäische Integrationsprobleme aus wirtschaftswissenschaftlicher Sicht*, Mohr Siebeck, Tübingen 1994.

[50] See G. Braunberger, 'Die Krise im EWS kann den Gewinn der Bundesbank schmälern', *Frankfurter Allgemeine Zeitung*, No. 183, 10 August 1993, p. 11.

[51] See Economic and Social Committee, 'Opinion of the Economic and Social Committee on "An Assessment of the Introduction of the Single Currency"', *Official Journal of the European Communities* C 117/3, 26 April 2000, pp. 23–27, Sections 7.1 and 7.2, available at: <http://eur-lex.europa.eu/LexUriServ/LexUriServ.do?uri=OJ:C:2000:1 17:0023:0027:EN:PDF>.

politicians then in office did not take the Pact seriously, and for another, they were in any case powerless to do anything about the excessive indebtedness in the private sector, which lies at the core of the crisis, as the Spanish and Irish examples show. The Stability and Growth Pact was a placebo given to appease the Germans, while at the same time the banks were given, under the table, a sort of dope in the form of generous accounting rules and the implicit protection granted by the ECB that encouraged lenders to literally close their eyes to risks.

CHAPTER 3

The Other Side of the Coin

*Euro Winners and Euro Losers—Capital Exports from the Core to the Periphery—
Mass Unemployment in Germany—Agenda 2010—The New Construction Boom—
Misunderstanding the Tango*

Euro Winners and Euro Losers

The near-catastrophic developments in the GIPSIC countries, i.e. Greece, Ireland, Portugal, Spain, Italy, and Cyprus, in particular their high rates of unemployment (Figures 1.2 and 1.3) and the burst property bubbles (Figure 2.11), coincided with sharp recessions in these countries during the crisis. Figure 3.1 shows the magnitude of the recessions, with the curves baselined on 2007, the year of the first breakdown of the interbank market. When the world sunk into what is now often called the Great Recession in 2008 and 2009, the GIPSIC countries, with the exception of Cyprus, followed suit. Unfortunately, most of them did not recover when the world economy subsequently picked up and experienced substantial growth as of 2010. On the contrary, some GIPSIC economies, including that of Cyprus, contracted even further. The recession hit hardest in Greece, where the economy shrank by 23%.

By contrast, Germany's economy, the largest in Europe, grew appreciably during the crisis,[1] while France's economy stagnated.

In view of the differences in performance, it would seem all too obvious that Germany has benefited most from the euro. Europe's largest economy flourishes while southern Europe suffers. Indeed, this fact has frequently been generalized to portray Germany as the winner of the euro. The European Commission has

---

[1] Among the euro countries, only Slovakia and Malta grew faster.

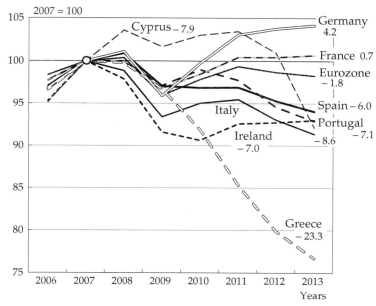

Figure 3.1 Growth of selected euro countries during the crisis (2006–2013, %)

Source: Eurostat, Database, *Economy and Finance*, National Accounts, GDP and its Main Components; European Commission, Economic and Financial Affairs, *Economic Databases and Indicators*, AMECO – the annual macro-economic database; Ifo Institute calculations.

Note: GDP growth rates measured in terms of chain-linked volumes at 2005 prices. The figures present the GDP growth rates for the period from 2007 to 2013. See also note to Figure 3.2. 2013 European Commission forecast, Autumn 2013.

expressed this view, and even the German government has endorsed it.[2] The truth, however, is quite different, as we will see, since Germany before the onset of the current crisis experienced its own euro crisis that required painful policy

---

[2] See P. Plickert, 'Die Vor- und die Nachteile des Euro', *Frankfurter Allgemeine Zeitung*, 22 June 2011, available at: <http://www.faz.net/aktuell/wirtschaft/europas-schuldenkrise/waehrungsunion-die-vor-und-die-nachteile-des-euro-1653839.html>; A. Merkel, *Regierungserklärung zum Europäischen Rat in Brüssel*, 24/25 March 2011, available at: <http://www.bundesregierung.de/ContentArchiv/DE/Archiv17/Regierungserklaerung/2011/2011-03-24-merkel-europaeischer-rat.html>; and 'Wie profitiert Deutschland vom Euro?', *ZDF heute-journal*, 8 September 2011, available at: <http://www.etwasverpasst.de/sendung/88591/zdf/zdf-heute-journal/zdf-heute-journal-vom-08-september-2011.html>; also 'Geben Sie Ihr Ehrenwort, dass wir Deutschen kein Geld verlieren?', Interview by K. Diekmann and D. Hoeren with José Manuel Barroso, *Bild*,

reactions. From a longer-term perspective, Germany's performance does not look all that great.

Figure 3.2 shows the growth of the same euro countries as in Figure 3.1, but starting in 1995, the year of the Madrid Summit at which the euro was irrevocably adopted, the timing for its introduction was specified, and markets started adjusting to the euro. The growth performance of the various countries before the outbreak of the crisis in 2007 appears to be nearly the exact opposite of what it was thereafter.

Germany in particular exhibited an entirely different performance relative to the other economies before and

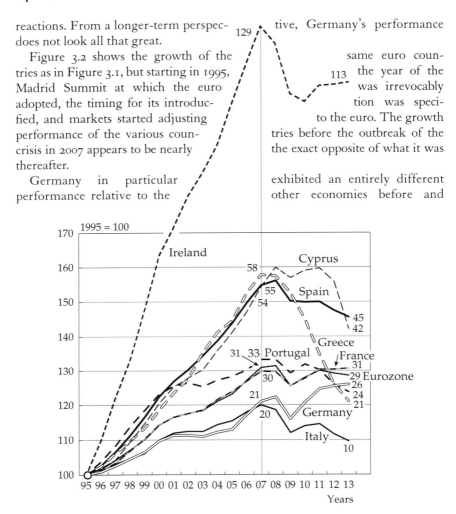

Figure 3.2 Growth of selected euro countries before and during the crisis (1995–2013, %)

Source: Eurostat, Database, *Economy and Finance*, National Accounts, GDP and its Main Components; European Commission, Economic and Financial Affairs, *Economic Databases and Indicators*, AMECO – the annual macro-economic database; Ifo Institute calculations.

Note: GDP growth rates measured in terms of chain-linked volumes at 2005 prices. The figures for the volumes are obtained by dividing GDP values by the respective national GDP deflator. While this is the usual statistical definition, it might be more appropriate in a currency union to deflate using the harmonized GDP deflator so as to capture quality changes that lead to relative price changes. In such a case, the German growth curve would look far worse, placing it well below Italy, at the very bottom of the ranking. 2013 European Commission forecast, Autumn 2013.

after the crisis. Over the twelve-year period from 1995 to 2007 it grew by just 21%, only one percentage point more than Italy, while the Eurozone on average grew by 31%. Until 2006, Germany's growth was even slower than Italy's, turning the country into the Eurozone's laggard. In fact, in the period from the announcement of the euro at the Madrid Summit to the year before the outbreak of the crisis, Germany experienced the lowest growth rate of all European countries, even if Europe's boundary were to be drawn at the Urals. In 2002, a member of the Bundestag walked down the aisle in the plenary room swinging a red railway lantern to signal that the German economy was the last carriage in the European train.[3]

The GIPSIC economies, by contrast, grew very rapidly, by 37% between 1995 and 2007. Ireland's economy even managed 129%, while the economies of Greece and Spain both expanded by around 55%. This performance is obviously the opposite of that shown in Figure 3.1 for the period since 2007. The former gazelles became turtles, and the turtles, gazelles. In a sense, as mentioned, the post-crisis performance is the mirror image of the pre-crisis one.

But not entirely. The initial growth phase was so strong that it more than compensated for the slump the GIPSIC economies have experienced since 2007. Over the entire period from 1995 to 2013, for instance, Ireland still grew by 113%, Spain by 45%, and Cyprus by 42%. Taken together, the GIPSIC economies grew by 25% over the entire period, which is very similar to the 29% growth for the Eurozone as a whole.

Germany, despite its recent growth, still ranks as an underperformer over the entire period. Its growth of only 26% over the period from 1995 to 2013 did not even reach the Eurozone average.

Portugal and Italy were also underperformers. Portugal started out superbly, boasting the highest growth after Ireland in the first five years after the announcement of the euro, but then it lost momentum and started to lag. Over the entire period, it grew at similar rate (24%) as Germany. Italy, by contrast, was a laggard before the outbreak of the crisis and has remained so ever since. Its GDP in 2013 was only 10% larger than in 1995. Over the whole period, it showed the worst performance of all countries (assuming that the data are correct and not blurred by Italy's incredibly large shadow economy).

10 October 2011, available at: <http://www.bild.de/geld/wirtschaft/jose-manuel-barroso/deutschland-euro-krise-20394200.bild.html>.

[3] See H.-W. Sinn, *Die rote Laterne. Die Gründe für Deutschlands Wachstumsschwäche und die notwendigen Reformen*, Nordrhein-Westfälische Akademie der Wissenschaften (ed.), Ferdinand Schöningh Verlag, Paderborn 2003; also *ifo Schnelldienst* 55, Special Issue, No. 23, 17 December 2002, pp. 3–32, available at: <http://www.cesifo-group.de/DocDL/SD23-2002.pdf>; and Deutscher Bundestag, 'Das Geschehen im Parlament festhalten', 12 February 2010, available at: <http://www.bundestag.de/dokumente/textarchiv/2010/28642186_kw06_stenografen/index.html>.

If one compares the growth rates of real GDP per capita, the figures look somewhat less dire for Germany than when considering the absolute values shown on the chart above. This is because Germany's population stagnated over the eighteen years considered, expanding by only 0.5%, well below the 9.5% average for the other Eurozone countries.[4] In fact, with barely 8.3 newborns for every 1,000 people, Germany had the lowest birth rate of all OECD countries.[5] Immigration was unable to offset the lack of births, as Germany's bad economic performance translated into declining immigration. After the massive inflow of people from eastern Europe in the 1990s, the number of immigrants came down when the euro was introduced and eventually even turned negative in 2008 and 2009, after the Great Recession broke out. A net emigration of native Germans has taken place since 2005, and since 2006 there has even been a net emigration of Germany's Turkish population. This all translated into a steady decrease in Germany's population from 2003 to 2010. Only the good post-crisis performance of the German economy has recently managed to reverse the population trend.[6]

Despite its meagre population growth, per capita GDP in Germany slipped in the Eurozone's ranking. Figure 3.3 shows the evolution since 1995 of the ranking positions of the seventeen countries that in 2013 were in the Eurozone. In 1995 Germany was number two in the ranking, although German reunification had reduced its average GDP per capita, being topped only by Luxembourg, whose large financial services industry makes its top position unassailable. Thereafter, the roaring growth of the smaller euro economies made Germany fall steadily back; by 2007 the country had slid to eighth place. It was not until after the crisis that it clawed its way back to seventh. (Compared to all the countries that were members of the EU in 2013, it slid from third behind Luxembourg and Denmark to 11th in 2007. By the end of 2013 it had regained ninth place.) No other country dropped quite that far. Portugal fell three places over that period, France and Belgium two places, and Italy one place. Ireland and Finland, with a four-place improvement, were the best performers, followed by Slovenia and Malta, with a two-place improvement.

These facts alone should dispel the often-repeated notion that Germany has been the greatest beneficiary of the euro. If truth were defined by the frequency of public assertions, Germany would have indeed profited more than anyone else from the euro. However, the statistics above show that these assertions are not even approximately true.

---

[4] This is overlooked by *The Economist*. See 'Vorsprung durch Exports. Which G7 Economy Was the Best Performer of the Past Decade? And Can It Keep It Up?', *The Economist*, 3 February 2011, available at: <http://www.economist.com/node/18061550>; as well as H.-W. Sinn, Letter to the Editor: 'Germany's Economy', *The Economist*, 23 February 2011, available at: <www.ifo.de/w/3UfDQuwzg>.

[5] See The World Bank, World Data Bank, *World Development Indicators*, available at: <http://databank.worldbank.org/data/home.aspx>.

[6] See The World Bank, World Data Bank, *World Development Indicators*.

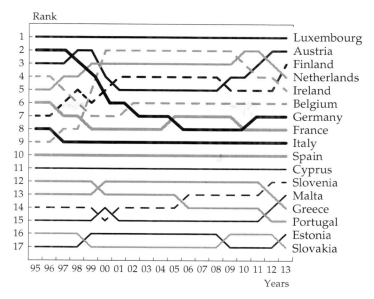

Figure 3.3 Per capita GDP ranking of euro countries

Source: Eurostat, Database, *Economy and Finance*, National Accounts, GDP and Main Components; European Commission, Economic and Financial Affairs, *Economic Databases and Indicators*, AMECO – the annual macro-economic database; Ifo Institute calculations.

Note: 2013 European Commission forecast, Autumn 2013.

Capital Exports from the Core to the Periphery

What happened in Europe during the period between the introduction of the euro and the outbreak of the crisis can best be understood in terms of capital movements, since the capital that created the bubble in southern Europe must have come from somewhere, and this somewhere was often Germany. Germany was by far the largest capital exporter at the time, to its own detriment.

From the time the euro was introduced, a growing fraction of German savings started to flow abroad, with very little investment being made at home, and it was this lack of investment that explains Germany's miserable growth performance shown in Figure 3.2. Germany had traditionally been a capital-exporting country. In 1991, it turned into a net capital importer, when it needed resources to nurture the ex-communist eastern part of its economy, and only reverted to being a net capital exporter in 2002, the year the euro was physically introduced. Shortly thereafter, German net capital exports surpassed those of China, Russia, and Saudi Arabia, and in 2006 those of Japan. From 2006 to 2010, Germany was

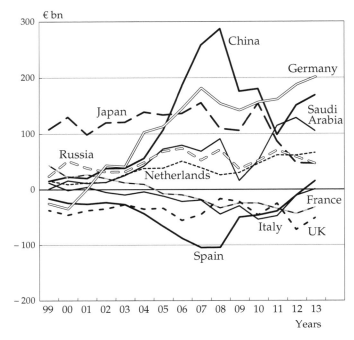

Figure 3.4 The world's largest capital exporters and a few other countries (1999–2013)

Source: International Monetary Fund, *World Economic Outlook Database*, October 2013; Deutsche Bundesbank, Time Series Databases, External Sector, Balance of Payments; and Exchange Rates; Ifo Institute calculations.

Note: For 2013 the graphs include IMF forecasts (except for Germany).

the second-largest net capital exporter in the world, behind China, and in 2011 it took over the leading position, as shown in Figure 3.4.

Germany's capital exports followed the announcement of the euro at the 1995 Madrid Summit with a certain delay, for the same reason as that explained in Chapter 2, namely the inertia of current accounts (Section *The Timing Problem*). When they finally became evident, around the time the euro was physically introduced, they triggered an anguished debate about Germany's future as a business location.[7] The Ifo Institute contributed to the debate in 2002 and 2003 with a proposal for the so-called 'Activating Social Assistance' and with a book on Germany's problems ('Can Germany be Saved?'), both of which influenced

---

[7] See H.-O. Henkel, *Die Kraft des Neubeginns: Deutschland ist machbar*, Droemer, Munich 2004; German Council of Economic Experts, *Jahresgutachten 2002/03: Zwanzig Punkte für Beschäftigung und Wachstum*, November 2002.

the reforms, known as Agenda 2010, eventually undertaken by the Schröder government.[8] The fact that Germany's industrial workers were the world's highest-paid at the time seemed at odds with:

—the growing industrial competition that globalization represented,

—the fall of the Iron Curtain,

—the eastward expansion of the EU and, not least,

—the introduction of the euro.

The euro starkly exposed the German workers' lack of competitiveness and increased the competitive pressure they were exposed to by bringing transparency to prices and wages, but most of all because it eliminated the exchange-rate uncertainty. Such uncertainty had kept capital from exploiting the advantages offered by moving to other places in terms of labour costs and returns on investment. Eliminating the impediments to the free movement of capital by removing exchange uncertainty was, as explained earlier, one of the driving factors for introducing the euro. Thanks to the euro, investors now dared to invest their resources in the Eurozone's low-wage countries. German banks and insurance companies, which had formerly been wary of investing in such countries, now saw them as attractive alternatives compared to investing in Germany, with the result that an increasing amount of German savings ended up wandering abroad.

Faced with this situation, Germany had no other option but to undertake wage-restraint reforms in order to avoid further damage to its industry and avert the risk of turning Germany into a bazaar economy, one which eliminates jobs in the domestic sector by importing an increasingly large amount of labour-intensive intermediary products, and displaces capital, talent and value-added towards the downstream sectors of the export industry.[9] While the displacement of value-added from the domestic sectors to the downstream sectors of the export industry was unstoppable, it could at least be slowed down

---

[8] In a letter to the Spiegel, Wolfgang Wiegard, then a member of the German Council of Economic Experts, argued that this literature was the 'intellectual basis' of the Agenda 2010. See W. Wiegard, *Letter to the Editor*, available at: <www.ifo.de/wiegard/w/j7yqcXB2>; also H.-W. Sinn, C. Holzner, W. Meister, W. Ochel, and M. Werding, 'Aktivierende Sozialhilfe. Ein Weg zu mehr Beschäftigung und Wachstum', *ifo Schnelldienst* 55, Special Issue, No. 9, 14 May 2002, available at: <http://www.cesifo-group.de/DocDL/SD9-2002.pdf>; H.-W. Sinn, *Ist Deutschland noch zu retten?*, Econ, Berlin 2003, English translation: *Can Germany be Saved?*, MIT Press, Cambridge 2007; see also D. Snower, A. J. G. Brown, and C. Merkl, 'Globalization and the Welfare State: A Review of Hans-Werner Sinn's "Can Germany Be Saved?"', *Journal of Economic Literature* 49, 2009, pp. 136–158.

[9] See H.-W. Sinn, *Die Basar-Ökonomie. Deutschland: Exportweltmeister oder Schlusslicht?*, Econ, Berlin 2005.

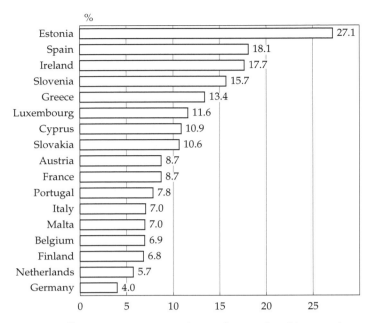

Figure 3.5 Overall net investment as a share of net national income (2003–2007)

Source: Eurostat, Database, *Economy and Finance*, National Accounts, GDP and its Main Components; and National Accounts, Income, Saving and Net Lending/Borrowing; Ifo Institute calculations.

Note: The chart shows the sum of private and public investment net of depreciation relative to net national income. (Net national income is arguably the best denominator for comparing the domestic use of savings. However, basing net investment on GDP or other income measures would not alter the ranking.)

through wage restraint. Wage restraint made it possible for some industries that were still relatively labour-intensive to retain their competitiveness, while a sufficient number of jobs were created in the service sector to compensate for the job losses in industry. The reforms were painful, but unquestionably necessary.

Whereas the elimination of exchange rate uncertainty was a boon for the countries in Europe's periphery, for Germany it was a problem, because savings capital flowed abroad instead of being invested at home. Germany posted the lowest net investment rate of all euro countries by far in the five years between the introduction of the euro (2002) and the year of the Lehman crisis (2008), as shown in Figure 3.5 above.[10]

[10] In 2011, a major revision of Germany's national accounts was performed leading to a complete overhaul of the calculations. Before this revision, Germany had had, for many years, the lowest net investment rate of all OECD countries.

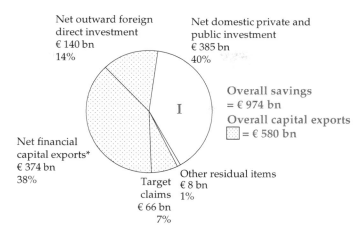

Net outward foreign
direct investment
€ 140 bn
14%

Net domestic private and
public investment
€ 385 bn
40%

I

Overall savings
= € 974 bn
Overall capital exports
☐ = € 580 bn

Net financial
capital exports*
€ 374 bn
38%

Target
claims
€ 66 bn
7%

Other residual items
€ 8 bn
1%

Figure 3.6 Use of German savings (2003–2007)

* Including statistically non-itemizable transactions.

Source: German Federal Statistical Office, *Fachserie 18*, Reihe 1.2; Deutsche Bundesbank, Time Series Databases, External Sector, Balance of Payments.

The grass appeared to be greener everywhere but in Germany. The investors did not see the risks that now are the focus of concern; they only saw the higher yields they were promised elsewhere. German life insurers and banks, most of all the Landesbanks that are now in the doldrums,[11] preferred to buy Greek, Portuguese, and Spanish government bonds over German bonds for a mere 20 to 35 extra basis points, i.e. barely 0.20 to 0.35 percent more in yields. That was the period when German savings capital was leaving the country in droves in search for yields abroad, where it created jobs and fuelled economic growth.

Figure 3.6 shows the share of overall savings accumulated from 2003 to 2007, which amounted to € 974 billion, going to net private and public investment at home, net financial capital exports, and net outward foreign direct investment. Over this period, 60% of German savings went abroad, a total of € 580 billion, and only 40% was invested at home for private and public purposes.[12] It would be difficult to find

---

[11] For an early criticism of the reckless investment strategy of the Landesbanks made possible by state guarantees, see H.-W. Sinn, *The German State Banks. Global Players in the International Financial Markets*, Edward Elgar, Cheltenham, UK, and Northampton, MA, USA, 1999.

[12] The data revision of the German Federal Statistical Office carried out in August 2011 has increased the share of domestic investment significantly. Based on the data before the revision, the share of German savings invested at home in the period 2002 to 2010 was only 34%. See H.-W. Sinn, 'Germany's Capital Exports

another country that at any time in its history exported such a high proportion of its savings to finance investment in other countries.

The chart also shows the increase in Target claims which, at € 66 billion, were still relatively small, as well as other residual items that are not detailed further, resulting from accounting errors, but which are still capital exports. Target claims, as will be explained in detail later on in this book, result from the cross-border relocation of central bank refinancing credit, being in effect a public capital export.[13] One remarkable aspect of the chart is that only a small portion of Germany's huge capital exports took the form of net foreign direct investment. The spectacular German industrial complexes located abroad, primarily in eastern Europe, account for only a small portion of capital movements, probably because they were largely overshadowed by German companies being bought by foreign investors. Much more important than direct investment were the financial capital outflows through the anonymous channels of the banks and insurance companies, which went largely unnoticed by the media.

Normally, a capital export is a benefit for the exporting country as a whole, because the gain in capital income outperforms the loss in labour incomes resulting from this export. However, this assumes that the capital was invested well. Savers in the northern European countries like Germany filled their savings books and paid their life insurance policies, and the banks and insurance companies sent their money abroad, in the hope of capturing higher yields than at home. The funds thus exported served to finance many a sensible project, but unfortunately they were also used to finance many ventures that were far less sensible. The funds flowed across the Atlantic into dodgy asset-backed securities (ABS) consisting of structured credit claims of US banks that, for political reasons, were intended to help the poor buy a home and were at the centre of the so-called subprime crisis.[14] The money also flowed into the government bonds of southern European countries, helping to finance salary increases for state employees, and to savings banks, such as the Spanish *Cajas*, that today are teetering on the brink of insolvency because they invested the money in risky real-estate projects. In hindsight, the return on this investment was not exactly what the investors had expected.

Under the Euro', *VoxEU*, 2 August 2011, available at: <http://www.voxeu.org/article/germany-s-capital-exports-under-euro>.

[13] Intra-Eurosystem claims and liabilities resulting from under- or over-proportionate banknote issuance are in many ways similar to Target balances, but unlike Target balances they are not included in balance-of-payments statistics. For details see Chapter 6, Section *Target Balances as a Public Capital Export*.

[14] Details can be found in H.-W. Sinn, *Kasino-Kapitalismus. Wie es zur Finanzkrise kam, und was jetzt zu tun ist*, Econ, Berlin 2009, English translation *Casino Capitalism. How the Financial Crisis Came About and What Needs to Be Done Now*, Oxford University Press, Oxford 2010, in particular chapter 6: *Hot Potatoes*.

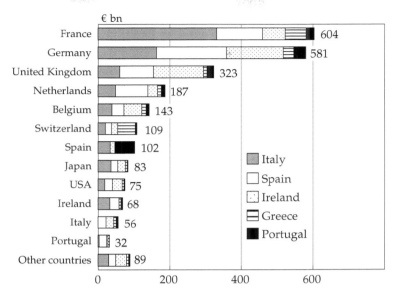

Figure 3.7 International bank claims vis-à-vis public and private sectors of Greece, Ireland, Portugal, Spain, and Italy at the time of the Lehman crisis

Source: Bank for International Settlements, Statistics, *Consolidated Banking Statistics*, May 2013.

Note: The figure shows cross-border claims and local claims of foreign affiliates, ordered according to their value at Q3 2008. Domestic claims are not included. The claims are vis-à-vis both private and public residents.

While Germany was by far the western world's largest capital exporter, the exposure of its banking system to the crisis countries was not the largest. As Figure 3.7 shows, the exposure of the French banking system was larger. The chart provides an overview of the exposure of national banking systems from around the world to the public and private sectors of Greece, Ireland, Portugal, Spain, and Italy (GIIPS), ranked by size at the time of the Lehman crisis (Q3 2008).[15]

The exposure of French banks amounted to € 604 billion, and that of German banks to € 581 billion, representing 31% and 24% of the respective GDP for 2008. Even in absolute terms, French exposure was a bit larger (4%) than that of Germany. Relative to GDP it was 33% larger.

French banks had invested particularly strongly in government bonds. The respective data are unfortunately not available for the time of the Lehman crisis, but in the first quarter of 2010, the Bank for International Settlements (BIS)

---

[15] The data for Cyprus are not available.

published, for the first time, data concerning bank exposure to the sovereign debt of Greece, Ireland, Portugal, and Spain. It turned out that the exposure of the French banks to these four crisis countries was 55% larger than that of German banks, and adjusted for the smaller French GDP it was even 95% higher, as already mentioned in Chapter 1.[16] All this explains why the French banking system has been more heavily affected by the European debt crisis than the German one, and also why, next to the borrowing countries themselves, it might be the greatest beneficiary of the bailout operations of the ECB and the community of states.

While Figure 3.7 only refers to financial claims on public and private GIIPS institutions, French banks were also heavily engaged via equity stakes in the banking systems of southern Europe. For example, Bank Geniki, Greece's ninth-biggest bank, is a subsidiary of Société Générale, and Emporiki Bank, the fifth-biggest, was a subsidiary of Crédit Agricole, before it was sold for a symbolic price of one euro to Greek Alpha Bank. Crédit Agricole, moreover, has ownership stakes in Italy's Intesa Sanpaolo and Cariparma, as well as Portugal's Banco Espirito Santo, while Banque Nationale de Paris owns the Italian Bank BNL.

The reason for the large French exposure is not that France was a large net capital exporter. As Figure 3.4 showed, it was in fact a net capital importer. The true reason is that the French banking system acted as a hub for international savings. French banks borrowed from the international markets and then distributed the capital to the Mediterranean countries, with which France has traditionally had close cultural ties, owing in particular to its geographical proximity and its common Romance language.

The United Kingdom, primarily the City of London, also played the role of a hub for southern Europe. While Britain was also a net capital importer (see Figure 3.4), it had nevertheless invested heavily in the European crisis-hit countries, its bank exposure to public and private institutions amounting to 18% of its GDP in 2008.

Next to the UK, the banks of the Netherlands, Belgium, Switzerland, and Spain (the latter not including the lending of Spanish banks to Spanish customers), in that order, also showed significant exposure to the crisis countries in absolute terms. Relative to GDP in 2008, Belgium (41%) tops the list, followed by Ireland (38%), the Netherlands (32%), France (31%), Switzerland (30%), Germany (24%), Portugal (19%), the United Kingdom (18%), Spain (9%), Italy (4%), Japan (3%), and the US (1%).

Mass Unemployment in Germany

The lack of investment in Germany shown in Figure 3.5 gave rise to mass unemployment that long appeared nearly intractable, peaking at rates similar to Italy's

---

[16] See Bank for International Settlements, *BIS Quarterly Review*, September 2010, p. 16.

unemployment rate today (see also Figure 1.2). While during the peak of the Internet boom it had seemed possible for Germany to break the trend towards steadily increasing unemployment that had prevailed since the early 1970s, the global slump after September 11, 2001 dashed this hope. German unemployment increased sharply and, with a peak rate of 11.5% in April 2005, even surpassed its level at the trough of the previous business cycle (9.7% in the period March 1997 to February 1998). At the time, Germany suffered by far the highest unemployment rate of all the current members of the Eurozone. Figure 3.8 shows the evolution of the German unemployment rate in comparison with the crisis-hit countries and with France.

Back in the years 2001 to 2006 Germany was the sick man of Europe, while the GIPSIC countries now mired in crisis enjoyed nearly unprecedented prosperity. In Ireland, Greece, and Spain in particular, unemployment decreased significantly, at times even dramatically, after the euro was announced. Ireland experienced a veritable explosion in employment between 2000 and the onset of the financial crisis. Portugal was clearly more sluggish in this respect, once

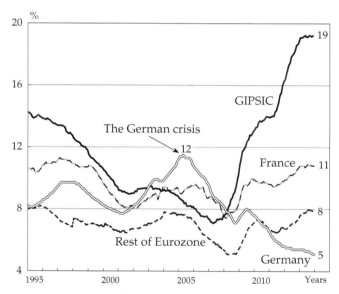

Figure 3.8 Unemployment rate in Eurozone countries, seasonally adjusted (1995–2013)

Source: Eurostat, Database, *Population and Social Conditions*—Labour Market—Labour Force Survey—LFS Main Indicators; Ifo Institute calculations.

Note: The curves refer to all countries now in the Eurozone, based on data published by Eurostat: Slovenia since January 1996, Slovakia since January 1998, Greece since April 1998, Cyprus and Malta since January 2000, Estonia since February 2000.

its initial momentum waned, but in April 2005 it still had a rate of unemployment that was three percentage points below that of Germany. Italy, despite its low growth, boasted a reduction in unemployment in almost every year between 1998 and 2007, which earned it one of the Eurozone's lowest jobless rates, at about 6%. As Figure 3.8 shows, the overall unemployment rate of the GIPSIC countries declined from 10.0% in 2000 to 7.3% in 2007. In April 2005, it was three percentage points below the German one.

In France the unemployment rate also fell strongly after the euro was announced, staying significantly below the German level from 2002 until 2007. In April 2005, it was 2.4 percentage points lower than Germany's.

The crisis reversed all these trends. Germany's employment situation, which had started to rebound in 2006 as the economy picked up, improved markedly, while in the other countries employment levels simply collapsed. By the end of 2013 Germany had a much lower unemployment rate than during the peak of its latest boom in 2008, whereas France had a much higher unemployment rate than at the trough of its latest slump, in the winter of 2004/2005.

Agenda 2010

The German euro crisis forced the Schröder government to undertake painful social reforms, announced under the name of Agenda 2010.[17] These reforms essentially meant that the government reshuffled funds from the long-term unemployed to low-income earners. The government abolished long-term

---

[17] See G. Schröder, 'Regierungserklärung von Bundeskanzler Gerhard Schröder am 14. März 2003 vor dem deutschen Bundestag', Deutscher Bundestag, *Plenarprotokoll* 15, 2003, No. 32, in particular p. 2479. The preparatory work that provided the basis for the Schröder reforms included the proposals for Activating Social Assistance prepared by the Ifo Institute in May 2002, a parallel proposal by the Economic Advisory Council to the Federal Ministry of Economics of August of that year, the proposals of the Hartz Commission of that same month, and most of all by the Twenty-Point Programme of the German Council of Economic Experts of November of that year. See H.-W. Sinn, C. Holzner, W. Meister, W. Ochel, and M. Werding, 'Aktivierende Sozialhilfe', 14 May 2002; Advisory Council to the Federal Ministry of Economics and Technology, 'Reform des Sozialstaats für mehr Beschäftigung im Bereich gering qualifizierter Arbeit', *BMWi Dokumentation*, No. 512, 2002; P. Hartz, N. Bensel, J. Fiedler, H. Fischer, P. Gasse, W. Jann, P. Kraljic, I. Kunkel-Weber, K. Luft, H. Schartau, W. Schickler, H.-E. Schleyer, G. Schmid, W. Tiefensee, and E. Voscherau, 'Moderne Dienstleistungen am Arbeitsmarkt', *Commission's Report*, 16 August 2002; German Council of Economic Experts, *Jahresgutachten 2002/03: Zwanzig Punkte für Beschäftigung und Wachstum*, November 2002.

unemployment insurance and let the long-term unemployment benefit fall to the level of ordinary welfare, which just provides a subsistence minimum, but added a wage subsidy element to welfare by reducing the benefit withdrawal rate for low income earners. The new welfare system was labelled Unemployment Benefit II. Around 1.3 million people in western Germany and one million people in eastern Germany were affected by the elimination of long-term unemployment assistance, and during the peak of the latest boom, in 2008, five million employable people were receiving Unemployment Benefit II, of which 1.3 million collected the wage subsidy.[18] Schröder's party did not forgive him for pushing through these reforms, and he lost his re-election bid to Angela Merkel, albeit by a fairly scant margin.

The reforms were certainly not easy on the German workers; they posed an extreme burden on them that massively affected the lives of many millions of people and tore at the fabric of German society. The thesis that Germany was the great euro winner is, in light of this development, simply absurd.

The Schröder reforms proved to be a blessing in disguise for Germany's labour market, since its citizens were paid less public money when staying out of work and more when participating in the labour force. The reform effectively cut the minimum wage implicit in the German welfare system by reducing the reservation wage at which workers were willing to accept a job. The lower reservation wage, in turn, implied a downward stretching of the wage distribution and kept the average wage increase below the increase in labour productivity for a number of years, raising the profit share in national income. This gradually improved the competitiveness of the German workforce and gave rise to the creation of more jobs, particularly in the low-wage segment.

A major reason for Germany's healthy economic and labour market situations after the onset of the financial crisis lies squarely with the Schröder reforms. This success was born out of the necessity brought about partly by the euro, and it is certainly not due to an advantage resulting from the euro itself. If Germany had failed to follow the low-wage strategy, it would have been much harder to bring unemployment down, and growth would have likely been less impressive after the outbreak of the crisis than it actually has been.

The New Construction Boom

There is a further reason for Germany's economic growth that is directly related to the crisis. Before the onset of the crisis, German savings flowed massively

---

[18] See Bundesagentur für Arbeit, *Grundsicherung für Arbeitsuchende: Erwerbstätige Arbeitslosengeld II-Bezieher: Begriff, Messung, Struktur und Entwicklung*, Appendix, table 1.

abroad because German banks and insurance companies, as well as private investors, underestimated the risks of foreign investment, if only because they expected bailouts for troubled countries. Once the crisis hit, they changed their mind and opted to keep their capital at home. They turned primarily to German real estate, triggering a huge construction boom that the country had not seen since reunification.[19] Money that was not invested directly in construction was lent to homebuilders. Mortgage rates in 2011 and 2012 were the lowest in the country's history. (They moved in a way similar to the government bond rates, shown in Figure 2.2.) Companies invested more in factories and machinery, pushing up demand in the toolmaking industries and providing another impulse to construction. New jobs were created in both sectors, the additional wage income in turn boosting consumption. Furthermore, new jobs were also created in the investing industries themselves, strengthening the trend even further. Ifo researchers had already forecast this development as early as summer 2010, speaking of a golden decade opening up because capital was once more being invested at home—duly mentioning that this was relative to other countries and that temporary slumps could be expected now and then for all countries.[20] Subsequent developments proved them right.

The investors' change of mind explains the boom and the increase in investment in 2010 and 2011, which became the motor for growth, surpassing external trade.[21] After real investment in construction had decreased almost continuously, by around one-fourth altogether over the one-and-a-half decades from 1994 to 2009, it picked up in 2010. In 2012 it was 8% higher than in 2009.[22]

[19] This section contains passages based on the Sohmen Lecture given by the author: H.-W. Sinn, 'Die Europäische Fiskalunion', *Perspektiven der Wirtschaftspolitik* 13, 2012, pp. 137–178; see also H.-W. Sinn, 'Genießt den Aufschwung!', *Wirtschaftswoche*, No. 18, 30 April 2012, p. 44, available at: <http://www.ifo.de/bauboom/w/nuQXV8ng>.

[20] The first forecasts of this construction boom can be found in H.-W. Sinn, 'Nachweisbare Wirkungen', *Wirtschaftswoche*, No. 23, 7 June 2010, p. 39, available at: <http://www.ifo.de/nachweisbare_wirkungen/w/3FZKYYgni>; also *Ifo Viewpoint* 115, 22 June 2010; and H.-W. Sinn, *Rescuing Europe, CESifo Forum* 11, Special Issue, August 2010, pp. 19–20, available at: <http://www.cesifo-group. de/DocDL/Forum-Sonderheft-Aug-2010.pdf>; see also *ifo Konjunkturprognose 2010/2011: Auftriebskräfte verlagern sich nach Deutschland*, Ifo Institute, 23 June 2010, available at: <http://www.cesifo-group.de/DocDL/ifosd_2010_12_3.pdf>; and H.-W. Sinn, 'Europa in der Krise', *Ifo Annual Meeting 2010*, available at: <http://mediathek. cesifo-group.de/player/macros/_v_f_750_de_512_288/_s_ifo/_x_s-764870657/ifo/ index.html>.

[21] See Projektgruppe Gemeinschaftsdiagnose, 'Gemeinschaftsdiagnose Frühjahr 2012', *ifo Schnelldienst* 65, No. 8, 26 April 2012 p. 29, available at: <http://www. cesifo-group.de/DocDL/SD-8-2012.pdf>.

[22] See German Federal Statistical Office, *Fachserie 18*, National Accounts, Series 1.2, Quarterly GDP Figures, Fourth Quarter 2012, table 3.10.

Construction permits for residential units were 37% higher in 2012 than in 2009, and for owner-occupied dwellings, 86% higher.[23] Orders for civil engineering projects climbed by 22%.[24] Architects have a right to rejoice: whereas their backlog amounted to only 4.7 months in 2007 and 5.3 months in 2009, it had risen to 5.9 months in 2012. This is its highest level since 1994, when Germany was enjoying its reunification boom.[25]

The improvement in Germany's economic performance is, in fact, just a correction of the devastating development before the crisis and after the announcement of the euro. At the time the capital sent to Spain was largely wasted in the ruins now surrounding the Spanish cities to meet a demand that could never have materialized, while both German housing stock and German infrastructure were degrading. Seen in this light, the recent reversal of capital movements seems to be efficiency-enhancing. The assertion that the post-crisis boom in Germany proves that the country is a euro winner follows the same logic as the assertion that a person who finds himself in convalescence after a serious illness is a beneficiary from his malaise.

Misunderstanding the Tango

But don't the persistent German trade surpluses indicate that the country has indeed been a beneficiary of the euro? After all, its export success generates profits and jobs, and is envied throughout Europe.

European politicians appear to think so, given how often the export argument is bandied about in order to demonstrate the benefits that Germany has derived

---

[23] See German Federal Statistical Office, press release of 17 March 2011, No. 110, and press release of 14 March 2013, No. 101.

[24] See German Federal Statistical Office, press release of 25 February 2010, No. 63, and press release of 25 February 2013, No. 69.

[25] See E. Gluch, 'ifo Architektenumfrage: Weiterhin hohe Auftragsbestände', *ifo Schnelldienst* 66, No. 5, 14 March 2013, pp. 49–50, figure 4, available at: <http://www.cesifo-group.de/DocDL/ifosd_2013_05_6.pdf>. Prices rose as well. According to data provided by real-estate agents, the number of owner-occupied dwellings climbed by around 7% in 2011, while for terraced houses (town houses), the rise was a bit more than 4% (see BulwienGesa AG, *BulwienGesa-Immobilienindex 1975–2011*, January 2012, p. 4). Agricultural plots were particularly sought after, their prices rising by 9.6% in 2009 and 8.7% in 2010 (see German Federal Statistical Office, *Fachserie 3, Reihe 2.4,* Kaufwerte für landwirtschaftliche Grundstücke 2010, p. 14). Behind all these rises were the investors' yearning for safe investments that would protect their money from the vagaries of the euro crisis.

from the euro. The German Chancellor is representative of many politicians when she says:[26]

> We in Germany are very well aware that we, as an exporting nation, profit particularly from the euro.

Similarly, while she was still the French finance minister, Christine Lagarde, now Managing Director of the IMF, time and again singled out the huge German current account surplus, pointing out that this was just the counterpart of the current account deficits of southern Europe.

> It takes two to tango,

she said in 2010, emphasizing that Germany was enjoying its surplus at the expense of other countries.[27]

As far as the statistics are concerned, Christine Lagarde is, of course, right. Given that the Eurozone as a whole had a balanced external current account when she made her statement, the German surplus must inevitably have had its mirror image in the deficits of other euro countries. Figure 3.8 compares the German and GIPSIC current account balances, which by definition are identical to the respective capital exports and imports shown in Figures 2.1 and 3.4. Evidently, the evolution of Germany's current account surpluses and net capital exports largely mirrors the deficits of these countries. When the euro was decided upon in 1995, there were no imbalances worth mentioning. Over the following years, however, imbalances literally exploded, peaking at about € 200 billion per year in the years 2007 and 2008, i.e. at the time the crisis began.

But did Germany really capture some advantages through its surplus and, most crucially, at the expense of other countries? This would be too hasty a conclusion, if only because Germany's current account surplus certainly did not result primarily from a net trade with other Eurozone countries. After all, as Figure 1.5 showed, only 36% of German exports go to other Eurozone countries, and while Germany's trade surplus at the start of the crisis in 2007 with the rest of the world was € 168 billion (6.9% of GDP), its trade surplus with the Eurozone was only € 64.6 billion (2.7% of GDP), of which the GIPSIC countries accounted for € 54 billion. Accounting for imported intermediate inputs and recalculating the net exports to the GIPSIC countries in value-added terms,

---

[26] See A. Merkel, 'Die Europa-Rede', Pergamon Museum Berlin, 9 November 2010, available at: <http://www.bundeskanzlerin.de/ContentArchiv/DE/Archiv17/Reden/2010/11/2010-11-09-merkel-europarede.html> (translated by the author).

[27] See C. Lagarde, Interview, *Financial Times*, 15 March 2010, available at: <http://www.ft.com/intl/cms/s/0/78648e1a-3019-11df-8734-00144feabdc0.html#axzz21iHcyCQk>.

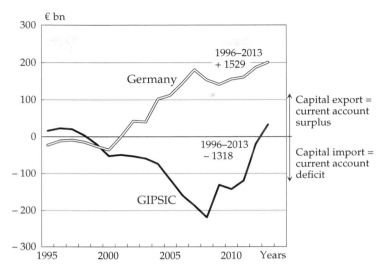

Figure 3.9 Capital flows and current account balances in the Eurozone—the European tango (1995–2013)

Source: Eurostat, Database, *Economy and Finance*, Balance of Payments—International Transactions, Balance of Payments Statistics by Country; European Commission, Economic and Financial Affairs, *European Economic Forecast*, Autumn 2013; Deutsche Bundesbank, Time Series Databases, *External Sector*, Balance of Payments; Ifo Institute calculations.

Note: GIPSIC 2013 European Commission forecast, Autumn 2013.

Germany's surplus with the GIPSIC countries amounted to just € 45.6 billion (1.9% of German GDP).[28]

The weak link between the current account balances is also apparent in the divergence of the current account figures after the crisis set in, as Figure 3.9 reveals. During the crisis, the current account deficits of the GIPSIC countries shrank, but the German current account surplus remained more or less unchanged, and even increased somewhat. Obviously, Germany's current account surplus does *not* measure a net amount of goods and services that it supposedly delivered to other Eurozone countries.

Moreover, the German surplus over the period in question was driven by capital movements that weakened the German economy instead of strengthening it. As explained at the beginning of Chapter 2, it resulted from the

---

[28] See R. Aichele, G. Felbermayr, and I. Heiland, 'Der Wertschöpfungsgehalt des Außenhandels: Neue Daten, neue Perspektiven', *ifo Schnelldienst* 66, No. 5, 14 March 2013, pp. 29–41, available at: <http://www.cesifo-group.de/DocDL/ifosd_2013_05_3.pdf>, forthcoming in English in CESifo Forum.

attempt of investors to restructure their international portfolios from Germany to southern Europe and elsewhere. As indicated by the convergence of interest rates (Figure 2.2), the announcement of the euro wiped out the perceived risk associated with investments in southern Europe, causing a readjustment of real economic activity that generated the current account imbalances and made the desired portfolio reallocations possible. However, capital flowed not only directly from Germany to the southern countries, but also to the international capital market, and from there also to the GIPSIC countries. Recall that, according to Figure 3.7, the French banking system had the largest, and the British the third-largest, exposure to the GIPSIC countries, even though the two countries weren't net capital exporters.

Since German domestic investment fell while the increased savings resulting from the rising profit share in national income sought higher returns abroad, the country went through a prolonged slump. There was a lack of domestic demand for consumption and investment goods, and not enough jobs were being created. German incomes rose little, and the demand for imports lagged in comparison to other countries. Exports, however, given that they were the imports of other countries, rose apace with the rising incomes of those other countries. Because of this the German export surplus was more an import deficit than anything else. A further boost to Germany's current account surplus came from its improved competitiveness. Indeed, the massive unemployment in Germany coupled with the Agenda 2010 reforms brought about significant wage moderation that translated not only into a higher profit share and a higher savings rate, but also into a lower inflation rate, improving the competitiveness of German products. Germany went through what is known as a real depreciation through a curbing of its inflation.

The situation was the exact opposite in the periphery countries. There, capital was flowing in, fuelling inflationary consumption and an investment boom, which in turn fuelled demand for imports, while rising wages and prices undermined the competitiveness of their export industries.

That is the law of capitalism. If capital flows from A to B, A will experience a slump and B a boom. The booming economy increases its imports and reduces its exports as a result of higher incomes and prices, while the opposite occurs in the sagging economy. Germany was the sagging economy, while the European periphery was the booming one. That explains Germany's surplus and the European tango, but it by no means supports the thesis that the German current account surplus materialized 'at the expense' of other countries. Nothing could be more absurd than accusing the country whose capital seeps away to other countries, creating jobs and income there rather than at home, of taking advantage of other countries. Seeing a trade surplus as a sign of special profits of the exporting country, a view shared by quite a number of leading German politicians, is nothing but crude mercantilism.

Of course, from a national perspective there is a good side to a current account surplus, inasmuch as it measures the accumulation of foreign assets or claims against other countries. Germany's current account surplus is, as it were, the main driver of the yearly increase in the German net foreign asset position (see Figure 2.9). From the time the euro was announced at the Madrid Summit in December 1995 until 2013, Germans accumulated a whopping € 1,529 billion abroad, represented by the area under the German curve in Figure 3.9. While these are claims against the rest of the world and certainly not primarily claims against the GIPSIC countries, if only because much of Germany's capital export was flowing via the French banking system, it is remarkable that the GIPSIC debt accumulated by way of current account deficits, amounting to € 1,318 billion, is of a similar order of magnitude.

The accumulation of foreign assets naturally benefits the German owners of these assets, since they receive the resulting interest income. That was the reason why they sent their money abroad in the first place. However, two qualifications to this statement are in order.

The first is that the ordinary German population, workers in particular who possess only negligible financial assets, certainly did not benefit from the capital exports, since the productivity gains and wage rises made possible by the investments financed with domestic savings occurred abroad rather than at home. Current account surpluses, contrary to widely held perceptions, are not really beneficial for domestic workers. It is true that jobs are created in the export sector, a trivial effect that is readily visible, but if capital had not been exported, as represented by the current account surplus, the funds would have fuelled domestic demand and created jobs in construction and the engineering industries at home. So there is no net gain for domestic labour from the demand effect that comes with a current account surplus, if this surplus is the result of a portfolio shift from domestic to foreign investment. What many people overlook is that it makes no difference to the demand for domestic products whether domestic savings are used for domestic or foreign investment. The former leads to as much demand in the domestic construction and equipment industries as the latter leads to a net demand among the industries engaged in foreign trade. A shift from domestic to foreign demand could only generate beneficial differential effects for domestic labour if the export industries were more labour-intensive than the domestic sector of non-tradeables, primarily the construction sector, but the opposite is the case. Thus, if anything, the demand effect represented by the export surplus is likely to be negative rather than positive for domestic labour.

The true difference between domestic and foreign investment comes from supply-side effects. Obviously, only domestic investment generates more domestic supply by increasing the domestic production capacity. If the supply effect takes place abroad, domestic workers get nothing out of it; they can only benefit if the supply effect occurs at home, as new jobs result from building new factories and installing machinery for domestic use.

A second qualification to the above statement is that there is reason to doubt whether the huge savings account that the Germans have filled abroad with their trade surpluses will be available when the need arises to draw funds from it. When the German baby-boomers reach their retirement age, which will be around the years 2025 to 2030, and wish to retrieve the funds that their life insurance providers have invested in southern Europe and elsewhere, Germany will have to build a current account deficit by importing all the goods and services that these citizens will need. Such a current account deficit would arise automatically when the population in question begins to put their savings to use. But this presupposes, of course, that the foreign credit-takers to whom the funds were lent will be in a position to actually repay them. Whether they will be able to, given their own demographic realities and level of indebtedness, remains to be seen. If the money does not return, the current account surpluses will have been for nought. Actually, as explained in Chapter 2, € 336 billion of the increase in Germany's net foreign asset position of € 1,328 billion built up through current account surpluses over the period 1996 to 2012 has already been written off by open haircuts and by reductions in the market value of assets in anticipation of future haircuts.

CHAPTER 4

The Competitiveness Problem

Why the Current Accounts Improved—Dying Industries—Too Expensive—The Necessary Real Depreciation—Little Progress—How Did Ireland Do It?— The Baltics: Austerity Works—The True Competitors—Caught in the Euro Trap: The Terrors of Deflation

Why the Current Accounts Improved

At the time this manuscript was finalized in February 2014, the European crisis had been rumbling on for six and a half years, since the interbank market seized up for the first time in August 2007. The citizens of the crisis-hit countries are increasingly worried about the rise in unemployment, and the taxpayers of the still-solid economies fret about increasing liabilities imposed on them through the rescue operations. On the other hand, financial markets have calmed down considerably, interest spreads have shrunk and some crisis countries, which had previously been shunned by the capital market, have been able to return. The international media have turned to other issues, and the world at large seems to have put the crisis out of the collective mind. There are even some signs that the real economies of southern Europe may be recovering.

One of the most frequently cited signs of progress is the reduction in the current account deficits of the GIPSIC countries, as shown in Figure 3.9, often combined with an allusion to the strong rebound in the exports of the crisis countries. The current account reduction is seen as a sign of recovery and improvement in competitiveness, the fruits of painful and courageous reforms carried out with the support of the EU and the ECB.[1]

---

[1] See Council of the European Union, press release of the 3220th Council Meeting, Economic and Financial Affairs, Brussels, 12 February 2013, available at: <http://www.

Unfortunately, however, such an interpretation is flawed, as Figure 4.1 shows. The chart depicts the imports and exports behind the current account balances separately for each of the six crisis-hit countries. In addition, it gives the pre-crisis trend lines for imports and exports, to illuminate the causes of the improvements in current account balances.

The charts show that imports and exports collapsed with the outbreak of the crisis and recovered partially thereafter. However, in all cases, imports declined more strongly than exports, explaining all of the current account improvements. In none of the countries did exports rise beyond their trend level. In Greece, Cyprus, and Italy exports even collapsed outright. In Portugal, Spain, and Ireland, exports have reached their pre-crisis trends, although they apparently are not about to surpass them. In short, exports recovered after the Great Recession of 2008/2009, but they have not surpassed their pre-crisis trend level, which an improvement in competitiveness would have accomplished.

The decline in imports resulted from the crisis itself. The collapse of the distressed economies has driven down employment and incomes, and has hence reduced imports via a mere income effect resulting from the austerity imposed by capital markets.

A sizeable contribution to the current account improvement also stems from a reduction in net investment income earned by foreign capital, caused by monetary easing on the part of the ECB, a profit squeeze of subsidiaries of foreign companies operating in the crisis countries, and the various fiscal or quasi-fiscal rescue operations, which replaced market credit with low-interest public credit or provided public insurance that enabled creditors to content themselves with lower yields. After all, a current account deficit is, roughly speaking, the sum of imports and net investment income paid to non-residents, minus exports.[2]

Figure 4.2 shows the potential effect of the rate of return reductions through the provision of rescue funds, ECB interventions, and a profit squeeze. It compares the actual net investment income the GIPSIC countries paid to the rest of the world (solid line) with hypothetical net investment income that the GIPSIC countries would have had to pay to the outside world (dotted line) if the average

---

consilium.europa.eu/uedocs/cms_data/docs/pressdata/en/ecofin/135438.pdf>; H. Van Rompuy, Speech by President of the European Council at the Annual 'State of Europe' Event, 11 October 2012, available at: <http://www.consilium.europa.eu/uedocs/cms_data/docs/pressdata/en/ec/132796.pdf>; 'On Being Propped up', *The Economist*, 25 May 2013, p. 29, available at: <http://www.economist.com/news/europe/21578394-spains-pain-likely-continue-despite-some-promising-reforms-unless-new-sources-growth>.

[2] Investment income here is meant in a broad sense of the word, including, e.g., interest income, dividends and retained earning of foreign subsidiaries. In addition to investment income, the current account includes other cross-border income payments as well as international transfers by governments, such as development aid, and by individuals, such as guest worker remittances.

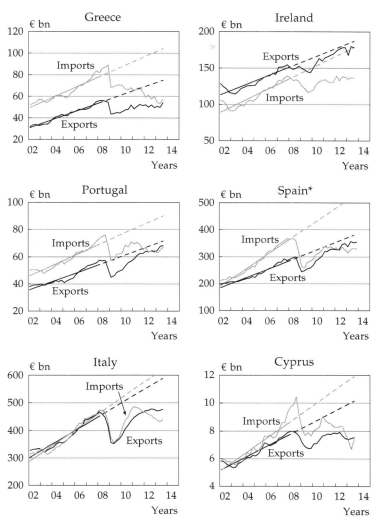

Figure 4.1 Components of the current accounts, seasonally adjusted (Q1 2002–Q3 2013)

* Q1 2002—Q4 2013.

Source: Eurostat, Database, *Economy and Finance*, Quarterly National Accounts, GDP and Main Components; Ifo Institute calculations.

Note: Exports and imports include manufactured goods and services (seasonally adjusted and adjusted for working days) as reported by Eurostat. The trend is calculated as a linear trend for the period Q1 2002 to Q4 2007. The chart shows annualized quarterly data.

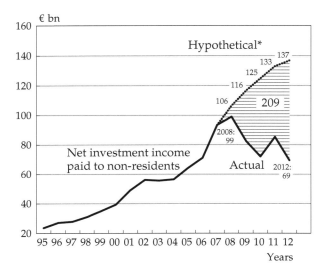

Figure 4.2 Net investment income paid by GIPSIC countries to non-residents

* Given the average rate of return of Q4 2007, in proportion to net foreign debt (without devaluation effects).

Source: Eurostat, Database, *Economy and Finance*, Quarterly National Accounts, GDP and Main Components; and Balance of Payments—International Transactions, Balance of Payments Statistics and International Investment Positions, Balance of Payments by Country; Ifo Institute calculations.

Note: The dotted curve depicts the notional annual burden on the GIPSIC economies from net investment income payments to non-residents if the average rate of return had remained at the Q4 2007 level, i.e. had the investment income payments grown in proportion to net foreign debt, assuming that this debt grew according to the GIPSIC current account deficits without potential write-offs in the market value of this debt.

rate of return on their net external debt position had remained constant at the level it had at the end of 2007, while their net external debt position grew according to the current account deficits. Interestingly enough, the investment income paid out by the crisis countries in 2012 was 26% *lower* than in 2007, even though the interest spreads increased—in fact exploded—as of 2008 (refer also to Figure 2.2) and the stock of GIPSIC net foreign debt (including revaluation effects) increased by € 347 billion, or by 22% of its 2007 level.

In the year 2012 alone, the GIPSIC countries gained € 67 billion from the rate of return reduction. Given that their net foreign debt was about € 2 trillion at the end of 2012, this corresponds to a rate of return reduction of about three percentage points (see Figure 2.10). In the five years from 2008 through to 2012, the GIPSIC countries reaped benefits of at least € 209 billion altogether, which on average amounted to € 1,558 per capita. The true gain, if measured against the sharply rising market rates, is much larger than this, but difficult to calculate in an unambiguous way. Thus, the sum mentioned is a very conservative estimate of the benefit brought about by monetary policy, rescue operations, and lower profit remittances.

Figure 4.3 shows what the interest savings implied for the current account. It depicts the aggregate goods and services exports and imports of the GIPSIC countries and, represented by the height of the dotted area, the GIPSIC countries' net interest burden (including profit remittances and retained earnings of foreign corporations), which in principle is a liability of the GIPSIC countries to the rest of the world and hence a negative entry to their current accounts, similar to the imports of goods. The dashed area above the dotted area shows a conservative estimate

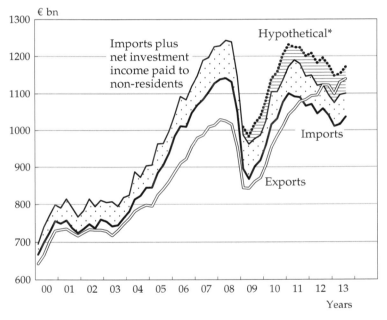

Figure 4.3 GIPSIC exports, imports, and net interest burden, seasonally adjusted

* Given the average 2007 rate of return, in proportion to net foreign debt (exclusive of revaluation effects).

Source: Eurostat, Database, *Economy and Finance*, Quarterly National Accounts, GDP and Main Components; and Balance of Payments—International Transactions, Balance of Payments Statistics and International Investment Positions, Balance of Payments by Country; Ifo Institute calculations.

Note: The dotted curve depicts the sum of imports and the hypothetical annual net investment income paid to foreigners according to the calculations underlying Figure 4.2. The chart shows annualized quarterly data.

of the additional interest burden that the GIPSIC countries would have had to bear without the public support provided by rescue funds, ECB interventions, and reduction in profit remittances as calculated above and shown in Figure 4.2. The most recent figures on the right-hand side of the chart show that imports and net interest payments to non-residents have now fallen below exports. But obviously this would not have happened, other things being equal, had the outside world not contented itself with a lower rate of return on the funds provided.

Dying Industries

The disheartening reason for the southern countries' current account improvements is unfortunately confirmed by the available data on the evolution of manufacturing output shown in Figure 4.4. Since manufacturing output is usually

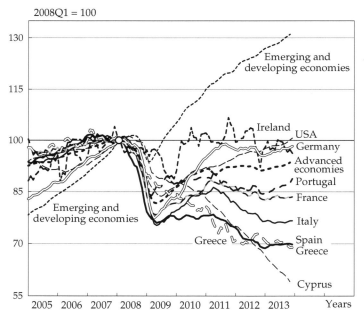

Figure 4.4 Escaping the crisis? Manufacturing output, seasonally adjusted

Source: Eurostat, Database, *Industry, Trade and Services*, Short-term Business Statistics, Industry, Production in industry; CPB Netherlands Bureau for Economic Policy Analysis, *World Trade Monitor*, Database; OECD, *OECD.StatExtracts*, Industry and Services, Production and Sale (MEI); Ifo Institute calculations.

Note: The monthly data are seasonally adjusted. In addition, monthly data are smoothed with an average over the last three months (including the month in question). The data are normalized such that their value at Q1 2008 is 100.

closely related to a country's exports and often the key to economic prosperity, it is essential for recovery to include this sector.

The chart shows that, by the end of 2013, the advanced economies had not succeeded in reaching their pre-crisis manufacturing output level, defined as the level at Q1 2008, while the emerging and developing economies had grown at a blistering pace. The US and Germany, which have been included as benchmarks, have just about reached their pre-crisis level. The GIPSIC countries—and France—have clearly performed miserably.

Developments in Italy, the largest of the crisis countries, are particularly disquieting insofar as the highly productive, family-owned manufacturing industries of northern Italy have always been the country's pride and stability anchor. Toolmaking, metal working, leather, fashion, and many other branches have been the region's traditional mainstays, but the firms in these sectors are currently dying like flies, which may be one of the reasons why the Italian statistical office has stopped publishing the data. Even Fiat, once one of Europe's biggest car manufacturers, is considering leaving the country. As the Italian curve in Figure 4.4 shows, there was some justified hope for an Italian recovery in 2010, but starting in 2011 the manufacturing sector nosedived. Small wonder that Silvio Berlusconi, the Italian Prime Minister at the time and a former successful entrepreneur, in autumn 2011 began secret negotiations about a euro exit, as mentioned in the Introduction. By the end of 2013, Italian production was at about the level it had reached in 2009 after the Great Recession of the world economy and 23% below the level before the crisis. Obviously, Italy shows all signs of a double-dip recession.

Even worse was the development in Spain. There was also a double dip here, but more of a double-dip depression rather than a mere recession, the second dip leading to an even lower level than the first one. By the end of 2013, industrial output in Spain had fallen by 30%. This is a catastrophic development that resembles that of the Great Depression from 1929 to 1933 in many industrialized countries.

Greece performed similarly, although there was no double dip. Output fell by 31% by the end of 2013. The industrial production of Cyprus declined by 41% (by November 2013).

Portugal and France have performed somewhat better, but with output reductions of 11% and 16% respectively, both still fall below the average of the world's industrialized countries (7%). While a turnaround seems to be underway in Portugal, the French economy seems to be stalling, where news of closing automobile factories are abundant. PSA Peugeot Citroën announced job cuts of 11,200, and Renault of 7,500.[3] The French government

[3] See 'Peugeot to Cut Added 1,500 Jobs as European Sales Plunge', *Bloomberg*, 12 December 2012, available at: <http://www.bloomberg.com/news/2012-12-11/peugeot-to-cut-added-1-500-jobs-as-european-sales-plunge.html>; and 'Renault to cut about 7,500 jobs in France', *BBC News*, 15 January 2013, available at: <http://www.bbc.com/news/business-21032990>.

is planning rescue operations by subsidizing the purchase of environmentally friendly cars.[4]

Among the crisis countries, only Ireland has performed well. This confirms the impression gained from Figure 4.1, which will be discussed in more detail later in this chapter.

Too Expensive

An improvement in competitiveness in the sense of a structural improvement in current accounts and a recovery of manufacturing output can only come from a substitution effect due to relative price changes, not from income effects or artificial measures that reduce the cost of credit. A country is uncompetitive if the prices of the goods it delivers are too high, and if it needs foreign credit to finance its imports and living standards. Conversely, even the world's least-productive economy can be competitive, in the sense that it can get along without foreign credit if its products are cheap enough and if it satisfies itself with a sufficiently low living standard. There is no such thing as a technical lack of competitiveness.

Politicians and the general public often speak of a lack of competitiveness in the sense of the low productivity of their economies because of poor infrastructure, inefficient legal systems, low innovation, lack of discipline, corruption and so on. Indeed, these elements can undermine a country's competitiveness, but if so, only because they imply excessively high prices, given the wages and other kinds of costs. If, on the other hand, productivity is given, there is always the possibility of making a country competitive by cutting wages and other kinds of income. A lack of competitiveness in the sense of trade deficits simply means overblown income aspirations relative to productivity, and hence overblown prices.

This will be the topic of the remainder of this chapter. This section shows that the GIPSIC countries lost their competitiveness by inflating their prices excessively during the credit bubble that the euro brought about, and the following sections will examine the possibilities for bringing these prices down through deflation in order to regain competitiveness, a task that is, as we will see, much more difficult than it sounds.

Figure 4.5 shows how strong inflation actually was in Ireland and southern Europe. The bars depict the price increases between the Madrid Summit of 1995 and 2007, the year the US subprime crisis spilled over to Europe. The

---

[4] See 'Frankreichs Regierung beschenkt Autoindustrie', *Zeit Online*, 25 July 2012, available at: <http://www.zeit.de/wirtschaft/2012-07/frankreich-autoindustrie-hilfen>; and 'Peugeot Citroen Secures Government Funds', *Bloomberg*, 24 October 2012, available at: <http://www.bbc.com/news/business-20054391>.

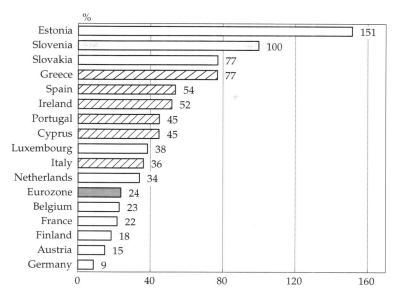

Figure 4.5 Price change from 1995 to 2007 of goods produced in the Eurozone countries (GDP deflator)

Source: Eurostat, Database, *Economy and Finance*, Annual National Accounts, GDP and Main Components, Price Indices.

changes shown are not those of consumer prices, which include imported goods, but of the GDP deflator, i.e. the price index for the domestically produced goods.

The GDP deflator is a good indicator for a country's competitiveness, since its evolution comes close to measuring the analogue to depreciation or appreciation of a currency. It makes no difference whether the domestic currency appreciates or domestic prices and incomes inflate: both make domestic products more expensive for foreigners and foreign products relatively cheaper for domestic residents. In either case foreigners and domestic residents alike will have an incentive to substitute foreign for domestic goods, and a trade deficit will emerge as a result.

The six troubled countries are indicated by the hatched bars, while the grey column shows the Eurozone average. It can be seen that the distressed countries' inflation rates all lay well above the Eurozone average. While prices rose on average by 24% in the Eurozone, Italian prices increased by 36%, Portuguese prices by 45%, Irish prices by 52%, and Spanish prices by 54%. Inflation in Greece was even worse, with a figure of 77%. Germany's prices, in contrast, rose over the 12 years by only 9%.[5] Thus, Germany underwent a real (or internal) depreciation

---

[5] The figures refer to the growth rate of the GDP deflator, which in the German case was below the inflation rate of consumer products.

relative to other countries, and the others a real appreciation. And to reiterate the point made above: in terms of the effects on competitiveness it makes not difference whether relative prices increase because of a currency appreciation or a genuine price increase.

In principle, the price increases could have resulted from the so-called Balassa–Samuelson effect.[6] This effect is based on the assumption of idiosyncratic productivity increases in a country's export sectors that result in wage rises in the export industry, which then spread to the domestic service sectors and increase service prices, assuming that the productivity in these sectors grows less than in the export sectors. In such a case, the price increases are not detrimental to competitiveness. However, as explained in Chapter 2, the price increases in the GIPSIC countries resulted instead from credit bubbles in the construction and government sectors, spreading from there via higher wages and intermediary costs to the export sectors, undermining their competitiveness. This is the opposite of the price transmission postulated by the Balassa–Samuelson effect.

Figure 4.6, which depicts data from Spain, shows that there is indeed little evidence for the Balassa–Samuelson effect. Evidently, after 1998, when interest rate convergence was completed (see Figure 2.2) and the foundation of the housing bubble was laid, construction wages increased relative to manufacturing wages, indicating that the former were pulling the latter and not the other way around. This confirms the credit bubble as the valid explanation rather than the Balassa–Samuelson effect.

The price increases measured by the GDP deflator were not homogeneous for all goods. Naturally, tradeable goods such as exported or imported manufactured products cannot easily become more expensive, since their prices are largely fixed by direct international competition. A small price increase suffices to wipe out much demand. Thus, the inflation pressure is relieved primarily through the so-called non-traded goods, such as household services, haircuts, restaurants and the like, for which the international competition is low. Still, as mentioned, the GDP deflator is an excellent measure for a country's competitiveness, since an increase in the price level of non-tradeables often results from wage increases and translates into higher production costs and lower profit margins

---

[6] See K. S. Rogoff, 'The Purchasing Power Parity Puzzle', *Journal of Economic Literature* 34, 1996, pp. 647–668; H.-W. Sinn and M. Reutter, 'The Minimum Inflation Rate for Euroland', *CESifo Working Paper* No. 377, December 2000, pp. 1–17; A. Alesina, O. Blanchard, J. Galí, F. Giavazzi, and H. Uhlig, *Defining a Macroeconomic Framework for the Euro Area*, Centre for Economic Policy Research, London 2001, chapter 3: *Country Adjustments within the Euro Area: Lessons after two Years*; É. Balázs, I. Drine, K. Lommatzsch, and C. Rault, 'The Balassa–Samuelson Effect in Central and Eastern Europe: Myth or Reality?', *Journal of Comparative Economics* 31, 2003, pp. 552–572; K. Rose and K. Sauernheimer, *Theorie der Außenwirtschaft*, Vahlen, Munich 2006, chapter 3.

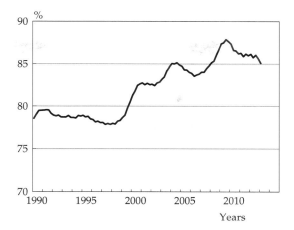

Figure 4.6 Spanish wage per worker in construction relative to manufacturing (Q1 1990–Q1 2013)

Sources: Instituto Nacional de Estadística, *INEbase*, Society, Labour Market, Wage Survey for Industry and Services (1990–1999), Main Series 1981–2000, Ganancia media por trabajador y mes. Pagos totales por sectores de actividad, periodo, categorías profesionales y unidad, empleados y obreros; *Quarterly Labour Cost Survey* (QLCS, since 2000), Main Series of the QLCS by Activity Sectors, Period, Cost Components and Measurement Unit, Total Wage Cost per Worker.

Note: The data are smoothed with a moving average.

for the tradeables, so that small price increases suffice to reduce exports and raise imports.[7] Apart from that, most goods are tradeable in a broader sense of the word. For example, even restaurant services, haircuts or housing rents are tradeable by migration and tourism.

Figure 4.5 only refers to nominal price changes of domestically produced goods. To assess the full effect on competitiveness it also has to be taken into account that some exchange rate realignments took place after the Madrid Summit of December 1995 and before the irrevocable fixation of conversion rates for a euro entry in May 1998. A case in point is Italy, where a revaluation of the lira by slightly more than 11% against the deutschmark was performed on 25 November 1996.[8] If the latter effect is combined with the real appreciation

---

[7] Competitiveness could also be measured by the ratio of the prices of non-tradeable and tradeable goods. This ratio would show the same evolution as the GDP deflator.

[8] Originally, when the Exchange Rate Mechanism (ERM) was introduced on 13 March 1979, one thousand liras was worth 2.19 deutschmarks, but a substantial bout of inflation in the 1980s eroded this parity. After the ERM ran into difficulties in 1992, the thousand liras even fell to 80 pfennig (cents of a deutschmark) on 19 April 1995. By the

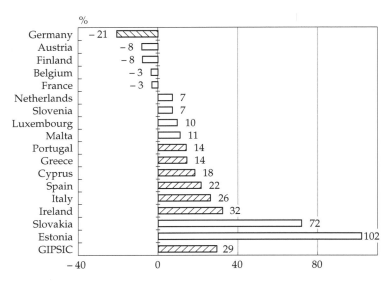

Figure 4.7 Real appreciations and depreciations relative to the respective rest of the Eurozone (1995–2007)

Source: European Commission, Economic and Financial Affairs, *Economic Databases and Indicators*, Price and Cost Competitiveness, Quarterly Real Effective Exchange Rates vs. (rest of) EA17, Price Deflator GDP, Market Prices; Ifo Institute calculations.

Note: The EU figures shown here refer to changes in the national GDP deflator relative to the average GDP deflator of the rest of the Eurozone, when trade shares are used as weights.

through inflation that occurred thereafter, it turns out that Italy became 44% more expensive relative to Germany in the period from the Madrid Summit in 1995 to 2007. The time when the Adriatic coast was the 'Teutonic barbecue', alluding to the Germans sunbathing there on account of everything being so cheap, is long gone. Germans looking for an inexpensive meal out now prefer to stay in Germany. Even pizzas offered by Italian restaurants in Germany are often cheaper than those offered by restaurants in Italy.

Figure 4.7 above shows the percentage of revaluation or devaluation for each country relative to its Eurozone trading partners over the period in question, taking potential realignments of exchange rates into account, as published by the European Commission. Clearly, all countries now in trouble appreciated significantly, led by Italy, with 26%, and Ireland, with 32%. Note that the percentage

time of the Madrid Summit, the thousand liras had climbed again to 90 pfennig, and a subsequent appreciation brought it to 1.01 deutschmarks.

for Italy is lower than the 44% appreciation relative to Germany mentioned earlier, since some of Italy's trading partners also appreciated relative to Germany over that period.

The last bar in the chart shows the appreciation of the six countries now in distress, if one considers them as one entity. The increase in the average price index of these countries relative to the trade-weighted rest of the Eurozone was a non-negligible 29%.

Over the period in question, Germany depreciated by 21% in trade-weighted terms. This is the main reason behind Germany's resilience during the euro crisis and behind its remarkable competitiveness. Whether the productivity of German industry has increased more than the productivity of other industries in the period in question is debatable. It is clear, however, that its products have become relatively cheaper. As described in Chapter 3, the real depreciation brought about through wage restraint was no walk in the park, but it paid off.

The Necessary Real Depreciation

The real appreciation evidently deprived the distressed countries of their competitiveness.[9] Prices and wages rose during the bubble-building period beyond the level that would have made sustainable economic development possible without depending on credit inflows. For a number of years, the current account deficits of the GIPSIC countries continued to grow unabated (Figure 3.9) and, with them, their need for foreign credit to finance the deficits. Everything went just fine for as long as the markets were willing to finance these deficits, but when they pulled back in the summer of 2007, the crisis set in.

Given that cheap credit is no longer available today, the real appreciation of the GIPSIC countries has to be undone. This can be achieved by rewinding the price clock through deflation in the GIPSIC countries, or by inflating the core, notably Germany. Outright deflation is a difficult undertaking, since the price clock only runs smoothly going forward. It is always a pleasure to raise wages and prices; lowering them, in contrast, provokes massive resistance. And outright inflation in Germany would also meet strong resistance, as will be discussed later on in this chapter. Nevertheless, there is no alternative to a realignment of relative prices in the Eurozone if the competitiveness of the crisis-stricken countries is to be re-established within the Eurosystem, and if this is to be achieved without inflation in the aggregate, deflation in some countries cannot be avoided.

It is somewhat surprising in this regard to hear the president of the ECB, Mario Draghi, expressing his concern about such a solution. Defending the

---

[9] See also H.-W. Sinn, 'Austerity, Growth and Inflation: Remarks on the Eurozone's Unresolved Competitiveness Problem', *The World Economy* 37, 2014, pp. 1-13, available at: <http://www.cesifo-group.de/sinn-world-econ-2014_pdf >.

ECB's OMT programme, which will be discussed in Chapter 8, he argued in the German parliament:[10]

> In our assessment, the greater risk to price stability is currently falling prices in some euro area countries. In this sense, OMTs are not in contradiction to our mandate: in fact, they are essential for ensuring we can continue to achieve it.

With this statement, Draghi implicitly refers to price stability as the main goal of the ECB's policy and defends the ECB's taking actions against the risk of deflation in some countries. This concern seems misplaced, since deflation in some countries would be useful and indispensable to restore their competitiveness.

To date, the ECB has always defined price stability in terms of the average Eurozone price level, rather than in terms of idiosyncratic country price levels. Given that the idea of fighting national changes in price levels was vigorously denied by ECB board members when the southern countries inflated at an above-average rate, it is mystifying to find the ECB now arguing that it needs to take action to counteract the trend towards deflation in those very same countries.[11] If country

---

[10] See M. Draghi, *Opening Statement at Deutscher Bundestag*, Speeches and Interviews, 24 October 2012, available at: <http://www.ecb.int/press/key/date/2012/html/sp121024.en.html>.

[11] For example José Manuel González-Páramo, at that time Member of the Executive Board of the European Central Bank, said in a speech: 'First, there is a broad consensus among academics, observers and policy-makers that monetary policy should focus on maintaining price stability in the single currency area as a whole. [...] By contrast, it is widely recognised that assigning to monetary policy the additional role of directly addressing the relative balance between the sectors or regions of the single currency area in the process of adjustment to shocks would overburden monetary policy to the detriment of its primary role'. See J. M. González-Páramo, *Inflation Differentials in the Euro Area*, Speech at Cámara de Comercio, Industria y Navegación de la Región de Murcia, 23 May 2005, available at: <http://www.ecb.europa.eu/press/key/date/2005/html/sp050523.en.html>. Lucas Papademos, at that time Vice President of the ECB, emphasized: 'Needless to say, but I will say it anyway to make it abundantly clear, the single monetary policy cannot address the ULC growth and inflation divergences in individual countries. And since it cannot do it, it should not attempt to do it and it will not do it. However, by ensuring the preservation of price stability in the euro area as a whole, it can help guide and anchor inflation expectations to price stability in all euro area countries and thus help consumers and firms to take appropriate economic decisions'. See L. Papademos, *Inflation and Competitiveness Divergences in the Euro Area Countries: Causes, Consequences and Policy Responses*, Speech at the conference 'The ECB and its Watchers IX', Frankfurt, 7 September 2007, available at: <http://www.ecb.int/press/key/date/2007/html/sp070907_2.en.html>. And even then-ECB President Jean-Claude Trichet made it clear in 2011 that 'temporary deviations from the euro area-wide inflation average should not be a matter of concern'. See J.-C. Trichet, *Competitiveness and the Smooth Functioning of EMU*, Lecture at the University of Liège, 23 February 2011, available at: <https://www.ecb.int/press/key/date/2011/html/sp110223.en.html>.

prices were to be stabilized, the ECB should have implemented restrictive monetary policies in the years during which inflationary credit bubbles accumulated; it is not the time for the ECB to intervene now that the mistakes need to be corrected by way of realigning relative prices.

It is true that there are reasons for protecting an economy against the mass unemployment and destabilization that usually precedes a deflation. This could justify expansionary monetary and fiscal policies, but the motivation for such policies lies outside the ECB's mandate. Supply-side policies to enhance the downward-flexibility of wages would also be very useful, as they would work towards reducing an economy's level of unemployment. Arguing that such policies should not be tolerated would be a tragically mistaken interpretation of the ECB's mandate.

How far back would the price clock have to be set in order to regain competitiveness? The answer is difficult, since part of the price hikes in the GIPSIC countries may have been justifiable and sustainable because of the above-mentioned Balassa–Samuelson effect. To the extent that this effect played a role, it seems that the price clock should not be set back all the way to 1995.

On the other hand, returning to old prices may not be sufficient for restoring competitiveness in the sense of having a balanced current account, since the GIPSIC countries have built up much foreign debt, which will lead to higher interest payments once markets have come back to normal and the rescue credits have been repaid. Thus, the price clock may have to be reset further back than only to the year 1995.

Researchers from the Goldman Sachs economics department have developed a model to simulate the necessary realignments.[12] The authors explored the question of how much realignment of relative goods prices in the Eurozone would be necessary in the long run (20 years) to reduce all net foreign asset positions to below 25% of GDP in absolute terms. They found that the troubled countries would have to cut their prices relative to the Eurozone average to improve their current accounts, and Germany would have to increase its prices relative to the Eurozone average to scale down its current account surplus. Recall that net foreign asset and debt positions result primarily from accumulating current account imbalances and that, as shown in Figure 2.9, Greece, Ireland, Portugal, Spain, and Cyprus all had net foreign debt positions in the neighbourhood of 100% of GDP in 2012, while Germany had a net foreign asset position of about 40%. The authors assumed an average Eurozone inflation rate of 2% and that the external value of the euro will adjust so as to keep constant the average relative price level of the euro countries, expressed in terms of foreign goods. Given that the euro has a flexible exchange rate, that the ECB refrains from manipulating

---

[12] The source is given under Table 4.1.

the exchange rate, and that the Eurozone as a whole had a balanced current account with the rest of the world before the crisis, this is a reasonable assumption. Table 4.1 shows the results of the calculations.

Table 4.1 Realignment needs in the Eurozone as of Q3 2010 relative to the Eurozone average

	Depreciation	Mean	Necessary price cut to be on a par with Turkey 2011–2013
Portugal	25–35 %	30 % (20 %*)	29 %
Greece	25–35 %	30 % (20 %*)	36 %
Spain	25–35 %	30 % (27.5 %*)	
France	15–25 %	20 %	
Italy	5–15 %	10 % (0 %*)	
	Appreciation	Mean	
Ireland	0–5 %	2.5 % (0 %*)	
Germany	15–25 %	20 %	

* As of Q3 2012, taking the haircut on Greek government debt, the rescue operations and interest-reducing policies into account.

Source: H. Pill, K. Daly, D. Schumacher, A. Benito, L. Holboell Nielsen, N. Valla, A. Demongeot, and A. Paul, Goldman Sachs Global Economics, 'Achieving Fiscal and External Balance (Part 1): The Price Adjustment Required for External Sustainability', *European Economics Analyst*, Issue No. 12/01, 15 March 2012; H. Pill, K. Daly, D. Schumacher, A. Benito, L. Holboell Nielsen, N. Valla, A. Demongeot, and S. Graves, Goldman Sachs Global Economics, 'External Rebalancing: Progress, but a Sizeable Challenge Remains', *European Economics Analyst*, Issue No. 13/03, 17 January 2013; OECD Database, *OECD. StatExtracts*, National Accounts, PPPs and Exchange Rates; Ifo Institute calculations.

Note: The calculations in the first two numerical columns show the realignments of the GDP deflators relative to the Eurozone average, as of Q3 2010, that would bring the absolute values of net foreign asset positions of all euro countries below 25% of GDP in the long run (20 years), assuming an adjustment of the external euro value so as to keep the average terms of trade of the Eurozone relative to the rest of the world constant. The figures in parentheses give the necessary realignments taking the Greek haircut as well as interest-reducing policies into account. The third numerical column gives the necessary realignments relative to Turkey for Greece and Portugal based on average price levels of the years 2011–2013.

The first numerical column shows the country-specific ranges of required depreciation and appreciation that result from different model specifications, while the second numerical column gives the mean of these ranges in a baseline scenario applying to Q3 2010. By construction, the need for realignment depends not only on assumptions about the real economy but also on debt levels and the interest rates. For the baseline scenario, moderate interest burdens on foreign debt similar to those prevailing at the time (refer also to Figure 4.2) have been assumed.

In addition to a baseline scenario, the Goldman Sachs study gives revised estimates that refer to the situation in Q3 2012. They are indicated in parentheses in the third column. The revision takes into account the additional intergovernmental rescue operations and the ECB's support, as well as the Greek haircut of € 105 billion, or 54% of GDP, which brought down the interest burden and facilitated the task of reducing net foreign debt positions.

The table shows that alarmingly high price cuts are necessary for Greece and Portugal (30%) in the baseline scenario. In the revised scenario, the price cuts are still substantial, at 20% each. The two estimates for Greece are of the same order of magnitude as that calculated by the EEAG, under alternative assumptions about the income elasticity of Greek imports, to eliminate the current account deficits.[13]

The orders of magnitude are also confirmed if the Greek and Portuguese price levels are compared with Turkey's price level according to the OECD's purchasing power statistics. The required devaluations resulting from this comparison, based on average prices and exchange rates of the years 2011–2013, are shown in the third numerical column. Purchasing-power parity is the level of an exchange rate at which the prices of a given basket of goods and services bought in two countries are equal. Comparing it with the actual exchange rate makes it possible to assess a country's over- or undervaluation relative to another country. While the price levels of developed and less-developed economies cannot be easily compared because of the Balassa–Samuelson effect, the price levels of countries of similar economic development, such as those of Turkey and Greece, can. Turkey's coast, food and temples are on a par with Greece's. For tourists, the services are of a comparable level. Their products are also comparable. In this light, Greece should not be any more expensive than Turkey if it wants to stay competitive relative to its neighbour which, being seven times as large, determines the local market conditions. But, in reality, Greece was 55% more expensive in the years 2011 to 2013 on average. It therefore would need to cut its prices by 36% to regain its competitiveness,[14] which is an even steeper drop than the Goldman Sachs researchers came up with, but still of the same order of

[13] See EEAG, *The EEAG Annual Report of the European Economy: The Euro Crisis*, CESifo, Munich 2012, chapter 2: *The European Balance-of-Payments Problem*.

[14] Note that $155^*(100\% - 36\%) \approx 100$

magnitude. Turkey has a customs union with the EU and there are no restrictions on tourism. It is simply impossible for Greece to be competitive against its mighty neighbour. Applying the same reasoning to Portugal, Portuguese prices would have to fall by 29% relative to their average 2011–2013 level to come to par with Turkey's.

Among the countries that need realignment, Spain stands out because of its size (46 million inhabitants) and the magnitude of the necessary realignment. According to the baseline scenario, its prices will have to fall by about 30%, and even in the revised scenario the necessary price cut, 27.5%, is still huge. This confirms the concerns expressed in Chapters 1 and 2 that Spain could be the Eurozone's biggest problem. Spain has by far the biggest external debt in absolute terms and, next to Greece, the largest unemployment rate in the Eurozone. The next section will discuss how much of the necessary realignment has already taken place.

Remarkably, France should also have to depreciate, by 20%, a figure that is not affected by the revision of the calculations. This result, which follows largely from France's growing current account deficit (1.8% of GDP in 2013) gives the issue an entirely new facet.

Italy, by contrast, needs only a small realignment. This is surprising, given Italy's huge inflation in the early years of the euro and the lira appreciation of 1996 (see Figure 4.5). The explanation is that, at only 24.8% of GDP in 2010, the year on which the Goldman-Sachs figures are based, Italy's net foreign debt was comparatively very low, even below the 25% threshold assumed by Goldman Sachs. However, the calculation may have been a bit too optimistic, given that Italy's net foreign debt position increased to 28% in 2012 (see Figure 2.9) and 29% in 2013. The calculations show that Italy does not need a positive current account balance to satisfy the debt sustainability criterion if the economy grows, but unfortunately it has shrunk instead since the calculations were made. Note, however, that the calculations are based on a long-run forecast (20 years) and do not hinge much on the performance of one or two years.

On the flip side of the coin are Ireland and Germany. According to Table 4.1, Ireland needs no price cuts—if anything, a small revaluation instead, while Germany would need to increase its prices by 20% relative to the average to rebalance the Eurozone, reducing its own competitiveness and net foreign assets to help the crisis countries improve their competitiveness and redeem their debt.

Little Progress

Could it be that the process of relative price adjustment has already taken place? Are the southern countries already on the way to restoring their competitiveness? If so, there would be reason to hope that they might soon be able to do without rescue funds, and it would make sense for the taxpayers of the still-sound econo-mies to continue standing by them for a while. If not, a more radical solution to the euro crisis may have to be sought.

Representatives of the financial industry and EU officials often point to the improvements in the crisis countries' unit labour costs, regarding them as a sign that the EU policies are on the right track and insisting that the taxpayers stay firm, because success is near. But unit labour costs are the wrong indicator. For one thing, they are instrumental variables that are subordinate to product prices when it comes to assessing a country's competitiveness. Their decline would indicate an improvement in competitiveness only if they induced a subsequent price decline. For another, a reduction in unit labour costs only signals improved competitiveness if employment stays constant, since an increase in unemploy-ment in itself leads to a reduction in the unit labour costs, given that the mar-ginal jobs that disappear first have a lower productivity and higher unit labour costs than average jobs.

If a country lurches into a crisis, most firms rationalize the jobs with high unit labour costs first, and firms with high unit labour costs that cannot rationalize them go bankrupt. Both effects naturally reduce the average unit labour costs of the remaining jobs, even if not a single competitive new job was created. This explains, to a large extent, the fall observed in unit labour costs. It is a mere sta-tistical artefact.

Germany suffered from a similar confusion in the public debate during its own euro crisis, since the crisis had also led to rapidly increasing unemploy-ment and falling unit labour costs.[15] While economists argued that German wages were too high, and that a welfare reform was necessary to reduce the social replacement incomes and the resulting wage demands to save jobs, unions pointed to the improving unit labour costs and argued that no harsh reforms were necessary, since the economy was already on the right track. In fact, how-ever, no wage cuts had taken place, and no surge in technological efficiency was occurring. The only reason for the improvement in unit labour costs, just as in southern Europe today, was the rationalization of marginal jobs and the result-ing increase in unemployment. The real breakthrough for the German econ-omy came only later, when the social reforms of the Schröder government led to substantial wage restraint (see Chapter 3, section *Agenda 2010*), which, in turn, increased growth and employment.

Figure 4.8 provides an overview of the changes in relative prices in the Eurozone since the Madrid Summit of 1995, also called 'real effective

---

[15] See H.-W. Sinn, *Ist Deutschland noch zu retten?*, Econ, Berlin 2003, English trans-lation: *Can Germany be Saved?*, MIT Press, Cambridge 2007, chapter 2: *How German Workers Lost Their Competitive Edge*.

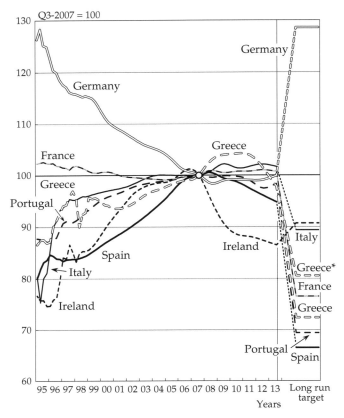

Figure 4.8 Real effective exchange rates (GDP deflator relative to the rest of the Eurozone)

* Revised calculation after the haircut on the Greek sovereign debt.

Sources: European Commission, Economic and Financial Affairs, *Economic Databases and Indicators*, Price and Cost Competitiveness, Quarterly Real Effective Exchange Rates vs. (rest of) EA17, Price Deflator GDP, Market Prices; H. Pill, K. Daly, D. Schumacher, A. Benito, L. Holboell Nielsen, N. Valla, A. Demongeot, and A. Paul, Goldman Sachs Global Economics, *European Economics Analyst*, Issue No 12/01, 15 March 2012; H. Pill, K. Daly, D. Schumacher, A. Benito, L. Holboell Nielsen, N. Valla, A. Demongeot, and S. Graves, Goldman Sachs Global Economics, *European Economics Analyst*, Issue No. 13/03, 17 January 2013.

Note: The chart shows the original values of the real effective exchange rates as published by the European Commission. As a rule, these refer to the ratio of the price level of the goods produced in a given country (GDP deflator) to the trade-weighted price average of its trading partners or, if the price index is not available, to a measure of the average total unit cost of goods produced. The last point in the diagram giving actual data instead of a long-run requirement is Q3 2013.

exchange rates'.[16] According to the European Commission's definition, the real effective exchange rate of a country is its GDP deflator relative to the weighted average of the GDP deflators of the rest of the Eurozone, where trade shares are used as weights. In the chart, the real effective exchange rates or relative prices are normalized to 100% in Q3 2007, the time of the first breakdown of the interbank market.

The chart shows that all GIPSIC countries appreciated dramatically relative to the respective rest of the Eurozone before the outbreak of the crisis. By contrast, Germany became steadily cheaper in relative terms until 2007. That was the real depreciation mentioned above, a respectable 21% between 1995 and 2007. All this is basically the same information given in Figure 4.7.

What the chart shows in addition is sobering, however. After the onset of the crisis and until 2009, there were grounds to hope that Germany's real depreciation process had bottomed out and that the trend would reverse. But what happened was largely the opposite. While Germany's inflation followed the average of its trading partners in the Eurozone, Italy and France, instead, inflated faster than their trading partners and faster than Germany, undermining their competitiveness even further. These countries show no signs of the real depreciation that would be necessary. With France in particular, a problem lurks here that could spell doom for the Eurozone. Surprisingly, Greece even accelerated its inflation after the crisis broke out. The sharp increase in the slope of the Greek price curve after 2007 depicts this clearly. In the three years from 2005 through 2007, the annual Greek inflation rate (GDP deflator) was 0.5 percentage points above the level for the rest of the Eurozone, but in the subsequent three years it accelerated to 1.5 percentage points above this level, its relative price inflation continuing until 2010. Only in 2011, with scant access to the capital markets and interest spreads rising rapidly (Figure 2.2), Greece was forced to reverse its inflation trend. It was not until the end of 2012, more than five years after the onset of the crisis, that Greece managed to once again reach the level of the real exchange rate with which it had entered the crisis.

It must be kept in mind, however, that Italy and Greece have raised their indirect taxes in this phase, which is not necessarily detrimental to competitiveness, since export goods, except for the export of tourism services, are exempt from these taxes while import goods are burdened with them. In the case of Italy, that accounts for less than one percentage point of appreciation so far, while in the case of Greece it accounts for three percentage points at most.[17]

---

[16] See H.-W. Sinn, 'Austerity, Growth and Inflation. Remarks on the Eurozone's Unresolved Competitiveness Problem', 2014.

[17] Italy raised its normal VAT rate from 20% to 21% on 17 September 2011. It also raised the petrol (gasoline) tax, increasing the price per litre by 16 cents of a euro (see 'Italien erhöht Benzinsteuer stark', *Der Standard*, 7 December 2011, available at: <http://

Spain and Portugal have depreciated in real terms relative to their trading partners. From Q3 2007 to Q3 2013, Spain managed a real devaluation of about 5% and Portugal one of about 1.5%.

With the exception of Ireland, none of the crisis countries has come anywhere near the required depreciations calculated by Goldman Sachs, as discussed in the previous section. The horizontal portions on the right-end of the curves show the long-run target values for the real exchange rates, according to the Goldman Sachs calculations for the baseline scenario relative to Q3 2010, which does not take into account all the interest-reducing measures of the ECB or the rescue funds.

Only for Greece does the chart show an updated calculation, which takes into account the country's huge debt relief of 54% of its GDP that, as mentioned above, took place in 2012. Since this is a permanent relief, Greece will continue to benefit from it even if the rescue operations come to an end and interest rates return to normal.

Recall that while the Goldman Sachs results are relative to the *average* of the Eurozone including the country considered, the European Commission (EC) data give each country's appreciation or depreciation relative to the respective *rest* of the Eurozone. In order to make the Goldman Sachs data compatible, it was recalculated to match the EC yardstick. For small countries this makes little difference, but for large countries the respective depreciation and appreciation figures are correspondingly higher.

One of the more alarming aspects of Figure 4.8 is that Germany did not appreciate during the crisis even though its goal should be to appreciate by 20% against the average, which is 30% against the rest of the Eurozone, to help improve the competitiveness of the GIPSIC countries and France. This all means that after six and a half years of crisis, in most of the GIPSIC countries the necessary realignments are not yet underway and there is little hope that they might be achieved in the near future. Small wonder then that none of the crisis countries has succeeded in raising its exports beyond trend, as shown in Figure 4.1. A drop in their relative prices is mandatory for them to translate the income effect resulting from the economic collapse and mass unemployment into an import-substitution effect. This is the only way for them to return to normal rates of unemployment.

derstandard.at/1323222432610/Monti-Sparplan-Italien-erhoeht-Benzinsteuer-stark>). Greece raised the reduced VAT rates from 4.5% and 9% to, respectively, 5% and 10%, and the normal VAT rate from 19% to 21% on 15 March 2010. On 1 July 2010, the reduced rates were again raised to 5.5% and 11%, respectively, and the normal VAT rate to 23%. A further hike came on 1 January 2012, bringing the reduced rates to 6.5% and 13%, respectively (European Commission, *VAT Rates Applied in the Member States of the European Union*, 1 July 2012).

Note that there are two reasons why competitiveness improves if the prices of non-traded goods fall. For one thing, it reduces the cost of intermediate goods used in exports and signals a fall in wage costs for the export industry. For another, consumers will then substitute domestic for foreign goods, which will reduce imports and create jobs at home. The latter effect is particularly important for a country like Greece, which no longer has a significant export industry other than tourism.

Greece has a huge current account deficit in agricultural products, which, considering its nearly ideal climate and given the huge success of Israel, which certainly enjoys no better conditions, seems downright preposterous. Its imports of agricultural goods exceed exports by one and a half times.[18] The country even imports tomatoes from the Netherlands and refined olive oil from Germany.[19] If prices and wages came down in Greece, Greeks would undoubtedly turn to their own products and shun imports, farmers would again cultivate their fields instead of letting them lie fallow, and the young would again find employment in the agricultural sector.

How Did Ireland Do It?

As crucial as a real depreciation is for regaining competitiveness, it can be very difficult to achieve. Within the Eurozone, it presupposes a very large economic contraction accompanied by massive unemployment, which no one would wish upon any country. Chapter 9 will analyse the real options for depreciation available inside and outside the Eurozone.

It is all the more surprising then that Ireland did find a way to engineer a real depreciation *within* the Eurozone. Relative to the other countries in the Eurozone, Ireland depreciated by a stunning 15% in the period from 2006 to 2012. This has no parallels in the other troubled countries.

And the depreciation has borne fruit. Whereas Ireland posted growing current account deficits in the years before the crisis, from 0.6% of GDP in 2004 to 6% in 2008, the deficit disappeared during the crisis. In 2010, it turned into a small surplus, which by 2013 had climbed to a quite respectable 4% of GDP.

It is true that part of this success is due to the interest-alleviating policies of the ECB and the community of states, as can be measured following the

---

[18] In 2010, imports of agricultural goods exceeded exports by 47%. See World Trade Organization, *Statistics Database*, Trade Profiles, Greece, April 2012, available at: <http://stat.wto.org/CountryProfile/WSDBCountryPFView.aspx?Language=E&Country=GR>.

[19] See 'Greece Importing Olive Oil from Germany', *ekathimerini.com*, 8 September 2011, available at: <http://www.ekathimerini.com/4dcgi/_w_articles_wsite1_1_08/09/2011_405493% CE%93%20%CE%B2%E2%82%AC>.

methodology discussed for Figure 4.3 above. Had Ireland's net investment income payments to the rest of the world grown from 2008 to 2012 in proportion to the growth of the Irish net foreign debt resulting from further current account deficits, Ireland's annual net interest burden would have consumed another 4.0% of its 2012 GDP. However, the improvement in the current account from 2008 to 2012 went from minus 5.6% to plus 4.4% of GDP, i.e. 10.0 percentage points of GDP, a significantly larger figure.

It is also true, of course, that the collapse of the Irish economy has driven down imports, as shown in Figure 4.1. The income effect was also in Ireland the primary driver behind the current account improvement.

Still, the relatively good performance of Irish exports (Figure 4.1) and, in particular, of industrial production (Figure 4.8) singles out Ireland as a success story. While other crisis countries suffered from a double-dip recession or even depression, Irish industrial production recovered more quickly from the crisis than even that of Germany or the United States.

Because of this superb performance, Ireland was able to actually pay back some of its external debt. This instilled more confidence among investors and led to lower yields on Irish debt. As Figure 2.2 shows, the only yields that managed to escape the upward trend in the crisis-stricken countries as early as summer 2011 were those of Ireland.

How did Ireland manage to cut its prices, while the other distressed economies still show no sign whatsoever of a similar development? There are several possible explanations.

First of all Ireland, for which the US social model was the one to follow, always had more flexible labour markets and weaker unions than the other countries, so that it was somewhat easier to push through wage reductions. Figure 4.9 shows the evolution of workers' compensation in the overall economy and in the public sector by country, before and after the onset of the crisis.[20]

It can be readily seen that Ireland suffered large wage reductions. Wages in the overall economy fell by 13% from 2007 to 2012. In contrast, they fell in Spain by only 4%, while in Portugal they rose by 3% from 2007 to 2011. In Greece, compensation kept increasing until 2009, to then sink significantly, falling by a total of 7% from 2007 to 2011.

It is noteworthy that, according to the information available as of this writing (February 2014), public sector wages have exhibited strong downward rigidity. During the crisis they only went down in net terms in Ireland, by 14% from 2007 to 2012. In Spain, by contrast, public sector wages initially kept rising rapidly, by 19% until 2010, to only then decline a bit. In net terms they increased by 11% from

---

[20] The data shown in the graph are the most recent available as of this writing (February 2014). Unfortunately, all countries publish their wage data after a long delay, Greece in particular.

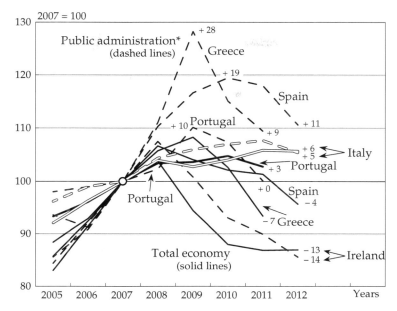

Figure 4.9 Labour income in the public sector and on average (2005–2012)

* Public Administration, Defence, Social Security.

Source: Eurostat, Database, *Economy and Finance*, Annual National Accounts, National Accounts Aggregates and Employment by Branch.

Note: The curves show the development of the aggregate compensation flowing to employees, not the wage per person.

2007 to 2012, despite the desperate situation of Spain's finances and its rising mass unemployment. In Portugal public wages stayed constant in net terms.

In Greece, public sector compensation increased by 28% from 2007 to 2009, to then fall by 15% from 2009 to 2011. The net result was an increase throughout the crisis of 9% from 2007 to 2011, i.e. during the same period in which the Irish government sector wages fell by 10%. This puts quite a damper on the assertion that Greece has implemented massive austerity measures. While the private sector shows signs of austerity, the public sector does not.

Secondly, Ireland has a powerful export industry. Irish exports amounted to 108% of GDP in 2012 given that exports, like everywhere else, have a high import component. Spain's exports amounted to barely 33%, Portugal's to 39%, and Greece's to 27% of their respective GDP. Countries with a significant export industry tend to have a strong export lobby that pleads for wage restraint. If, by contrast, a country has a strong import lobby, as Greece does, pushing through a real depreciation is much harder, because it hurts import businesses. When the prices of domestic goods fall, as they would in the case of a real depreciation, people will shun imports, hurting importers. The importance of the export sector was highlighted by the Greek Minister of Economics, Michalis Chrysochoidis, in February 2012 in an interview with the daily *Frankfurter Allgemeine Zeitung*, when he complained that the many EU subsidies had destroyed his country's export industry, driving the better companies and talents from the export to the import business.[21] The minister made plain what in economic theory is known as the Dutch Disease, namely that inflowing capital makes exports disposable and increases the demand for imports. In the Netherlands's case, which gave the disease its name, it was not EU money that was behind the inflows of funds, but the country's gas exports.[22]

Thirdly, and most importantly, the crisis reached Ireland earlier than the other troubled countries. This is clearly evident in the early bursting of the Irish property bubble in 2006 (Figure 2.11) and naturally in the sharp downward shift of goods prices starting in the same year (Figure 4.8). Ireland stood alone at the time. There were no intergovernmental rescue packages and no special ECB programmes. The country had to help itself—and so it did, by lowering its wages and prices.

The rest of the stricken countries were hit by the crisis two or more years later, after the collapse of Lehman Brothers in September 2008. Instead of taking Ireland's path of austerity and social parsimony, they preferred to look for alternative solutions, in particular resorting to the local printing presses. This issue will be discussed in depth in the subsequent chapters.

The Baltics: Austerity Works

The Baltic states undertook measures similar to Ireland's. Latvia and Lithuania have been members of the ERM–II system since 2005 and 2004 respectively, a preliminary stage to joining the Eurosystem in which the exchange rate may not move more than ±15% relative to the euro. Estonia introduced the euro in 2011, while Latvia did so on 1 January 2014. Lithuania wants to join as soon as possible.

Just like the other former Communist countries, the Baltics have seen significant increases in their prices and wages since 1995, with Estonia's price level

---

[21] See M. Chrysochoidis, 'Die Gesellschaft ist reifer als ihr System', Interview by M. Martens, *Frankfurter Allgemeine Zeitung*, 9 February 2012, available at: <http://www.faz.net/aktuell/politik/europaeische-union/griechischer-wirtschaftsminister-die-gesellschaft-ist-reifer-als-ihr-system-11642768.html>.

[22] See N. M. Corden and J. P. Neary, 'Booming Sector and De-Industrialization in a Small Open Economy', *Economic Journal* 92, 1982, pp. 825-848.

doubling by the time the crisis hit. To be sure, the price increases are largely a statistical artefact, because the goods produced by these countries at the time of the transition, essentially identical to those of the Communist era, cannot be compared to those being produced now.

Still, the countries became too expensive for reasons similar to those of the now-stricken countries, and eventually had to break this trend. As Figure 4.10 shows, they did so by imposing austerity, reducing their wages dramatically after the onset of the crisis. From 2007 to 2012 Latvian wages plunged by 9% in net terms in the overall economy, and by 16% in the public sector. For the sub-period 2008 to 2010, the decline in both public and overall wages was a staggering 34%, a record among the countries considered, even surpassing the decline in Ireland.

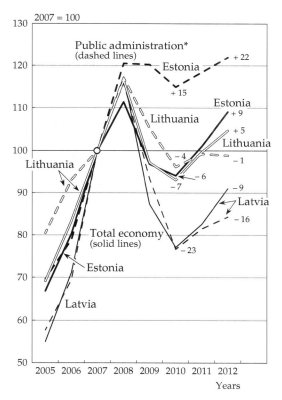

Figure 4.10 Wages in the Baltics (2005–2012)

Source: Eurostat, Database, *Economy and Finance*, Annual National Accounts, National Accounts Aggregates and Employment by Branch.

In Lithuania the wage reductions from 2008 to 2009 amounted to 17% (overall economy) and 10% (public sector). Over the period from 2007 to 2012, however, wages in the public sector remained stable, while they increased by 5% in the economy as a whole. In Estonia wages increased by 9% (whole economy) and by 22% (public sector) over the entire period.

All three countries suffered from a sharp recession. Real GDP in Latvia plunged by 12% between 2007 and 2012, in Estonia by 4%, and in Lithuania by 2%.

Latvia's performance is quite remarkable. The big question is: why did Latvia bite the bitter bullet of a real depreciation voluntarily, although it still had the possibility of carrying out an outright devaluation of its currency? The answer was provided by former Latvian Prime Minister, Valdis Dombrovskis, at the Munich Economic Summit policy forum: doing otherwise would have imperilled his country's prospects for Eurozone accession.[23] Using this argument, he was able to bring all social partners on board for a policy of massive wage cuts. And, as he summed up,

> To get into the Eurozone you do anything. Once in, you can evidently do whatever you want.

Figure 4.11 shows that wage restraint in Latvia and Lithuania did have positive implications for competitiveness. While imports declined more than exports, just as in the GIPSIC countries (see Figure 4.1), exports even surpassed their pre-crisis trend in both countries. Lithuania in particular shows a remarkable success.

> Austerity works

beamed former Lithuanian Prime Minister, Andrius Kubilius.[24]

The True Competitors

The relative flexibility of the Baltic countries points to a particular problem that the southern European economies face: the new competition from eastern Europe. While such competition did not seem an issue when the euro was announced in 1995, it has became a growing concern for the southern economies ever since the bulk of eastern European countries joined the EU in the years 2004 to 2007. Most eastern European countries have shaken free of the yoke

[23] See V. Dombrovskis, 'Managing the Crisis. The Case of Latvia', 9th Munich Economic Summit, CESifo and BMW Stiftung Herbert Quandt, 30 April 2010. Dombrovskis made this remark during the discussion following his presentation.

[24] At the 12th Munich Economic Summit, CESifo and BMW Stiftung Herbert Quandt, 16 May 2013.

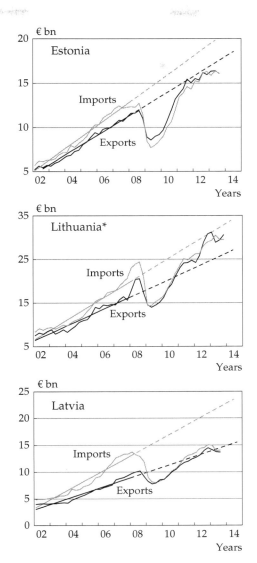

Figure 4.11 Exports and imports in the Baltics, seasonally adjusted (Q1 2002–Q3 2013)

* Q1 2002–Q4 2013.

Source: Eurostat, *Economy and Finance*, Quarterly National Accounts, GDP and Main Components; Ifo Institute calculations.

Note: Exports and imports include manufactured goods and services (seasonally adjusted and adjusted by working days) as reported by Eurostat. The trend is calculated as a linear trend in the period Q1 2002 to Q4 2007. The charts show annualized quarterly data.

of Communism and overcome their transition problems. The Baltics, Poland, the Czech Republic, Slovenia and, with some reservations, Hungary are now well-established, functioning market economies with a skilled labour force. All are attractive as business locations and have already been able to build up highly competitive industrial sectors, largely due to foreign direct investment from Germany and other countries. There is no parallel to this strength in southern Europe, except perhaps in Italy. In addition, the eastern EU countries have one further big advantage over the southern European countries: they are cheap.

Figure 4.12 compares the hourly wages for industrial workers in the six euro crisis countries and the eastern EU countries. Clearly, nearly all crisis countries have substantially higher wages than the eastern EU countries. The only exception is Slovenia, which has surpassed Cyprus and Portugal. On average, the wages of the southern euro countries and Ireland shown in the chart are 247% higher than those in eastern Europe, if the respective shares in hours worked are used as weights. Wages in the Czech Republic, Slovakia and Hungary, three countries that host huge Volkswagen plants (Skoda and Audi), compete directly with those in Spain, which also hosts a sizeable car company owned by Volkswagen (Seat), but they are only about half or one-third of the Spanish ones. And the biggest eastern country, Poland, has hourly wages of only about € 7, which is less than half of those in Greece and one-third of those in Spain.

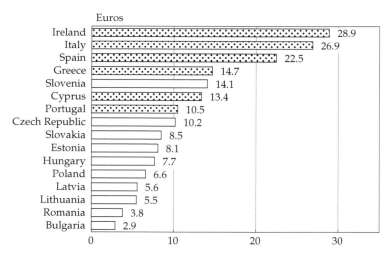

Figure 4.12 Wages per hour in manufacturing in the GIPSIC countries in comparison with eastern EU countries (2012)

Source: German Federal Statistical Office, 'Arbeitskosten in Deutschland 2012 um 32% höher als im EU-Durchschnitt', press release of 26 March 2013, No. 116, available at: <https://www.destatis.de/DE/PresseService/Presse/Pressemitteilungen/2013/03/PD13_116_624.html >.

These wage differences are huge by any standards, and one does not have to be an economist to expect southern Europe to face a long period of hardship until eastern Europe has prospered sufficiently to give the southern European countries a second chance.

The problem for southern Europe is that eastern Europe is large. Were it a small region, the low-wage competition from there might not pose much of a threat to the domestic upswing. In fact, eastern EU countries are home to 101 million inhabitants.[25] While this is less than the population of the southern European crisis countries, which stands at 130 million,[26] it is of a similar order of magnitude and certainly large enough to imply painful reallocations of capital. This statement is true a fortiori when considering that the EU has signed association agreements with Turkey and Serbia, two countries with even lower wages, that give these countries preferential access to EU markets. Their joint population is currently 81 million.[27] There is such an abundance of highly profitable investment opportunities in southeastern Europe and Turkey that the southern euro countries will have a hard time competing.

Caught in the Euro Trap: The Terrors of Deflation

Correcting the overblown wages and prices in southern Europe is indispensable for a recovery of that part of the European Union, but the task will be hard and possibly insurmountable within the currency union. At first glance, the necessary realignment of relative prices in the Eurozone seems not too difficult to achieve. After all, if wrong prices arose through differential inflation rates over a few years, it should be possible to correct the mistake over a similar period of time by reversing the structure of inflation rates. However, this optimism is ill-founded, since the price clock cannot easily be wound backwards.[28]

---

[25] Bulgaria, Czech Republic, Estonia, Hungary, Latvia, Lithuania, Poland, Romania, Slovakia and Slovenia. Eurostat, Database, *Economy and Finance*, National Accounts, Annual National Accounts, Auxiliary Indicators to National Accounts.

[26] Cyprus, Greece, Italy, Portugal, and Spain.

[27] See Eurostat, Database, *Economy and Finance*, National Accounts, Annual National Accounts, Auxiliary Indicators to National Accounts.

[28] See H.-W. Sinn, 'Reining in Europe's Debtor Nations', *Project Syndicate*, 23 April 2010, available at: <http://www.project-syndicate.org/commentary/reining-in-europe-s-debtor-nations>; and P. Krugman, 'The Euro Trap', *New York Times*, 29 April 2010, available at: <http://www.nytimes.com/2010/04/30/opinion/30krugman.html>. See also H.-W. Sinn (interview), 'Schuldenbegrenzung nicht ernst genommen', *Berliner Zeitung*, 29 March 2010, No. 75, p. 12, available at: <http://www.cesifo-group.de/w/3MaFL6G8B>, 'Das zwingt uns in die Knie', *Spiegel online*, 26 April 2010, available at:

The countries that inflated after the euro announcement are those that were long accustomed to inflation. Unions, governments, banks, households, and firms had all been used to substantial inflation, to which they adjusted their expectations, purchasing habits, wage demands, and price-setting behaviour long before the euro was introduced. Conversely, those countries that underwent a real devaluation, Germany in particular, were accustomed to a low inflation rate before the euro was introduced. It will not be easy for these countries to simply trade places, because this would require overcoming well-established national habits, traditions, and preferences that are deeply ingrained in their psyche.

As mentioned above, the difficulty is particularly large insofar as the path back towards equilibrium prices will in some cases be even longer than the path towards today's prices, because the distressed countries have accumulated much external debt in the meantime, which have contributed to deteriorating the current accounts. The Goldman Sachs study clearly reflects this aspect in the cases of Spain, Portugal, and Greece, calculating that these countries would have to lower their relative prices to *below* their level at the time of the Madrid Summit in 1995.

To illustrate the difficulties, suppose the realignment of the Eurozone according to the Goldman Sachs study were to be achieved without deflation in any of the member countries. Then Germany would have to inflate by 5.5% per year for ten years, entailing a total price level increase of 71% and a reduction of 42% in the real value of nominal savings. The average Eurozone inflation rate in this case would be 3.6% p.a. Even if it were technically possible for the ECB to manage such a level of inflation, it would violate the Maastricht Treaty and create an uproar in Germany, where the trauma of the hyperinflation experienced from 1915 to 1923 still sits deep in the German psyche. At the time, hyperinflation deprived the middle class of its wealth and drove it to look for radical political solutions. This is the reason why Germany accepted giving up the deutschmark only under the condition that the maintenance of price stability be the goal of the ECB. The first sentence of article 105 TFEU reads: [29]

> The primary objective of the ESCB shall be to maintain price stability.

Apart from that, it would be difficult to create inflation, given that the Eurozone is close to a liquidity trap, i.e. a situation where the interest rates are already close to zero and monetary policy has lost its effectiveness. Japan provides a useful warning. After its housing bubble burst in 1990 and a banking

<http://www.cesifo-group.de/w/Kcf7SuQZ>, and 'Das Griechen-Drama wird schrecklich enden', *Focus online*, 19 March 2010, available at: <http://www.cesifo-group.de/w/3Fzcg9dcq>.

[29] See EU, 'Treaty on European Union', *Official Journal* C 191, 29 July 1992, available at: <http://eur-lex.europa.eu/en/treaties/dat/11992M/htm/11992M.html>.

crisis in 1997 drove 40% of the banks to the brink of bankruptcy and into government rescue operations, the Bank of Japan set the short-term interest rate at close to zero, a level it has kept to this day, flooding the economy with money. However, despite all its efforts, the Bank of Japan was not able to avoid a protracted bout of deflation and secular stagnation, to use Alvin Hansen's term.[30] After an inflation rate of about 20% from 1980 to 1994, the Japanese GDP deflator has fallen by about the same amount so that now, a third of a century later, it is back at its 1980 level.

Thus, a realignment of the Eurozone may require the crisis-stricken countries to actually deflate. As this deflation would affect only a subset of countries in the Eurozone, it would not be sterilized by an outright currency appreciation as in the case of Japan, but would improve the deflating countries' competitiveness as it did in the case of Ireland, Latvia or Lithuania.

An additional reason why deflation is needed is that, unlike those countries that underwent real depreciations before the crisis, the GIPSIC countries are being shunned by the capital markets and therefore do not have much time for a gradual realignment through reduced inflation. Capital markets are impatient and have exerted a great deal of pressure to accomplish the required price adjustments quickly, enforcing outright deflation.

However, deflation would impose much hardship and strain on countries like Greece, Portugal, or Spain, as evidenced by their current unemployment levels, particularly among the young (see Figure 1.2 and 1.3). While the economy would prosper after the deflation has run its course, the process itself of deflating is painful and tears at the very fabric of society. The political systems are strained by factional conflicts and by strong unions that are not easily moved to compromise.

This is the argument John Maynard Keynes used in his essay on 'The Economic Consequences of Mr. Churchill' in 1925, which he repeated in his General Theory.[31] Keynes had warned Churchill not to bring Great Britain back to the gold standard, since this would force it to undergo a real depreciation that, due to the resistance of the unions, would result in mass unemployment. Every union, he argued, would object to wage cuts given that it could not assume that other unions would simultaneously accept such cuts. Thus, services like restaurants or hairdressers would not be expected, by a single trade union deciding in isolation, to become cheaper after accepting a wage cut, thereby mitigating the real income loss. Moreover, the relative income position of its members would deteriorate. Resistance would be weaker if a simultaneous cut in all wages could be orchestrated, but given that this is impossible,

---

[30] See A. Hansen, *Full Recovery or Stagnation*, Norton, New York 1938.

[31] See J. M. Keynes, *Essays in Persuasion*, Macmillan, London 1931, chapter 5: *The Economic Consequences of Mr. Churchill (1925)*, and J. M. Keynes, *The General Theory of Employment, Interest and Money*, Palgrave Macmillan, London 1936, here Macmillan 1960, p. 267.

nominal wages tend to be downward-sticky, causing mass unemployment when demand falls. During the Great Depression, Britain indeed suffered from the effects Keynes had described, and was forced to leave the gold standard again.

Germany, under the Weimar Republic, provided another example of the effects Keynes described. Under the Dawes Plan, which codified the Treaty of Versailles, Germany was prevented from devaluing its currency as a vehicle to improve its competitiveness. A key element of the treaty resulting from the Dawes Plan was the German banking law of 1924, which set an immutable exchange rate between the Reichsmark and gold. Any attempt to change it would have led to calamitous conflicts with Germany's public and private creditors. Not even Hitler dared to tamper with this.[32] In the years following the onset of the 1929 economic depression, some of Germany's competitors devalued their currencies, in particular Great Britain, Japan, and some of the Scandinavian countries. After the UK gave up its gold peg in 1931, the British pound fell by around 30% against the gold standard. (Later, in 1934, the US devalued by around 40%, spelling the beginning of the end of the gold standard.) In view of this, the only solution for Germany to regain its competitiveness was through a real depreciation by way of reducing prices and wages, a course that was followed with remarkable doggedness by the government of Chancellor of the Republic Heinrich Brüning through harsh austerity measures.[33]

As a result, German wages plummeted by 27% between 1929 and 1933,[34] while consumer prices fell by 23%.[35] This real depreciation was brought about by

---

[32] See C. G. Dawes and R. McKenna, *Die Sachverständigen-Gutachten, Der Dawes- und McKenna-Bericht, mit Anlagen*, literal after the original text, Frankfurter Societäts-Druckerei, Frankfurt am Main 1924, pp. 10, section VI and pp. 12 f., sections IX and X. See also P. Heyde, *Das Ende der Reparationen. Deutschland, Frankreich, und der Youngplan; 1929–1939*, Ferdinand Schöningh Verlag, Paderborn 1998, pp. 48 and 51.

[33] See K. Borchardt, 'Zwangslagen und Handlungsspielräume in der großen Wirtschaftskrise der frühen dreißiger Jahre: Zur Revision des überlieferten Geschichtsbildes', Commemorative speech of 2 December 1978, *Jahrbuch der Bayerischen Akademie der Wissenschaften*, Beck, Munich 1979, pp. 85–132; detailed descriptions of the situation during the German inflation of the 1920s can also be found in N. Ferguson, 'Keynes and the German Inflation', *English Historical Review* 110, 1995, pp. 368–391; N. Ferguson, 'Constraints and Room for Manoeuvre in the German Inflation of the Early 1920s', *Economic History Review* 49, 1996, pp. 635–666; N. Ferguson and B. Granville, '"Weimar on the Volga": Causes and Consequences of Inflation in 1990s Russia Compared With 1920s Germany', *Journal of Economic History* 60, 2000, pp. 1061–1087.

[34] See J. H. Müller, *Nivellierung und Differenzierung der Arbeitseinkommen in Deutschland seit 1925*, Duncker & Humblot, Berlin 1954.

[35] See German Federal Statistical Office, *Fachserie 17*, Preise, Reihe 7, p. 2.

mass unemployment of around 30%, not cushioned by a welfare state supported with public credit from other countries,[36] and a 16% drop in GDP from 1928 to 1932.[37] While the countries that had left the gold standard performed reasonably well, Germany's depression pushed the country to the brink of a civil war, with left-wing and right-wing hordes brutally battling each other on the streets. What came in 1933 turned out to be worse than any civil war.

What the German example shows is that real depreciations of the magnitude of those needed by Portugal, Greece, and Spain can have dire consequences in politically divided countries. The unions will oppose such a step with all their might, even taking to the streets to defend their members' standpoint. Theoretically, the unions could be talked into accepting this if wage cuts were coordinated across a wide front, because the nominal lowering of wages would lead to a drop in the price of domestically produced goods. In reality, however, it is inordinately difficult to orchestrate such a wide-ranging wage cut. The consequence is that every single union will fight tooth and claw to preserve their members' wages. None will want to be the first to cave in, hoping that the others will take the plunge instead. Keynes himself pointed to the trap into which Germany had fallen during the Weimar Republic because of its fixed exchange rate.[38] Interestingly, Keynes' great opponent, Milton Friedman, agreed with him on this point.[39] Since nominal wages in a modern economy exhibit downward rigidity, the possibilities for performing a real depreciation through wage cuts and price reductions are limited.

And even if the unions came around to accepting it, there is still the problem that a real depreciation would lead to severe distortions in individual balance sheets. With price reductions of the magnitude envisaged here, many normal companies that own assets such as machinery and buildings and owe debts to domestic banks would run into difficulties, because the value of their assets as well as their cash flow would diminish, while their debts and their debt service would remain unchanged. Many companies would go bankrupt, even if at first glance the lower prices ought to make them more competitive.[40] Likewise, many private households that bought property on credit would be unable to service

---

[36] See D. Petzina, 'Arbeitslosigkeit in der Weimarer Republik', in W. Abelshauser (ed.), *Die Weimarer Republik als Wohlfahrtsstaat. Zum Verhältnis von Wirtschafts- und Sozialpolitik in der Industriegesellschaft*, Vierteljahrschrift für Sozial- und Wirtschaftsgeschichte, Beiheft 81, Stuttgart 1987.

[37] See A. Maddison, *The World Economy. Historical Statistics*, OECD, Paris 2003, p. 50.

[38] See J. M. Keynes, *The General Theory of Employment, Interest and Money*, 1936 (1960, p. 267).

[39] See M. Friedman, *Essays in Positive Economics*, University of Chicago Press, Chicago 1953, chapter: *The Case for Flexible Exchange Rates*, especially p. 165 and p. 173.

[40] These problems stood in the centre of Irving Fisher's debt deflation theory. See I. Fisher, 'The Debt-Deflation Theory of Great Depressions', *Econometrica* 1, 1933, pp. 337–357.

their debt after a balanced wage and price cut, and would be driven into insolvency. The distortion of the domestic debt-to-asset ratios is an insurmountable problem that would doom every attempt to carry out a sizeable real depreciation by way of actual and not relative price reductions.

The internal debt problem is particularly severe for the GIPSIC countries, since all of them lost their competitiveness because of the credit bubble that the euro brought about. Thus, typically, their firms, private households, and governments are overburdened with debts and debt service obligations that make it impossible for them to accept a significant real depreciation even if prices and incomes could all be cut simultaneously and in proportion. And if a real depreciation via deflation nevertheless happens, there will inevitably be a massive surge of bankruptcies of firms and households.

This, by the way, is a major difference between the Baltics and the GIPSIC countries. The former had just escaped Communism and were too expensive because they had entered the ERM II with overvalued currencies, but their governments, households and firms did not hold much debt. Thus, it was relatively easy to convince the various groups of society of the merits of austerity programmes. Obviously, this example cannot easily be translated to southern Europe and Ireland.

That is the real dilemma, the blind alley the Eurozone is stuck in. 40% of the population of the Eurozone, namely the population of the GIPSIC countries, and perhaps even France, which accounts for 20%, are trapped in a dreadful situation where competitiveness has been lost due to excessive credit-financed inflation and from which the escape route by way of price cuts is blocked by the internal debt problem.

In such a situation, an outright depreciation through exiting the currency union remains the only practicable possibility. However, the fear of an exit causes bank runs and capital flight that could drive the banking sector into bankruptcy, forcing the affected countries to introduce capital controls and limit the amounts that can be withdrawn from bank deposits. The bankruptcy of the Cypriot banking system in early 2013 demonstrated very clearly which ramifications could be expected, suggesting that the set of solutions for the Eurozone, at least the set of easy solutions, may be empty.

That said, the big advantages of an outright devaluation should not be overlooked. It boosts demand for locally produced goods, since imports become more expensive and prompt people to switch to the local equivalents. It stimulates export demand. And it leaves the domestic debt obligations relative to people's incomes unchanged, avoiding the distortion to balance sheets of individuals and institutions holding domestic debt. All debts held with domestic lenders are included automatically in the currency conversion, so that no one needs to declare insolvency on account of his local banking debts or other domestic debt contracts.

But foreign debts continue to be a problem. In this respect, however, there is no difference between an internal, real depreciation and an outright depreciation by changing the value of the currency. In both cases foreign debts will rise relative to the value of domestic assets, whose value will decline with the depreciation of the domestic currency.

The increase in the relative size of the foreign debt is used sometimes as an argument against allowing such an open depreciation. But the argument is flawed. A sufficiently large depreciation will boost a country's competitiveness in such a way that it once again will be able to post current account surpluses that, in turn, will enable it to repay at least part of its debts. Seen in this light, the path to a sustainable foreign debt, in the absence of debt forgiveness, would seem to go through an initial increase in the foreign debt-to-GDP ratio. Only after increasing this ratio as a result of a devaluation is it possible to lower it through current account surpluses to the pre-devaluation level.

That said, a country could still go bankrupt and become unable to repay its foreign debt. In that case, either its creditors would have to give up some of their claims to allow the country a restart, or the taxpayers of other countries would have to bail the country out. But this issue is largely independent of the competitiveness problem.

Even in cases where the debt problem can be resolved, some countries may only be able to regain their competitiveness by leaving the Eurozone and devaluing their new currency. The last chapter of this book will discuss the possibilities of minimizing the risks that such a solution would entail.

CHAPTER 5

The White Knight

The Crash—Help from the Printing Press—Lowering Collateral Standards and Extending Maturities—Moral Hazard—ELA Credit

The Crash

The derailment of the European express, hurtling along with no private or public debt brakes, started when the US financial crisis engulfed the European banks. The write-offs of now-toxic US securities deprived the European banks of capital and destroyed the illusion that a triple A rating equalled safety. The growing number of ailing banks contributed mightily to the increasing insecurity. This led, in August 2007, to the first breakdown of the European interbank market. The result was a change in the risk assessment of securities from the European periphery and in the willingness to hold such instruments, as reflected in the yawning, and growing, spreads that became evident at that time (see Figure 2.2).

The many banks that folded did so spectacularly. Just one month after the ECB had alleviated the first small collapse of the interbank market in August 2007 with a generous injection of liquidity, the first bank run occurred, affecting the UK's Northern Rock bank. The difficulties of that bank to borrow from other banks fed the fear that it faced looming insolvency. Its customers rushed to have their demand deposits paid out in cash, but given that no bank ever has all the cash on hand that is shown on its depositors' account balances, panic broke out. The Bank of England, which had at first refused to come to the rescue, had no other option but to restore confidence in the bank by providing financial assistance and, ultimately, by nationalizing the bank in February 2008. Then the US bank Bear Stearns started wobbling, while at the same time Germany's Saxony state bank (Landesbank Sachsen) took a hit through the businesses of its Irish special purpose vehicle, Sachsen LB Europe. In July 2008, the US mortgage lender IndyMac filed for bankruptcy, while in Germany one state bank after another went into a tailspin in the first half of 2008.[1]

After the collapse of the Lehman Brothers investment bank in September 2008, the interbank market seized up around the world, with hundreds of banks folding in the aftermath.

The financial markets calmed down somewhat in the following months, thanks to substantial fiscal and monetary rescue programmes, and a global upswing started in the second half of 2009. But the days of low market interest rates for the banks and governments of the Eurozone's periphery, and with it the attendant overheating of the economy, were over. What had started as a desirable convergence process turned out to be a bubble that eventually burst. As Figure 2.2 showed, the spreads went up to levels not seen since before the euro was announced.

Figure 5.1 depicts bank exposure and capital flight in the crisis countries according to official data of the Bank for International Settlements (BIS). Clearly, nearly all national banking systems (see also Figure 3.7) reduced their gross exposure to the private and public sectors of the crisis countries quite substantially after the collapse of Lehman Brothers.[2] They typically stopped rolling over their loans and demanded redemption of the existing debts at maturity, thus reducing their overall exposure to the GIIPS countries (GIPSIC minus Cyprus) from € 2.449 trillion in Q4 2007 to € 1.349 trillion in Q3 2013, i.e. by € 1.100 trillion. Capital fled massively back to the home country or to countries considered safe havens.

The only nation whose banking sector significantly increased its exposure to the crisis countries was the United States, going from € 85 billion in Q4 2007 to € 121 billion in Q3 2013. Obviously, US banks were less risk-averse than their European counterparts, stepping in when the latter stepped out, and seeking profit opportunities.

---

[1] See W. Münchau, *The Meltdown Years. The Unfolding of the Global Economic Crisis*, McGraw-Hill, New York 2009; H.-W. Sinn, *Casino Capitalism. How the Financial Crisis Came about and What Needs to Be Done Now*, Oxford University Press, Oxford 2010; and A. S. Blinder, *After the Music Stopped*, Penguin Press, New York 2013.

[2] As the data depicted in the graph stem from the consolidated balance sheets of banks, they include changes in the market value of claims to the extent the claims were reported in the banks' trading books as well as write-off losses at maturity. However, this effect cannot be dominant insofar as market values had plummeted up to the peak of the crisis in August 2012 and went up thereafter, as markets calmed and interest rates came down again. Obviously the graph does not show any particular abnormality around Q3 2012, as it should if the market revaluation were a strong effect. One of the reasons for the absence of visible revaluation effects could be that, particularly in troubled times, banks tend to hold their claims in the banking books, which spares them the task of reporting losses in market values.

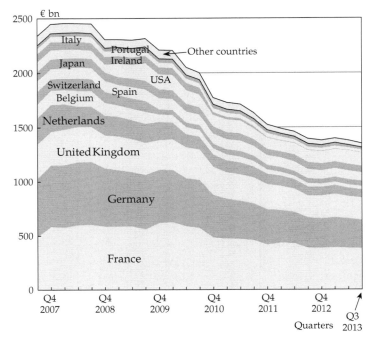

Figure 5.1 International bank claims vis-à-vis private and public sectors in Greece, Ireland, Portugal, Spain, and Italy

Source: Bank for International Settlements, Statistics, *Consolidated Banking Statistics*.

Note: The figure shows cross-border claims and local claims of foreign affiliates, ordered according to their value at Q3 2008 (Lehman crisis). Domestic claims are not included.

The reader should be warned, however, that the chart only shows the reduction in the *gross* exposure of lending banks with regard to the private and public sectors of the GIIPS economies, concealing the fact that the GIIPS banks in turn changed their exposure vis-à-vis other countries as well.[3] Thus, for example, Italian banks recalled funds from abroad to the tune of € 131 billion in the period considered, presumably to partly compensate for the € 334 billion that foreign banks had withdrawn from Italy. Similarly, Irish banks recalled € 414 billion from abroad, while foreign banks recalled € 264 billion from Ireland.

---

[3] For this and the following see Bank for International Settlements, *Consolidated Banking Statistics*, table 9E, available at: <http://www.bis.org/statistics/consstats.htm>.

Interestingly enough, however, Spanish banks lent an additional € 289 billion to other countries over that period, while foreign banks withdrew € 298 billion from Spain, both figures representing outright capital flight in the face of an impending collapse of the Spanish banking system. Most of the Spanish flight money, about € 139 billion, was brought to Latin America including the Caribbean, Brazil alone receiving € 78 billion. Britain ended up with € 55 billion, the US with € 65 billion.

A similar phenomenon was observed in Greece. While foreign banks withdrew € 145 billion from Greece, Greek banks transferred € 69 billion to a large range of countries, the list of known and reported money transfers being topped by Turkey and Cyprus, followed by Bulgaria, Romania, the UK, the Marshall Islands, Liberia, Serbia, Germany, Albania, the Ukraine, Panama, and the Maldives. In addition, there were probably many transfers to countries not captured by the BIS statistics. For example, it has been reported that Greeks have parked € 200 billion in Switzerland.[4]

Moreover, capital often flowed through other countries before it reached, or after it left, the GIIPS countries. This is clearly shown by the BIS statistics on cross-country banking exposure. While French gross bank exposure to the GIIPS countries (all sectors) shrank by € 204 billion from Q4 2007 to Q3 2013, Belgian banks reduced their exposure to France by € 68 billion, Dutch banks by € 56 billion, and British banks by € 27 billion, giving a combined total of € 151 billion. Thus, in effect, much of the capital that France had lent to the GIIPS countries and that it recalled during the crisis may originally have come from other countries, via the European interbank market. Figures 3.7 and 5.1 show that the French banking system had lent more funds than other banking systems to the crisis-hit countries, but given that France was not a net capital exporter (Figure 3.4), it must have been other countries' savings that it was lending out. Indeed, thanks to France belonging to the Romance language family, the French banking system served as a hub for the distribution of savings to southern Europe.

All of this is interesting, but confusing. The complex structure of financial capital flows does not lend itself to a simple narrative and is rather incomplete, since many agents involved in financial capital flows such as insurance companies, private equity companies, hedge funds, and companies of the real economy are not banks and hence not included in the BIS statistics.

The Bundesbank statistics on the nature of private capital flows between Germany and the rest of the world shed some light on the importance of

---

[4] See 'Leveraging the Backstop: A Trillion Euro Insurance Policy for the Common Currency', *Spiegel Online International*, 19 October 2011, available at: <http://www.spiegel.de/international/europe/leveraging-the-backstop-a-trillion-euro-insurance-policy-for-the-common-currency-a-792641.html>.

other sectors.[5] While the BIS statistics reveal that German banks recalled € 902 billion from other countries in the period Q4 2007 to Q3 2013, € 304 billion from the GIIPS alone, and that foreign banks, in turn, recalled € 173 billion in net terms from Germany, the Bundesbank reports that German enterprises and private households at the same time exported capital worth € 1,026 billion in net terms through lending, the purchase of foreign securities, and direct investment.[6] Thus, it seems that the private capital flows into and out of Germany roughly balance out. But even this information is incomplete as it excludes, among others, recalls of funds by foreign financial institutions like hedge funds and investment funds as well as investments in Germany by foreign enterprises and households.

As the German balance of payments statistics reveal, which in principle comprise all capital flows, there were no private capital flows in net terms to Germany since the beginning of the crisis; on the contrary, a net export of capital amounting to € 521 billion occurred from the beginning of 2008 to 2013.[7] Only in one year, 2010, was there a net private capital inflow (about € 100 billion), but this was more than offset by the net outflows of other years.[8] Thus, even though German banks recalled some of the credit they had given to other countries, international financial institutions as well as German firms and households exported even more private capital from Germany in the period considered. This is important insofar as it has been claimed over and again in opinion columns that a huge capital flight to Germany occurred during the crisis.

However, even the information that the private net capital export was € 521 billion from 2008 to the end of 2013 is puzzling, as it seems to be at odds with the fact that Germany had a huge current account surplus of € 1,001 billion over this period, and hence overall net capital exports of that same magnitude (refer also to Figure 3.4).[9] This puzzle will be solved in Chapter 7.

There is little doubt, though, that the net flow of private capital to the GIPSIC countries shrank substantially, and that it even reversed direction for some

[5] See also H.-W. Sinn and T. Wollmershäuser, 'Target Balances and the German Financial Account in Light of the European Balance-of-Payments Crisis', *CESifo Working Paper* No. 4051, 2012, figure 5, available at: <http://www.cesifo-group.de/DocDL/cesifo1_wp4051.pdf>.

[6] See Deutsche Bundesbank, *Zahlungsbilanzstatistik*, January 2014, p. 58, available at: <http://www.bundesbank.de/Redaktion/DE/Downloads/Veroeffentlichungen/Statistische_Beihefte_3/2014/2014_01_zahlungsbilanzstatistik.pdf?__blob=publicationFile>.

[7] See Deutsche Bundesbank, *Zahlungsbilanzstatistik*, January 2014, pp. 58–59.

[8] In 2011 and 2012, Germany's private capital export was small, however, at € 14 billion and € 35 billion, respectively.

[9] See Deutsche Bundesbank, *Zahlungsbilanzstatistik*, January 2014, p. 7.

periods and some countries, as will be shown in more detail in Chapter 7. This turned out to be a huge problem for the GIPSIC countries, since the inflationary credit bubble analysed above had deprived them of their competitiveness and had created huge current account deficits that needed to be financed (see Figure 2.1). This raises one question: who was the white knight who came to the rescue and financed the current account deficits and the private capital flow reversal? The answer is: the Eurosystem.

Help from the Printing Press

The Eurosystem was the white knight who initially rescued the troubled countries. In accordance with the rules set by the ECB Governing Council, the national central banks (NCBs) of the GIPSIC countries offered the local commercial banks refinancing credit at generous rates; in other words, they helped them with the printing press. That help began in October 2008, after the Lehman debacle. In addition, from May 2010, all NCBs and the ECB itself purchased a substantial amount of the GIPSIC countries' government bonds, and in September 2012 the ECB announced that it would henceforth do it without limit (through the so-called OMT programme). This came in addition to the intergovernmental rescue operations that had started in May 2010. The rest of this chapter, as well as the two following ones, will concentrate on the role of local refinancing credit. Government bond purchases and intergovernmental rescue operations will be discussed in Chapter 8.

Refinancing credit is granted by an NCB through the issuance of self-created money to commercial banks in its jurisdiction, typically against adequate collateral, in line with the rules of the Eurosystem and normally with shared responsibility and risk. In Europe, refinancing credit is the main channel through which the NCBs issue money. It is subdivided into main refinancing operations, long-term refinancing operations, and credit from the so-called marginal lending facility. In addition, however, the local NCBs, and to a limited extent even the ECB itself, issue money by way of open-market purchases of assets held by the banking sector, which is the predominant method of money creation used in the USA. The assets bought include gold, foreign currency, government bonds, and, temporarily, covered bonds issued by the private sector. The rest of this book will refer to refinancing credit and asset purchases to summarize all of these sources of money creation.

The money issued can take the form of banknotes, but it typically first comes as book money credited to the demand deposits that commercial banks hold with their respective NCB. Unless otherwise noted in this book, money is meant to be central bank or base money, i.e. banknotes in circulation and demand deposits that commercial banks hold with their NCBs, called 'current accounts' and 'deposit facilities'. As the former term in economics is already used in foreign trade accounting, where it means something entirely different, it will be avoided here. Moreover, deposit facilities in the Eurozone have lost most of their practical importance since banks no longer receive interest on them. In addition, commercial banks hold term deposits with the central banks against interest, i.e. they lend money to their NCB. These term deposits are not part of the monetary base.

Moreover, whenever the term 'money printing' is used in this book, it means money creation in a broader sense of the word, and not only the physical process of printing banknotes.[10] Similarly, the terms money shredding and money transfers will later be used in this metaphorical sense.

Refinancing credit used to be given at very short maturities—a couple of days up to at most three months used to be the norm—and had to be renewed constantly. Today, longer maturities are common. The NCBs create the money, credit it to the account of the commercial banks that request it in their jurisdiction, and charge a given interest rate, typically the main refinancing rate. This rate has been reduced repeatedly during the crisis, standing at 0.25% as of this writing.

Normally, a bank gets the money that it lends out to its customers from depositors or from other lenders, which, in turn, have received the money from their clients. The money, in other words, comes from the private sector and flows back to it. However, a growing economy needs an increasingly large amount of money for general transactions, since a good portion of the money is always circulating and kept temporarily in wallets and accounts. For this reason, given a country's payment habits, additional money has to be created by its central bank every year in proportion to the nominal growth of the economy and, through lending it to the commercial banks, brought into private circulation. The stock of refinancing credit that lies behind the money circulating in a growing economy must also be increased accordingly. This brings in a growing amount of interest revenue to the central bank, the so-called seignorage, which it then passes on to the treasury.[11] As mentioned in Chapter 1, the stock of seignorage capital of the Eurosystem in 2013 was about € 1.3 trillion in a static calculation, and could be about € 2.9 trillion in a dynamic one. Since the NCBs act under

---

[10] International payments, which will be considered below, are also purely electronic transactions that do not involve transporting cash. The printing-press metaphor is common in technical discussion when referring to creating and transferring money and should not be taken at face value. In cases referring to physical money, the context will make it clear.

[11] Incidentally, the German interest revenue resulting from refinancing credit was greatly reduced after the introduction of the euro, because the special profits that the Bundesbank used to make as a result of the extensive use of the deutschmark in eastern Europe and Turkey are now socialized. See H. Feist und H.-W. Sinn, 'Eurowinners and Eurolosers: The Distribution of Seignorage Wealth in EMU', *European Journal of Political Economy* 13, 1997, pp. 665–689.

common rules, their interest income is pooled, each NCB receiving a fraction of it depending on the size of its sovereign's economy. The fraction is called its 'capital key' after the relative, and minuscule, equity injections into the ECB system upon its foundation.[12]

In addition to the central bank's creation of base money, commercial banks create book money by lending out demand deposits that serve the same purpose as bank notes and are also needed in proportion to the economic activity level of a country. They earn seignorage income on the self-made deposit money, just like the central banks on base money. Given the cash withdrawal rate of private agents, and given the minimum reserve needed to ensure liquidity (and possibly to satisfy legal constraints), a commercial bank cannot, however, arbitrarily create book money beyond a certain proportion of the central bank money it holds without risking illiquidity. Thus the stock of book money made by a commercial bank is endogenously determined by its stock of base money and is not a separate explanatory variable for the issues considered in this book.

During an economic crisis, which is accompanied by a loss of confidence between creditors and debtors, more fresh money from the central bank is needed, since potential creditors prefer to hoard their base and book money instead of lending it on to others, out of fear that they won't see it again. A sudden increase in liquidity preference, however, destabilizes the economy, since the additional liquidity hoarded ceases to be available for credit that final investors could use for purchasing investment goods. The flow of funds from savers to real investors is disturbed, implying a lack of aggregate demand. To avoid this destabilizing effect, the central bank must issue additional money to make up for the leakage in the savings–investment flow that occurs through hoarding.

Hoarding is a graver problem when savers' money must pass through several financial institutions, like banks and insurance companies, before it reaches the final borrower, who wishes to use it to purchase real goods, typically investment goods. When a widespread loss of confidence occurs, many different cash hoards in these intermediary financial institutions are filled at the same time. At every step of the flow of credit from the saver to the final investor, a portion of the money disappears into a hoard, meaning that in some cases very little reaches the real investor. This turns a financial crisis into a crisis of the real economy, which can cause massive unemployment. The interbank market is one such many-staged system. As a result of the sudden hoarding of money, it broke down temporarily in August 2007 and then again, massively, after the collapse of the Lehman Brothers investment bank in September 2008. The effects on the

---

[12] Including retained revaluation profits, the ECB's equity capital was € 21 billion on 31 December 2013.

real economy were dire, pushing the global economy in 2009 into its worst recession in the post-war period, the Great Recession.

The ECB tried, initially somewhat hesitantly and then more vigorously, to replace the extra money being hoarded. Except for a direct intervention on 9 August 2007 and on the following days, when it offered commercial banks unlimited liquidity overnight,[13] it limited itself to the normal refinancing operations available to all banks. But when the crisis grew more acute and the interbank market seized up after the collapse of Lehman Brothers, it implemented a wide-ranging Enhanced Credit Support programme with which it generously provided liquidity.[14] After years of having auctioned only limited amounts of central bank money to commercial banks, starting in October 2008 it allowed its NCBs to grant unlimited refinancing credit at gradually reduced rates of interest (first 1% and eventually as low as 0.25%), provided sufficient eligible collateral was pledged. The new policy, which still is in place at this writing, was called the Full Allotment Policy.

These measures offered the commercial banks an alternative to the faltering interbank market. Instead of getting money from other banks, which now preferred to keep it to themselves, the indebted banks now turned to their respective NCBs.

At the same time, the ECB continued to allow the banks with excess liquidity to deposit it at the ECB itself for a moderate rate of interest, instead of keeping it in their demand deposits and drawing no interest income. With this policy, the ECB claimed to take the position of an intermediary between creditor and debtor banks, channelling lending through its books in order to guarantee the security of credit operations.[15] This is only a heuristic description of the procedure, however, since the Eurosystem's lending operations do not depend in any way on how much money commercial banks deposit with their central banks. Later the ECB preferred to speak of improving the 'functioning of the monetary policy transmission mechanism'.

The generous provision of refinancing credit by the Eurosystem was a complete success. It contributed very quickly to restoring confidence among the

---

[13] See J.-C. Trichet, 'Supporting the Financial System and the Economy: Key ECB Policy Actions in the Crisis', *Speech at a conference in Madrid organised jointly by Nueva Economía Fórum and the Wall Street Journal*, 22 June 2009, available at: <http://www.ecb.int/press/key/date/2009/html/sp090622.en.html>.

[14] See J.-C. Trichet, 'The ECB's Enhanced Credit Support', *CESifo Working Paper* No. 2833, October 2009, available at: <http://www.cesifo-group.de/DocDL/cesifo1_wp2833.pdf>. An overview of the monetary policy of the West's central banks and other rescue operations can be found in H.-W. Sinn, *Casino Capitalism*, 2010, chapter 9: *Rescue Attempts*, in particular pp. 206 ff. and 215 ff.

[15] See J.-C. Trichet, 'The ECB's Enhanced Credit Support', October 2009.

healthy banks of the still-sound economies, the necessary ingredient for a functioning interbank market. Just a few months after introducing such measures, around the turn of the year 2008/2009, the interbank market got going again and could have quickly returned to an arguably healthier situation, given that markets had begun to differentially reassess country and institutional risks, if the continued application of these measures had not provided a more attractive alternative for the commercial banks.

The reassessment of risks by markets meant that the GIPSIC countries had to pay higher risk premia than they were used to. Confidence in the solvency of these countries was damaged, because now, during the crisis, investors were keeping a watchful eye on such countries' exorbitant foreign and sovereign debts. Their commercial banks were regarded as increasingly vulnerable, since they had gorged themselves on government bonds (as a result of not being obliged to hold equity against them, as explained above). In addition, they had given huge volumes of mortgage loans to the private economy that turned sour because of the collapsing real-estate market. For this reason, they had to pay ever larger risk premia for interbank loans from countries that had surplus savings. This pushed up the commercial banks' demand for cheap refinancing credit from the respective NCBs, and the ECB saw itself under increasing pressure to extend the planned duration. It kept setting termination dates, but as they came nearer, they were postponed again and again, despite the fact that a global upswing had started to be felt in summer 2009, which gained enormous impetus in the years 2010–2012. At this writing, the emergency measures are still in place and have been announced to remain so at least until 7 July 2015, which would be eight years after the outbreak of the crisis and nearly seven years after they had first been adopted.

Even though the ECB refinancing policy was designed for the entire Eurozone and did not contemplate any special measures for individual countries, after the Lehman shock was overcome it started to function as a special operation to finance southern and western countries, since that was where financing problems persisted and markets demanded higher yields. The ECB's refinancing policy then ceased to be a policy aimed at battling the crisis in general, metamorphosing instead into a creative measure to benefit the GIPSIC countries by providing credit from the printing press at below-market conditions. The credit flowed via the commercial banks to private companies and to local governments, whose bonds and securities were used as collateral for obtaining refinancing credit.

In practice, the ECB's refinancing policy was a rescue facility for the peripheral economies that preceded by two-and-a-half years the multilateral rescue programmes introduced in May 2010. By the time this manuscript hits the bookstores, the Eurozone will have nearly completed its seventh year of crisis and the sixth year of the ECB's rescue programmes for the countries in the Eurozone's periphery.

Before the introduction of the euro, the countries making up the Eurozone today had already had the possibility of resorting to the money-printing press, since they followed an autonomous monetary policy. They had to be careful, however, since excessive money printing would necessarily bring about inflation and a devaluation of the currency, with the result that its purchasing power abroad would diminish. The euro offered them the apparent advantage of being free of the risk of devaluation, even if they made generous use of the printing press, since they were now part of a currency union in which no exchange rates existed among the member countries. Furthermore, the additional money printed by one NCB was offset by the reduced creation of money by other NCBs, so that there was not even an inflation risk.

This advantage was small when the Eurosystem offered only short-term liquidity against high-quality collateral, and the auctioning of this liquidity kept refinancing credit in short supply. However, when the Eurosystem eased access to central bank credit during the crisis, the advantage became far more evident and the money-printing press was actively used by a number of countries to avoid the comparatively more onerous credit conditions demanded by the interbank market. This enabled these countries to continue financing their current account deficits, despite the bursting of the credit bubble and the refusal of private investors to provide funding, simply by printing the money that they could not, or at unfavourable conditions, borrow in the market. In addition, resorting to the printing press made it possible for them to create the funds they needed to compensate for temporary waves of capital flight to France and northern European countries, as well as to the UK, the US, and many other countries. Chapter 7 will document the financing from the printing press, country by country.

The reader may be excused for doubting that this is actually so. Is it really possible for the Eurozone's NCBs to print as much money as they wish and then lend it out via their banks to their domestic economy and government? Are there no allotted stocks of central bank money that may be created according to the size of the respective economy, like 'small country, small printing press—big country, big printing press'? It cannot really be that countries may simply print money that they can no longer borrow cheaply elsewhere and go on as if nothing had changed, can it?

The answer is that, whether right or wrong, they can. Neither the ECB statutes nor the European treaties contemplate an apportionment of central bank money dependent on the size of the member countries' economies. On the contrary, it is widely accepted that it does not matter where the Eurosystem's refinancing credit is issued. This view stands in striking contrast to the facts that banks are not subject to common regulation, that countries have different propensities to make use of the local printing press, that collateral standards are low and interpreted differently, and in particular, that the unitary European state, which could separate the bankruptcy risk of financial institutions from the respective country risk by embedding the banks and their clients into a common fiscal system, has not been founded yet and, unfortunately, will not be founded in the foreseeable future. The last chapter of this book will return to these issues.

There is, however, an indirect way to apportion money creation according to economy size, in the form of borrowing banks having to pledge eligible collateral to their NCB. Since it can be assumed that a smaller economy will have less collateral of sufficient quality available than a larger one, this could indirectly limit money creation. The ECB Governing Council, alas, which defines the rules for eligible collateral, has done everything in its power to lift this restriction.

Lowering Collateral Standards and Extending Maturities

Before the crisis, banks had to secure the refinancing credit they received from their NCBs with agency-rated collateral, the minimum rating being single A in the ECB's internal rating scale, which, for example, corresponds to Standard & Poor's rating of A–.[16] The credit was only short-term, typically being provided for a week. The lots of refinancing credit offered were limited and had a maximum maturity of three months, the general idea being that the ECB provided the amount of liquidity necessary for commercial banks and the rest of the private sector to carry out their internal transactions, rather than providing funding to the financial sector to make up for the lack of domestic savings or foreign credit. If a country wanted to purchase more goods abroad than it sold there, it couldn't just turn to the central bank to get the money, unless it offered absolutely safe collateral; it had to tap the international capital markets for funding, at increasingly higher rates of interest. The higher interest rates moderated import wishes and made it attractive for foreigners to provide the required funds.

When the US financial crisis spilled over to Europe, this sort of monetary policy was severely challenged. As lenders, in particular foreign banks providing funds through the interbank market, shied away from countries burdened with huge current account deficits, withdrawing their funds or demanding higher yields, the commercial banks of these countries faced a liquidity crisis, if not a solvency crisis. They tried to overcome the shortfall by borrowing from their NCBs, pledging collateral in exchange. However, they were quickly running out of sufficiently good collateral, and the maturities of the ECB credit were too short to replace foreign private credit.

When the crisis came to a head with the collapse of Lehman Brothers in autumn 2008, the ECB Council helped the commercial banks with various policy changes. The most visible one concerned the above-mentioned move from

---

[16] According to the ECB's harmonized rating scale, a 'single A' rating is a rating of at least 'A3' from Moody's and 'A-' from Fitch or Standard & Poor's, while a 'triple B' rating is a rating of at least 'Baa3' from Moody's and 'BBB-' from Fitch or Standard & Poor's. See European Central Bank, *Eurosystem Credit Assessment Framework (ECAF)*, available at: <http://www.ecb.int/paym/coll/risk/ecaf/html/index.en.html>.

auctioning limited money tenders to the establishment of the Full Allotment Policy. More importantly, however, it dramatically reduced the quality requirements for eligible collateral and extended the maturities of refinancing loans.[17] These measures, as well as subsequent measures taken during the course of the crisis, are summarized in Table 5.1 and will be described below.

In October 2008, the ECB doubled the maximum maturity of its refinancing credit to six months, providing € 265 billion with such maturity in 2008 and 2009.[18] It granted this credit under the acronym of LTRO, which stands for Long-Term Refinancing Operations. In May 2009, the ECB decided to offer three twelve-month LTROs in full allotment mode, the first of which was launched in June and met a total demand of € 442 billion. By the end of 2009 the overall volume of such LTROs had increased to € 614 billion.[19] On 21 December 2011, the Eurosystem even began to offer refinancing credit for up to three years.[20] In two tranches, the latest of which was made available on 29 February 2012, the ECB lent a total of € 1.019 trillion. President Draghi called his programme the 'Big Bazooka'.[21] Out of the total, € 566 billion was used to replace existing short-term refinancing credit, but the rest (€ 453 billion) was provided in addition to that. Some banks hoarded the money; others used it to replace private credit they had received from other banks. In total, the banks of the Eurosystem parked almost € 600 billion with the ECB's deposit facility in order to build up a safe buffer stock of liquidity for later use rather than lending it out higher market interest rates.[22]

---

[17] Cf. also European Central Bank, *Collateral Eligibility Requirements – A Comparative Study Across Specific Frameworks*, Frankfurt, July 2013; European Central Bank, 'The Eurosystem Collateral Framework throughout the Crisis', *ECB Monthly Bulletin,* July 2013, p. 71 – 86; C. Hofmann, 'Central Bank Collateral and the Lehman Collapse', *Capital Markets Law Journal* 6, 2011, pp. 456 - 469; J. Eberl and C. Weber, 'ECB Collateral Criteria: A Narrative Database 2001-2013', *ifo Working Paper* No. 174, February 2014, pp. 14–15.

[18] See European Central Bank, *Measures to Further Expand the Collateral Framework and Enhance the Provision of Liquidity*, press release, 15 October 2008, available at: <http://www.ecb.int/press/pr/date/2008/html/pro81015.en.html>.

[19] See European Central Bank, Monetary Policy, Instruments, Open Market Operations, Tender Operations History, *History of all ECB Open Market Operations*, available at: <http://www.ecb.int/mopo/implement/omo/html/top_history.en.html>.

[20] See European Central Bank, *ECB Announces Measures to Support Bank Lending and Money Market Activity*, press release, 8 December 2011, available at: <http://www.ecb.int/press/pr/date/2011/html/pr111208_1.en.html>.

[21] See 'Stabile Preise ohne monetäre Staatsfinanzierung', *Frankfurter Allgemeine Zeitung*, No. 47, 24 February 2012, p. 14.

[22] Between calendar week 50/2011 and calendar week 10/2012, deposit facilities increased by € 584 billion. See European Central Bank, *Consolidated Financial Statement of the Eurosystem as at 16 December 2011* and *9 March 2012*, press release, 20 December 2011, available at: <https://www.ecb.int/press/pr/wfs/2011/html/fs111220.en.html> and 13 March 2012, available at: <http://www.ecb.int/press/pr/wfs/2012/html/fs120313.en.html>, respectively.

Table 5.1 Changes in the ECB's refinancing policy (date of implementation)

Date	Policy measure
15 October 2008	Full allotment policy
Until 24 October 2008	Minimum rating of collateral: single A
As of 25 October 2008	Minimum rating reduced to triple B for all assets except ABS[1]
	Securities issued by credit institutions on non-regulated markets accepted (includes STEP[2] market)
30 October 2008	Maturity of LTROs[3] extended to six months
1 February 2009	Acceptance of government guaranteed own-use bonds as collateral
1 March 2009	Minimum rating of ABS: triple A
23 June 2009	First of three LTRO tenders with a maturity of 12 months
6 May 2010	Rating requirement waived for bonds issued or guaranteed by Greece
1 April 2011	Rating requirement waived for bonds issued or guaranteed by Ireland
7 July 2011	Rating requirement waived for bonds issued or guaranteed by Portugal
19 December 2011	Lowering of rating requirement to single A for specific ABS[4]; acceptance of ACC[5]
21 December 2011	First of two LTRO tenders with a maturity of 3 years
29 June 2012	Lowering of rating requirement to triple B for all ABS
3 May 2013	Rating requirement waived for debt instruments issued or guaranteed by countries that are under an EU-IMF programme
9 May 2013	Rating requirement waived for bonds issued or guaranteed by Cyprus

1) Asset-backed securities.

2) Short-term European Paper, unregulated market (see Box 5.1).

3) Long-term Refinancing Operations.

4) Asset-backed securities consisting of residential mortgages or loans to small and medium-size enterprises.

5) Additional credit claims.

The measures reducing the quality requirements for eligible collateral were sophisticated, multiple, and dramatic. The first measure was taken shortly after the introduction of the Full Allotment Policy on 15 October 2008. On 25 October 2008 the minimum for eligible collateral, except asset-backed securities (ABS), was reduced from single A to triple B, which is one grade above junk status. The ECB announced on various occasions that it would return to normal rating requirements at pre-specified dates, but when the dates arrived it always extended them; this policy remains in effect to this day.[23]

The lowering of the rating requirement to triple B helped for a while, since it liberated a substantial fraction of bank assets to be used as collateral and allowed banks to acquire more such assets with fresh refinancing credit. However, even the collateral that satisfied this reduced standard was soon exhausted. The ECB reacted by reducing collateral requirements even further to allow crisis-ridden countries to draw more credit from the printing presses at the disposal of their NCBs. The relief was always short-lived, lasting only until the latest collateral category accepted was exhausted. But when this happened, the ECB liberated more collateral by further reducing its quality requirements.

Government bonds have played a major role in the collateral pledged by commercial banks to draw refinancing credit from their NCBs. Banks borrow freshly printed money from their NCBs, buy government bonds with this money, and use these same government bonds as collateral for the credit. This has always been a

---

[23] On 15 October 2008, the ECB announced the 'Temporary expansion of the collateral framework' to be effective from 22 October 2008 until the end of 2009, lowering the rating requirement for all assets except ABS from single A to triple B. On 7 May 2009 it said that this expansion was to be extended until the end of 2011. In March 2010, President Trichet signalled that it was the intention of the ECB Governing Council to keep up this minimum credit threshold beyond 2011, which was then also officially announced on 8 April 2010. This prolongation lacked an expiration date and is still in force. Refer also to European Central Bank, *Measures to Further Expand the Collateral Framework and Enhance the Provision of Liquidity*, 15 October 2008; European Central Bank, *Technical Specifications for the Temporary Expansion of the Collateral Framework*, press release, 17 October 2008, available at: <http://www.ecb.int/press/pr/date/2008/html/pr081017_2.en.html>; European Central Bank, *Longer-Term Refinancing Operations*, press release, 7 May 2009, available at: <http://www.ecb.int/press/pr/date/2009/html/pr090507_2.en.html>; J.-C. Trichet, *Introductory Statement Before the Plenary of the European Parliament*, Brussels, 25 March 2010, available at: <http://www.ecb.int/press/key/date/2010/html/sp100325.en.html>; European Central Bank, *ECB Introduces Graduated Valuation Haircuts for Lower-Rated Assets in its Collateral Framework as of 1 January 2011*, press release, 8 April 2010, available at: <http://www.ecb.int/press/pr/date/2010/html/pr100408_1.en.html>; European Central Bank, *ECB Reviews Risk Control Measures in its Collateral Framework*, press release, 28 July 2010, available at: <http://www.ecb.int/press/pr/date/2010/html/pr100728_1.en.html>.

convenient process for indirect government financing. The process stalled, however, when the rating agencies published negative outlooks for the government bonds of Greece, Portugal, and Ireland and subsequently downgraded these bonds to non-investment grade (Greece in April 2010, Portugal and Ireland in July 2011).[24] The ECB Governing Council reacted by simply exempting the respective government bonds, as well as private securities guaranteed by these governments, from the minimum rating requirements (Greece in May 2010, Portugal in April 2011, Ireland in July 2011, and Cyprus in May 2013).[25] On 3 May 2013 the ECB generalized these exemptions by waiving the minimum rating requirements for countries supported by and compliant with an EU-IMF programme.[26] Moreover, the ECB decided to buy the government bonds of the crisis-stricken countries through its SMP and OMT programmes in order to maintain the value of collateral, as will be discussed in more detail in Chapter 8. All this enabled indebted states to place new government bonds in the market, since the banks were able to buy them with fresh

[24] On 27 April 2010 Standard & Poor's reduced the rating of Greece to BB+, see Standard & Poor's, *Greece Long- and Short-Term Ratings Lowered to 'BB+/B', Outlook Negative, '4' Recovery Rating Assigned to Sovereign Debt*, 27 April 2010, available at: <http://www.standardandpoors.com/products-services/articles/en/us/?assetID= 1245211893945>. Moody's downgraded Portugal on 5 July 2011 to Ba2 and Ireland on 12 July 2011 to Ba1, see Moody's, *Rating Action: Moody's Downgrades Portugal to Ba2 with a Negative Outlook from Baa1*, 5 July 2011, available at: <http://www.moodys.com/ research/Moodys-downgrades-Portugal-to-Ba2-with-a-negative-outlook-from?do cid=PR_222043>; and Moody's, *Rating Action: Moody's Downgrades Ireland to Ba1. Outlook remains negative*, 12 July 2011, available at: <http://www.moodys.com/research/ Moodys-downgrades-Ireland-to-Ba1-outlook-remains-negative?docid=PR_222257#>.

[25] See European Central Bank, *ECB Announces Change in Eligibility of Debt Instruments Issued or Guaranteed by the Greek Government*, press release, 3 May 2010, available at: <http://www.ecb.int/press/pr/date/2010/html/pr100503.en.html>; European Central Bank, *ECB Announces the Suspension of the Rating Threshold for Debt Instruments of the Irish Government*, press release, 31 March 2011, available at: <http://www.ecb.int/ press/pr/date/2011/html/pr110331_2.en.html>; European Central Bank, *ECB Announces Change in Eligibility of Debt Instruments Issued or Guaranteed by the Portuguese Government*, press release, 7 July 2011, available at: <http://www.ecb.int/press/pr/date/2011/html/ pr110707_1.en.html>; European Central Bank, *ECB Announces Change in Eligibility of Marketable Debt Instruments Issued or Guaranteed by the Cypriot Government*, press release, 2 May 2013, available at: <http://www.ecb.int/press/pr/date/2013/html/pr130502_3. en.html>.

[26] This decision made it possible to end the idiosyncratic exceptions for Greece, Ireland and Portugal. See European Central Bank, 'Decision ECB/2012/18', *Official Journal*, L 218/20, 15 August 2012, available at: <http://www.ecb.europa.eu/ecb/legal/pdf/ l_21820120815en00200023.pdf>; also European Central Bank, 'Decision ECB/2013/5',

money that they were drawing from the national printing presses in exchange for pledging these bonds as collateral.

According to the ECB's accounts, the total volume of such indirect state finance, including regional and central governments, was € 452 billion in Q1 2013, most of which was concentrated in the crisis countries.[27] According to J. P. Morgan, by February 2011 39%, or € 56 billion, of the collateral pledged at the Greek central bank consisted of Greek government bonds. Moreover, another 38%, or € 55 billion, was accounted for by securities guaranteed by the Greek state.[28] The measures constituted indirect government financing through the ECB, and prevented the collapse of these states. State guarantees enabled commercial banks to pledge non-tradeable claims and securities as collateral. Since the true value of these assets was not known, given that they were not traded, banks tended to price them at their face value and asked the respective national governments to issue guarantees for them, which the governments did to safeguard cheap ECB credit for their economies. The only problem was that the governmental guarantees were worthless, given that the guaranteeing sovereigns themselves were threatened by insolvency, according to the judgement of the rating agencies.

An important role in the ECB's collateral policy was played by asset-backed securities (ABS). These are structured composite claims on a portfolio of assets that are supposedly safer than the original assets, thanks to internal risk diversification within the portfolio and thanks to the creation of a hierarchy of claims according to the waterfall principle.[29] Banks were allowed to compose these ABS papers from claims they held on private companies and other banks and to pledge them as collateral to their respective NCBs in the Eurosystem. ABS had been explicitly allowed as collateral since at least 2004, provided that they were traded in the market and had a rating of at least single A. As mentioned above, they were left out in the general reduction of collateral requirements to triple B that took place on 25 October 2008. Nevertheless, when the crisis induced commercial banks to replace interbank credit with refinancing credit

---

Official Journal, L 95/21, 5 April 2013, available at: <http://www.ecb.int/ecb/legal/pdf/l_09520130405en00210021.pdf>.

[27] See European Central Bank, *Payments and Markets, Collateral, Collateral Data*, 16 May 2013, available at: <http://www.ecb.europa.eu/paym/pdf/collateral/collateral_data.pdf?d8fde58106fc320aa93eb9244a487513>.

[28] See N. Panigirtzoglou, G. Koo, S. MacGorain and M. Lehmann, '*Flows & Liquidity. Who are the Losers from Greek Debt Restructuring?*', J. P. Morgan, *Global Asset Allocation*, 6 May 2011.

[29] For a detailed description see H.-W. Sinn, *Casino Capitalism*, 2010, chapter 6: *Hot Potatoes*, in particular p. 115 ff.

from their NCBs, ABS became an attractive way to generate the necessary collateral. The stock of ABS used for this purpose increased dramatically, from an average of € 182 billion in 2007 to € 490 billion in 2010.[30] To avoid any potential misuse, the ECB tightened the standard for ABS from single A to triple A on 1 March 2009.[31] However, as the ingredients for such good ABS became scarce, the Governing Council could not maintain this policy. On 19 December 2011 it decided to reduce the minimum rating requirement for ABS backed by residential mortgages or by loans to small and medium-size enterprises to the single A category once again.[32] Moreover, in June 2012 it lowered the minimum rating further, to triple B, the lowest possible investment grade, and applied this reduction to a broad range of securities including residential mortgages, loans to small and medium-size enterprises, commercial mortgages, car loans as well as leasing and consumer loans.[33]

The use of ABS gave banks ample room to mix in dubious claims that would otherwise have been difficult to pledge as collateral on their own. In Ireland, property loans were bundled into packages worth billions and submitted as collateral to the ECB. The resulting non-traded ABS papers were often protected by state guarantees in order to make them eligible as collateral for refinancing operations, despite the low quality of the original securities. Spanish banks were also able to bundle vast amounts of real-estate claims into ABS and to pledge these as collateral to the ECB.

It is well known that ABS instruments played an inglorious role in the US financial crisis, because they had permitted banks to bundle securities of differing quality to receive a better rating, pretending that the diversification would eliminate stochastically independent risks whereas, in fact, many such securities bore highly correlated risks. After the institutional swindle was detected at the outset of the crisis, new issues largely disappeared from the markets,[34] but

---

[30] See European Central Bank, *Payments and Markets, Collateral, Collateral Data*, 16 May 2013.

[31] See European Central Bank, 'Guideline ECB/2009/1', *Official Journal*, L 36/59, 5 February 2009, available at: <http://www.ecb.int/ecb/legal/pdf/l_03620090205en00590061.pdf>.

[32] See European Central Bank, 'Decision ECB/2011/25', *Official Journal*, L 341/65, 22 December 2011, available at: <http://www.ecb.int/ecb/legal/pdf/l_34120111222en00650066.pdf>.

[33] See European Central Bank, 'Decision ECB/2012/11', *Official Journal*, L 175/17, 5 July 2012, available at: <https://www.ecb.int/ecb/legal/pdf/l_17520120705en00170018.pdf>. The lowering to triple B is part of the 'temporary framework', which the ECB introduced in response to the crisis.

[34] For the evolution of issuance volumes before and after the beginning of the crisis, see H.-W. Sinn, *Casino Capitalism*, 2010, chapter 6, Fig. 6.1, p. 114.

they still flourish in the refinancing operations that the ECB permits its banks to perform. The world's savviest investor, Warren Buffet, once called them 'weapons of mass destruction'.[35] Another metaphor often used to describe them is 'sausages' because, as with real sausages, one does not necessarily want to know exactly what ingredients they contain.

The bits of meat that were fed into the ABS sausages were sometimes no longer edible. For instance, a claim was found in a Spanish ABS paper against the Real Madrid football club that had resulted from a loan to purchase football player Cristiano Ronaldo, while in Portugal some securities maturing on 31 December 9999 (this is no typing error) found their way into other ABS.[36] In the meantime, large haircuts for the hopelessly over-indebted football clubs in Spain have been discussed.[37] Such haircuts would deprive the ECB of part of its collateral. Should the banks become insolvent, wobbling as they are from massive volumes of toxic property loans, and fail to repay their refinancing loans, other countries' taxpayers will end up paying for the Real Madrid football players as well.

A strange aspect of the collateral policy is that banks are able to pledge securities issued by the banking sector itself, rather than by other parties such as governments or companies. The condition for accepting such bank bonds is that they be traded on regulated markets or certain non-regulated markets accepted by the ECB. The latter possibility was opened on 25 October 2008.[38]

The possibility of using bank bonds as collateral was closely linked to the so-called STEP market, which is a sort of French enclave controlled by the Banque de France that is run according to national rules. In July 2013, the total amount of outstanding STEP debt securities accepted as collateral and treated as 'eligible marketable assets', even though the STEP market itself was not regulated by the ECB, was € 404 billion, of which € 341 billion was debt issued by financial institutions.[39] The role of the STEP market and other details are explained in the box below.

[35] See 'Buffett Warns on Investment "Time Bomb"', *BBC News*, 4 March 2003, available at: <http://news.bbc.co.uk/2/hi/2817995.stm>.

[36] See 'Zweifelhafte Werte', *Der Spiegel*, No. 23, 6 June 2011, p. 62f, as well as 'Auf schmalem Grat', *Der Spiegel*, No. 21, 23 May 2011, p. 60 f.

[37] See 'Fußball Spanien: Spanische Klubs dürfen auf Schuldenschnitt hoffen', *Handelsblatt*, 12 March 2012, available at: <http://www.handelsblatt.com/fussball-spanien-spanische-klubs-duerfen-auf-schuldenschnitt-hoffen/6314162.html>.

[38] See European Central Bank, 'Decision ECB/2008/11', *Official Journal*, L 282/17, 25 October 2008, available at: <http://www.ecb.int/ecb/legal/pdf/l_28220081025en00170018.pdf>.

[39] See European Central Bank, *Monetary and Financial Statistics, Short-Term European Paper (STEP)*, available at: <http://www.ecb.int/stats/money/step/html/index.en.html>.

BOX 5.1 The STEP market

STEP stands for Short-Term European Paper, commercial securities, including papers issued by financial institutions, with maturities of between a few days and one year, which are not traded on the stock exchange. The STEP market was initiated in 2006 with the aim of integrating European markets for short-term securities through the convergence of market standards and practices. It was first accepted as a non-regulated market for collateral purposes in Eurosystem credit operations in April 2007, but at that time it was taboo to accept securities issued by financial institutions.[40] The ECB broke this taboo in October 2008 for the first time, when it declared STEP-labelled securities issued by banks temporarily eligible as collateral in Eurosystem credit operations, their acceptance being prolonged for another year in December 2009.[41] In September 2011, the ECB made a fundamental change to its 'General documentation on Eurosystem monetary policy instruments and procedures'.[42] It approved the suspension of the eligibility requirement, according to which debt instruments issued by credit institutions are only eligible if traded on a regulated market. Since January 2012, STEPs issued by financial institutions have been eligible for use as collateral in Eurosystem credit operations without any time limitation.

In July 2013 the stock of outstanding STEP securities pledged as collateral was € 404 billion, of which about 84% consisted of papers issued by commercial banks.[43]

The STEP market is managed by EURIBOR-EBF, an organization of the European Banking Federation (EBF) that was recently suspected of having manipulated the prime rate Euribor,[44] and it is supervised by Banque de

(continued)

---

[40] See European Central Bank, *Assessment of STEP for Collateral Purposes in Eurosystem Credit Operations*, press release, 15 September 2006, available at: <http://www.ecb.europa. eu/press/pr/date/2006/html/pr060915.en.html>.

[41] See European Central Bank, *Measures to Further Expand the Collateral Framework and Enhance the Provision of Liquidity*, 15 October 2008; for the prolongation see European Central Bank, *Longer-Term Refinancing Operations*, 7 May 2009.

[42] See European Central Bank, 'Guideline ECB/2011/14', *Official Journal*, L 331, 20 September 2011, available at: <http://www.ecb.int/ecb/legal/pdf/0201100014-20130103-en. pdf>.

[43] For statistical data on the STEP market, see European Central Bank, *Monetary and Financial Statistics, Short-Term European Paper (STEP),* available at: <http://www.ecb. europa.eu/stats/money/step/html/index.en.html>.

[44] See A. White, 'Euribor Should Be Overseen by EU Regulators, EBF Chief Says', *Bloomberg*, 20 July 2012, available at: <http://www.bloomberg.com/news/2012-07-12/ euribor-should-be-overseen-by-eu-regulators-ebf-chief-says.html>.

BOX 5.1 (Continued)

France according to criteria that do not satisfy the ECB's definition of 'regulated markets'.[45]

Detailed data on securities traded are provided by Euroclear France to the Banque de France, but they are not fully reported to the ECB. Euroclear France is an associate of the Euroclear Bank, which is one of the big players in the STEP market. By its own account, it is the world's second largest broker of short-term papers. All this is suggestive of a French monetary policy enclave within the Eurosystem. This impression is corroborated by observing that French banks rely heavily on the STEP market as a means of rapid borrowing. French banks have issued about € 190 billion worth of STEP-labelled bonds altogether, and effectively run the market.[46] It seems that the STEP market is still growing, attracting many new customers, such as banks from Spain and Portugal.

The problem with this acceptance of bank bonds was that banks could mutually issue and trade self-made bonds, which were then eligible as collateral for drawing refinancing credit from their respective NCBs. The only safeguard against misuse was initially that the bank bonds needed to be traded.[47] However, a couple of banks could issue such bonds, mutually trade them, and then use them to draw refinancing credit from their respective NCBs. In effect, this was as if the banks borrowed from the printing press without having to pledge any collateral. The ECB tried to prevent misuse by imposing quantity constraints on the use of uncovered bank bonds from closely linked issuers.[48] Nevertheless, by the end of 2012, the stock of uncovered bank bonds that were in principle eligible as collateral for refinancing operations was € 2.5 trillion, while the stock of such bonds used as collateral was about € 329 billion.[49]

---

[45] See European Central Bank, *Payments and Markets, Collateral, Eligibility Criteria and Assessment, Marketable Assets*, available at: <https://www.ecb.int/paym/coll/standards/marketable/html/index.en.html>.

[46] Refer also to M. Brendel and S. Jost, 'Die europäische Notenpresse gerät außer Kontrolle', *Die Welt*, 6 January 2013, available at: <http://www.welt.de/finanzen/article112420942/Die-europaeische-Notenpresse-geraet-ausser-Kontrolle.html>.

[47] See European Central Bank, 'Guideline ECB/2011/14', 20 September 2011.

[48] See European Central Bank, *Adjustment of Risk Control Measures for Newly Issued Asset-Backed Securities and for Uncovered Bank Bonds*, press release, 20 January 2009, available at: <http://www.ecb.int/press/pr/date/2009/html/pr090120.en.html>.

[49] European Central Bank, *Payments and Markets, Collateral, Collateral Data*, 16 May 2013.

A convenient side-effect of this trade was that it could be used to create equity out of nothing if trading took place above the bonds' face value. In principle, every bank participating in symmetric circular trading could book asset values above the liability it incurred by issuing its own bonds. This is a well-known aspect of circular trading of assets in general.[50]

Another variant of the use of bank bonds is own-use bonds, i.e. bonds that are not traded but issued and provided as collateral by the same bank that requested the refinancing credit. Such own use bonds were accepted by NCBs provided that a national government guaranteed them. Italian banks, for example, pledged € 40 billion worth of own-use bonds as collateral in 2011, and Irish banks did so to the tune of € 18 billion in 2011, and another € 8 billion in March 2013.[51] Greek banks reportedly pledged own-use bonds totalling € 6.4 billion in 2011.[52]

Non-marketable assets accepted as collateral also include direct credit claims on companies. After a heated discussion and against the vote of the Bundesbank, the ECB Council decided on 8 December 2011 to give up the idea of uniform minimum quality standards for collateral by leaving it to individual NCBs to 'accept as collateral for Eurosystem monetary policy operations credit claims that do not satisfy the Eurosystem eligibility criteria'.[53] This policy, which is known as the Additional Credit Claims Framework (ACC), was implemented on 19 December 2011; it meant that individual NCBs were allowed to accept,

---

[50] M. Lewis gave a funny and telling example: 'You have a dog, and I have a cat. We agree that they are each worth a billion dollars. You sell me the dog for a billion, and I sell you the cat for a billion. Now we are no longer pet owners, but Icelandic banks, with a billion dollars in new assets'; see M. Lewis, *Boomerang. Travels in the New Third World*, W.W. Norton & Company, New York 2011, p. 17.

[51] See S. Sirletti and E. Martinuzzi, 'Italy Banks Said to Use State-Backed Bonds for ECB Loans', *Bloomberg*, 21 December 2011, available at: <http://www.bloomberg.com/news/2011-12-20/italian-banks-are-said-to-use-state-guaranteed-bonds-to-receive-ecb-loans.html>; and J. Brennan, 'Irish Banks Aid Funding With Own-Use Bonds Amid Cyprus Woes', *Bloomberg*, 28 March 2013, available at: <http://www.bloomberg.com/news/2013-03-28/irish-banks-aid-funding-with-own-use-bonds-amid-cyprus-woes-1-.html>. See also European Central Bank, *Adjustment of Risk Control Measures for Newly Issued Asset-Backed Securities and for Uncovered Bank Bonds*, 20 January 2009; and European Central Bank, 'Decision ECB/2013/6', *Official Journal*, L 95/22, 5 April 2013, available at: <http://www.ecb.europa.eu/ecb/legal/pdf/l_09520130405en00220022.pdf> (accessed 7 February 2014).

[52] See T. Alloway, 'Greek Banks in € 6.4bn Bond Switch', *Financial Times*, 6 November 2011, available at: <http://www.ft.com/intl/cms/s/0/a008a664-0898-11e1-9fe8-00144feabdco.html#axzz2Z7qWa4rG>.

[53] See European Central Bank, 'Decision ECB/2011/25', 22 December 2011, article 4, paragraph 1.

at their own risk, credit claims with a credit rating below the ECB's scale of acceptable collateral, provided they developed their own eligibility criteria and had them approved by the Governing Council.[54] Only seven out of the 17 NCBs of the Eurosystem, among them most prominently the Banque de France and Banca d'Italia, made use of this option and submitted their idiosyncratic eligibility criteria for approval at the Council Meeting of 9 February 2012.[55] In Q1 2013, the volume of credit claims used as collateral amounted to € 472 billion, which corresponds to 19% of all collateral pledged.

Non-marketable assets accepted as collateral moreover include the above-mentioned government-guaranteed credit claims and other collateralized credit claims, retail mortgage-backed securities and fixed-term deposits from eligible counterparties such as public sector entities or international and supranational institutions. They became a major tool for expanding refinancing credit, and in fact they are the collateral category showing the greatest dynamism. The volume of assets in this category more than tripled from 2007 to 2010, from an average of € 109 billion to € 359 billion, and almost doubled once again to € 644 billion in Q1 2013.[56] The share of all collateral pledged that falls under this category increased from 10% of the total to 26% over this period.

In summary, the combination of longer maturities, extremely low collateral requirements, and a low interest rate meant that the ECB has in effect been significantly underbidding the interbank market for bank credit. This kept the troubled banks and their clients afloat, but it also meant that the role of the private capital market as a screening device for good and bad investment opportunities was largely undermined, an issue upon which this book will elaborate in several later sections. Quite a number of zombie banks were sustained with the implemented measures, and they now need to be recapitalized with public funds in a banking union (see Chapter 8).

To reiterate the point made above, the higher the interest rates the Eurozone banks had to pay in the market, the more the lowering of collateral standards and the prolongation of maturity helped them. Thus, even if strictly identical, but equally generous, collateral policies had been applied in all countries of the

---

[54] European Central Bank, 'Decision ECB/2011/25', 22 December 2011, article 4, paragraph 1; refer also, European Central Bank, *Eurosystem Credit Assessment Framework (ECAF)*.

[55] See European Central Bank, *ECB's Governing Council Approves Eligibility Criteria for Additional Credit Claims*, press release, 9 February 2012, available at: <http://www.ecb.int/press/pr/date/2012/html/pr120209_2.en.html>; also Banque de France, *Eligibility Criteria Regarding Additional Credit Claims*, press release, 9 February 2012, available at: <http://www.banque-france.fr/uploads/tx_bdfgrandesdates/2012-02-9-eligibility.pdf>.

[56] See European Central Bank, *Payments and Markets, Collateral, Collateral Data*, 16 May 2013.

Eurozone, the ECB's risk absorption through the lowering of collateral standards would still have distorted the markets.

However, not even that condition holds, since collateral policies are not as uniform as they seem. The ECB accepts about 38,000 different assets as collateral and uses detailed descriptions and rules for the respective country provisions, acknowledging the different national histories of collateral formation.[57] It has been accused of losing oversight of this system and of being unable to effectively limit the NCBs' scope for idiosyncratic interpretations of the general rules, which has effectively resulted in different eligibility criteria for collateral in the various countries.

A particular problem is the application of haircuts on the collateral pledged to minimize the risk of under-collateralization.[58] While the Eurosystem does use a general system of haircut rules, the NCBs' application of these rules has diverged substantially, because the necessary evaluation is carried out locally. The individual NCBs in particular circumvented the lexicographic ordering of evaluation criteria defined by the ECB, manipulating the ratings of the collateral they accepted so as to increase the stock of eligible collateral that banks could use to draw more refinancing credit.[59]

Moral Hazard

There is broad agreement that the ECB carried out the right policies in the immediate aftermath of the Lehman crisis, when the breakdown of the interbank market called for swift action. However, the long duration and successive extension of the ECB policies, even after the world economy started to recover strongly in the second half of 2009, and in particular the policy of lowering eligible collateral standards to junk levels, gave cause for growing concern.[60] It was

[57] See M. Brendel and S. Jost, 'EZB leistet sich gefährliche Regelverstöße', *Die Welt*, 11 July 2013, available at: http://www.welt.de/wirtschaft/article115063852/EZB-leistet-s ich-gefaehrliche-Regelverstoesse.html; also European Central Bank, *Payments and Markets, Collateral, Eligibility Criteria and Assessment, Marketable Assets*.

[58] See M. Brendel and C. Pauly, 'Europe's Central Bad Bank: Junk Bonds Weigh Heavy on ECB', *Spiegel Online International*, 6 June 2011, available at: <http://www.spiegel. de/international/europe/europe-s-central-bad-bank-junk-bonds-weigh-heavy-on-ecb-a-766856.html>; M. Brendel and S. Jost, 'EZB leistet sich gefährliche Regelverstöße', 11 July 2013.

[59] See M. Brendel and S. Jost, 'EZB leistet sich gefährliche Regelverstöße', 11 July 2013, and J. Eberl and C. Weber, 'ECB Collateral Criteria: A Narrative Database 2001-2013', February 2014, pp. 14–15.

[60] See, for example, J. Rocholl, 'Die Finanzflut der EZB ist gefährlich', *Handelsblatt*, 29 February 2012, available at: http://www.handelsblatt.com/meinung/gastbeitraege/ gastkommentar-die-finanzflut-der-ezb-ist-gefaehrlich/6267948.html>; and J. Rocholl,

feared that the ECB was bailing out banks and their creditors, interfering in the process well beyond the realm of monetary policy.

Bundesbank president Jens Weidmann expressed these concerns when he wrote a widely cited letter to ECB President Mario Draghi in early 2012, the content of which was leaked to the press, complaining about the low quality of the collateral being pledged by banks when drawing refinancing credit from their local central banks.[61] The smouldering conflict between the Bundesbank and the ECB, which started with the ECB's government bond purchases in May 2010 (SMP, see Chapter 8) and led to the resignations in 2011 of Bundesbank President Axel Weber and the ECB chief economist, Jürgen Stark, flared up with this letter.

In theory, the ECB was carrying out monetary policy, helping out with liquidity where needed. In practice, it was bailing out private banks and their creditors with credit from the printing press. In order for the liquidity interpretation to prevail, it would have been necessary for the ECB to stick to a policy of requiring first-rate collateral. Obviously it not only deviated from this policy, but turned it on its head by throwing all caution to the wind with its multifaceted and opaque system of collateral standards.

One may wonder where the incentives for reducing the collateral requirements so dramatically came from. An explanation lies in a classical moral hazard problem resulting from the fact that the cost of bank failures, in terms of write-off losses on the ECB's refinancing credit, is being socialized within the Eurosystem, which pools the returns and losses from monetary policy operations among the participating central banks and hence the national budgets, to which the profit distribution of the Eurosystem flows (see Chapter 1). This moral hazard effect explains the controversial collateral decisions taken by a majority of the ECB Governing Council against the fierce, but futile opposition of a minority. It also explains why the governments and NCBs of the crisis-stricken countries were eager to resort to the local printing presses by stretching the Eurosystem's collateral rules to the limits, enabling local banks to buy government bonds and lend funds to the private economy even though private investors were shunning

'Die EZB und die Kunst des Unmöglichen', *Handelsblatt*, 14 May 2012; see also M. J. M. Neumann, 'Die Europäische Zentralbank auf Abwegen', *Argumente zu Marktwirtschaft und Politik*, No. 116, Stiftung Marktwirtschaft und Politik, March 2012; A. Sibert, 'The Damaged ECB Legitimacy', *VoxEU*, 15 September 2011, available at: <http://www.voxeu.org/article/damaged-ecb-legitimacy>; S. Eijffinger and L. Hoogduin, 'The European Central Bank in (the) Crisis', *CESifo DICE Report*, 10, No. 1, pp. 32–38, January 2012, available at: <http://www.cesifo-group.de/DocDL/dicereport112-forum6.pdf>.

[61] See S. Ruhkamp, 'Die Bundesbank fordert von der EZB bessere Sicherheiten', *Frankfurter Allgemeine Zeitung*, 2 February 2012, available at: <http://www.faz.net/aktuell/wirtschaft/schuldenkrise-die-bundesbank-fordert-von-der-ezb-bessere-sicherheiten-11667413.html>.

domestic borrowers. The immediate benefits of the cash flow generated by the new credit, in terms of preserving asset prices, the infrastructure, jobs, pensions and wages, remained in the national economy, whereas if the debtors and the banks that lent them the money should fail, part of the losses would be shared by the community of Eurosystem states.[62] Actually, this incentive is particularly large for small countries, whose own proportional share in a euro lost by providing unsound refinancing credit is negligible. The fact that the smaller countries, in turn, have much larger voting rights per capita than the bigger ones (see Chapter 1) appears very problematic in this regard.

A counterargument to this interpretation could be that the ECB thus far has avoided major losses from its risk-taking strategy. But, as will be argued in Chapter 8, this argument overlooks the fact that the prior decisions of the ECB Governing Council to impose the risk of bankruptcies on the taxpayers of the Eurozone prejudiced the subsequent choices of parliaments and forced through a later repackaging of risks by establishing huge fiscal rescue funds. Eventually it may even turn the Eurozone into a transfer union, forcing one group of countries to transfer resources to another so as to prevent the latter's banks from defaulting.

The ECB has not openly reacted to these concerns, but has repeatedly stated that, despite the lowering of collateral standards, it sees no risk in the credit granted, since the haircuts it applies to the collateral are sufficient. It observes the market value of collateral on a daily basis and if this value falls, it will immediately demand additional collateral or withdraw the credit.[63] Unfortunately, however, the ECB has to this date published no statistics on which securities it has accepted as collateral and which deductible it has applied; nor has it published information on how well this safeguarding strategy has functioned in practice.[64]

---

[62] A similar argument was made by C. B. Blankart 'Goldgräber bedrohen Euroland', in D. Meyer (ed.), *Die Zukunft der Währungsunion. Chancen und Risiko des Euros*, LIT-Verlag, Berlin 2012, pp. 291–295. Another type of common-pool problem is described by Aaron Tornell and Frank Westermann. They argue that under the euro, each single NCB has an incentive to over-extend the printing press as the burden of higher inflation is imposed on all countries, while the benefits accrue at home. See A. Tornell, 'Target2 Imbalances and the Dynamic Tragedy-of-the-Commons in the Eurozone', *UCLA Mimeo*, September 2012; A. Tornell and F. Westermann, 'The Tragedy-of-the-Commons at the European Central Bank and the Next Rescue Operation', *VoxEU,* 22 June 2012, available at: <http://www.voxeu.org/article/tragedy-commons-european-central-bank>. See also C. B. Blankart, 'Oil and Vinegar—A Positive Fiscal Theory of the Euro Crisis', forthcoming in *Kyklos*.

[63] See also European Central Bank, 'Guideline ECB/2011/14', 20 September 2011, especially p. 51.

[64] There is only general information available in European Central Bank, 'Haircut Schedule for Assets Eligible for Use as Collateral in Eurosystem Market Operations', *Monetary Policy*, Collateral, Risk Mitigation, Liquidity Categories, available at: <http://www.ecb.int/press/pr/date/2010/html/sp090728_1annex.en.pdf?56d9b9db6fddaf7fcd28e bcd6706e630>.

Moreover, of course, adjusting the haircuts to daily fluctuations in market values only makes sense for traded assets, not for the 26% of all collateral that is non-traded.

Even when assets are traded, the haircut policy is no safeguard against the ECB incurring losses. By reducing the rating quality requirement to extremely low levels, even below investment grade, the ECB has subjected itself to the risk of a sudden default on a country's debt, which could instantly reduce its bonds' market value by a multiple of the haircut applied, without it being possible for the ECB to demand additional collateral. If the ECB, in a financial crisis, declared only some collateral insufficient, it would limit the banks' access to refinancing credit, which would reduce their demand for the bonds they could submit as collateral, thereby annihilating the available collateral.

Such a situation occurred in late February 2012 with Greek government bonds accepted as collateral by the Greek NCB, after the Greek parliament increased its pressure on holders of Greek government bonds to 'voluntarily' accept relinquishing part of their claims. The parliament announced that it would change the contractual conditions for government bonds (the so-called collective action clauses) from that point on in such a way that cuts would be forced upon those bondholders who did not voluntarily agree to waive part of their claims, an agreement as voluntary as a confession before the Spanish Inquisition.[65] After this announcement, the value of Greek bonds plummeted and the collateral for the outstanding refinancing credit provided by the Greek central bank was apparently no longer sufficient. Neither was it possible for the Greek commercial banks to provide additional collateral. As a result, the ECB saw itself forced on 28 February 2012 to waive the collateral requirement altogether, and to ask the Greek NCB to convert the collateralized refinancing credit into mere ELA credit, a form of emergency credit available at milder conditions.[66] When the debt moratorium was completed, it again accepted Greek government bonds as collateral, but on 25 July 2012 Greek bonds came under so much renewed pressure that the ECB had to ask the Greek NCB to resort to ELA loans once again.[67]

---

[65] See Greek Ministry of Finance, *Rules for the Amendment of Securities, Issued or Guaranteed by the Greek Government by Consent of the Bondholders*, 23 February 2012, available at: <http://www.hellenicparliament.gr/en/Nomothetiko-Ergo/Anazitisi-Nomothetikou-Ergou?law_id=3b426740-db7b-471a-9829-80a89a6518b5>.

[66] See European Central Bank, *Eligibility of Greek Bonds Used as Collateral in Eurosystem Monetary Policy Operations*, press release, 28 February 2012, available at: <http://www.ecb.int/press/pr/date/2012/html/pr120228.en.html>.

[67] See European Central Bank, *Collateral Eligibility of Bonds Issued or Guaranteed by the Greek Government*, press release, 20 July 2012, available at: <http://www.ecb.de/press/pr/date/2012/html/pr120720.en.html>; and D. Szarek, 'Jetzt drucken sich die Griechen ihre Euro selbst', *Focus*, 25 July 2012, available at: <http://www.focus.de/finanzen/

When the euro was first discussed some 20 years ago, one of the arguments for it was that it would impose more debt discipline on the countries of southern Europe that were used to solving their debt problems with the printing press. When national currencies prevailed, governments borrowed excessively and used to sell some of their bonds to commercial banks, which bought them with refinancing credit from the national printing press, a process that led to both inflation and currency depreciation. The euro, so the argument went, would induce more discipline because governments would have to borrow in a currency that they could not print, akin to borrowing in a foreign currency.

This view unfortunately turned out to be wrong, since the indebted countries had the majority in the ECB Governing Council and could, in fact, change the rules of local money printing at their discretion. The situation was even better than before, as the currency they allowed their local central banks to print and issue as refinancing credit was accepted as legal tender elsewhere in the Eurozone and could be used to buy goods or assets there. This will be discussed in more detail in the following two chapters.

And not even a majority in the ECB Governing Council was necessary to activate the local money printing presses. The ELA credit mentioned above clearly resembled a self-service facility.

ELA Credit

ELA is an acronym for 'Emergency Liquidity Assistance'. It consists of credit that the NCBs can give their commercial banks at their own risk, unless two-thirds of the ECB Governing Council oppose the operation.[68] In 2013, 8 out of 23 members of the Governing Council, i.e. slightly more than a third of the council members, were nationals of GIPSIC countries (see Figure 1.6) that needed cheap credit. In other crisis years the GIPSIC countries accounted for an even higher share of the votes. (Only with the entry of Latvia in 2014 have the GIPSIC countries lost the necessary quorum.) Thus, a blocking coalition of other nationals in the Governing Council was impossible. Theoretically, the nationals of the GIPSIC countries in the Council could have provided their countries with as much credit from the printing press as they wished, and no one would have been able to stop them.

news/staatsverschuldung/banken-refinanzieren-sich-ueber-notkredite-die-ezb-schal tet-auf-stur-also-schoepfen-sich-die-griechen-ihr-geld-selber_aid_786691.html>.

[68] See also article 14.4. of the ECB Statute, *Protocol of the Statute of the European System of Central Banks and of the European Central Bank*, available at: <http://www.ecb.int/ecb/ legal/pdf/en_statute_2.pdf>; and European Central Bank, *Annual Report 1999*, p. 98 f, available at: <http://www.ecb.europa.eu/pub/pdf/annrep/ar1999en.pdf>.

Voluminous ELA credit has been drawn from the Eurosystem by the central banks of Greece, Ireland, and Cyprus, and they indeed were close to bankruptcy when they used this tool. For Ireland the maximum stock of ELA credit was € 70 billion (February 2011), or 43% of 2012 GDP, for Greece it was € 126 billion (May 2012) or 64% of 2012 GDP, and for Cyprus it was € 11 billion (April 2013) or 64% of 2012 GDP.[69] In total it seems that the ECB Council tolerated ELA credit of up to € 251 billion, the peak reached in June 2012. By December 2013, the outstanding stock of ELA credit had declined to € 75 billion, largely because it had been replaced with other rescue credit.[70]

The reason for the low hurdle to using ELA credit is the assertion that this credit does not impose a liability risk upon other countries, as the issuing NCB itself would have to bear any write-off losses. Basically, it is seen as a country's own affair without implications for the rest of the Eurozone as long as it does not interfere with the single monetary policy. This has been repeatedly stressed by ECB representatives including, for example, Jörg Asmussen, a member of the ECB board, at an official hearing of the German Constitutional Court on 11 June 2013.[71] This view is at best a half-truth, since the Eurosystem does indeed bear a liability risk if the ELA credit is large enough, as will be explained below.

As Chapter 1 showed, income from monetary operations is normally pooled among the Eurosystem members. Formally, ELA credit is an exception, but the actual way of calculating interest remittances in the Eurosystem qualifies this exception. ELA credit is lent out by an NCB to commercial banks at a rate of interest that is usually one percentage point higher than the ECB's

---

[69] See Central Bank of Ireland, *Financial Statement of the Central Bank of Ireland*, items 'Other Claims on "Euro Area Credit Institutions" and "Other Assets"', available at: <http://www.centralbank.ie/polstats/stats/cmab/pages/money%20and%20obanking. aspx>, Central Bank of Greece, *Monthly Balance Sheet*, May 2013, items 'Other Claims on Euro Area Credit Institutions Denominated in Euro' and 'Sundry', available at: <http://www.bankofgreece.gr/BogEkdoseis/financialstat201205_en.pdf>; and Central Bank of Cyprus, *Monthly Balance Sheets*, April 2013, item 'Other Claims on Euro Area Credit Institutions Denominated in Euro', available at: <http://www.centralbank.gov.cy/media/pdf/BALANCE_SHEET_APRIL_2013_EN.pdf>. As of December 2013, the stock of ELA credit granted in Greece was € 19 billion, in Ireland € 2 billion, and in Cyprus € 10 billion.

[70] See European Central Bank, *Consolidated Financial Statement of the Eurosystem as at 31 December 2013*, available at: <http://www.ecb.europa.eu/press/pr/wfs/2014/html/fs140108.en.html>. ELA credits are not explicitly reported in the ECB balance sheet. However, the term 'Other Claims on Euro Area Credit Institutions in Euro' is usually taken as an approximation. It reached a maximum of € 251 billion in June 2012.

[71] See J. Asmussen, *Statement by the ECB in the Proceedings Before the Federal Constitutional Court*, Karlsruhe, 11 June 2013, to the Constitutional Complaint 2 BvR 1390/12, 2 BvR 1439/12 and 2 BvR 1824/12, 2 BvE 6/12.

main refinancing rate. While the interest surcharge remains with the NCB as compensation for the risk it is claimed to be assuming, the NCB effectively has to share the portion of the interest that it would have collected from normal refinancing credit with the other NCBs. The reason for this is that, given the monetary base of the Eurosystem, ELA credit reduces the scope for ordinary refinancing credit elsewhere in the Eurosystem, together with the corresponding interest revenue.[72]

To understand the risk that ELA credit imposes on the Eurosystem, it is useful to note that the value of a loan is equal to the present value of an infinite interest stream generated by this loan and a chain of equal replacement loans that finance the payment of principal at maturity. Normally, when a bank cannot repay its refinancing credit and the collateral pledged turns out to be worthless, the losses are borne by the entire Eurosystem, in the sense that the interest stemming from the corresponding credit chain no longer flows into the pool, while the country in question still receives its share of the overall remaining Eurosystem interest revenue from monetary policy operations. Despite the short maturity of refinancing credit, the Eurosystem's loss is permanent since, given the time path of the monetary base, it is not possible to recoup the interest losses by issuing more refinancing credit to replace the defaulting refinancing credit. The interest losses are permanently shared among the members of the Eurosystem in proportion to their respective capital keys. This is true regardless of the accounting rules that specify how the write-off losses are to be booked.

By contrast, in the case of default on an ELA loan, liability falls upon the issuing NCB, and thus on the state it belongs. The NCB in this case has to accept forever a liability that leads to a corresponding permanent reduction in interest received from the Eurosystem. This seems to fit the above narrative.

However, when an NCB has issued so much ELA credit that its entitlement to the Eurosystem's pool of interest revenue is smaller than the interest on ELA credit that it has to deliver to the pool, that NCB has to consume the income from assets financed with equity capital to fulfil its obligations. If that income is not high enough, the Eurosystem will share in the ELA losses. Thus, the

---

[72] Information provided by the Bundesbank. Contrary to this, it has been argued that the interest remains with the NCB and flows to the national treasury. See W. Buiter, J. Michels, and E. Rahbari, 'ELA: An Emperor Without Clothes?', *Global Economics View*, Citigroup Global Markets, 2011; on p. 2 the authors claim: 'article 14.4 thus highlights that, as the decisions regarding ELA are taken by the NCBs themselves, the costs and liabilities arising from ELA support are not pooled or shared by the other members of the Eurosystem. In particular, unlike operations carried out as part of the functions of the Eurosystem, any resulting gains or losses are not pooled and shared with the other members of the Eurosystem'.

Eurosystem will risk ELA write-off losses if a country's ELA credit exceeds the sum of the present value of this country's entitlement to the pool's interest income and its own equity capital. While legally the NCB remains liable, in such a situation it actually cannot fulfil its payment obligations.

It may be speculated that the state has an implicit liability, forcing it to endow its NCB with new equity capital, but this is a grey zone without clear and binding rules. The statutes of the Eurosystem definitely do not foresee such a recapitalization.[73] In all likelihood, therefore, the Eurosystem will itself suffer the losses.

Under static conditions, the critical level beyond which the liability for additional ELA credit becomes indistinguishable from that of a normal refinancing credit is where an NCB's stock of ELA credit (the present value of its ELA interest obligations) equals the sum of its equity capital and its capital-key share in the Eurosystem's monetary base (the latter being the present value of the NCB's entitlements to the Eurosystem's interest pool). During the crisis, the total stock of ELA credit exceeded this critical level by up to 144% in Greece, 276% in Ireland and 244% in Cyprus.[74] This shows that the idea of ELA credit being issued at an NCB's own risk (and therefore not needing a majority in the Governing Council) is a myth.

Given that an NCB can itself decide on the provision of ELA credit, it is tempting for officials faced with the near-bankruptcy of their country's banking system to use this kind of credit to delay the bankruptcy and bail out important bank creditors, allowing them to bolt before disaster strikes. This seems to have occurred with at least some of the € 11 billion in Cypriot ELA credit, of which

---

[73] See 'Protocol (No 4) on the Statute of the European System of Central Banks and of the European Central Bank', *Official Journal of the European Union*, C 83/230 EN, 30 March 2010, article 33.2.

[74] The equity capital in all cases is measured including the revaluation reserves. The figures mentioned refer to November 2012 (Greece), February 2011 (Ireland) and April 2013 (Cyprus). To understand the calculation, let us look at the Irish figures in detail. In February 2011, the Irish stock of ELA credit (other claims on euro area credit institutions in euro and other assets) was € 70.3 billion. However, as the Irish capital key was 1.6% and the aggregate stock of base money in the Eurosystem was € 1.057 trillion, the present value of the Irish interest entitlement from this pool under static conditions was only € 16.8 billion. The Bank of Ireland's capital and reserves amounted to € 1.7 billion, and its revaluation account, which is also equity capital, was € 0.2 billion, the total stock of equity therefore being € 1.9 billion, and the sum of equity and present value of interest entitlements was € 18.7 billion. Thus, the ratio of ELA credit generated in the Irish banking system, implying interest to be delivered to the pool, and the sum of equity and the present value of interest entitlements from the pool, was 3.76, implying that the former was 276% bigger than the latter.

€ 9.5 billion, or over half of Cypriot GDP, went to Laiki Bank.[75] This was clearly stated by Cyprus's President Nicos Anastasiades in a letter to ECB President Mario Draghi that was leaked to the public. According to Anastasiades, Laiki Bank was already bankrupt when it received the ELA credit, but the credit was used to bridge a change in government and make elections possible.[76] The bank eventually defaulted in March 2013.[77] An intergovernmental rescue package of € 10 billion, 56% of GDP, was then provided to Cyprus to avoid a sovereign default. While this protected the ECB from write-off losses, because it shifted its risk onto the rescue funds, it makes little difference to the taxpayers. They will either have to replace the ECB's seignorage losses, stand in for the losses of the rescue funds, or finance subsequent transfers to Cyprus to protect the rescue funds from admitting the losses.

ELA credit is supposed to help banks overcome liquidity crises but not to delay insolvency. It is also not meant to provide relief to local governments, which might wish to rescue banks in trouble, because this would violate article 123 TFEU, which forbids a state finance with the printing press. However, these constraints have not always worked in practice.

A clear abuse occurred in Greece in the last quarter of 2012, when the Troika had temporarily stopped the disbursement of a new tranche of intergovernmental rescue credit, because Greece hat not fulfilled all of its conditions. As this would have triggered a default of Greece, the Greek central bank issued ELA credit to the banks, which then helped the government. The ECB Governing Council tolerated this use of the ELA credit to bridge the gap, as no one wanted to pull the plug on the country.

[75] See K. C. Engelen, 'From Deauville to Cyprus', *The International Economy*, Spring 2013, pp. 51–53, 73–76.

[76] Anastasiades further cites the confession made at a press conference on 28 March 2013 by the Greek NCB Governor at the time of the ELA credit, Panicos Demetriades: 'Emergency Liquidity Assistance for Laiki reached 60 percent of the GDP of Cyprus. This was not pleasant, but we had to sustain Laiki in order for the elections to take place'; see also K. C. Engelen, 'From Deauville to Cyprus', Spring 2013.

[77] See H.-J. Dübel, *Bewertung des Bankenrestrukturierungsprogramms in Zypern und seiner Auswirkungen auf Konzepte und Institutionen der Bankenunion*, Kurzgutachten im Auftrag der SPD-Bundestagsfraktion, Finpolconsult, Berlin, 18 April 2013, available at: <http://www.finpolconsult.de/mediapool/16/169624/data/Zypern_Bankenrestrukturierung_Finpolconsult_4_18_13.pdf>; and H.-J. Dübel, *Creditor Participation in Banking Crisis in the Eurozone—A Corner Turned? Empirical Analysis of Current Bank Liability Management and Restructuring Policies with Conclusions for the European Bank Restructuring and Resolution Framework*, Finpolconsult, Berlin, 28 June 2013, available at: <http://www.finpolconsult.de/mediapool/16/169624/data/Duebel_Bank_Creditor_Participation_Eurozone_Final.pdf>.

In the case of Ireland, the stock of ELA credit was used to compensate for two rapid waves of capital flight that took place in 2008 and 2010 (see Chapter 7, Figure 7.3). In the meantime, the outstanding credit has come down from the € 70 billion mentioned to only € 2.4 billion. The reason was partly that Ireland's economy recovered rapidly thanks to a huge real devaluation, as shown in the previous chapter, but also, and more importantly, to Ireland having received intergovernmental aid in exchange (see also Chapter 7). The largest chunk of the reduction can be attributed to the fact that € 40 billion in ELA credit granted to the Irish Bank Resolution Corporation (IBRC), the bad bank created out of the remainders of the near-bankrupt Anglo-Irish bank, was converted into low-interest long-term government bonds with an average maturity of over 34 years and handed over to the Bank of Ireland when IBRC defaulted in February 2013.[78] That way the potential write-off losses were converted into long-term interest losses, which are basically the same in present-value terms, but have the advantage of not having to be reckoned in today's accounts by the Bank of Ireland.

For the Eurosystem, this conversion of ELA credit into government bonds held by the Bank of Ireland was neutral, inasmuch as it continued to receive the same interest from the Bank of Ireland as if the ELA credit had persisted. However, by accepting the deal, the Eurosystem has effectively extended the maturity of a refinancing credit, which originally was intended to be extremely short-term, to the maturity of long-term government bonds, without demanding a higher yield as the market would have done. This deal has nothing to do with monetary policy, but is outright state financing, blatantly violating article 123 of the EU Treaty and imposing part of the risk of default of the Irish state on the Eurosystem without paying a risk premium.

The Irish example aroused the interest of other countries too. Cypriot President Nikos Anastasiades wrote a letter to the EU Commission, the ECB, and the IMF in June 2013 suggesting the same deal for his country.[79] However, his request has been rejected for the time being.

The repackaging from ordinary refinancing credit to ELA credit, and from ELA credit to a more direct credit at reduced interest rates from the ECB system or the rescue funds, shows that the ECB's collateralization strategy is not at all

---

[78] See Central Bank of Ireland, *Central Bank Statement*, 7 February 2013, available at: <http://www.centralbank.ie/press-area/press-releases/Pages/CentralBankStatement. aspx>. The former ECB chief economist Jürgen Stark classified this as prohibited state financing; see J. Stark, 'Irlands verbotener "Deal" mit der Notenbank', *Die Welt*, 14 March 2013, available at: <http://www.welt.de/finanzen/article113645427/Irlands-verbotener-D eal-mit-der-Notenbank.html>.

[79] See R. Berschens, 'Wieder Notruf aus Zypern', *Handelsblatt*, No. 116, 20 June 2013, p. 10.

riskless, and wholly insufficient to protect the member states of the Eurosystem from losses in the case of a sovereign bankruptcy. Repackaging risks does not make them smaller, it only changes their appearance. With its policies, the ECB has drifted far from its duty of conducting monetary policy, increasingly acting instead as a lender of last resort for countries on an ongoing basis. Eventually, EU taxpayers will be hurt by this strategy, as they will have to bear the ECB's losses or those of the intergovernmental rescue funds that bail out the ECB, or the losses of subsequent transfer systems, yet to be established in the Eurozone, that bail out the rescue funds.

CHAPTER 6

The European Balance-of-Payments Crisis

The Target Balances—Ballooning Target Balances—Why Target Balances are a
Measure of Credit—Target Balances as a Public Capital Export—Inside Money, Outside
Money, and the Local Printing Press—Crowding out Refinancing Credit in the North

The Target Balances

While it is extremely difficult to understand and keep an overview of the multitude of ECB policy decisions that helped the crisis countries to draw replacement credit from the local printing presses, the so-called Target balances—first published and analysed by the Ifo Institute—make starkly, and accurately, clear the full dimension of the ECB's rescue activities.[1] Until recently, political decision-makers at the European or national level knew very little about Target balances and, apparently, often preferred it that way in order to spare

---

[1] This and the following sections are based on H.-W. Sinn and T. Wollmershäuser, 'Target Loans, Current Account Balances and Capital Flows: The ECB's Rescue Facility', *International Tax and Public Finance* 19, 2012, pp. 468–508, available at: <http://www.cesifo-group.de/DocDL/sinn-itax-2012-target.pdf>, previous versions of which were published as *NBER Working Paper* No. 17626, November 2011, <http://www.cesifo-group.de/DocDL/NBER_wp17626_sinn_wollm.pdf>, and *CESifo Working Paper* No. 3500, June 2011, available at: <http://www.cesifo-group.de/DocDL/cesifo1_wp3500.pdf>. See also H.-W. Sinn, 'Die Target-Kredite der deutschen Bundesbank', *ifo Schnelldienst* 65, Special Issue, 21 March 2012, pp. 3–34, available at: <http://www.cesifo-group.de/DocDL/Sd_Sonderausgabe_20120321.pdf>. These scholarly publications followed short opinion pieces written previously by the author that defined Target

themselves the burden of having to deal with the issue, exculpating themselves with an allusion to the independence of the ECB. However, after the
issue became a much-talked-about topic in financial circles and the rating agency
Moody's changed the outlook of Germany from 'stable' to 'negative', emphasizing

balances in terms of current accounts and capital accounts and explained the basic
issue: H.-W. Sinn, 'Die riskante Kreditersatzpolitik der EZB', *Frankfurter Allgemeine
Zeitung*, No. 103, 4 May 2011, p. 10, available at: <http://www.faz.net/aktuell/wirtschaft/
europas-schuldenkrise/target-kredite-die-riskante-kreditersatzpolitik-der-ezb-1637926.
html>, and, similarly in English, H.-W. Sinn, 'The ECB's Stealth Bailout', *VoxEU*, 1
June 2011, available at: <http://www.voxeu.org/article/ecb-s-stealth-bailout>. The first
public statement about the alarming levels that the balances had reached was published
in H.-W. Sinn, 'Neue Abgründe', *Wirtschaftswoche*, No. 8, 21 February 2011, p. 35. An
English translation was published as an international press release by the Ifo Institute
as: 'Deep Chasms', *ifo Viewpoint* No. 122, 29 March 2011, available at: <http://www.ifo.
de/Viewpoint_122/w/4XRFPXeMj>. Two days later the first statement, containing similar information, appeared on the internet: see J. Whittaker, 'Intra-eurosystem Debts',
Lancaster University Working Paper, 31 March 2011, available at: <http://eprints.lancs.
ac.uk/51933/4/eurosystem.pdf>. The first calculation of the Bundesbank's exposure to
other countries' Target liabilities, as determined by its share in the ECB's capital key, was
presented in H.-W. Sinn, 'Tickende Zeitbombe', *Süddeutsche Zeitung*, No. 77, 2 April
2011, p. 24. There were some early misinterpretations of the author's opinion pieces,
which led to an internet debate that rapidly snowballed and cannot possibly be documented here. For this see the appendix to the above mentioned CESifo working paper, as
well as H.-W. Sinn, 'On and off Target', *VoxEU*, 14 June 2011, available at: <http://www.
voxeu.org/article/and-target>. Target imbalances were originally thought to be limited
to the transition period from fixed exchange rates to the introduction of the euro (stage
III of the currency union). The problems that could arise during this period were discussed by P. M. Garber, 'Notes on the Role of Target in a Stage III Crisis', *NBER Working
Paper* No. 6619, 1998, and, P. M. Garber, 'The Target Mechanism: Will it Propagate
or Stifle a Stage III Crisis?', *Carnegie—Rochester Conferences on Public Policy* 51, 1999,
pp. 195–220. Later, in December 2010, Garber reportedly also wrote an internal text for
Deutsche Bank about which this author was informed, after his own publications in
spring 2011, by Thomas Mayer, Deutsche Bank, and which was *subsequently* published
on the internet. See P. M. Garber, 'The Mechanics of intra Euro Capital Flight', *Deutsche
Bank Economics Special Report*, December 2010. Garber, however, did not have at his
disposal, at the time of his writing, the panel data set on Target balances of the Eurozone
countries that Sinn and Wollmershäuser assembled, and did not discuss the macroeconomic relationships between capital accounts, current account balances and Target balances, or the relationship between the balance of payments and Target balances. The
author himself was made aware of the Target problem by former Bundesbank President
Helmut Schlesinger in early autumn 2010, during a meeting of the Scientific Advisory
Council of the German Ministry of Economics. Up to this day, the ECB has not published a coherent set of Target statistics.

Germany's Target risk,[2] the political silence has come to an end and spawned a wide range of scholarly publications.[3]

The issue became a hot political topic when Jens Weidmann, the Bundesbank president, expressed his concern about the Bundesbank's Target

---

[2] Moody's, *Moody's Changes the Outlook to Negative on Germany, Netherlands, Luxembourg and Affirms Finland's AAA Stable Rating*, 31 July 2012, London, available at: <https://www.moodys.com/research/Moodys-changes-the-outlook-to-negative-on-Germany-Netherlands-Luxembourg--PR_251214>. The agency's statement read: 'The second and interrelated driver of the change in outlook to negative is the increase in contingent liabilities [...] The contingent liabilities stem from bilateral loans, the EFSF, the European Central Bank (ECB) via the holdings in the Securities Market Programme (SMP) and the Target 2 balances, and—once established—the European Stability Mechanism (ESM)'.

[3] Following the initial articles of H.-W. Sinn and T. Wollmershäuser, 'Target Loans, Current Account Balances and Capital Flows: The ECB's Rescue Facility', 2012, a first round of scholarly responses, including authors from the ECB and the Bundesbank, was published by the Ifo Institute in August 2011, in a special issue of Ifo Schnelldienst: 'Die europäische Zahlungsbilanzkrise', *ifo Schnelldienst* 64, No. 16, 31 August 2011, available at: <http://www.cesifo-group.de/DocDL/SD-16-2011.pdf>. An English translation of this volume was published as a special issue of CESifo Forum in January 2012; see, H.-W. Sinn (ed.), 'The European Balance of Payments Crisis', *CESifo Forum* 13, Special Issue, January 2012, available at: <http://www.cesifo-group.de/DocDL/Forum-Sonderheft-Jan-2012.pdf>. The following provides the names of contributing authors, the respective titles of their articles in English and page references: H.-W. Sinn, 'The European Balance of Payments Crisis: An Introduction', pp. 3–10; H. Schlesinger, 'The Balance of Payments Tells Us the Truth', pp. 11–13; W. Kohler, 'The Eurosystem in Times of Crises: Greece in the Role of a Reserve Currency Country?', pp. 14–22; C. B. Blankart, 'The Euro in 2084', pp. 23–28; M. J. M. Neumann, 'The Refinancing of Banks Drives Target Debt', pp. 29–32; P. Bernholz, 'The Current Account Deficits of the GIPS Countries and Their Target Debts at the ECB', pp. 33–34; T. Mayer, J. Möbert, and C. Weistroffer, 'Macroeconomic Imbalances in EMU and the Eurosystem', pp. 35–42; G. Milbradt, 'The Derailed Policies of the ECB', pp. 43–49; S. Homburg, 'Notes on the Target2 Dispute', pp. 50–54; F. L. Sell and B. Sauer, 'Money, Capital Markets and Welfare: An Analysis of the Effects of Target2 Balances', pp. 55–62; I. Sauer, 'The Dissolving Asset Backing of the Euro', pp. 63–72; J. Ulbrich and A. Lipponer, 'Balances in the Target2 Payments System—A Problem?', pp. 73–76; C. Fahrholz and A. Freytag, 'A Way to Solve the European Balance of Payments Crisis? Take a Chance on Market Solutions!', pp. 77–82; U. Bindseil, P. Cour-Thimann, and P. J. König, 'Target2 and Cross-border Interbank Payments during the Financial Crisis', pp. 83–92; F.-C. Zeitler, 'Ways Out of the European Sovereign Debt Crisis after the Decisions of the July 2011 Summit', pp. 93–95; K. Reeh, 'Balance of Payments Adjustment in the Monetary Union: Current Events Help Shed New Light on an Old Question', pp. 96–101, and A. Tornell and F. Westermann, 'Greece: The Sudden Stop That Wasn't', pp. 102–103. See moreover U. Bindseil and P. J. König, 'TARGET2 and the European Sovereign Debt Crisis', *Kredit und Kapital* 45, 2012, pp. 135–174; U. Bindseil and A. Winkler, 'Dual Liquidity Crises - A Financial Accounts Framework', *Review of International*

claims, asking in the letter mentioned in the previous chapter for them to be collateralized, and complaining about the low collateral standards for refinancing credit.[4] Weidmann waited several months to write his letter, during which the Bundesbank kept quiet about the Target issue while it debated it internally in depth. With this letter, Weidmann distanced himself from the previous stance of the Bundesbank, which had maintained that the Target balances were mere statistical entries, a normal by-product of money creation in the European monetary system.[5] This position had been criticized, amongst others, by former Bundesbank President Helmut Schlesinger, during whose tenure in office the Maastricht Treaty was adopted.[6] With Weidmann's letter the Bundesbank now made its concern clear, namely that the Target balances amongst the national central banks (NCBs) had grown very large and

Economics 21, 2013, pp. 151–163; J. Pisani-Ferry, 'The Known Unknowns and Unknown Unknowns of European Monetary Union', *Journal of International Money and Finance* 34, 2013, pp. 6–14. An extensive recent overview of additional literature and a summary of the issues from the perspective of the ECB's specialist on Target balances can be found in P. Cour-Thimann, 'Target Balances and the Crisis in the Euro Area', *CESifo Forum* 14, Special Issue, April 2013, available at: <http://www.cesifo-group. de/DocDL/Forum-Sonderheft-Apr-2013.pdf>. Also see T. Mayer, *Europe's Unfinished Currency*, Anthem Press, London 2012; R. A. Auer, 'What Drives Target2 Balances? Evidence from a Panel Analysis', *CESifo Working Paper* No. 4216, April 2013, available at: <http://www.cesifo-group.de/DocDL/cesifo1_wp4216.pdf>, and N. Potrafke and M. Reischmann, 'Explosive Target Balances', *CESifo Working Paper* No. 4297, June 2013, available at: <http://www.cesifo-group.de/DocDL/cesifo1_wp4297.pdf>.

[4] S. Ruhkamp, 'Die Bundesbank fordert von der EZB bessere Sicherheiten', *Frankfurter Allgemeine Zeitung*, 29 February 2012, available at: <http://www.faz.net/aktuell/wirtschaft/ schuldenkrise-die-bundesbank-fordert-von-der-ezb-bessere-sicherheiten-11667413. html> and, S. Ruhkamp, 'Bundesbank geht im Targetstreit in die Offensive', *Frankfurter Allgemeine Zeitung*, 12 March 2012, available at: <http://www.faz.net/aktuell/ wirtschaft/wirtschaftspolitik/f-a-z-gastbeitrag-bundesbank-geht-im-targetstreit-in- die-offensive-11682060.html>. The article, translated freely, reads: 'In a letter whose content is known to the F.A.Z., Weidmann refers explicitly to the growing Target claims. He suggests collateralising the claims of the ECB on the financially weak national central banks in the Eurosystem, which he said have reached an amount exceeding € 800 billion'.

[5] Deutsche Bundesbank, *Bundesbank Target2 Balances*, press release, 22 February 2011, available at: <http://www.bundesbank.de/Redaktion/EN/Pressemitteilungen/ BBK/2011/2011_02_22_Bundesbank_TARGET2_balances.html>, and Deutsche Bundesbank, 'The Evolution of the Bundesbank's TARGET2 Balances', *Monthly Report* 63, No. 3, March 2011, pp. 34–37. The Bundesbank took a similar stance in a letter to the Ifo Institute dated 18 March 2011.

[6] H. Schlesinger, 'The Balance of Payments Tells Us the Truth', January 2013.

could pose a significant burden for the Eurozone's NCBs. While the ECB has not published Target balance panel data up to this day, it has in the meantime acknowledged the accuracy and definition of the data in a semi-official publication in CESifo Forum,[7] as well as, indirectly, through statements by its President confirming that the ECB monitors the data virtually on a daily basis.[8]

Behind the Target balances is the same refinancing credit given by the NCBs that was discussed in the previous sections. At first sight they appear to be nothing special, but they actually reflect the amount of central bank credit that has been issued *in excess* of the liquidity needs for transactions within the NCBs' national jurisdictions. This excess money is used by the economic agents of the country in question to purchase goods and assets abroad, and to pay off external debt. Thus, the Target balances mean something fundamentally different from simply providing the necessary liquidity for a national economy to conduct its transactions, i.e. the liquidity that moves from one account to another, but stays within the country. In fact, the balances enable a country to sustain a net inflow of goods or assets from abroad, or to repay foreign credit, by virtue of its NCB providing a continuous overflow of refinancing credit, akin to a personal overdraft facility being added to the personal checking account.

This excess liquidity is a direct consequence of the lowering of the standards for eligible collateral that the country's commercial banks must pledge at their NCB to receive refinancing credit. Conversely, in the core countries, economically speaking, the Target balances measure the public international credit provided to the GIPSIC countries through the refinancing operations of the ECB system. This, in effect, is nothing other than the public rescue packages EFSF, ESM, and whatever else they are called, which the parliaments in Europe have laboriously agreed on. The differences lie in the national recipients—banks or states— and the credit conditions in detail, but not in the economic substance.

The extra refinancing credit measured by the Target balances explains why the capital imports of the crisis-hit countries were able to continue during the first years of the crisis (as Figure 2.1 showed), albeit at reduced volumes, despite the crisis having had its roots precisely in the fact that the capital markets

---

[7] See P. Cour-Thimann, 'Target Balances and the Crisis in the Euro Area', April 2013.

[8] See M. Draghi, *Transcript of the questions asked and the answers given by Mario Draghi, President of the ECB, and Vítor Constâncio, Vice-President of the ECB*, press conference, 4 April 2012, available at: <http://www.ecb.int/press/pressconf/2012/html/is120404.en.html>: '...we have to look at the consolidated bank balance sheets, country by country. And, as you can imagine, we look at them every day. As well as inflation expectations and TARGET2 balances. These are three things that we look at almost every day. Every day actually, not almost every day!' The author had informed M. Draghi about the Target balances on the occasion of a scholarly PowerPoint presentation at Banca d'Italia on 22 April 2011.

shunned these countries. This extra refinancing credit was a rescue package that predated all other rescue packages—or, to recall the above image, it was the weapon wielded by the ECB which, as a white knight, came to the rescue when the capital markets ceased to be available. For reasons that will become clearer later, the extra refinancing credit showing up in the Target balances is called 'Target credit' in this book. The volume of Target credit that the GIPSIC countries have drawn far exceeds the volume of the official rescue credit.

The issue is technically complex, and the casual reader cannot be expected to be able to understand it all at first go. It is, however, of paramount importance to understanding what is going on in the Eurozone, much more important than all the rest of the rescue packages combined. The dynamics of the evolution of Target balances has ended up putting a substantial share of the foreign wealth of the creditor nations on the line. This and the following chapters will attempt to untangle this complexity, step by step, and make the issue understandable to everyone.

Target is the name of the settlement system through which international euro transactions between banks in the Eurozone are processed. It is an acronym for a complex expression (Trans-European Automated Real-time Gross settlement Express Transfer system) that does not convey much about its meaning. The Target system channels and measures payment orders between the national central banks (NCBs) in the Eurozone that result from orders given by public and private financial institutions to their respective commercial banks. A Target deficit of an NCB is a net outflow of payment orders to other countries, or, in economics parlance, a balance-of-payments deficit. Conversely, a Target surplus is a net inflow of payment orders from other countries, or a balance-of-payments surplus.[9] Heuristically, we may also speak of international money flows, although this is not entirely precise, since the money, in the sense of deposits of commercial banks with their respective central banks, is eliminated in the country from where the payment order originated and created anew in the country of destination.

Sometimes, the term Target2 is used instead of Target, in order to refer to the second iteration of the system, which came into force in 2007. But this is of little relevance. The differences between the first and the second Target systems are only of a technical nature and have no bearing upon the economic interpretation of the Target account as measuring balance-of-payments imbalances.[10] Thus the '2' behind the acronym has no real economic meaning and will be disregarded in this book.

---

[9] This was first explained in H.-W. Sinn, 'Die riskante Kreditersatzpolitik der EZB', 4 May 2011, and H.-W. Sinn, 'The ECB's Stealth Bailout', 1 June 2011. The first formal analysis was provided in H.-W. Sinn and T. Wollmershäuser, 'Target Loans, Current Account Balances and Capital Flows: The ECB's Rescue Facility', 2012.

[10] When the Eurosystem started to operate, only large payment orders were channelled through the ECB's payment system. In addition to Target, the banks of each country can use private payments systems; originally most payments were processed and netted off through those systems. Since the payments from country A to country B are

The Target system captures only the electronic movement of money, i.e. the international money transfers. There are no statistics on the physical flow of money, of the kind that would be transported in a suitcase. Since the payment flows in the Eurozone are not restricted, while cash transport is controlled, it can be assumed that physical cash transport within the Eurozone is relatively small. A certain movement of cash across borders occurs, of course, through tourism and guest workers paying visits to their home countries inside and outside the Eurozone (such as Turkey and the eastern European EU countries), which is an effect of some importance in Germany. Potentially, an issue similar to that of the Target balances arises, an aspect that will be discussed in Chapter 8.[11]

usually offset by payments from country B to country A, the Target system was only used for surplus settlement among the private payments systems. This changed with the introduction of the Target2 system in 2007. Increasingly, smaller payments were also processed directly through the Target accounts at the ECB. According to recent data, two-thirds of the Target transactions had a volume of less than € 50,000, with the median at only € 10,000. See European Central Bank, *Target Annual Report 2010*, Frankfurt 2010; and European Central Bank, *The Payment System—Payments, Securities and Derivatives, and the Role of the Eurosystem*, Frankfurt am Main 2010. While it is true that this change exerted a significant influence on the Target system's transaction volume, the balances booked annually in the system were *not* affected. From the beginning, they captured the whole of the net deficits and surpluses in the transfer of payments between the banks of the individual Eurozone member countries. This makes it possible to make a consistent interpretation of the time series, such as that shown in Figure 6.2 below. The rise in Target balances since 2007 shown is no statistical artefact.

[11] Refer also to J. Whittaker, 'Eurosystem Debts, Greece, and the Role of Banknotes', *Lancaster University Working Paper*, 14 November 2011, available at: <http://eprints.lancs. ac.uk/51935/1/eurosystemNov2011.pdf>. The Bundesbank balance sheet, for example, distinguishes between 'statutory' banknote circulation and the banknote circulation that goes above and beyond it. The statutory banknote circulation is measured in accordance with the share of the country in the capital of the ECB, which itself is an average of the country's population and GDP share and denotes a normal value. If the effective banknote circulation lies above this value, a cash outflow to other countries is assumed, which measures a similar debt as the electronic outflow of money through the Target system. This debt is booked under 'Intra-Eurosystem liabilities from the issuance of euro banknotes'. It increased from € 100 billion at the end of 2007 to € 224 billion at the end of December 2013. This change stands vis-à-vis a change in the Bundesbank's Target claims on the ECB system, which increased by € 439 billion over the same period (from € 71 billion to € 510 billion). This must be accounted for mostly by euro banknotes that are issued in Germany, but are circulating abroad (mostly in eastern Europe and Turkey, as mentioned above, but also in Russia and other countries.) and that have taken over the role of the former deutschmark that used to circulate in those countries, which at the time accounted for about one-third of the amount of the German monetary base. With the currency union, Germany gave its seignorage capital in the form of

Within the Eurozone, payments are continuously flowing to and from merchants and financial institutions both within countries and across borders, but only cross-border transactions are captured by the Target balances. People live in one country, buy from another, and export to a third. Shares of stock, bonds, property, and whole factories are bought and sold across borders. New credit will be drawn, and old debts will be repaid. These transactions always lead to payment orders, but as a rule to no net payment orders that would build up a balance for a given country, since inflows and outflows net each other out. Such a situation is known as a balance-of-payments equilibrium.[12]

A balance-of-payments equilibrium between countries is not the same thing as a current account equilibrium. The latter means, roughly speaking, that a country exports as much in goods and services as it imports. However, a country can have a current account deficit because it imports more than it exports, while its balance of payments is in equilibrium, because it is receiving an inflow of credit that finances the current account deficit.

Let's take Greece. Greece buys more goods from abroad than it exports. Therefore, it requires money to cover the shortfall. To get the funding, it taps the international capital markets. Money flows, for example, from a French bank through a Greek bank to one of its customers, who in turn transfers it to Germany because he wants to import a German car. The money comes from abroad and flows abroad once again. The Greek balance of payments is in equilibrium. This is the way it was before the financial crisis.

In a country like Germany, which has an export surplus, it was the other way around. Germany enjoyed an inflow of money from abroad because it exported more than it imported; it used the funds to purchase bonds, shares of stock,

---

deutschmark banknotes circulating abroad to the other member countries. See H. Feist and H.-W. Sinn, 'Eurowinners and Eurolosers: The Distribution of Seignorage Wealth in EMU', *European Journal of Political Economy* 13, 1997, pp. 665–689; and H. Feist and H.-W. Sinn, 'The Accidental Redistribution of Seignorage Wealth in the Eurosystem', *CESifo Forum* 1, No. 3, Autumn 2000, pp. 27–29, available at: <http://www.cesifo-group.de/DocDL/Forum300-special.pdf>, and H. Feist and H.-W. Sinn, 'Der Euro und der Geldschöpfungsgewinn: Gewinner und Verlierer durch die Währungsunion', *ifo Schnelldienst* 53, No. 31, 17 November 2000, pp. 14–22. The value of this 'gift' has grown apace with general economic growth. It must account for the lion's share of the € 204 billion mentioned above. Unlike the Target claims and liabilities, claims and liabilities from over-proportionate banknote issuance are *not* included in the calculation of net foreign asset positions as considered, e.g., in Figure 2.9.

[12] In statistical reporting, a balance of payments is by definition always in equilibrium. This is because a disequilibrium in payments of private agents and fiscal authorities (payments 'above the line') will be matched by a change in the position of the monetary authority vis-à-vis the rest of the world (payments 'below the line'). By contrast, the definition of equilibrium used here refers only to the balancing of payments above the line.

property or other assets abroad, or to provide credit to foreign borrowers. Money flowed for instance from Germany via the Benelux countries to French banks, from where it was forwarded to Greece.

In all countries, money flowed in both directions across borders, but there were no net flows of money across borders. The Target balances or the balance of payments were roughly zero, i.e. there was a balance-of-payments equilibrium. Figure 6.1 illustrates the situation by way of a three-country example where, for the moment, only the solid arrows are considered.

A balance-of-payments imbalance occurs when more money flows across borders in one direction than in the other, i.e. when outflows and inflows don't net out and a balance remains. If, for instance, the Greek car buyer does not get a loan from France, but wishes to purchase the car nonetheless by transferring money already existing in Greece, a Target deficit or balance-of-payments deficit will result, since now the same amount of money will have left Greece as before, but less money will have flowed into the country. If all other things remain equal, a surplus will arise in France, since less money has been transferred to Greece, while the German balance of payments remains in equilibrium. Of course, in this situation it is likely that the flow of credit from Germany to France ceases, since France no longer needs the credit. In this latter case, the balance-of-payments surplus in our example occurs in Germany, not France.

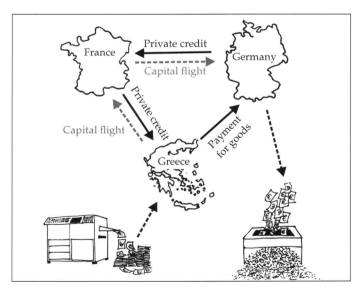

Figure 6.1 Payment flows in a balance-of-payments equilibrium and a balance-of-payments crisis

Source: Illustrated by the Ifo Institute.

Note that this example is for didactical purposes only. In reality, the flow of credit went from Germany into the large pool represented by the international capital market, from where France was drawing its funds before it lent them to Greece, without France being able to assess the origins of these funds. Moreover, there were substantial direct flows from Germany to Greece. At the present level of abstraction, however, these qualifications can be disregarded.

During the crisis, private capital flows not only dried up, for some countries and over certain periods, they even reversed their direction, since there was outright capital flight, primarily taking the form of lenders deciding not to roll over outstanding loans and demanding repayment. This happened in particular with European interbank credit, which is typically short-term and can easily be repatriated by not rolling it over.

In the above example this is represented by the dashed arrows from Greece to France and from France to Germany. Greece now has to issue net payment orders to other countries not only for buying goods from there, but also for redeeming the existing debt.

Balance-of-payments imbalances such as those between Eurozone countries can also occur in principle among regions within a country, or between the Eurozone and the rest of the world. However, the probability of such imbalances emerging on a large scale is very small.

Within individual European countries, fiscal equalization schemes make sure that regional and local administrations are supported and strictly controlled if they run into financial problems. The restrictions prevent excessive borrowing and thus make a sudden stop of private capital flows or even a capital flight unlikely. Moreover, if a region nevertheless does run into financial stress that the market does not alleviate, there is often public credit from other regions to help out, which means that such regions will be able to avoid balance-of-payments deficits. That is why no shunning of particular regions by private lenders within the European states has been observed.

In the US things are a bit different, as there is no formal fiscal equalization scheme between the different federal states and the implicit shock absorption through federal institutions or the federal unemployment system is very small.[13] However, there are other institutional constraints that imply a limitation and

---

[13] The automatic shock absorption through fiscal mechanism amounts to around 13% to 15%, i.e. a local gross income loss of $ 1 billion leads to a net income loss of $ 870 million to $ 850 million. See P. Asdrubali, B. E. Sorensen, and O. Yosha, 'Channels of Interstate Risk Sharing: United States 1963–1990', *Quarterly Journal of Economics* 111, 1996, pp. 1081–1110, who estimate 13%; or D. Gros, *Fiscal Union after Banking Union or Banking Union instead of Fiscal Union?*, unpublished note for the Austrian Government, June 2013, which estimates 15%; as well as D. Gros and E. Jones, 'External Shocks and Unemployment: Revisiting the Mundellian Story', unpublished manuscript, *Centre for European Policy Studies*, February 1995; see also J. von Hagen, 'Achieving Economic

settlement of Target-like imbalances. (See Chapter 7, Section *How Target-Like Balances are Settled in the USA*.)

Externally, with regard to countries outside the currency zone, flexible exchange rates and different currencies usually make sure that goods and capital flows balance out. Larger cross-border currency movements occur only when the central banks hoard foreign currency in order to influence the exchange rate. Between the private sectors of different currency areas there are no significant net flows of foreign currency, since there is usually not much use for a currency outside the country where it serves as legal tender. A notable exception is the dollar, which is a medium of exchange throughout the world.

A distinction is normally made in international payment transactions between payments within the framework of the current account, and the capital account. The current account balance covers transactions related to the acquisition of goods of current production, services—including interest on credit operations—and gifts. The capital account, in turn, measures payments resulting from the exchange of assets, in particular the granting or repayment of credit. The cross-border sale of an asset makes it possible for the seller to buy something else, just as when s/he 'sells' an IOU, which is one way to interpret the taking out of a loan. IMF statistics sometimes define the capital account much more narrowly and use the term 'financial account' for most of what economists label capital account. This terminology is, however, not common in economics parlance. For the purposes of this book, the term 'capital account' covers credit of all kinds, including short-term interbank credit and direct investment, as well as all kinds of asset purchases, including financial assets and real assets such as stocks or real estate, the latter qualifying as direct investment if the buyer acquires a sufficiently large ownership share. Although we will see that changes in Target imbalances also measure a public capital flow between the NCBs, the term 'capital flows' will usually, unless otherwise stated, be meant to refer to what is ordinarily understood by a capital flow, i.e. credit provided by private agents and by fiscal entities.

Based on the above, one can say that a balance of payments is in equilibrium when the capital account and the current account net each other out, and in disequilibrium when they don't. In the Eurozone, therefore, a balance-of-payments or Target deficit can be defined as the portion of the current account deficit that is not financed by net private and fiscal capital imports, or, equivalently, as the sum of the current account deficit and the net private and fiscal capital export. This definition will be useful later when the relationship between the Target balances and the current account balances is discussed.[14]

Figure 6.1 also shows a printing machine and a paper shredder, both being meant metaphorically only. They come into play because the activities of commercial and central banks automatically sterilize the effects of international money flows on the stocks of money circulating within the countries. The outflow of money from Greece goes hand-in-hand with the creation of new money by way of refinancing operations, since otherwise the stock of money circulating in Greece would shrink and internal transactions would be hindered. The inflow of money into Germany, in turn, leads to additional liquidity that German banks do not need and which they therefore choose to lend to the Bundesbank, with the effect that the money is removed from the economy. These aspects will be discussed in more detail below.

Ballooning Target Balances

Whereas Figure 6.1 only serves to provide a basic understanding of the processes involved, Figure 6.2 shows exact figures from a database that Timo Wollmershäuser and the author compiled from the balance sheets of the Eurozone's NCBs or, in the cases where individual NCBs do not or did not publish such data, from the statistics of the IMF.[15] This panel data set has been replicated by many researchers after we published and interpreted it.[16] The figures are contained in the balance sheets of the NCBs because, as will be discussed later in more detail, they constitute claims and liabilities among the central banks. Usually they are fairly well tucked away under obscure headings and mixed

[14]   This definition was first stated in H.-W. Sinn, 'Die riskante Kreditersatzpolitik der EZB', 4 May 2011; or, in English, in H.-W. Sinn, 'The ECB's Stealth Bailout', 1 June 2011. A brief mathematical interpretation can be found in H.-W. Sinn and T. Wollmershäuser, 'Target Loans, Current Account Balances and Capital Flows: The ECB's Rescue Facility', 2012; or also in S. Homburg, 'Notes on the Target2 Dispute', January 2013.

[15]   See H.-W. Sinn and T. Wollmershäuser, 'Target Loans, Current Account Balances and Capital Flows: The ECB's Rescue Facility', 2012; in particular the preceding working paper versions as well. Regularly updated Target data are available at: <http://www.cesifo-group.de/ifoHome/policy/Haftungsspegel.html>.

[16]   The figures were first presented by the author to an audience at Banca d'Italia during a lecture on 22 April 2011, and then at the Munich Economic Summit on 19 May 2011, from where they found their way into the Financial Times with the permission of the author and were commented upon by Martin Wolf. See M. Wolf, 'Intolerable Choices for the Eurozone', *Financial Times*, 31 May 2011, available at: <http://www.ft.com/intl/cms/s/0/1a61825a-8bb7-11e0-a725-00144feab49a.html#axzz2Z7HBqk4Z>. The formal working paper appeared a few days later. This made them immediately known worldwide.

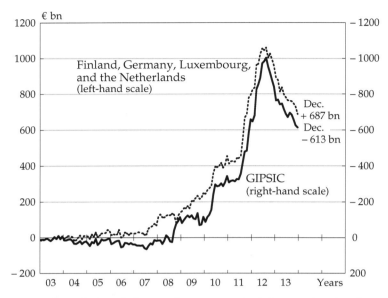

Figure 6.2 Cumulative balance-of-payments imbalances in the Eurozone (January 2003— December 2013)

Sources: Deutsche Bundesbank, Database, Time series BBK01.EU8148B; De Nederlandsche Bank, Statistics, Financial Institutions, Domestic MFI-statistics (monetary), Balance sheet of the Nederlandsche Bank; Banco de España, Boletín Estadístico, Balance sheet of the Banco de España; Banca d'Italia, Statistical Database, Bank of Italy balance-sheet aggregates; for the other countries see International Monetary Fund, International Financial Statistics, net claims on Eurosystem (IFS code xxx12eoszkm), Currency issued (IFS code xxx14aoozkm), and Currency put into circulation (IFS code xxx14moozkm).

Note: The Target balance data for Germany, the Netherlands, Italy, and Spain stem directly from their central bank balance sheets. For the other countries, we calculate a precise proxy from the International Financial Statistics of the International Monetary Fund, following the methodology of H.-W. Sinn and T. Wollmershäuser, 'Target Loans, Current Account Balances and Capital Flows: The ECB's Rescue Facility', 2012, Appendix, p. 504ff. The 'Target claims' are computed as the difference between 'Net claims on Eurosystem' and the 'Intra-Eurosystem claims related to banknote issuance'. The latter is calculated as the difference between 'Currency issued' and 'Currency put into circulation'. This chart was created with the newest data available as of 26 February 2014, which includes the values for all countries as of December 2013.

with other entries, so that it is not very easy to extract them. Some countries give the data only to the IMF, from whose publications it must then be extracted. The deadlines for publication vary as well. To this day, no comprehensive primary statistic on Target balances is available from the ECB itself. But the way we calculate these balances based on the NCB balance sheets and complemented by the IMF statistics is now even being used by the ECB itself, and has become the norm around the world.[17]

The figure shows the evolution within the Eurozone of the balance-of-payments or Target balances for a northern euro bloc that includes Germany, the Netherlands, Finland, and Luxembourg, and the GIPSIC countries (Greece, Ireland, Portugal, Spain, Italy and Cyprus). As before, GIPSIC stands for those countries receiving official aid from intergovernmental rescue programmes or in the form of government bond purchases by the ECB. The dotted curve for the northern euro bloc shows the accumulated balance-of-payments surpluses, known as Target claims, measured by the left-hand scale, and the solid curve for the GIPSIC shows the accumulated balance-of-payments deficits, i.e. the Target liabilities, the values of which can be read on the right-hand scale. All figures refer to stocks and not current flows; the flows are illustrated by the slopes of the curves. Both scales are divided into identical intervals and differ only in their algebraic sign. It can be seen that until the summer of 2007 the balances were roughly zero, Target claims amounting then to just around 1.3% of the Eurozone's 2007 GDP.

After August 2007, however, when the European interbank market stumbled for the first time, significant imbalances started to develop. Quite remarkably, the curves for the GIPSIC countries and the northern euro bloc paralleled each other, even though they refer only to subsets of euro countries and the balances add up to zero only in the aggregate, as will be explained further below. Since the banks of the northern euro bloc, as well as the banks of countries that acted as intermediaries for European capital flows such as France or Belgium, were now lending abroad only hesitantly, the GIPSIC countries, all of which had inherited large current account deficits from the pre-crisis credit bubble, had to finance their goods purchases with money that was not being replenished with inflows from abroad. What is worse, in some cases they also had to

---

[17] The ECB's first statement on the economic significance of the Target balances appeared in its October 2011 Monthly Report. See European Central Bank, 'TARGET2 Balances of National Central Banks in the Euro Area', *Monthly Bulletin*, October 2011, pp. 35–40, in particular p. 37. In footnote 5, the Bank stated that there is no single database grouping together the statistics, but that the data can be calculated on the basis of IMF data and from the balance sheets of the individual central banks. It thus advocated using exactly the same method that Sinn and Wollmershäuser had used for their working paper of June 2011. See *CESifo Working Paper* preliminary version by H.-W. Sinn and T. Wollmershäuser, 'Target Loans, Current Account Balances and Capital Flows: The ECB's Rescue Facility', June 2011. In fact, it would be possible to further refine this method by also subtracting the intra-Eurosystem balances related to the transfer of foreign reserves, as explained by P. Cour-Thimann, 'Target Balances and the Crisis in the Euro Area', April 2013, Annex D.

finance the repayment of prior credit taken abroad. They covered the shortfall, as discussed above, by drawing refinancing credit from their NCBs, something made possible by the lowering of collateral requirements that enabled more and more collateral to be eligible for refinancing credit purposes. The NCBs provided this additional credit by printing the money and lending it to their commercial banks, which then, in turn, used it to carry out net payments to other euro countries in a volume that is measured by the Target balances.

In spring 2011, when the Ifo Institute figures on Target balances were first published, with Germany holding just over € 300 billion in Target claims, some readers said that the sums would go back down soon and that the latest developments already showed that things were quieting down. Far from it. From April 2011 to August 2012, Germany's Target claims rose by around € 85 billion per quarter, or € 28 billion per month. Germany's Target claims peaked in August 2012 at € 751 billion. Similar developments occurred in the other countries of the northern euro bloc. In August 2012, the total Target claims held by the northern bloc amounted to € 1,060 billion, or 11.2% of the Eurozone's GDP of that year. On the flip side of the coin, by August 2012 the Target liabilities of the GIPSIC countries had reached a level of € 1,002 billion. As it turned out, the Target balances exploded.[18]

However, as the chart shows, the balances declined after September 2012. As will be explained in more detail in Chapters 7 and 8, this happened because intergovernmental fiscal rescue credit was being paid out to the crisis countries and because the ECB and the rescue fund ESM promised to buy the government bonds of crisis-afflicted countries should these countries run into acute financial difficulties. These guarantees have induced foreign investors to buy the government bonds of the GIPSIC countries and, indirectly, rekindled confidence in these countries' private assets. The incoming public and private payment orders have reduced these countries' Target debt.

For the discussion of the economics involved it is useful to differentiate between domestic and external money or, in short, inside and outside money.[19] I label outside money the money which circulates in one Eurozone country, but originated in another through liquidity-creating operations, i.e. refinancing credit given to commercial banks or asset purchases from them, that was then transferred to this country by way of payment orders through the Target system. Inside money, in turn, is defined as money that was created by refinancing credit or asset purchases in the same country where it circulates. Given these definitions, the dashed curve in Figure 6.2 thus measures the stock of outside money

---

[18] See N. Potrafke and M. Reischmann, 'Explosive Target Balances', June 2013.

[19] The definition follows Gurley and Shaw's definition, but is not identical to it. See J. G. Gurley and E. S. Shaw, *Money in a Theory of Finance*, Brooking Institutions, Washington, DC, 1960.

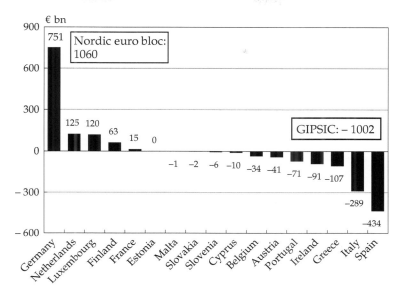

Figure 6.3 Target balances by country (peak values August 2012)

Source: See Figure 6.2.

Note: The countries not mentioned in Figure 6.2 are calculated in the same manner as Greece, Cyprus, Finland, Portugal, or Luxembourg from IMF data. For the calculations, see H.-W. Sinn and T. Wollmershäuser, 'Target Loans, Current Account Balances and Capital Flows: The ECB's Rescue Facility', 2012, Appendix, p. 504ff.

that arrived in the northern euro bloc, while the solid curve shows money created in the GIPSIC countries that was used for international payment orders and became outside money elsewhere. The similarity of the curves suggests that the outside money circulating in the northern euro bloc did indeed largely originate in the GIPSIC countries.

Figure 6.3 provides a more differentiated depiction of the Target balances at the time of their peak, in August 2012. It can be seen that Germany, Luxembourg, the Netherlands, and Finland had all amassed significant stocks of outside money or, equivalently, Target claims, while the GIPSIC countries had become Target debtors, because they produced more money via refinancing credit or asset purchases than they needed for internal circulation, sending it abroad to redeem their debts or to buy assets and goods. The GIPSIC countries are joined by Austria, Belgium, Slovakia, Slovenia, and Malta, but the liabilities of the latter are relatively small. The Target balances within the Eurosystem add up to zero, including an own Target balance that accumulated for the ECB itself, whose origin is explained in a footnote.[20]

Obviously, the Deutsche Bundesbank was, by a wide margin, the Eurosystem's largest Target creditor. By August 2012 it accounted for no less than 70% of the total Target claims in the Eurosystem, although it held only 27% of the ECB's liable capital. In per capita terms, however, Luxembourg topped the list with € 226,400, followed by Finland with € 11,700, Germany with € 9,200, and the Netherlands with € 7,500.

On the side of the Target debtors, Spain stood out with a Target debt of € 434 billion, followed by Italy with € 289 billion, Greece with € 107 billion, Ireland with € 91 billion, Portugal with € 71 billion, and Cyprus with € 10 billion. It is noteworthy that Belgium and Austria, with € 34 billion and € 41 billion, respectively, also showed substantial Target debt levels. In per capita terms Ireland topped the list, with a Target debt of € 19,800, followed by Cyprus with € 11,600, Greece with € 9,500, Spain with € 9,400, Portugal with € 6,700, Austria with € 4,900, Italy with € 4,700, and Belgium with € 3,100.

Why Target Balances are a Measure of Credit

Balance-of-payments imbalances always measure international credit between monetary authorities, a form of public credit. Usually they occur when foreign currency reserves are depleted or accumulated in exchange for goods or assets. In the Eurosystem, what is accumulated are Target claims and liabilities instead of foreign currency reserves, but otherwise the situation is similar.

Nevertheless, the case is not obvious to the non-economist, since normally the granting of credit is accompanied by a handing over of money. It is legitimate to wonder whether, and how, a creditor NCB holding a Target claim has lent

---

[20] In addition to the country Target balances, by the end of 2013 the ECB had itself incurred an intra-Eurosystem Target claim of € 1 billion. This basically resulted from a dollar-euro swap agreement with the US Federal Reserve. The ECB sold the dollars it borrowed from the Fed to some Eurosystem NCBs, the Banque de France in particular. By doing so, it received a Target claim against the Eurosystem NCBs and incurred an external liability with the Fed. See European Central Bank, *Annual Accounts 2013*, p. 27. On the flip side of the coin, the ECB participated in the SMP programme and bought € 13 billion worth of GIPSIC government bonds, which created Target claims elsewhere in the Eurosystem and a corresponding Target liability for itself. See European Central Bank, Annual Accounts 2013, p. 19. The ECB moreover holds external Target liabilities vis-à-vis Bulgaria, Denmark, Latvia, Lithuania, Poland, and Romania, which, as associated members of the Eurosystem, are allowed to accumulate Target claims, but not to incur Target liabilities. The counterpart to these ECB liabilities are claims of the ECB on Eurosystem NCBs that issued payment orders to the associated NCBs. See also P. Cour-Thimann, 'Target Balances and the Crisis in the Euro Area', April 2013, p. 48.

money to another NCB that bears a Target liability. The answer is, of course, that it hasn't. The credit relationship arises in an entirely different sense.

Consider the example of a Spaniard purchasing an asset from a seller in the Netherlands. This purchase causes the Dutch central bank to carry out a payment order on behalf of the Central Bank of Spain, which itself acts on behalf of the Spanish commercial bank of the buyer of the asset. The Dutch central bank makes the payment to the commercial bank of the Dutch seller, and in exchange it acquires a claim against the Spanish central bank, or, more precisely, against the Eurosystem, which itself receives a claim against the Spanish central bank. The Dutch central bank pays the Dutch seller, and by doing so on behalf of the Spanish central bank, in effect it gives the latter a credit.

It is akin to me lending money to a friend who forgot his wallet so that he can pay, say, the plumber's bill. By carrying out the payment, I am granting my friend credit (giving him a loan), acquiring in the process a claim against him.

The only difference is that, come evening, my friend will repay the loan, whereas the Target claim can remain in principle for ever, and can never be called due. Spain, then, receives the assets without having to deliver any goods or assets in return other than the Target debt title. And this does not only apply to assets. It doesn't make any difference what is acquired with the money that the Dutch central bank pays out to the seller's account—goods, services or securities, property or a company, or a simple debit note that ceases to exist when the debt is repaid. The procedure is always the same.

The analogy with the friend also differs from the Target case insofar as I can always decide whether I want to help my friend out of the tight spot or not. In the Target case, the Dutch central bank has no leeway to decide. It is obliged to carry out the payment. That is the way the Eurosystem operates.

By carrying out the payment order, the Dutch central bank creates money that then circulates in the Netherlands. Normally, it creates money by giving refinancing credit to commercial banks or buying assets from them. In the example explaining the Target balances, however, it does not receive a claim on the commercial banks nor titles to private assets, but claims on the ECB system instead.

The net payment orders from Spain, both in the example and in reality, reduce the stock of money circulating in Spain, since the buyer of the asset relinquishes a deposit with his commercial bank, which in turn relinquishes money deposited with its central bank. This is the link between the generous refinancing policy of the ECB system, made possible by lowering the collateral requirements as discussed above, and the rise in the Spanish Target balance. The last section of this chapter will explain this in greater detail. With a less generous policy, the credit from the printing press would have been scarcer, credit conditions would have been more attractive for foreign lenders to Spain, in the sense that Spanish interest rates net of risk premia would have been higher, prompting more foreign credit to flow to Spain, and implying a higher volume of reverse payment orders from other countries to Spain that would have reduced Spain's Target liabilities. And perhaps the Spanish buyer of the Dutch asset would have purchased domestic assets instead.

Target was not originally intended to serve as a source of credit between the NCBs. As Helmut Schlesinger, a former president of the Bundesbank, explained, the Target system was supposed to serve solely as a clearing house for financial flows without credit-granting arising as a result.[21] It was thought at the time that the Target credit would only remain overnight and be netted off almost at once, and so indeed it was until 2007.

Schlesinger also argued that, at the time, the idea was that international payment orders would be carried out by private clearing houses that provided credit to one another in case the balances between them did not net out to zero, rather than having the Eurosystem provide the credit. Indeed, there are private payment orders between commercial banks in Europe, as well as within multinational banks that maintain internal payment systems, that do not go via Target. When these payments are not settled, a private international credit flows between these institutions which is not, and should not, be tallied to the Target balances, given that these balances measure public rather than private international credit.[22]

As will be explained in detail in Chapter 7, Target-like balances can also arise in the US, but as the US payment system is basically private, though publicly controlled, they must be settled annually. Thus, imbalances of the European magnitude cannot happen in the US system. In the Eurozone the Target positions are kept open and there is no settlement mechanism. The creditor countries' NCBs must content themselves with an everlasting bookkeeping claim, and can find relief only in the fact that the entire ECB system guarantees the Target claims by socializing bilateral claims on a daily basis. In the above example, the Dutch NCB first acquires a claim on the Spanish NCB; at the end of the day, however, this claim is transformed into a claim on the ECB and, conversely, the liability of the Spanish NCB becomes one to the ECB, or better, to the Eurosystem.[23] Therefore, should the Spanish NCB default, all surviving NCBs share in the losses, provided the Eurosystem as such survives.

[21] See H. Schlesinger, 'The Balance of Payments Tells Us the Truth', January 2013.

[22] The ECB rightly points out that such private payment systems within international institutions result in different Target balances than would have prevailed without such systems. It does not mention, however, that that is exactly the reason why Target is a measure of public international credit. See European Central Bank, *Monthly Bulletin*, May 2013, p. 106.

[23] See Taxpayers Association of Europe (TAE), 'Target2: Die finanzielle Atombombe', *MMnews*, 24 February 2012, available at: <http://www.mmnews.de/index.php/wirtschaf t/9560-target2-die-finanzielle-atombombe>.

Given that the Target stocks are credit, it is logical that they yield interest revenue. Indeed, the interest rate equals the main refinancing rate, i.e. the rate applied to commercial banks that receive refinancing credit from their respective NCBs.[24] Until October 2008, this rate was 4.5%, but was thereafter steadily lowered until it reached a level of only 1% in May 2009. On 11 July 2012 it was lowered even further, to 0.75%, on 8 May 2013 it was lowered to 0.5%, and on 13 November 2013 to 0.25%, where it stands as of this writing. This rate is far lower than the average inflation rate in the Eurozone, which hovered around 2% between 2008 and 2012, and decreased to 1.4% in 2013 and to 0.8% in January 2014. The interest accrued is added yearly to the Target stocks and carried over from year to year as compound interest.

The fact that interest is charged and added to the balance qualifies somewhat the above assertion regarding Figure 6.1, according to which the chart's curves depict the stocks of central bank money flowing electronically across borders. The assertion has to be modified to take account of the interest accrued, which is included in the balance sheets as well. But since this rate was nearly always at or below 1% over the period in question, the quantitative difference between the balances and the sum of cross-border money flows is negligible. In fact, the interpretation of the balances as credit is all the more accurate as a result, since credits that have been granted at different times can only reasonably be compared when cumulative interest payments are added.

Thus, an NCB with a negative Target balance must pay interest to the ECB and, conversely, the NCBs of countries with a positive Target balance receive interest income from the Eurosystem. The question arises, why is this so? After all, interest payments among the Eurozone NCBs are irrelevant, since interest charges and interest income are distributed among the NCBs according to their respective capital keys at the ECB. It is as if one spouse in a community–property marriage pays the other spouse interest on the purchase of a car. The money paid in interest is not gone from the household, since it belongs to the partners, before and after payment, in equal measure. The answer can only be that the creators of the system took into account the possibility of insolvency of one of the NCBs or an exit from the Eurosystem, since in that case the interest charged to this NCB goes into the remaining claims of the ECB system. If, say, Greece should leave the Eurozone, the remaining NCBs keep their claims on Greece, including

---

[24] Reply 2011/003864 of the Bundesbank to a question by the Ifo Institute, dated 11 March 2011, and letter from the ECB to the Ifo Institute, dated 15 March 2012. Article 2 paragraph 1 of the unpublished decision ECB /2007/NP10 on the interest yield of intra-Eurosystem net balances states: 'Intra-Eurosystem balances [. ..] are remunerated at the latest available marginal interest rate used by the Eurosystem in its tenders for main refinancing operations'.

interest and compound interest. Without this possibility in the background, the interest on the Target debt is meaningless.

Target Balances as a Public Capital Export

The reason for the credit-like nature of the balances lies deeper than in the necessities of double bookkeeping, since the net flow of money that leads to Target balances stands vis-à-vis a real flow of goods and/or assets (including the 'repurchase of private debt titles', i.e. the redemption of a debt). This net flow of goods and assets must be booked in the NCBs' balance sheets as claims and liabilities, since it would otherwise amount to gifts from one national economy to another. To be sure, the private sellers of export goods receive their money and are therefore content enough. But this money is actually a claim on their own NCB that sits on the liability side of its balance sheet. The claim of this NCB on other NCBs, or the Eurosystem, represents the sole countervalue for the national economy of the country that has exported these goods or assets.

It is therefore logical for the change in the Target balances to be indeed booked as capital flows under the line labelled 'Capital Investments Abroad' (or with a similar label) in the national balance-of-payments statistics. It is also logical for the Target stock, as reported in the NCB balance sheets, to be tallied as part of a country's net foreign asset position. The reader may recall the discussion on the rapid rise in the net foreign asset positions after the euro announcement in Chapter 2, in the context of Figures 2.9 and 2.10. As will be shown in Chapter 7, a substantial part of this rise, in particular after 2008, was due to the increase in Target balances. Figure 6.4 shows the fraction of the net foreign asset position of a selected number of euro countries that is officially accounted for by Target credit, with both the net foreign asset position and the Target balance expressed as a portion of GDP.

It is noteworthy that for some of the troubled countries, notably Greece and Ireland, Target liabilities account for a major share of their net foreign debt, if one considers this debt as composed of two elements: ordinary (private and fiscal) credit and asset titles on the one hand, and Target liabilities on the other. Of Greece's net foreign debt of 109% of GDP in 2012, 50 percentage points was accounted for by Greek Target liabilities; of Spain's 91%, 33 percentage points; of Italy's 28%, 16 percentage points; of Portugal's 115%, 39 percentage points; and of Ireland's 112%, 48 percentage points. If countries are ranked by the share of Target liabilities in their total net foreign debt, Italy would top the list, with more than 50%.

Conversely, in the Netherlands and Germany, net foreign assets, considering a similar decomposition, consist to a large extent of mere Target claims. In Germany, 25 percentage points out of a net foreign asset position of 42% of GDP in 2012 was accounted for by the Bundesbank's Target claim. In absolute

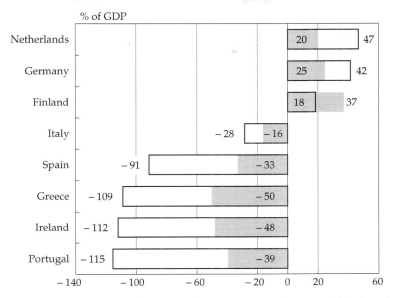

Figure 6.4 Target balances (grey) and foreign assets, relative to GDP (2012)

Sources: Eurostat, Database, *Economy and Finance*, Balance of Payments—International Transactions; Target balances: see Figure 6.2.

terms, this was € 656 billion out of € 1,107 billion. In the Netherlands, Target claims accounted for 20 percentage points out of a total of 47% of GDP.

   In Finland the situation was unusual, since the Finnish Target claims exceeded its net foreign asset position, which is 18% of GDP, by 19 percentage points. This indicates that the Finnish economy no longer held ordinary net claims on the rest of the world; what is more, if the Eurosystem had defaulted on the Finnish Target claims, Finland would have fallen into a net debtor position to the tune of 19% of its GDP.

Inside Money, Outside Money, and the Local Printing Press

We should now return to the relationship between Target balances and the ECB's refinancing policy, alluded to briefly in the context of Figure 6.1, which explained the basic mechanics of the Target system (recall the printing press image). No economy can cope with ever-increasing amounts of money being sent abroad, unless the money leaving the country is replenished, since otherwise a liquidity crisis will inevitably occur. The stock of central bank money in a modern economy is quite small. While the wealth of the citizens typically amounts to three to five times the country's GDP, the stock of central bank money, as defined by the so-called monetary base, has an order of magnitude of only one-tenth to one-fifth of GDP. In 2011, for example, the stock of central bank money in the Eurozone amounted to 12.3% of GDP, in Germany 17.8%, and in Greece 19.7%. Greece, however, had a 9.9% current account deficit in 2011. Even if Greece had suffered no capital flight and its current account deficit had to be financed solely with existing money, the stock of money would have been exhausted within two years if no fresh funding from the Greek NCB had been forthcoming, making it impossible to conduct any domestic transactions.

This makes it clear that the outflow of money measured by the Target balances must be compensated by printing fresh money—indeed, that money printing made such outflow possible in the first place. To be sure, there is a certain flexibility in the economy that makes it possible to produce a given GDP with a somewhat smaller stock of money in circulation, as has always been pointed out by Keynesian economists who stress the flexibility of money demand and the velocity of money circulation. It is possible to get by, given one's income and expenditure, with a lower average stock of money in the wallet and on the checking account by filling the savings account more frequently with smaller quantities and withdrawing smaller sums from the ATM while paying it more frequent visits. Similarly, a commercial bank can get by with a lower average stock of central bank money on its account with its NCB by resorting to a more sophisticated and risky liquidity management. The necessary change in the stock of liquidity carried around can be induced by a rise in the short-term interest rate, since this raises the opportunity cost of holding liquidity. But this flexibility is utterly insufficient to cope with the net outflow of money that the troubled countries have experienced since the crisis broke out.

It is the same with an individual. If income disappears and the individual does not want to give up his/her interest-bearing physical and financial assets, the living standard can be maintained for as long as the liquid money in the wallet and on the bank account lasts. While it lasts, the person will have a negative balance of payments, because the bank account will be depleted fairly quickly, and the wallet even faster. But the money will eventually be gone and something will have to be done to improve the balance of payments, either by finding a job or getting a loan or selling part of one's assets. If the balance of payments fails to be improved with a paying job, and the person does not want to sell assets and the bank not only refuses to provide credit, but starts to demand repayment of outstanding credit, this person has a problem. It is not advisable for him or her to try to solve the problem by printing in his basement the money needed, since that is severely punishable by law. But in the case of the Eurozone countries, the situation is a bit different.

Figure 6.5 shows what happened during the crisis. The dotted curve depicts the evolution of the GIPSIC monetary base, i.e. the stock of money circulating there, since the first year of the crisis. The monetary base of a country consists of the banknotes that the country's NCB has issued and the demand deposits held by the commercial banks at the NCB. It can be seen that the monetary base of the GIPSIC countries did not decline, despite their huge balance-of-payments deficits, initially following a rising trend that later flattened somewhat. The money sent abroad by way of payment orders must therefore have been reprinted, for if not, their monetary base would have declined on a par with the rise of Target balances.

The steeply rising solid curve gives the overall amount of money created in the GIPSIC countries by refinancing credit and asset purchases. This is indeed much more money than is circulating within these countries. The difference between this curve and the dotted curve measures the net amount of central bank money that flowed out of these countries by way of payment orders, as measured by the Target balances. It is what was called outside money above in the Section *Ballooning Target Balances*, as opposed to the inside money that circulates in the country where it was created through refinancing operations and asset purchases.

Figure 6.5 provides a deeper economic interpretation to complement the analysis of the Target balances conducted so far. As discussed above, these balances represent credit flowing between NCBs resulting from mutual payment orders. The balances accurately measure the cross-border net flow of money, because the monetary base shrinks in the country where the payment order is issued and expands where the payment is received. But there can be no overflow of money if no additional money is created in the originating country. As the chart shows, the point in time at which the stock of outside money equalled the stock of inside money was already reached in July 2011. Thereafter, no central bank money would have been left in the GIPSIC countries if it had not regularly been replenished with the printing press. Indirectly, therefore, the Target balances measure the additional money creation and, with it, the additional granting of refinancing credit (or money through asset purchases) above and beyond the liquidity needs of the economy. As shown above, this additional refinancing credit was made possible by the lowering of collateral standards and the extension of maturities. It enabled banks to deliver the freshly printed money to the local economy, making it possible for citizens to continue purchasing goods or assets from abroad, or to pay off foreign debt. Without the cheap credit from the printing press, which undercut market conditions, there would have been a shortage of liquidity in those countries, leading to higher interest rates being demanded of them. Their citizens would have been able to buy fewer goods and assets from abroad, and foreign investors would have been inclined to provide more private credit, since yields net of risk premia would have been higher. All of this would have kept the net payment orders measured by the Target balances from rising as explosively as they did.

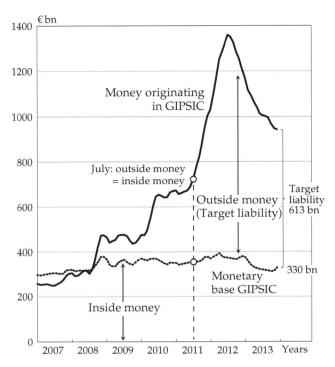

Figure 6.5 Inside money and outside money of the GIPSIC countries (January 2007—December 2013)

Sources: Balance Sheets of the ECB, Central Bank of Ireland, Central Bank of Greece, Banco de Portugal, Banco de España, Banca d'Italia, Central Bank of Cyprus; International Monetary Fund, *International Financial Statistics*; H.-W. Sinn and T. Wollmershäuser, 'Target Loans, Current Account Balances and Capital Flows: The ECB's Rescue Facility', 2012, figure 3, updated with a slightly changed definition of the monetary base (now including deposit facilities, according to the official definition.)

Note: The monetary base of a country or a group of countries is defined as demand deposits of commercial banks with their NCBs (including deposit facilities) plus statutory banknotes (banknote issuance in proportion to size of economy) plus related 'intra-Eurosystem liabilities' (over-proportionate issuance of banknotes), the latter item netting out to zero if the group of countries comprises the entire currency area. Inside money is the central bank money that has been created locally by refinancing operations or asset purchases and has not been sent, in net terms, to other countries by way of international payment orders. Outside money, the money that the Target balances measure, is the net portion of money created by a country's NCB through refinancing operations or asset purchases that have flowed out of the country by means of international payment orders and circulates abroad. The charts were smoothed by using rolling three-month averages. In December 2013, the monetary base of the GIPSIC countries amounted to € 330 billion, the demand deposits of commercial banks to € 56 billion, statutory bank notes to € 335 billion, and there were € 61 billion in intra-Eurosystem claims from under-proportionate banknote issuance, so that the actual banknote issuance was € 274 billion.

In the United States, it was a great cause for concern that the Federal Reserve System tripled the monetary base during the crisis.[25] All the more alarming then is that the volume of money created in the GIPSIC countries by way of domestic credit operations including asset purchases in a span of five years, from summer 2007 to summer 2012, has grown more than fivefold, as the chart shows.[26]

The self-service at the printing press was carried out to an extreme that is truly astounding. At its peak, in July 2012, before the ECB calmed the markets with the announcement of its OMT programme, the stock of credit money originating in the GIPSIC countries had grown to € 1,359 billion in the six crisis-hit countries, with € 985 billion of this sum having been used to buy goods and assets abroad and repay external debt. This was a stealth rescue facility provided by the Eurosystem of which the public knew little, and which dwarfed all of the official rescue programmes.

Crowding out Refinancing Credit in the North

The question now is how the enormous increase in money creation in the crisis-hit countries has affected the rest of Europe. In public discussion, the issue raised most often is inflation. Politicians and economists warn against this danger,[27] while the ECB reassures everyone that there are no signs of an inflationary trend.[28]

One thing is certain: a vast amount of liquidity has been created in the GIPSIC countries that has landed in the other countries of the Eurozone. The money that had flowed from the core to the GIPSIC countries before the crisis, in the form of private credit, now ceased to flow, while the money that the core countries' banks had lent to the now-troubled countries fled back home because investors were afraid of the risks, and unwilling to compete with the local printing presses, which were offering credit regardless of these risks at conditions private lenders could never meet. Moreover, as documented at the beginning of

---

[25] For the policy responses of the Federal Reserve Bank to the financial crisis starting in 2007, which lead to this tripling, see B. S. Bernanke, *The Federal Reserve and the Financial Crisis*, Princeton University Press, Princeton 2013.

[26] A similar point was made by A. Tornell and F. Westermann, 'Europe Needs a Federal Reserve', *New York Times*, 21 June 2012, available at: <http://www.nytimes.com/2012/06/21/opinion/the-european-central-bank-needs-more-power.html?_r=1>.

[27] See M. Feldstein, 'Is Inflation Returning?', *Project Syndicate*, 29 August 2012, available at: <http://www.project-syndicate.org/commentary/is-inflation-returning-by-martin-feldstein> or 'The World from Berlin: "High Inflation Causes Societies to Disintegrate"', *Spiegel Online International*, 11 May 2012, available at: <http://www.spiegel.de/international/germany/fear-of-inflation-in-germany-after-bundesbank-comments-a-832648.html>.

[28] See M. Draghi, 'Stabile Preise ohne monetäre Staatsfinanzierung', Interview by H. Steltzner and S. Ruhkamp, *Frankfurter Allgemeine Zeitung*, 24 February 2012, available at: <http://www.ecb.int/press/key/date/2012/html/sp120224_1.en.html>.

Chapter 5, there was large-scale capital flight from Greek and Spanish banks to safer places abroad.

All of this translated into a surplus of liquidity and credit in the rest of the euro countries, which pushed interest rates to a historical low and triggered a construction boom in Germany (see Chapter 3). The upswing in Germany absorbed only a small portion of the liquidity, using it as additional transaction cash. The banks of the northern euro bloc found themselves flush with liquidity and had difficulty disposing of it.

While this could mean that there may have been forces stoking inflation in these countries, no sizeable inflation differentials between the GIPSIC countries and the rest of the Eurozone have yet materialized, as Figure 4.8 in Chapter 4 showed (bar Ireland). The harmonized inflation rate in the Eurozone, in turn, gives no reason for concern: while it was 2.1% on average in the five crisis years from 2008 to 2012, it averaged 2.2% in the previous five years.

The reason was probably that the monetary base in the Eurozone did not, in fact, expand extraordinarily in the aggregate during the crisis. The more than three-fold increase mentioned above in the stock of money balances created in the GIPSIC countries in the period 2007–2012 contrasts sharply with the increase in the stock of money balances in the aggregate of all euro countries, which amounted to 'only' 71%.

Figure 6.6 shows what happened. Obviously the explosion of the stock of money balances created in the GIPSIC countries by way of refinancing credit, caused or made possible by the ECB's collateral and maturity policies, only moderately expanded the aggregate monetary base, because it reduced the inside money circulating in the rest of the Eurozone. This happened because the commercial banks of the other Eurozone countries took countervailing actions to get rid of at least some of the inflowing liquidity, since they did not need it, by repaying their own refinancing credit or lending the surplus cash to their NCBs by investing in fixed-term deposits.

Remarkably, the expansion of the stock of money created in the GIPSIC countries had become so large that by April 2012 it eventually reached the trend value for the aggregate stock of money balances in the entire Eurozone, € 1,189 billion. At that point, all the money normally needed for transactions in the Eurozone was created in the six crisis countries. True, there was an additional stock of € 493 billion of inside money in the non-GIPSIC countries at that time,[29] but that money was not needed for transactions; it was nevertheless held in NCB demand deposits by commercial banks and as bank notes by the public, because the ECB had only auctioned limited slots for fixed-term deposits among the commercial banks. In addition, the interest for money parked in the deposit facility,

---

[29] This figure includes a minor amount of money created through the ECB's own asset purchases.

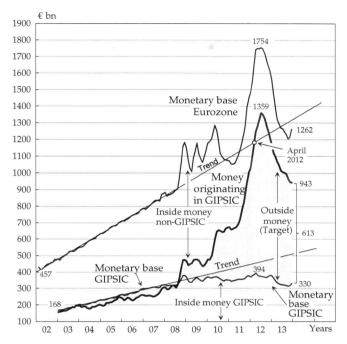

Figure 6.6 The structure of the monetary base and the role of Target balances (January 2002—December 2013)

Note: For the definitions and sources see Figure 6.5. The inside money of the non-GIPSIC countries includes money created by asset purchases by the ECB itself.

which used to absorb much liquidity, had been set to zero on 11 July 2012. This reduced the incentive to park the liquidity there.

At the peak of the aggregate value of the monetary base in July 2012, 77% of the base money circulating in the Eurozone had originated in the six crisis countries through refinancing operations or asset purchases. This share itself peaked in April and September 2013 at 81%. Figure 6.7 shows this quite graphically by providing the information given in Figure 6.6 in relative terms, all variables being expressed in relation to the aggregate stock of base money in the Eurozone.

The rising solid line in the centre of the chart shows which fractions of the total stock of base money available in the Eurozone were created in the GIPSIC countries (the distance from the abscissa) and in the non-GIPSIC countries (the distance from the upper boundary) by way of refinancing credit and asset purchases.[30] Similarly, the dotted line shows which fractions of the total monetary

---

[30] The latter includes money created through the ECB's own asset purchases.

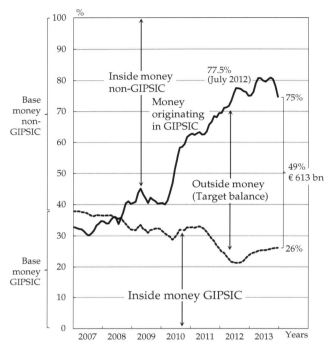

Figure 6.7 International shifting of refinancing credit as a result of net payment orders (January 2007–December 2013)

Note: For definitions and sources see Figure 6.5 as well as the balance sheet of the ECB.

base were actually circulating in the GIPSIC (the distance below the line) and non-GIPSIC countries (the distance above the line). The distance between the solid and the dotted lines is the Target balance, i.e. the outside money that was created by refinancing credit and asset purchases in one group of countries, flowed through payment orders into another group, and now circulates there.

It is clearly evident that the liquidity flowing into the non-GIPSIC countries through the payment orders measured by the Target balances gradually crowded out the liquidity created by asset purchases and refinancing credit in these countries. The alternative source of liquidity available to commercial banks has constrained the NCBs' ability to issue refinancing credit.[31] The crowding-out process

---

[31] The term 'crowding out' has created some confusion in the debate as non-economists active in the internet re-interpreted it as a supply-induced crowding out, and disseminated this interpretation across the English-language blogosphere. Someone even implied that Sinn and Wollmershäuser had argued that the Target balances created a credit

lasted until April 2013, when the percentage of the monetary base consisting of the Target debt of the GIPSIC countries, i.e. the outside money circulating in the non-GIPSIC countries, peaked. At that time, only 19% of the Eurozone's monetary base had originated in the non-GIPSIC countries (or from the ECB itself), even though these countries accounted for 68% of the Eurozone's GDP. Fully 81% of the money circulating in the Eurozone originated in the GIPSIC countries. 25 percentage points of this money was used for providing liquidity to these countries, and 56 percentage points was Target credit that enabled the GIPSIC countries to buy goods and assets elsewhere and redeem their foreign debt. After September 2013, the percentage of money created declined somewhat. Nevertheless, by the end of 2013, 75% of the Eurozone's monetary base was created in the GIPSIC countries. Fully 49% of the Eurozone's monetary base, € 613 billion in absolute terms, originated from Target credit provided to the GIPSIC countries.

It is a matter of debate whether this helped these countries more than their creditors, who otherwise might not have been able to get their money back. However, it definitely was a huge bailout operation by the ECB that was implicit in the rules of the Eurosystem and was not understood by the public, and initially not even by economic specialists. This is why the English version of the original article on this issue bore the title 'The ECB's Stealth Bailout'.[32]

In Germany the crowding-out process was particularly pronounced.[33] There, the net refinancing credit, calculated by subtracting the fixed-term

---

crunch. However, the crowding out of refinancing credit in the non-GIPSIC countries occurs because the demand for, rather than the supply of, liquidity is given. It constrains the ECB, not the commercial banks. This is the exact opposite of a credit crunch. This use of the term crowding-out harks back to the beginning of the crowding-out debate in monetary economics, starting with Milton Friedman's argument that useful public goods crowd out private goods because they are substitutes for them. See M. Friedman, *Capitalism and Freedom*, University of Chicago Press, Chicago 1962, chapter VI: *The Role of Government in Education*. As an example, Friedman used free school meals that crowd out meal provision by the parents, since the demand for meals is limited. It is precisely this kind of crowding out, resulting from a reduction in demand, that the inflowing Target money has caused. Another example is the crowding out of one supplier in a market through the entry of another. A detailed analysis of this issue can be found in H.-W. Sinn and T. Wollmershäuser, 'Target Loans, Current Account Balances and Capital Flows: The ECB's Rescue Facility', 2012; see in particular the preceding working paper versions as well. See also H.-W. Sinn, 'On and off Target', 14 June 2011, which discusses this and other misunderstandings.

[32] See H.-W. Sinn, 'The ECB's Stealth Bailout', 1 June 2011. For a scholarly analysis see H.-W. Sinn and T. Wollmershäuser, 'Target Loans, Current Account Balances and Capital Flows: The ECB's Rescue Facility', 2011 and 2012.

[33] Unfortunately the Dutch central bank does not publish data on the aggregate monetary base. Thus, it is not possible to report on its particular situation in this regard.

deposits that commercial banks hold with their central bank, turned negative as early as August 2011.[34] The only inside money existing in Germany at
that time had originated from the Bundesbank's prior asset purchases. After
August 2011, the net creditor position of German commercial banks with the
Bundesbank remained negative for many months, peaking at –€ 99 billion,
or –17% of the German monetary base, in February 2012. Only in December
2013 the Bundesbank's refinancing credit turned positive again, with a value
of € 5 billion, or 0.9 % of the German monetary base.

In Finland the situation was even more extreme. There, the net refinancing
credit turned negative in October 2010 and has remained negative ever since,
peaking at –€ 21 billion, or –42% of the Finnish monetary base, in January
2012. By December 2013, the last data point available at this writing, it was
–€ 11 billion, or –34% of the monetary base.[35] The Bank of Finland, even in
net terms, borrowed funds equal to one-third of its monetary base from its
commercial banks to absorb the excess liquidity that capital flight had washed
ashore.

However, sterilizing changes in the stock of central bank money not only
originated from the NCBs' borrowing and lending operations, but also from
their buying and selling of marketable assets. Figure 6.8 shows the overall effect
of all money-creating and -absorbing operations for Germany and Finland.

Obviously, by June 2012 even the stock of money created by the Bundesbank's
asset purchases and refinancing operations taken together had been crowded
out in net terms. The stock of inside money vanished, as the Target balances
reached the level of the entire German monetary base.[36] The monetary base
was created exclusively by the Bundesbank's fulfilling of net payment orders
on behalf of other central banks of the Eurozone. By the end of June 2012
and in the following months, the Bundesbank's Target claims even slightly
exceeded the German monetary base, the excess peaking at € 61 billion, or

---

[34] See also H.-W. Sinn and T. Wollmershäuser, 'Target Loans, Current Account
Balances and Capital Flows: The ECB's Rescue Facility', 2012, p. 485; see also A. Tornell
and F. Westermann, 'Has the ECB Hit a Limit?', *VoxEU*, 28 March 2012, available
at: <http://www.voxeu.org/article/has-ecb-hit-limit>.

[35] See Balance Sheet of the Bank of Finland, available at: <http://www.suomen-
pankki.fi/en/tilastot/tase_ja_korko/Pages/tilastot_rahalaitosten_lainat_talletukset_ja_
korot_taseet_ja_raha_aggregaatit_SP_tase_en.aspx#Pebaf7b6c85a04fcf91c867a3091f99
3b_6_51iToRox55>, and International Monetary Fund, *International Financial Statistics*,
Datastream.

[36] It is worth remembering that the monetary base of a country is defined as including
over-proportionate banknote issuance, and it is not known whether these banknotes are
circulating in Germany or elsewhere in the world. See footnote to Figure 6.5.

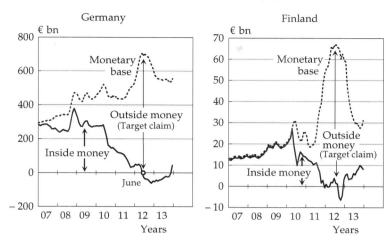

Figure 6.8 Crowding out inside money in Germany and Finland

Sources: Deutsche Bundesbank and Bank of Finland balance sheets; International Monetary Fund, *International Financial Statistics*.

Note: For the underlying Target balances see Figure 6.2. The corresponding chart for the Netherlands cannot be constructed, since the Dutch central bank does not publish data on the monetary base.

9% of the German monetary base, in November 2012.[37] The Bundesbank had effectively stopped being a central bank that lends out its self-created money against interest and collateral, turning instead into a sort of paper shredder mopping up huge amounts of liquidity that had been generated in other Eurozone countries by way of asset purchases and lending to commercial banks, receiving Target claims in exchange. The period of negative inside money lasted about one-and-a-half years, until November 2013. Germany's 'self-made' monetary base did not turn positive again until December 2013, with a value of € 46 billion, or 8% of Germany's monetary base. During the crisis, Germany had lent out its entire stock of money balances to rescue Europe (including its own banks).

The same was true for Finland, as shown on the right-hand chart. In Finland, the inside money was entirely crowded out by the end of 2011, then came a short

---

[37] The difficulties that the Bundesbank would encounter when its entire monetary base was turned into Target credit were discussed and forecast for 2013 in H.-W. Sinn and T. Wollmershäuser, 'Target Loans, Current Account Balances and Capital Flows: The ECB's Rescue Facility', *CESifo Working Paper* No. 3500, June 2011; see in particular figure 15. As it turned out, they arrived a year earlier than expected.

period when the stock of inside money again was slightly positive, then it turned negative again, and did not return to the normal, positive range until the end of 2012, after the crisis had calmed, as Finnish Target claims again fell below the monetary base level. By the end of 2013, still about one-third of the Finnish monetary base was inside money and two-thirds were outside money, stemming from credit operations or asset purchases elsewhere in the Eurozone.

What all this shows is that the Target balances do not represent an increase in the monetary base, but a mere shifting of refinancing credit from the north to the south. One could say that the Target balances measure the extent to which the (electronic) printing press has been lent to the southern NCBs. This lends a stronger foundation to the interpretation of the Target balances as a measure of intergovernmental credit, which follows from the way such balances sit in the respective NCB balance sheets.[38] While the southern NCBs printed and lent out large amounts of money so as to give their economies the possibility of continuing to import goods and assets from other countries and pay off their foreign debt, the northern NCBs 'shredded' the inflowing money by becoming net debtors to their commercial banks, or by giving them less refinancing credit.

The ECB was, of course, aware of this situation. It justified its policy by claiming to assume the role of a credit intermediary among the banks. Since banks hesitated to provide credit to each other, concerned that they would not get their money back, they preferred to park it at the ECB; and the ECB itself then took on the task of lending out the money. This had advantages for both sides, according to the ECB. The borrowing banks received the money on cheaper terms, and the lending banks enjoyed more security on their investment.[39] However, this view hides the fact that with its policy the ECB systematically redirected savings capital from one group of countries to another, a process that may have slowed down the correction of the current account imbalances between the Eurozone countries and *constituted an international public capital flow* performed by the central banks of the Eurosystem. The volume of this international capital flow is measured by the Target balances.

[38]   This interpretation was first posited in H.-W. Sinn, 'Die riskante Kreditersatzpolitik der EZB', 4 May 2011; and H.-W. Sinn, 'The ECB's Stealth Bailout', 1 June 2011.

[39]   See J.-C. Trichet, 'Enhanced Credit Support: Key ECB Policy Actions for the Euro Area Economy', Lecture given at *Munich Seminar*, CESifo and Süddeutsche Zeitung, 13 July 2009; and J.-C. Trichet, 'The ECB's Enhanced Credit Support', *CESifo Working Paper* No. 2833, October 2009, available at: <http://www.cesifo-group.de/DocDL/cesifo1_wp2833.pdf>.

CHAPTER 7

Current Accounts, Capital Flight, and Target Balances

Financing Balance-of-Payments Deficits—Greece, Portugal, and Cyprus Living off the Printing Press—Irish Capital Flight—The Flight from Italy and Spain—France in Between—Germany: Exporting for Target Claims—Finland and the Netherlands—Bretton Woods and the European Payment Union—Transfer Roubles—The Swiss Example—How Target-Like Balances are Settled in the USA—A Fundamental Dichotomy in the Rescue Policies

Financing Balance-of-Payments Deficits

Chapters 2 and 4 showed that the countries now in crisis (Greece, Ireland, Portugal, Spain, Italy, and Cyprus, grouped under the acronym GIPSIC) lost their competitiveness and ran up massive current account deficits as a result of an inflationary credit bubble induced by reduced borrowing costs brought about by the introduction of the euro. When the US crisis spilled over to Europe, the capital markets were no longer willing to finance such deficits. Chapters 5 and 6 discussed how and in what sense the GIPSIC countries made use of their money-printing presses as a replacement for funding unavailable at more desirable conditions from the capital markets. This chapter will look at the countries individually and attempt to ascertain the degree to which they actually financed their current account deficits with freshly created money, which portions were financed through other channels, and what role capital flight played, in the sense of a reversal of the flow of capital, a case discussed in the previous chapter in the context of Figure 6.2.

A current account deficit, i.e. the excess of imports and interest payments on net foreign debt over exports and net transfers received, needs to be financed.

Assuming that the local stock of central bank money is being held constant, a country has only three possibilities:[1]

1. Incoming payment orders associated with private capital import. These normally result from the investment decisions of foreign private investors and their financial institutions, including portfolio decisions and foreign direct investment (such as the acquisition of a company), as well as from a repatriation of capital by domestic residents. This is the normal option, and the one that actually financed the current account deficits until the crisis struck.

2. Incoming payment orders associated with fiscal credit provided by other states or international organizations. This is basically intergovernmental credit from multilateral institutions such as the Eurozone, IMF or ESM. This type of credit started flowing in May 2010, and will be discussed in further detail in Chapter 8.

3. Local money creation through refinancing operations and asset purchases by the national central bank (NCB). For the reasons explained in Chapter 6, this book calls 'Target credit' the extra money created to make net payment orders possible without eroding the monetary base.

The relationship between these three variables and a country's current account balance results from a national budget constraint that cannot be altered except by theft, and of course, it holds algebraically: if one of the items changes its sign, the others must compensate for it. If, for example, a country's private capital import is negative because the capital inflow not only stops, but reverses its direction, Target credit or fiscal credit have to make up for it. Otherwise, either the current account deficit could not occur or the capital flow could not reverse its

[1] See H.-W. Sinn, 'Die riskante Kreditersatzpolitik der EZB', *Frankfurter Allgemeine Zeitung*, No. 103, 4 May 2011, p. 10, available at: <http://www.faz.net/aktuell/wirtschaft/europas-schuldenkrise/target-kredite-die-riskante-kreditersatzpolitik-der-ezb-1637926.html>; H.-W. Sinn, 'The ECB's Stealth Bailout', *VoxEU*, 1 June 2011, available at: <http://www.voxeu.org/article/ecb-s-stealth-bailout>; H.-W. Sinn and T. Wollmershäuser, 'Target Loans, Current Account Balances and Capital Flows: The ECB's Rescue Facility', *International Tax and Public Finance* 19, 2012, pp. 468–508, specifically section 9, available at: <http://www.cesifo-group.de/DocDL/sinn-itax-2012-target.pdf>; the latter appeared as *CESifo Working Paper* No. 3500, June 2011, available at: <http://www.cesifo-group.de/DocDL/cesifo1_wp3500.pdf> and as *NBER Working Paper* No. 17626, November 2011, available at: <http://www.cesifo-group.de/DocDL/NBER_wp17626_sinn_wollm.pdf>; S. Homburg, 'Anmerkungen zum Target2-Streit', *ifo Schnelldienst* 64, No. 16, 31 August 2011, p. 46, available at: <http://www.cesifo-group.de/DocDL/ifosd_2011_16_9.pdf>; G. Milbradt, 'Die EZB auf der schiefen Bahn', *ifo Schnelldienst* 64, No. 16, 31 August 2011, p. 39, available at: <http://www.cesifo-group.de/DocDL/ifosd_2011_16_8.pdf>.

direction. Note that if country A uses Target credit to finance its current account deficit vis-à-vis country B (or a capital flight to country B), this means that country B's NCB issues the money in exchange for a claim on the ECB system instead of a claim on commercial banks in its own jurisdiction, while the ECB receives a claim on the NCB of country A, which receives a claim on its banks by giving them refinancing credit (or buys assets from them) in the first place. This was explained in the previous chapter.

This statement needs to be qualified if a euro country has a current or a capital account imbalance with countries outside the Eurozone. While such imbalances by themselves lead to flows of euros or other currencies across borders, they normally do not last long, as economic agents in each currency area usually try to get rid of excess stocks of money that is legal tender only in other jurisdictions.[2] Exchange rate adjustments will usually induce countervailing transactions in the reverse direction that have the effect of absorbing the excesses. Imbalances can only occur if central banks manipulate the exchange rate by accumulating foreign currency, which is typically the case in fixed-exchange rate systems, or if there are sizeable changes in the stocks of currencies held outside their currency areas for international transaction purposes. While it is true that both the dollar and, to a limited extent, the euro are used as a means of payment outside their respective jurisdictions, there are usually no significant increases or reductions in their respective stocks of dollars or euros.

In the Eurozone the exchange of foreign currency is operated by the ECB itself, which allocates Target liabilities and Target claims to NCBs according to the currency they buy or sell abroad. Suppose a citizen of a particular euro country buys a Chinese product, to be paid for in dollars. The citizen draws up the payment order in euros, but his bank converts the euros into dollars, which it receives from its NCB; the latter, in turn, receives the dollars from the ECB in exchange for a Target liability. However, with a flexible exchange rate, there will be a similar inflow of dollars into the Eurozone, as foreigners buy Eurozone goods or assets, which the ECB converts into euros. This reverse payment order means that the ECB allocates a Target claim to the NCB of the recipient of the payment. Similarly, if the citizen pays for the Chinese product in euros, which are then used to buy goods or assets from another other euro country, his NCB has to accept a Target liability with regard to the ECB, while the other euro country's NCB receives a Target claim on the ECB.

Thus, it is not the euro-internal current account and capital account imbalances of a country to which the above accounting identity refers, but to the one with the entire rest of the world, including euro and non-euro countries.

---

[2] Bulgaria, Denmark, Latvia, Lithuania, Poland, and Romania have an associate status with the Eurosystem. They are allowed to hold Target claims, but not to incur Target liabilities. This, however, is only a minor item.

The question that now arises is in which proportion Target credit, private capital imports, and, if any, fiscal capital imports contributed to financing the current account deficits. Whatever the answer, it shouldn't be interpreted as if Target credit was the cause of current account deficits or that the two are correlated. Given that the current account deficits of the crisis countries react only sluggishly and must be financed somehow, as was discussed in Chapter 2 (Section *The Timing Problem*), it is clear that the main short-term correlation is between Target and the other two variables (private capital flows and fiscal rescue credit). Nevertheless, it is useful to find out what contributions the separate items have made.

A first overview is provided by Figure 7.1, which reviews the combined budget constraints of the GIPSIC countries. This is a very rich and informative chart whose reading requires close attention and, since it forms the basis

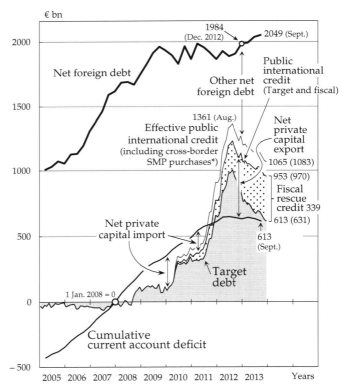

Figure 7.1 Net foreign debt, cumulative current account balances, Target liabilities, and open rescue operations (GIPSIC)*

* Securities Markets Programme (SMP): book value of GIPSIC government bonds held by non-GIPSIC central banks.

for the rest of this chapter, it should be studied carefully. The figure shows the time paths of:

—the cumulative GIPSIC current account deficit, 1 January 2008 being the base point, set at zero,

—the stock of GIPSIC Target liabilities,

—the stock of fiscal rescue credit paid out to the GIPSIC countries (added to the Target balances),

—the stock of GIPSIC government bonds purchased by non-GIPSIC NCBs and the ECB itself (again added to the former two items), and

—the stock of net foreign debt of the GIPSIC countries evaluated at market prices. (Basically, this stock is the sum of current account deficits

Figure 7.1 (Continued)

Sources: Eurostat, Database, *Economy and Finance*, Balance of Payments—International Transactions; European Commission, *Economic and Financial Affairs*, The EU as a Borrower; European Commission, *EU Budget 2011*, Financial Report; European Commission, *The Economic Adjustment Programme for Greece: Fifth Review*; European Financial Stability Facility, *Lending Operations*; IMF, *Financial Activities*; IMF, *SDR Exchange Rate Archives by Month*; IMF, *Updated IMF Quota Data*; European Stability Mechanism, *Financial Assistance*; European Stability Mechanism, *ESM Factsheet*; ECB, *Open Market Operations*; Banca d'Italia, *Base Informativa Pubblica*, Balance of Payments and International Investment Position; for Target balances, see Figures 6.2 and 6.3.

Note: The figures in brackets show the respective increments of the curve values as of 1 January 2008. In this diagram they differ from the curve values by the value of the GIPSIC Target claim on 31 December 2007, which amounted to € 18 billion.

The fiscal rescue credit is calculated net of the six crisis countries' own contributions to rescue operations and net of debt redemptions (€ 1.7 billion up to December 2013), only actual payments being tallied. It includes all financial help disbursed by the EU, IMF, the euro countries, EFSF, and ESM (monthly data). Greece: first rescue package of the euro countries and IMF, second rescue package of the EFSF and the IMF. Ireland: EFSF, EFSM, and IMF. Portugal: EFSF, EFSM, and IMF. Spain: ESM. Cyprus: ESM and IMF. By December 2013, this had translated into a net fiscal rescue credit of € 339 billion. The countries' own contributions follow from the rescue agreements in the case of the first Eurozone package, from the share in the revenues of the EU budget in 2011 in the case of EU contributions, and from their contributions to ESM's paid-in capital.

Government bond purchases by the ECB: since all the euro countries' NCBs participated in the purchase of sovereign bonds according to their share in the ECB's capital, the GIPSIC share (37%) is subtracted from the overall total. This and the following charts are based on data available as of 24 February 2014.

accumulated from far back in the past, adjusted for a revaluation of outstanding debt and liability titles as shown in the context of Figure 2.9 in Chapter 2.)

Since all the curves show stocks, their slopes indicate the respective flows.[3] Thus, for example, the slope of the cumulative current account curve shows the current account deficit, whose level the reader already knows from Figure 2.1. As can be seen, the deficits existed before the crisis broke out in 2007 and have persisted thereafter. Only with a delay of a couple of years did they gradually come down, as shown by the flattening and eventually downward-pointing slope.

The figures at the end of the curves refer to the values at the end of 2013, unless otherwise noted. The figures in brackets give the corresponding increments as of 1 January 2008. By the end of 2013, GIPSIC Target debt was € 613 billion, as shown in Figure 6.2, while the increment as of 1 January 2008 was € 631 billion, given that the starting stock of Target debt at that point in time was –€ 18 billion.

As explained in Chapter 2, before the outbreak of the crisis markets were still willing to finance the current account deficits. Thus, the Target balances were vanishingly small until 2007. However, since autumn 2008, when the Lehman debacle brought the crisis to full swing, the Target balances started to rise sharply because the measures described in Chapter 5, particularly the lowering of collateral standards for local refinancing credit and the extension of its maturity, cranked up the printing presses, given that ECB funding became available at below-market conditions. The Target curve shows which part of the current account deficits, accumulated since 1 January 2008, was financed at various points in time by Target credit, i.e. the ECB internal credit among the NCBs. Strictly speaking, the contribution of Target credit is given by the increase in the height of the curve from 1 January 2008 to the respective date, but given that Target credit was close to zero at the starting point, this is of little relevance in the chart.

However, the GIPSIC countries not only received credit from the ECB, but also from fiscal institutions. The fiscal capital flows resulting from the various rescue operations are measured by the height of the dotted area placed on the Target curve. The rescue programmes began with the decisions adopted by the EU countries on 10 May 2010. These decisions paved the way for the intergovernmental aid for Greece and the establishment of the European Financial Stability Facility (EFSF), which in January 2011 began to issue credit to Ireland, and in May 2011 also to Portugal. In addition there were rescue credits from the IMF and the EU, the latter in the form of the European Financial Stabilisation Mechanism (EFSM). Later, in 2012, the permanent rescue fund ESM was added. The credit flows are calculated here net of the GIPSIC countries' own

---

[3] This chapter uses and expands the methodology of H.-W. Sinn and T. Wollmershäuser, 'Target Loans, Current Account Balances and Capital Flows: The ECB's Rescue Facility', 2012.

contributions to the rescue programmes and net of repayments. The figures shown include only the actual disbursements, not the total programme volumes. As the dotted area demonstrates, the net flow of these rescue credits increased sharply after May 2010 and contributed to funding the crisis-stricken countries. By the end of 2013 the stock of fiscal rescue credit received by the GIPSIC countries was € 339, as indicated by the curly bracket. In the following, the upper boundary of the dotted area will be labelled 'public credit,' as it measures the sum of the Target and fiscal credits.

The difference between the current account curve and the public credit curve by definition gives the net private capital import into the GIPSIC countries accumulated since 1 January 2008 (minus the small starting Target claim of € 18 billion). The two double-arrowed lines on the left show this difference at alternative points in time referring to the initial phase of the crisis. Obviously, up to these points private capital still had co-financed the current account deficits. The third double-arrowed line, further to the right, refers to the reverse situation. As the sum of Target and fiscal credits exceed the accumulated current account, in net terms private capital had left the GIPSIC countries during the crisis up to that point in time. Public credit, fiscal and Target, had not only financed the current account deficits, but also an outright capital flight.

At the last data point available as of this writing, December 2013, the public credit, i.e. the sum of the Target and the fiscal rescue credits, net of the countries' own contributions, was € 953 billion (the increment of this sum since 1 January 2008 being € 970 billion). About two-thirds of this sum was Target credit, and one-third was fiscal rescue credit, an issue that will be discussed in more detail in Chapter 8 in the context of Figure 8.2.

In addition, the chart shows two further curves that provide complementary information on the financing of the GIPSIC countries. The first is the curve labelled 'effective public international credit (including cross-border SMP purchases)'. The distance between it and the upper boundary of the dotted area measures the stock of GIPSIC government bonds bought by non-GIPSIC central banks (including the ECB itself) under the ECB's Securities Markets Programme (SMP) introduced in May 2010. This is not a direct entry to the balance-of-payments statistics, because the NCBs buy the bonds only from the banks in their jurisdictions. When those banks or other market agents purchase such government bonds from the GIPSIC countries, the purchases are counted as a private capital import for the GIPSIC countries, although they are publicly induced. To be specific: when the non-GIPSIC central banks buy GIPSIC government bonds from their local commercial banks, a local shortage of such bonds occurs that banks will likely, though not necessarily, refill by repurchasing the bonds in the international market. This induces a net flow of such bonds from the GIPSIC countries, where the bonds are issued by the respective states, and results in a private capital import and a corresponding reduction in their Target debt. Thus the height of the area corresponding to the cross-border SMP purchases can be assumed to roughly measure a publicly induced, albeit privately processed, capital flow to the GIPSIC countries.

Subject to this qualification, the second curve from above indeed shows what was labelled 'effective international public rescue credit,' incorporating all programmes. This overall public credit reached a total of € 1,065 billion by December 2013, as indicated on the right-hand edge of the chart.[4] The curve peaked in August 2012 at a value of € 1,361 billion.

The effective overall sum of public international credit could even be augmented by the ECB's Covered Bond Purchase Programmes I and II (CBPP), which obliged all NCBs to buy well-specified private collateralized bonds. By the end of 2013 the stock of assets purchased under these programmes was € 57 billion, of which the non-GIPSIC countries and the ECB accounted for € 36 billion.[5] However, given that the ECB has not revealed in detail what it has bought, it can only be surmised that these programmes concentrated on covered bonds of the GIPSIC countries. If so, the total fiscal and quasi-fiscal credit provided to the GIPSIC countries and showing up directly or indirectly in the balance-of-payments statistics would have been € 1.101 trillion by December 2013.

The second curve added as complementary information is the curve at the top of the chart; it shows the net foreign debt position of the GIPSIC countries, which the reader knows already from Figure 2.9. The slope of that curve, in the absence of revaluation effects, would be equal to the slope of the curve showing the accumulated current account deficit. However, as discussed in Chapter 2, Eurostat wrote off some of the debt of the GIPSIC countries because of the decline in its market value. By September 2013 (the last data point available at this writing), GIPSIC net foreign debt was € 2,049 billion. At the end of 2012, GIPSIC net foreign debt amounted to € 1,984 billion, of which 42% was Target debt, 15% fiscal rescue credit, and 7% credit from other central banks resulting their purchases of GIPSIC government bonds.[6] Only the remaining 26% was truly private. This qualifies the information about the share of Target

---

[4] Another break-down of the rescue credits is shown in Figure 8.2 in the next chapter. Note that that figure also takes into account that the GIPSIC countries hold a small claim against the rest of the Eurozone because they issued an underproportionate stock of banknotes. This is not included in the analysis of this chapter since this claim, unlike the Target balances, does not lead to entries in the countries' official balance-of-payments statistics.

[5] See European Central Bank, *Consolidated Financial Statement of the Eurosystem as at 31 December 2013*, press release, 8 January 2014, available at: <http://www.ecb.int/press/pr/wfs/2014/html/fs140108.en.html>. Assumption: The GIPSIC NCBs participated in the purchase according to their share in ECB capital.

[6] The respective data for 2013 were not yet available as of this writing.

debt in the 2012 net foreign debt positions of the individual GIPSIC countries as given above in Figure 6.4.

The relationship between the public credit curve (Target and fiscal) and the curve showing the cumulative current account deficit tells the story of the crisis. When both curves have the same slope, the current account deficit in the respective period is entirely financed by new public credit and there are no other net capital flows across borders, although of course the gross flows in all directions are always huge. When the public credit curve's slope is steeper than that for the cumulative current account deficit, public credit finances more than just the current account deficit at the respective point in time, indicating that private capital is being exported in net terms. When the public credit curve is flatter, public credit finances less than the current account deficit, indicating that there is still a net private capital import.

Public credit increased endogenously, through market forces, and exogenously through the policy measures of the ECB Governing Council as discussed in Chapter 5, as well as through fiscal policy decisions that will be discussed in Chapter 8. It came in three waves: during the second half of 2008 (Lehman Brothers), in the first half of 2010, and again from summer 2011 to summer 2012. During these periods the slope of the public credit curve was steeper than the curve of cumulative current accounts, indicating outright capital flight.[7] Private capital in net terms was relocated by foreign investors to other countries, mostly in the sense that the banks of creditor countries recalled their interbank credit and placed it elsewhere. Foreign investors were no longer willing to finance the current account deficits and, in addition, they also wanted their money back when loans matured, rather than rolling over the debt. The GIPSIC countries largely filled the financial gap with the printing press, which was activated by lowering the collateral standards for refinancing credit as discussed in Chapters 5 and 6. They used the printing press to finance their current account deficits and to redeem part of their existing debt as demanded by their foreign creditors. In addition, after May 2010 fiscal rescue credit started to arrive, which was used for essentially the same purposes.

While it was predominantly foreign investors who fled, residents of the GIPSIC also fled into safe havens. The case of Greek and Spanish banks shifting € 358 billion to other countries in the period 2008 to September 2013 was documented at the beginning of Chapter 5. The banks borrowed money

---

[7] The capital flight was documented in the various versions of the Sinn-Wollmershäuser Target paper, once the respective data had become available. Ireland: June 2011 CESifo version; Italy: November 2011 NBER version; Spain: May 2012. See H.-W. Sinn and T. Wollmershäuser, 'Target Loans, Current Account Balances and Capital Flows: The ECB's Rescue Facility', 2012.

from their central banks and lent it to other countries. Or the banks used the money they borrowed from their central banks to buy assets, typically government bonds, from domestic investors, and these invested the funds in other countries.

During the year 2009 and again in the period from autumn 2010 to spring 2011, markets had calmed temporarily, after the first two waves of capital flight. In these periods the public credit curve was rather flat, while the cumulative current account curve remained steep, indicating that the markets were again willing to finance an increasing portion, if not all, of the current account deficits. On balance, until the autumn of 2009, there was no capital flight in net terms and in the aggregate. The increasing distance between the curves depicting the cumulative current account and the Target debt shows that a sizeable private capital import financed most of the current account deficits.

But then came two stormy periods of capital flight, the first in spring 2010, and the second from summer 2011 to summer 2012.[8] During these periods more private capital left the crisis countries than had entered since the beginning of 2008. In the autumn of 2011, a point was reached where the Target credit just sufficed to finance the current account deficit that had accumulated since 1 January 2008. But this was obviously only a snapshot, as the capital flight continued until the summer of 2012, driving the public credit curve way above the current account curve.

After the summer of 2012, markets calmed down and the capital flow even reversed its direction, as can be seen by the sharply declining public credit curve. Even the curve showing the effective public credit, including the cross-border SMP purchases of government bonds by NCBs, was coming down in this period. The calming of markets was presumably due to the establishment of the permanent rescue fund ESM and to the ECB's announcement of its OMT programme, both of which promised buyers of GIPSIC government bonds much more safety, inducing investors to send fresh money to these countries. This will be discussed in more detail in Chapter 8.

However, the decline in Target debt itself was not only attributable to the increasing confidence of the markets. It also resulted from the surge of fiscal rescue credits, which reduced Target debt through the associated issuance of net payment orders to the GIPSIC countries. The decline in the Target balances from the peak of the Target curve in August 2012 to December 2013 was € 389 billion. Over the same period, the fiscal rescue funds gave rise to a flow of payment orders from the non-GIPSIC to the GIPSIC countries amounting to around € 112 billion. Thus, 29% of the decline in Target balances over that

---

[8] For an early assessment of this capital flight see H.-W. Sinn, 'Italy's Capital Flight', *Project Syndicate*, 25 October 2011, available at: <http://www.project-syndicate.org/commentary/italy-s-capital-flight>.

period was attributable to the fiscal rescue funds alone. The rest can be attributed to the ECB's OMT programme and the announcement of the ESM.

In principle, the actual cross border purchases under the SMP could also have contributed to bringing down the Target balances, as they induced private international payment orders to the GIPSIC countries, but the SMP ended in February 2012, and therefore could not exert any effect. It did exert an effect, however, before this date. As mentioned above, the peak of the effective public credit curve was reached in August 2012, with € 1,361 billion. Other things equal, this would have been the GIPSIC Target debt at that point in time, had there been no SMP and no fiscal rescue programmes. By the same token, in the absence of fiscal rescue credit and the SMP, the GIPSIC Target debt would have been € 1,065 billion by the end of 2013. Both the fiscal rescue credit and the credit granted through the SMP programme merely repackaged Target credit, distributing the overall sum to various other types of rescue credit whose economic similarities the public would not normally be able to discern.

It is important to note what this means for the way current account deficits were financed during the crisis. From the beginning of 2008 to September 2013 (the last current account data point available as of this writing), Target credit and fiscal rescue credit financed the entire € 613 billion of cumulative current account deficits of the GIPSIC countries and, in addition, a capital flight of around € 425 billion. Thus, in net terms, 59% of the public credit provided to the GIPSIC countries (Target and fiscal) served to finance the current account deficits and 41% compensated for the net capital flight. Taking the SMP into account, which by September 2013 likely had induced a public capital inflow into the GIPSIC countries of around € 113 billion, the true private capital flight that was financed in addition to the current account deficits may have even been € 538 billion.

To reiterate a point made earlier, the statement of how the GIPSIC current account deficit was financed is an accounting statement, not one about economic causality, correlation or the like. It is on the same logical level as saying that, over a certain time span, x% of the government budget was tax-financed and y% was debt-financed. It is tempting to rework such a statement using one of the modern econometric toolboxes, but an accounting identity simply does not lend itself to such an exercise.[9] The inertia of the current account logically implies that

[9] Various authors have claimed that Sinn and Wollmershäuser posited such a positive correlation, going on to show that it does not exist. However, the claim is simply not true. Saying that a current account deficit was financed with Target credit rather than private credit from abroad is logically not a statement about correlation. See H.-W. Sinn and T. Wollmershäuser, 'Target Loans, Current Account Balances and Capital Flows: The ECB's Rescue Facility', 2012.

there should have been a nearly perfect negative correlation between the short run Target deficit and private capital imports during the time span considered.[10] Short-term capital, as always, was jittery and jumping across borders in both directions, and the buffer was the Target credit.

Note also that the accounting statement not only includes current account deficits with the rest of the Eurozone, but also deficits with the rest of the world, outside the Eurozone. Buying goods in net terms from non-euro countries requires credit from someone else, and if this credit is not being provided by the capital market, it must come from public sources such as intergovernmental credit or extra credit from the printing press. As explained above, an international money order to a country outside the Eurozone also leads to a Target liability for the originating country and to a Target surplus somewhere else in the Eurozone, unless the ECB or other central banks influence the exchange rate by hoarding or dishoarding currency reserves.

Overall, the chart thus confirms the overwhelming role of public credit in maintaining the living standards of the crisis-stricken countries and compensating for the capital flight that affected them. Target credit is the most important part, but the least known form of this support. The fact that it carries a minuscule interest rate given by the ECB's main refinancing rate (held for long at only 1% and currently just 0.25%) is probably the main explanation for the puzzle presented in Figure 4.3, namely that the net investment income that the GIPSIC countries paid to other countries declined during the crisis in absolute terms, even though they kept borrowing abroad in net terms and had to pay higher rates in the markets. Since the GIPSIC countries' additional credit taken during the crisis was just Target credit, and since Target credit even replaced some of the existing credit that had to be serviced at market conditions, the decline in net interest payments should not be all that surprising.

Greece, Portugal, and Cyprus Living off the Printing Press

The same analysis as that carried out for the GIPSIC countries as a group can be made for each individual country, except for the curve of the ECB's government

---

[10] Auer shows, however, that from a longer-term perspective there is a statistically significant positive correlation between current account deficit and Target deficit. See R. A. Auer, 'What Drives Target2 Balances? Evidence from a Panel Analysis', *CESifo Working Paper* No. 4216, April 2013, available at: <http://www.cesifo-group.de/DocDL/cesifo1_wp4216.pdf>.

bond purchases in the SMP programme, for which no country-specific panel data have been published.[11]

Let us start with Greece, Portugal, and Cyprus, the first two of which, according to the analysis presented in Chapter 4, are among the least competitive. All three countries had enormous current account deficits even before the crisis started. In 2007, Greece's deficit amounted to 14.6% of GDP, Portugal's to 10.1% and Cyprus's to 11.7%.[12] In the case of Greece and Portugal, the deficits would have been about 1.5 percentage points higher if these two countries hadn't already been receiving significant public transfers from the EU. It will be difficult to find examples in history of such huge levels of net absorption of external resources by independent states. And unfortunately, as shown in Figure 2.6, the excess absorption served consumption rather than investment purposes.

In the meantime, the current account deficits have come down, but only due to the collapse of incomes during the crisis, not due to a realignment of relative prices, as would be required for an improvement in competitiveness. This was discussed in the context of Figure 4.1.

Figure 7.2 shows the situation in the three countries in an analogous way to Figure 7.1. All the curves have the same meaning as before. It can be seen that in the initial years of the crisis the Target credit provided in all three countries was about the same as their cumulative current account deficit. In fact, it is surprising that the coincidence lasted roughly until the fiscal rescue credits began to flow, which was May 2010 for Greece, May 2011 for Portugal, and May 2013 for Cyprus. Thus, up to these points in time the cumulative net private capital

---

[11] The allocation of the stock of purchased assets to different countries has only become known for two points in time, 31 December 2012 and 31 December 2013. See European Central Bank, *Details on Securities Holdings Acquired under the Securities Markets Programme*, press release, 21 February 2013, available at: <http://www.ecb.int/press/pr/date/2013/html/pr130221_1.en.html>, and European Central Bank, *Annual Accounts of the ECB for 2013*, press release, 20 February 2014, available at: <http://www.ecb.europa.eu/press/pr/date/2014/html/pr140220.en.html>. These are the figures published: 31 December 2012: Italy: book value € 99.0 billion (47.4%); Spain: book value € 43.7 billion (20.9%); Greece: book value € 30.8 billion (14.8%); Portugal: book value € 21.6 billion (10.3%); Ireland: book value € 13.6 billion (6.5%); 31 December 2013: Italy: book value € 86.8 billion (48.5%); Spain: book value € 38.4 billion (21.5%); Greece: book value € 25.4 billion (14.2%); Portugal: book value € 19.0 billion (10.6%); Ireland: book value € 9.2 billion (5.1%). In addition, there is a private estimate of the county break-up as shown in the next chapter Figure 8.1. However, it ends in February 2012 and does not incorporate the partial sterilization that has taken place in the meantime.

[12] See Eurostat, Database, *Economy and Finance*, Balance of Payments—International Transactions, Balance of Payments Statistics and International Investment Positions, Balance of Payments by Country.

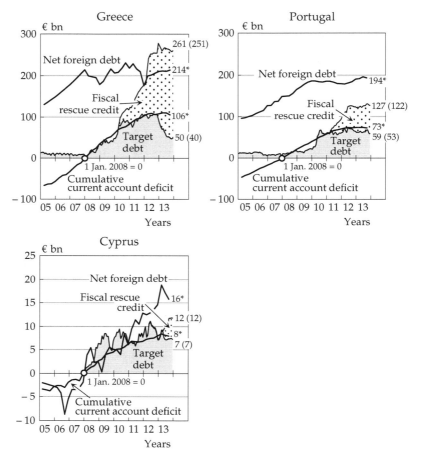

Figure 7.2 Greece, Portugal, and Cyprus

* September 2013

Sources: See Figure 7.1.

Note: The fiscal rescue credit here and in the following graphs is calculated net of the respective country's own contributions to the rescue programmes and net of debt redemption, if any. Cf. the explanations given below Figure 7.1. The figures in brackets show increments from 1 January 2008 to end of December 2013. For Cyprus no Target data before 2008 are available.

movements were close to zero. This clearly indicated a sudden stop of private capital imports, not of a reversal of capital flows, to use the terminology introduced when the Target balances were explained in Figure 6.2. The cumulative current account deficit up to these points in time was indeed financed with refinancing credit from the central bank, i.e., to be blunt, with the printing press.

The charts show once again, however, that the capital flows were more volatile than the trade flows. There were always short periods during which the slope of the Target curve exceeded that of the current account curve, indicating net private capital outflows, followed by short periods of capital inflows, albeit at a lower level. Thus, the statement that the printing press financed the current account deficits over the period in question should not be taken to imply a correlation. It is a mere statement about an accounting identity. Since private capital flows did not contribute to financing the current account deficits, and the fiscal rescue credits were not yet available, the Eurosystem's Target credit must, by definition, have done the entire job.

The situation changed dramatically when huge fiscal rescue packages became available. By September 2013, three and a half years after the first fiscal credit had been released for Greece, the sum of Target and fiscal rescue credit exceeded the cumulative current account deficits, by € 148 billion in Greece and € 52 billion in Portugal. This shows that in the later phase of the crisis fiscal and Target credit not only financed the net import of real economic resources as measured by the current account deficits, but also an outright capital flight. Although it is not possible to say what type of public credit financed what—current account or capital flight—the charts do suggest that the fiscal rescue operations induced or enabled a capital flight of a similar magnitude, for without the possibility of tapping public credit—refinancing credit from the printing press (Target) or fiscal credit from other states—it would not have been possible for debtors to redeem their debt, or for investors to sell their local assets and send the proceeds abroad.

It is worth noting that, in the case of Greece, Target liabilities have come down significantly since November 2012, when they peaked at € 107 billion, or 55% of GDP. At first glance this could be taken as proof that capital is now returning to Greece and that the situation is calming down. However, this would be a misinterpretation, since the sum of Target credit and fiscal rescue credit roughly stayed constant over this period,[13] while the current account curve began to flatten out, indicating a reduction in the Greek current account deficit. Thus, the reduction in the Greek Target debt can entirely be attributed to the surge of fiscal rescue credit paid out to Greece, which, by virtue of the mechanics of Target accounting, reduces the Target credit one-to-one. The reduction in the Greek Target debt shows nothing but a repackaging of public rescue credits, definitely *not* a return of private capital to Greece. As the reader can easily verify, exactly the same situation prevailed in Portugal. No private capital has returned to Portugal as of this writing.

---

[13] From November 2012 to December 2013, the Greek Target liability fell by € 57 billion, while the stock of fiscal rescue credit Greece had received increased by € 64 billion.

In Cyprus, where capital controls were introduced in March 2013 after the collapse of Laiki Bank, the sum of Target credit and fiscal rescue credit continued to increase, while the current account turned positive. Thus, private capital flight from this country continued up to this writing as fast as the capital controls allowed it.

Irish Capital Flight

The situation in Ireland differs markedly from the one in Portugal and Greece, since Ireland's current account deficit was smaller and capital flight played a far larger role. The relative Irish current account deficit, which in 2007 amounted to 5.3% of GDP and 5.6% the following year, was very large by international standards, but still less than two-fifths of Greece's and only about half as large as Portugal's. As a tax haven, Ireland's problem was, as Figure 7.3 shows, very clearly capital flight, or repatriation of capital by the core countries. The mountain of Target liabilities amassed by Ireland was significantly larger than what it needed to finance its current account deficit. It reflects primarily the capital flight from the country.[14]

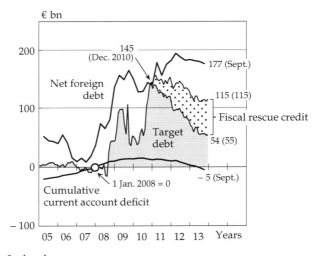

Figure 7.3 Ireland

Sources: See Figure 7.1.

Note: See Figures 7.1 and 7.2.

[14] See also H.-W. Sinn and T. Wollmershäuser, 'Target Loans, Current Account Balances and Capital Flows: The ECB's Rescue Facility', in particular *CESifo Working Paper* No. 3500 of June 2011, which elaborated on the special role played by Ireland.

As the Section *The Foreign Debt Problem* in Chapter 2 discussed, the transformation of maturities, i.e. borrowing short-term to finance long-term loans, brought Ireland's banks into enormous difficulty. The yields they had to offer for fresh capital climbed ever higher, while at the same time their long-term loans lost value. In only two years, from September 2007 to September 2009, this increased Ireland's net external debt by € 147 billion, equivalent to almost its entire GDP (€ 162 billion in 2009). The government tried to calm the markets by offering huge guarantees for the banks, worth over 200% of GDP. It failed. As discussed in Chapter 2, the country was caught in the global financial maelstrom and within a year its budget deficit had soared to 30% of GDP, forcing it to seek the help of the official rescue packages, which cost it part of its sovereignty.

Figure 7.3 shows that Irish capital flight occurred in two waves. The first came directly after the collapse of Lehman Brothers in the autumn of 2008. The Bank of Ireland made large use at that time of ELA (Emergency Liquidity Assistance) credit from its central bank, probably because there was not enough eligible collateral available for the enormous volume of refinancing credit needed (see Chapter 5). The situation subsequently calmed down somewhat and some capital flowed back to the country in the winter of 2009/2010. But in the autumn of 2010 the second wave hit, much stronger than the previous one, forcing Ireland to seek the help of the fiscal rescue programmes. Up to December 2013, a total gross amount of € 62 billion, or € 60 billion net of own contributions, was disbursed for Ireland.

As in the case of Greece, the fiscal rescue funds paid out to Ireland accounted in large part for the reduction in Irish Target liabilities. From January 2011, when the first fiscal rescue credit was paid out to Ireland, until December 2013, Irish Target debt came down by € 90 billion, while at the same time a total of € 60 billion in rescue credit was given to the country. Thus, two-thirds (67%) of the reduction in Irish Target debt was simply a repackaging from Target to fiscal credit, while the remainder is explained by a return of private capital, presumably induced by the ECB's provision of insurance through it OMT programme.

Indeed, the expectation that the reliance on central bank liquidity and thus Target credit could be reduced was one of the reasons why the then-president of the ECB, Jean-Claude Trichet, pressed Ireland to seek the help of the rescue programme. Ireland at that time did not want rescue money, since it carried a 5.8% interest rate, while Target credit cost it only 1% in interest. But Trichet insisted on replacing the money-printing press with intergovernmental and IMF help in order to bring the ECB balance sheet under better control. By the end of 2013, Ireland still held € 54 billion in Target liabilities, equivalent to 33% of its GDP.

The Flight from Italy and Spain

The year 2011 was the euro's *annus horribilis*. Target credit and fiscal rescue packages had more or less brought under control the first wave that hit the smaller economies, but then a second and far bigger wave struck; it left Italy and Spain reeling.

Some observers declared themselves absolutely stunned. Who would compare Italy with Greece? Italy is a productive, rich country, with 41% more private wealth per household or 14% more per capita than Germany.[15] The northern Italian economy is one of Europe's most productive. The fact that Italy had long managed with public debt exceeding 100% of GDP and a small foreign debt, amounting to less than 30% of GDP (29% at the end of September 2013), appeared to be enough to calm the markets. By comparison, the other crisis-hit countries' foreign debt amounted to about 100% of GDP (see also Figure 2.9).

And yet, Italy was now stumbling too.[16] Spreads on Italian debt started to rise against Germany's benchmark in July 2011 (see Figure 2.2), and the first foreign banks started to pull capital out of the country, turning Italy's Target claims into a Target liability that soared after August 2011. Silvio Berlusconi's government tried to soothe the markets with austerity programmes hastily put together in August, to no avail. By the end of 2011, Italy's Target liabilities, fuelled by capital flight and the granting of fresh refinancing credit, had shot to € 191 billion, from € 6 billion in June of that year. That was the time when Prime Minister Silvio Berlusconi initiated secret negotiations about Italy's exiting the euro, as cited in the Introduction. By August 2012, Italy's Target liabilities had soared to € 289 billion, as Figure 7.4 shows, marking a total increase of € 295 billion as of 1 January 2008.

The situation in Spain was similar. Before the summer of 2011, Spain's Target liabilities increased somewhat, but remained moderate. From January 2008 until June 2011, the Spanish NCB had taken on € 42 billion in Target credit, whereas the country's cumulative current account deficit had risen to € 227 billion by that time. Thus, approximately one-fifth of the current account deficit of those three-and-a-half years was financed with the money-printing press. The rest was financed by normal capital imports.

The situation in Spain also changed dramatically in July 2011. From June 2011 to August 2012, Spain's Target liabilities rose from € 45 billion to € 434 billion. The € 389-billion increase was even larger than Italy's € 295 billion over the same period. As discussed at the beginning of Chapter 6, foreign banks withdrew huge amounts of funds from Spanish banks, but Spanish banks also shifted deposits abroad.

---

[15] See Chapter 2, Figure 2.2, and the related discussion.

[16] See H.-W. Sinn, 'Italy's Capital Flight', 2011. An early prediction of the difficulties to come can be found in H.-W. Sinn, *Casino Capitalism. How the Financial Crisis Came About and What Needs to Be Done Now*, Oxford University Press, Oxford 2010, chapter 10: *Will the West Retain its Stability?*, section: *Will Greece and Italy Have to be Bailed Out?*

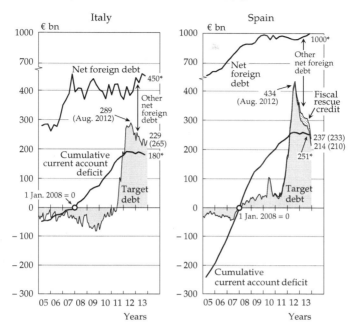

Figure 7.4 Italy and Spain

* End of September 2013.

Sources: See Figure 7.1.

Note: See Figures 7.1 and 7.2. Unlike the other GIPSIC countries, Italy made a net contribution to fiscal rescue operations of € 27 billion. This is not shown in the diagram.

The capital flight that gave rise to these Target liabilities was much larger than the private capital import that occurred in the first period of the crisis, before the summer of 2011, which is approximately measured by the distance between the curve of cumulative current account deficits and the Target curve at that point in time, given that the Spanish Target liabilities were only € 3 billion at 1 January 2008.

By the end of 2011, Spain's Target curve had already reached the cumulative current account curve. Thus, summed over the four acute-crisis years from 2008 to 2011, Spain's cumulative € 242 billion current account deficit was not financed with private capital imports, but exclusively with the money-printing press, because the capital that had been imported until the summer of 2011 left Spain again within just a few months.

In Italy the Target and current account curves also met by the end of 2011, but since the Italian Target debt in 2008 started with a negative value

(–€ 36 billion) rather than about zero as in Spain, the Italian printing press financed even more than the cumulative current account deficit over that period. Capital flight was so large that within only half a year it more than offset Italy's total capital imports since the beginning of 2008.

Whereas Greece, Portugal, and Ireland had all received fiscal rescue credit, this was not yet the case for Italy. Italy has benefited from the ECB's purchasing of its government bonds, but it has not received funds from any of the rescue programmes. It has instead itself made contributions, through its provision of equity capital for the ESM and, in particular, its additional guarantees for the ESM, which, however, do not show up in Italy's international payment statistics until they lead to payment flows.[17] Spain, by contrast, after a short period of being a contributor to the fiscal rescue programmes, became a recipient in December 2012 with an inflow of funds, net of Spain's own contributions, as illustrated by the dotted area above the Target curve on the right. Relative to the huge Target credit that Spain received, however, the fiscal rescue funds appear small.

What exactly triggered the unease in the capital markets in the summer of 2011 is unclear. The GIPSIC countries had accumulated a rising amount of external debt, their loss of competitiveness was manifest, the housing bubble had burst, banks were suspected of concealing huge quantities of toxic assets, unemployment was soaring, and the hope had vanished that the real economy would soon recover. All of this was reason enough for investors to become increasingly nervous, but it does not explain the trigger event in the summer of 2011, as the respective processes had already been underway for a while then. Whatever it was, once a seed of distrust was sown, contagion was swift among investors, which, in turn, provided a new boost to capital flight and generated a self-fulfilling process of confidence destruction.[18]

There are reasons to suspect that the capital flight out of Spain and Italy was encouraged by the ECB's rescue operations themselves. The Big Bazooka offer of December 2011, the Long-Term Refinancing Operation (LTRO) described in Chapter 5 that eventually provided up to a trillion euros in three-year refinancing credit in two tranches, had considerable effects. Spanish banks, for example, took more than € 250 billion of this long-term refinancing credit, using it to repay their interbank credit and replace funds that Spanish investors had whisked abroad to protect them from a possible wave of bankruptcies. Spanish banks also bought € 85 billion in additional Spanish government bonds over that period, offering a chance for other investors to unload these bonds and bring the proceeds out of the

---

[17] The calculation is explained in a footnote to Figure 7.1.

[18] See P. De Grauwe, *Economics of Monetary Union*, Oxford University Press, Oxford 2012, for a thorough analysis of confidence building and confidence destruction in the capital market.

country.[19] Spanish banks themselves also invested huge amounts abroad, often in Latin America, as shown at the beginning of Chapter 5. The consequence of this policy was a jump of about € 101 billion in Spanish Target liabilities from January through late April 2012, as the chart shows.

Italian banks made use of the LTRO to take on € 201 billion in long-term refinancing credit from the Banca d'Italia from December 2011 to June 2012.[20] They used the money to redeem interbank credit taken abroad, buy domestic securities, including government bonds, and give new loans to private customers.[21] The money either flowed directly abroad or was paid out to Italians first, who then brought it to safe havens abroad. In this respect, the Big Bazooka stabilized the prices of Italian and Spanish bonds in the short-term, but at the price of bolstering the capital flight it was meant to combat.

The Italian crisis led, in November 2011, to the fall of the Berlusconi government. The new Prime Minister, Mario Monti, a former EU Commissioner and professor of economics at the University of Milan, started out with sweeping reforms. He pushed his first € 30-billion austerity package through parliament in 2011. It included, among other things, a rise in the retirement age, cuts in health spending, and a VAT rise.[22] However, when he tried to liberalize the labour market by breaking the tenure rights of older workers in order to help younger ones enter the market, he did not achieve much because the unions, heartened by the ECB's help, did not feel any sense of urgency to relinquish

---

[19] See Banco de España, Boletín Estadístico, *Net Lending to Credit Institutions and its Counterparts*, Net Lending in Euro, Open Market Operations, LTROs, table 8.1.b, available at: <http://www.bde.es/webbde/es/estadis/infoest/e0801e.pdf>; and Banco de España, Boletín Estadístico, Credit Institutions, *Aggregated Balance Sheet from Supervisory Returns*, Assets, Securities, Domestic, General Government, Total, table 4.4, available at: <http://www.bde.es/webbde/es/estadis/infoest/a0404e.pdf>.

[20] See Banca d'Italia, Central Bank: Assets—Lending to Euro-Area Financial Sector Counterparties Denominated in Euros: Longer-Term Refinancing Operations, *Base Informativa Pubblica*, Supplements to the Statistical Bulletin, Bank of Italy Balance-Sheet Aggregates: Assets, June 2012, available at: <http://bip.bancaditalia.it/4972unix/homebipentry.htm?dadove=corr&lang=eng>.

[21] See Banca d'Italia, General Government: Securities Held by Other Monetary Financial Institutions *Base Informativa Pubblica*, Supplements to the Statistical Bulletin, The Public Finances, Borrowing Requirement and Debt, General Government Debt: By Holding Sector, June 2012, available at: <http://bip.bancaditalia.it/4972unix/homebipentry.htm?dadove=corr&lang=eng>.

[22] See 'Italy Senate Passes Monti's Austerity Package', *BBC News Europe*, 22 December 2011, available at: <http://www.bbc.co.uk/news/world-europe-16301956>.

social achievements they had fought for decades to obtain.[23] Like nearly all of his predecessors, Monti had to step down after only a few months in office. He failed miserably in the elections of February 2013, giving way to a new government under Enrico Letta, who in the meantime has been replaced by Matteo Renzi.

France in Between

The great unknown in the European calculation is France. On the one hand, the Grande Nation should be well above suspicions of financial instability. France possesses a functioning state endowed with the power to tap its own citizens for financial resources at any time and to bring forward European solutions to its domestic problems, if necessary. A sovereign default is *a priori* unlikely.

On the other hand, the French state has quite nearly exhausted its potential. In 2013 the country had the second largest public sector (57% of GDP), after Denmark, among the OECD countries,[24] while its public debt amounted to 93% of GDP. The French unemployment rate was 10.8% as of December 2013, about as high as the German rate at the peak of Germany's own euro crisis in 2005 (compare Figure 3.8). During the financial crisis (2008–2013), when the current account deficits of many countries decreased as a result of the reduction in imports triggered by the recession, the French current account, which before the crisis had been in equilibrium, worsened to 1.8% of GDP in 2013. According to the analysis by the economics department of Goldman Sachs cited in Chapter 4 (see Table 4.1 and Figure 4.8), France needs a real depreciation of 20% relative to the Eurozone average in order to achieve debt sustainability. The Standard & Poor's rating agency downgraded France from top-notch to AA- in January 2012, followed by downgrades by Moody's in November 2012 and the French-owned agency, Fitch, in July 2013.

France's particular disadvantage is that its banks acted as a hub for European savings. French banks borrowed in the European interbank market, often from Belgium, the Netherlands, and the UK, who in turn borrowed from other countries, Germany in particular, and distributed the funds around southern Europe, an area to which it is closely tied for historical and cultural reasons (refer also to the discussion of Figure 5.1). Whereas Germany's banks had concentrated on the American business and got a bloody nose from the write-off losses on US structured securities, French banks were hardly affected, since they had specialized

---

[23] See 'Monti bringt Arbeitsmarktreform durchs Parlament', *Handelsblatt*, 27 June 2012, available at: <http://www.handelsblatt.com/politik/international/italien-monti-bringt-arbeitsmarktreform-durchs-parlament/6807276.html>.

[24] See OECD, *Economic Outlook* 2013, No. 94, Statistical Annex, table 25.

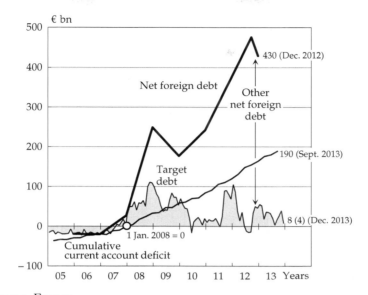

Figure 7.5 France

Sources: See Figure 7.1; for the Target balance, see Figure 6.3.

in southern Europe.[25] When the fiscal rescue operations were agreed, at the end of Q1 2010, French banks held 95% more government bonds of Greece, Ireland, Portugal, and Spain in their books relative to the size of the French economy than did German banks.[26]

France's nail-biting is reflected in its Target curve, depicted in Figure 7.5. France evidently had to battle against some capital flight during the first wave of the crisis (notably related to difficulties in refinancing markets in US dollars), which pushed its Target liabilities to around € 100 billion. The balance declined in 2010, only to rise once again during the second wave that began in the summer of 2011. However, in the spring of 2012, when capital flight was in full swing in the Eurozone, as the overall rise in Target balances (see Figure 7.1) clearly shows, the French Target debt declined, indicating that in all the turmoil France was considered a relatively safe haven by the capital markets. By the end of 2013 the French Target debt was close to zero, only € 4 billion higher than at the beginning of the crisis.

---

[25] See H.-W. Sinn, *Casino Capitalism*, chapter 8: *The Extent of the Damage*, figure 8.6.

[26] See Bank for International Settlements, BIS Quarterly Review, September 2010, available at: <http://www.bis.org/publ/qtrpdf/r_qt1009.htm>.

It is noteworthy that while France had no net external debt before the crisis, it did accumulate such debt during the crisis. With a volume of € 430 billion by the end of 2012, equivalent to 21% of GDP, it shows a significant change with respect to the onset of the crisis. The fact that the increase in this debt, like in Ireland's case, is much larger than that which could be accounted for by its current account deficits, suggests that France's banks were also acting as credit intermediaries, borrowing short-term to lend long-term to countries that were later swamped by the crisis, ultimately taking large losses on their investments. Thinking of French banks as institutions that borrowed short-term in the interbank market to lend long-term at enticing interest rates to southern European entities does not appear to be too wide of the mark.

When assessing the French Target debt, account must be taken of the fact that the French participation in the rescue operations, taken by itself, would have resulted in Target debt. The Banque de France, for example, had to buy € 45 billion worth of GIPSIC government bonds through the ECB's SMP programme. Since these bonds came from abroad, French participation induced payment orders to other countries, building up a corresponding Target debt. In addition, French contributions to fiscal rescue operations and potential sales of ESM securities in the French capital market will have also contributed to the French Target debt. Since France's actual Target debt is nevertheless close to zero, there must have been a private capital import above and beyond the current account deficit to accommodate the public capital outflows.

Germany: Exporting for Target Claims

With a current account surplus of € 201 billion in 2013, Germany was the world's largest capital exporter (see Figure 3.4). As the country accumulated huge Target claims, the question is what fraction of the capital export was accounted for by such Target claims and what was the contribution made by the rescue credit. Figure 7.6 provides the answer. It resembles the previous charts, except that, since Germany's net foreign asset position is positive rather than negative, the chart now shows assets and claims, rather than liabilities and debt.

There are two curves for Germany's cumulative current account surplus. The solid one depicts the surplus against the rest of the world, and the dashed one the surplus against the rest of the Eurozone. Interestingly, the solid curve roughly reaches about the same altitude as the Target curve at the peak of the intra-euro balance-of-payments crisis in June 2012. In the first five years of the crisis (2008–2012), the increase in German Target claims amounted to € 585 billion, while the cumulative German current account surplus was € 800 billion. Thus, 73% of Germany's cumulative current account surplus in the first five years of the crisis was not paid for with money foreigners had collected by selling marketable assets

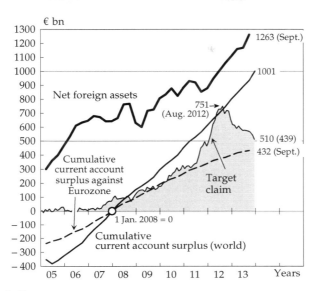

Figure 7.6 Germany

Sources: See Figure 7.1 as well as Deutsche Bundesbank, Time Series Databases, *External Sector*, Current Account by Country and Group of Countries.

Note: The numbers in brackets give increments as of 1 January 2008.

to, or borrowing from, Germany, but with money borrowed from the printing press elsewhere in the Eurozone. In exchange, all that the Bundesbank received was a compensating Target claim. Only 27% of Germany's current account surplus during this period was used to accumulate private claims against foreign countries and institutions.

In 2013, the German Target balance came down significantly, indicating a strong increase in private capital export from Germany that began in the second half of 2012 and gained momentum in 2013. The situation had improved dramatically because the OMT and the ESM had calmed the markets. By the end of 2013, Germany's accumulated current account surplus was € 1,001 billion, of which € 439 billion, or 44%, was Target-financed and 56% was accommodated with private capital export.

At the beginning of Chapter 5 it was shown that despite the substantial retreat of German banks from the GIPSIC countries, Germany still posted a considerable net private capital export of € 521 billion during the first 6 years of the crisis (1 January 2008 to 31 December 2013), and that it was puzzling that this capital export was much smaller than the country's overall capital export, in terms of its persistent current account surplus, which reached a cumulative € 1,001 billion during the period considered. The information given in Figure 7.6 solves this puzzle: the public capital flow through the printing press largely filled the gap. In addition, Germany's participation in the first intergovernmental rescue programme for Greece, which induced direct payment orders from government to government, contributed with € 15 billion to filling this gap, admittedly a small sum.

In all likelihood, however, a large part of the € 521 billion in private capital export was also caused by public interventions.

Firstly, private funds moved into the Luxembourg-based rescue fund, which then distributed them as public credit to the crisis-stricken countries. The overall rescue credit provided by international institutions in the period considered (net of the direct intergovernmental aid to Greece) was € 340 billion, to which German investors have contributed an unknown share. Since investors from all euro countries bought a good 40% of the European rescue credit titles, the German share may have been in the range of € 30 to € 60 billion.[27]

Secondly, as the Bundesbank participated in the SMP programme, Germany's Target claims were reduced through the issuance of payment orders to other countries as part of the process of bringing the GIPSIC government bonds to Germany. Germany's participation in the SMP alone could therefore have reduced its Target claims by € 48 billion, or about 5% of Germany's cumulative net capital exports during the period from 2008 to 2013.

Thirdly, private funds moved directly to the crisis-stricken countries under the protection of the ECB's OMT programme and the permanent rescue fund ESM, a topic that will be studied at length in Chapter 8. This also might explain a considerable share of private capital exports.

It is true that German firms earning export revenues did not care whether the money they received came out of other countries' printing presses or had previously been acquired by selling assets to, or borrowing from, Germany. For them Target finance is of no concern. However, in the aggregate the origin of the money is important insofar as Target finance means that a corresponding part of the German savings that people bring to their banks is not used by these banks to acquire foreign assets, but to redeem the refinancing credit they have drawn from the Bundesbank, or to transfer funds to term deposits

---

[27] The share of German investors in EFSM bonds amounts to 29.4%, that of French investors to 11.1%, and that of the Benelux to 8.5% (see European Union, Investor Presentation, February 2014, p. 20, available at: <http://ec.europa.eu/economy_finance/eu_borrower/documents/eu_investor_presentation_en.pdf>). The share of German investors in EFSF Bonds and ESM Bonds is not known. However, Eurozone investors hold 46% of the largest EFSF Bond issue, and 39% of the first ESM Bond issue (see European Financial Stability Facility & European Stability Mechanism, Investor Presentation, November 2013, p. 23 and 25, available at: <http://www.esm.europa.eu/pdf/EFSF%20ESM%20New%20Investor%20presentation%2027%20November%202013.pdf>).

with the Bundesbank. Thus, it was not private individuals, but ultimately the Bundesbank, a public institution, which acquired most of the claims against the rest of the world in exchange for the German export surplus. It acted similarly to a sovereign wealth fund investing domestic savings abroad, the only difference from a true wealth fund being that it did not invest its funds deliberately, but built up accounting claims on the Eurosystem through other countries using their printing presses and exerting their implicit drawing rights within the ECB system. These claims can never be called due, bear a paltry rate of interest equal to the ECB's main refinancing rate, and are at risk should the euro break up, as will be discussed in Chapter 8.

Instead of comparing the Target flow with the current account surplus, Germany's Target stock may also be compared with its net foreign wealth, resulting from previous current account surpluses. The data underlying Figure 7.6 show that, by the end of 2012, German Target claims accounted for 59% of the net foreign wealth (see also Figure 6.4) that Germany had acquired over its history. By the end of September 2013, they still accounted for 45% of the country's net foreign wealth.

All this does not mean that the Target debtors just used the fresh money from their printing presses to buy German goods, having the corresponding sums chalked up to their accounts at the ECB. The true relationship between Germany and the Target debtors is more complicated than this, involving many other countries inside and outside the Eurozone.

Recall that, in principle, the Eurosystem allows a country to finance not only the euro-internal balance-of-payments deficit with credit from the local printing press, which is then converted into Target debt, but also its balance-of-payments deficit with the rest of the world. The country receives goods or assets from the rest of the world for the money it prints, and this money then flows to another country of the Eurozone in exchange for goods or assets, leading to a Target claim for the respective central bank that has to carry out the payment orders.

Consider an example. Suppose a Chinese businessman buys a German car with dollars he received from a Spanish buyer of a Chinese product, who in turn received the dollars from the ECB in exchange for new euros borrowed from Banco de España, and let's assume that the German carmaker hands the dollars via his bank to the Bundesbank to convert them into euros. In this case the Banco de España builds up a Target liability and the Bundesbank acquires a Target claim. The Bundesbank essentially credits the delivery of goods from Germany via China to Spain.

Or think of a capital flight from Spain to Britain by way of payment orders in euros. The euros from the Spanish printing press allow Spanish banks to repay their debt with British investors, who then lend them to US borrowers who use them to buy the German car. Even in this case, a Spanish Target debt corresponds to a German Target claim, because, in a sense, Germany repaid the Spanish foreign debt with a car delivery in exchange for receiving a Target claim against the ECB system.

This latter example is particularly relevant insofar as it may explain why the parallelism between Germany's Target claims and the cumulative German current account surplus, as shown by Figure 7.6, is closer than the respective parallelism between the Target liabilities of Ireland, Spain, and Italy and their cumulative current account deficits. The money fleeing from these countries presumably went to a large number of countries inside and outside the Eurozone, before it eventually was lent to foreign importers of German goods. Think for example of the substantial flight of Spanish capital to Latin America documented at the beginning of Chapter 5, or the retreat of British capital from Cyprus and Ireland. All these capital movements involved euro payment orders from GIPSIC countries that consumed the GIPSIC monetary base, which would not have been possible without the NCBs of the GIPSIC countries activating their (electronic) printing presses to replenish this base. After crisscrossing the world, the new euros printed in the GIPSIC countries ended up buying German goods, replacing a potential German accumulation of marketable assets with mere Target claims.

This may also help to explain the puzzle of why the German current account surplus did not fall during the crisis with the collapse of Germany's GIPSIC customers and the corresponding disappearance of their current account deficits, as documented in Figure 3.9, but remained stable and even increased somewhat, reaching a record level of about 7.3% of German GDP in 2013, a level heavily criticized by EU politicians. The likely cause is the ECB's financing of the capital flight from the GIPSIC countries to non-euro countries. The global abundance of fresh euros that came out of the GIPSIC printing presses induced a depreciation of the euro (13% from 2008 to 2012 against the dollar) and sustained Germany's huge current account surplus, by now the largest in the world (see also Figure 3.4). Without the ECB's collateral policy cranking up the local printing presses, interest rates in the GIPSIC countries would have been higher, capital flight would have been lower, fewer euros would have been supplied to the currency markets, the value of the euro would have been higher, and the German current account surplus lower. And, instead of being compensated for three-quarters of its current account surplus in the years 2008–2012 with mere Target claims, Germany would have been able to convert its somewhat lower current account surplus into marketable foreign assets. Thus, to some extent, Germany effectively exported its goods to redeem the private foreign debt of southern European countries, replacing these countries' private creditors with the ECB system, which in turn became a debtor to the Bundesbank.

It could be objected that the German current account surplus stayed high and gained strength in 2013 even though the private capital flows reversed and the euro appreciated against the dollar (3% from 2012 to 2013). However, this is likely due to the well-known anomaly of current account reactions in the short run, i.e. the combination of sluggishness of export and import quantities and a price reduction of goods imported from non-euro countries.[28]

---

[28] Compare with Section *The Timing Problem* in Chapter 2.

It is an irony that Germany is being disparaged for its current account surplus, when in fact the persistence of this surplus has largely resulted from the rescue credits that the Bundesbank was forced to provide, and it is a sign of blunt ignorance of basic economic accounting identities when EU officials ask Germany to both export more rescue capital and fewer goods to other countries. They demand the impossible.

Finland and the Netherlands

The last two countries considered explicitly in this chapter are Finland and the Netherlands, which have also accumulated huge Target claims, at least until recently, as the last chapter documented (Figure 6.4). Figure 7.7 shows simplified versions of the respective charts (without the contributions to fiscal rescue credits and without the net foreign asset position—for this see Figure 2.9).

The charts show rather different patterns of Target balances for these two countries. In the case of the Netherlands, which has traditionally had a sizeable current account surplus, the additional Target claims that De Nederlandsche Bank built up from the beginning of 2008 to June 2011 accounted for just 34% of the country's cumulative current account. Afterwards, however, a lot of capital fled to the Netherlands which, in quantitative terms, meant that the private

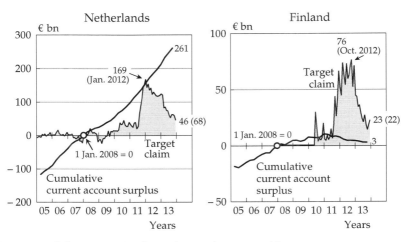

Figure 7.7 Other countries from the northern euro bloc

Sources: See Figure 7.1.

Notes: Unlike for Germany, intra-Eurozone current account data for the rest of the Eurozone have not been published. The figures in brackets give increments as of 1 January 2008.

capital that had been exported returned in net terms. This follows from the fact that, by January 2012, the Dutch Target curve temporarily reached the cumulative current account curve (while it was close to zero on 1 January 2008). After that point in time, however, the Dutch continued to export private capital. Over the whole span of the crisis, from 1 January 2008 to September 2013, the latest month for which data are available as of this writing, 33% of the Dutch current account surplus was paid for with money from foreign printing presses, while the rest was used for private capital exports or fiscal rescue credit.

The situation in Finland was obviously very different. While the Finnish current account surplus disappeared in 2011, as the slope reversal of the cumulative current account curve shows, there was a huge capital flight towards Finland after the summer of 2011, which came to a halt a year later when the ESM was ratified and the OMT was announced. Just like the Netherlands, Finland was considered a safe haven to safeguard against the risk of a currency breakup.[29] The insurance was provided by Suomen Pankki, Finland's central bank, which credited the payment orders for the investors who deposited funds in Finland, and received claims on the Eurosystem in exchange.

Bretton Woods and the European Payment Union

The significance of the Target balances is made clearer by reflecting on the Bretton Woods system, the monetary order that governed currency relations among the world's major industrial countries in the post-war period until 1973, with a gold-backed system that tied individual currencies to the dollar.[30]

---

[29] The investors seem to have been predominantly British financial institutions. See S. G. Cecchetti, R. N. McCauley, and P. M. McGuire, 'Interpreting TARGET2 Balances', *BIS Working Papers* No. 393, December 2012, available at: <http://www.bis.org/publ/work393.pdf>. While the point Cecchetti et al. make is correct, they misrepresent the work by T. Wollmershäuser and the author by implying that we had argued that the Target imbalances were *caused* by current account imbalances. This is a false interpretation. We analysed the role of capital flight and current account imbalances in the context of the Target balances in all our papers, and we always made clear that the current account imbalances, which had developed earlier and for other reasons, now needed an alternative source of financing. We also documented capital flight from the outset, as explained in footnote 7.

[30] See W. Kohler, 'The Eurosystem in Time of Crisis: Greece in the Role of a Reserve Currency Country?', *CESifo Forum* 13, Special Issue, January 2012, pp. 14–22, available at: <http://www.cesifo-group.de/DocDL/forum-0112-special-3.pdf>, and C. B. Blankart, 'The Euro 2084', *CESifo Forum* 13, Special Issue, January 2012, pp. 23–28, available at: <http://www.cesifo-group.de/DocDL/forum-0112-special-4.pdf>. For a comparison with the Mexico crisis, see A. Tornell and F. Westermann, 'Greece: The Sudden Stop

During the 1960s, US products had become increasingly expensive, and a US current account deficit developed. European visitors found the US expensive, while Americans went on shopping sprees in Europe. They purchased with abandon, be it companies, cars or shares of stock. American tourists were as ubiquitous back then as the Japanese are today.

But the Americans were not borrowing the money that they were spending abroad: they were printing it. Not for nothing was the dollar the world's reserve currency, accepted around the globe. Many countries actually *had* to accept it, since the fixed-currency system forced the other countries' central banks to hoard dollars when there was excess supply in the market. This way, the US Federal Reserve could provide the US economy with ever larger quantities of dollars through asset purchases and refinancing operations for people's shopping tours abroad. The US built up a huge balance-of-payments deficit, while the European countries accumulated corresponding surpluses. The excess dollars flowed mainly to Europe and were exchanged into national currency by the European central banks. The Banque de France and the Bundesbank accumulated growing hoards of dollars over the years, which were often converted to US Treasury Bills.

By virtue of the conversion of dollars into national currency, an amount of deutschmarks and francs got into circulation in Germany and France that did not result from domestic asset purchases or refinancing operations by their respective central banks, since such activities had already taken place in the US.

The resulting 'dollar-deutschmarks' and 'dollar-francs' circulating in Europe, in effect outside money originating in the US, crowded out the European inside money, i.e. the money created domestically through refinancing operations and asset purchases by the Bundesbank or the Banque de France.

The outside money that came to circulate in Germany and France in this way was of exactly the same nature as the outside money that came from the GIPSIC countries during the crisis. And the stocks of dollars and US Treasury Bonds in the European central banks then are now the Target claims of northern bloc euro countries against the Eurosystem.

The international credit shift through the central banks was also similar. While the European central banks saw their refinancing credit retrench, the Fed provided ever more credit to the US economy by buying predominantly public securities from banks. The US back then was in a very similar situation to the

that Wasn't', *VoxEU*, 28 September 2011, available at: <http://www.voxeu.org/article/greece-sudden-stop-wasn-t>. For a comparison of the Bretton-Woods system with the European Monetary System in the context of Bretton Woods, see also H. James, 'The Multiple Contexts of Bretton-Woods', *Oxford Review of Economic Policy* 28, 2012, pp. 411–430. For an analysis which draws an analogy between today's international financial system and the Bretton Woods system, see B. Eichengreen, *Global Imbalances and the Lessons of Bretton Woods*, MIT Press, Cambridge 2006.

current position of the GIPSIC countries. It was said at the time that Europe had indirectly helped to finance the Vietnam war.[31]

French President Charles de Gaulle, who disliked the US engagement in what had been French Indochina, in 1968 took literally the US assertion that the dollar was a gold-backed currency and demanded that France's dollar reserves be converted into gold. He sent his submarines to the US to escort the gold from New York back to France. That spelled the end of the Bretton Woods system, since the US did not possess enough gold to satisfy all conversion wishes and had to give up the gold standard.[32] Five years after de Gaulle's subs went to pick up the French gold, Bretton Woods was history. Since then, most exchange rates in the world have been determined by market supply and demand.

The Bundesbank, in contrast, had given assurances that it would not convert its dollar reserves into gold.[33] It had at the time, however, amassed large balance-of-payments surpluses against other European countries within the European Payment Union (EPU).[34] The EPU was established on 1 July 1950 as the result of a US endeavour to create a multilateral payment system within Europe as a sub-system to the Bretton Woods system created in 1944. This endeavour was marked by three intra-European clearing agreements between 1947 and 1949, which differed in signatory states, clearing categories and linkages to the European Recovery Program. The clearing of imbalances within the EPU was done monthly by the Bank for International Settlements.[35]

An increasing fraction of the imbalances within the EPU, ultimately 75%, had to be settled at the debtor's choice with either dollars or gold at the official parities, but since the market price of gold was below the parity, the debtors

---

[31] See R. D. Hormats, *The Price of Liberty: Paying for America's Wars*, Henry Hold and Company, New York 2007, in particular p. 255.

[32] For this and a further discussion of the collapse of the Bretton Woods system, see T. Mayer, *Europe's Unfinished Currency*, Anthem Press, London 2012, especially chapter 3: *A History of Failures*.

[33] See letter of Bundesbank President Karl Blessing, dated 30 March 1967, to the President of the Federal Reserve System, W. M. Martin Jr., available at: <http://www.mmnews.de/index.php/gold/7201-der-blessing-brief>.

[34] For a comparative work on the EPU versus the EMU, see J. C. Martínez Oliva, 'The EMU versus the EPU. A Historical Perspective on Trade, Payments and the European Financial Crisis', *World Economics* 14, 2013, pp. 126–144.

[35] For a detailed study of the European Payment Union, see E. Tuchtfeldt, *Die europäische Zahlungsunion*, Forschungsstelle Völkerrecht und Recht, Frankfurt am Main 1953.

preferred gold settlement.[36] By 1958, the Bundesbank had accumulated a gold stock of 2,346 tonnes.[37]

The EPU was replaced in 1958 by the European Monetary Agreement, which demanded the settlement of imbalances with dollars, but due to the official gold parity of the dollar, the actual settlement continued to be carried out with gold. So in the following ten years, the Bundesbank's physical stock of gold reserves increased by another 55%, to a total of around 4,000 tonnes (or 18 billion deutschmarks) in 1968.[38] This stock, minus around 6% that was ceded to the ECB in early 1999, still belongs to the Bundesbank.[39] The Bundesbank's gold today is worth about 15 times more in nominal terms than its value back then, which in real terms is 4.4 times, corresponding to an annual real rate of return of 3.4%. [40] By contrast,

[36] See C.-L. Holtfrerich, 'Geldpolitik bei festen Wechselkursen', in Deutsche Bundesbank (ed.), *50 Jahre Deutsche Mark—Notenbank und Währung in Deutschland seit 1948*, Beck, Munich 1998, in particular p. 400. After the establishment of the EPU in July 1950, the portion to be settled in gold or dollars was only 25%, from 1954 it was 50%, and since 1955, 75%.

[37] See C.-L. Thiele, *Pressegespräch 'Deutsche Goldreserven'*, Presentation, 16 January 2013, available at: <http://www.bundesbank.de/Redaktion/DE/Downloads/Presse/ Publikationen/ 2013_01_16_thiele_praesentation_pressegespraech_gold.pdf?__blob= publicationFile>.

[38] C.-L. Thiele, *Pressegespräch 'Deutsche Goldreserven'*, and Deutsche Bundesbank, Statistics, Time Series Databases, *Macroeconomic Time Series*, Time Series BBK01. EU8201: External Position of the Bundesbank up to 1998/Gold, available at: <http:// www.bundesbank.de/Navigation/EN/Statistics/Time_series_databases/Macro_eco- nomic_time_series/its_details_value_node.html?tsId=BBK01.EU8201&listId=www_ s201_b1005.>; see also P. Bernholz, 'Die Bundesbank und die Währungsintegration in Europa', in Deutsche Bundesbank (ed.), *50 Jahre Deutsche Mark—Notenbank und Währung in Deutschland seit 1948*, Beck, Munich 1998, in particular p. 828, for a chro- nology of European monetary integration; and J. H. Furth, 'The European Monetary Agreement', *Review of Foreign Developments*, 6 September 1955.

[39] A total of 7 million Troy ounces, or 218 tonnes, of gold were transferred to the ECB, out of a total stock of 119 million Troy ounces at the end of 1998. See Deutsche Bundesbank, *Annual Report 1999*, 6 April 2000, in particular p. 168, available at: <http:// www.bundesbank.de/Redaktion/EN/Downloads/Publications/Annual_Report/1999_ annual_report.pdf?__blob=publicationFile>; as well as Deutsche Bundesbank, *Annual Report 1998*, 1 April 1999, in particular p. 176, available at: <http://www.bundesbank. de/Redaktion/EN/Downloads/Publications/Annual_Report/1998_annual_report. pdf?__blob=publicationFile>.

[40] See Deutsche Bundesbank, *Annual Report 2011*, 13 March 2012, in particular p. 142, available at: <http://www.bundesbank.de/Redaktion/EN/Downloads/Publications/ Annual_Report/2011_annual_report.pdf?__blob=publicationFile>; as well as Deutsche Bundesbank, Statistics, Time Series databases, *Macroeconomic Time Series*, Time

its Target claims currently bear an interest rate of 0.25% in nominal terms and about −1% in real terms. Because of the need to settle the balance-of-payments imbalances under the Bretton Woods system, the European deficit countries tried to avoid them and kept their local money supply scarce. This kept the interest rates up, which discouraged local borrowing, kept the current account deficit in check, and encouraged capital imports, which financed the current account deficit and limited the balance-of-payments deficit. The basics of this mechanism were described by classical economist David Hume as early as the nineteenth century.[41] It was almost certainly the need to settle the balances that explains why the imbalances at the time were much smaller than those under the Eurosystem today, even in relative terms. In 1968, the Bundesbank's dollar reserves amounted to 1.6% of German GDP, and the gold reserves to 3.4%. Together, they were equivalent to 5% of GDP, or 26.72 billion deutschmarks.[42] The Bundesbank's Target claims, by contrast, amounted in August 2012 to € 751 billion, or 28.4% of German GDP.[43] The Bundesbank has kept the dollar reserves to this day, not as cash, but typically in the form of US government bonds and Treasury bills.

Series BBK01.TUB600: Gold und Goldforderungen Bundesbank, July 2012, available at: <http://www.bundesbank.de/Navigation/EN/Statistics/Time_series_databases/ Macro_economic_time_series/its_details_value_node.html?tsId=BBK01.TUB600>; and C.-L. Holtfrerich, 'Geldpolitik bei festen Wechselkursen', in particular p. 351; and Deutsche Bundesbank, Time Series BBK01.EU8201: External Position of the Bundesbank up to 1998/Gold.

[41] See M. Burda, 'Hume on Hold?', *VoxEU*, 17 May 2012, available at: <http:// www.voxeu.org/article/hume-hold-consequences-not-abolishing-euro- zone-national-central-banks>; M. D. Bordo and H. James, 'The European Crisis in the Context of the History of Previous Financial Crises', *NBER Working Paper* No. 19112, June 2013.

[42] At the end of 1968, the Bundesbank's gold reserves stood at 18.156 billion deutsch- marks, equivalent to 3.4% of GDP, which at the time was 553.71 billion deutsch- marks. The dollar reserves amounted then to 8.561 billion deutschmarks, or 1.6% of GDP. See Deutsche Bundesbank, Time Series BBK01.EU8201: External Position of the Bundesbank up to 1998/Gold; Deutsche Bundesbank, Statistics, Time Series Databases, *Macroeconomic Time Series*, Time Series BBK01.EU8215: External Position of the Bundesbank up to 1998/Foreign Exchange Reserves/US dollar Assets, avail- able at: <http://www.bundesbank.de/Navigation/EN/Statistics/Time_series_databases/ Macro_economic_time_series/its_details_value_node.html?tsId=BBK01.EU8215>; as well as German Federal Statistical Office, *Gross Domestic Product, Gross National Income, and Net National Income at Factor Cost*.

[43] € 2,644.2 billion: Eurostat, Database, *Economy and Finance*, National Accounts.

Transfer Roubles

As far removed as the Soviet empire was from a market economy, it also needed an internal payment system to allow for mutual transactions. Such a system was introduced in 1964 among the socialist countries of the world assembled under the Council for Mutual Economic Assistance (CMEA, but usually known as Comecon), including the Soviet Union, the eastern European countries, and other socialist countries such as Cuba and Vietnam. It replaced the ineffective system of barter trade that had existed before.[44] Every state had an account with the International Bank for Economic Co-operation (IBEC) in Moscow that it could use for payment orders to other states, the unit of account being the so-called transfer rouble.[45]

Since the system imposed no limits to balance-of-payments imbalances, member states took advantage and built up growing debt positions that basically were credited by the Central Bank of Russia. This led to inflation and growing political tensions within the system, as Russia was unable to cope with the export of real economic resources that it had to credit to the member countries.[46] These tensions ultimately contributed to the fall of the Soviet system. In 1992, after the Wall had come down, Russia changed the system by introducing bilateral overdraft limits.[47] This, however, reduced its attractiveness for the member states and induced them to exit it, which led to the collapse of the Rouble Zone in September 1993.[48]

Russian credit to the former Soviet republics amounted to 9.3% of Russian GDP, and the debts built up ranged from 11% of the debtor countries' GDP (Belarus and Moldova) to 91% (Tajikistan).[49] The end of the system was a great mess, and Russia was unable to have its claims settled.[50]

---

[44] See P. J. J. Welfens, *Market-oriented Systemic Transformations in Eastern Europe*, Springer, Berlin 1992, especially p. 151.

[45] See P. B. Kenen, 'Transitional Arrangement for Trade and Payments Among the CMEA Countries', *IMF Staff Papers* 38, June 1991, pp. 235–267, especially p. 238.

[46] See L. S. Goldberg, B. W. Ickes, and R. Ryterman, 'Departures from the Rouble Zone: The Implications of Adopting Independent Currencies', *World Economy* 17, 1994, pp. 293–322.

[47] See L. S. Goldberg, B. W. Ickes, and R. Ryterman, 'Departures from the Rouble Zone: The Implications of Adopting Independent Currencies', p. 303.

[48] See A. Åslund, 'Why a Collapse of the Eurozone Must Be Avoided', *VoxEU*, 21 August 2012, available at: <http://www.voxeu.org/article/why-collapse-eurozone-must-be-avoided-almost-any-cost>.

[49] See T. Wolf and J. Odling-Smee, 'Financial Relations among Countries of the Former Soviet Union', *IMF Economic Reviews*, 1994, and A. Åslund, 'Why a Collapse of the Eurozone Must Be Avoided', 21 August 2012.

[50] See P. Conway, 'Currency Proliferation: The Monetary Legacy of the Soviet Union', *Princeton Essays in International Finance* 197, June 1995.

The Swiss Example

Another useful comparison that helps understand the Target imbalances in the Eurozone is Switzerland. Switzerland is in a similar situation today as Germany was under the Bretton Woods system or is now in the Eurosystem. The return of Swiss investment capital from abroad, together with capital flowing in from distressed countries, has brought about a strong appreciation of the Swiss franc, reducing the competitiveness of Swiss industry. This prompted the Swiss National Bank to apply the emergency brakes. On 6 September 2011, it announced that it would henceforth tolerate no fall in the price of the euro below 1.20 francs or, equivalently, no increase in the price of the Swiss franc above 83 euro cents. The announcement was credible, since while no central bank can permanently protect its currency against devaluation—because in order to accomplish that it would need to sell foreign currency, of which it only has a finite amount—it can indeed protect it against appreciation by simply printing money or issuing bonds in order to meet the demand of domestic or foreign investors for Swiss francs or financial investments. The result of the market intervention was a surplus in the Swiss balance of payments that brought a very large amount of euros to the Swiss central bank. The central bank did not hold the euros as cash, however, but invested them promptly in European securities, and particularly in German sovereign bonds. Today it is the largest holder of German government bonds in the world.[51]

The stock of German bonds held by the Swiss central bank is the analogue to the Bundesbank's Target claims.[52] The only difference is that, in this case, these claims consist of marketable securities that can be exchanged at any time into other assets. The claims that Swiss commercial banks have amassed on the Swiss National Bank, unlike those that the German commercial banks have accumulated on the Bundesbank, can be serviced at any time by the Swiss National Bank without resorting to inflationary money printing, even if the exchange rate regime should be terminated.

---

[51] The Swiss central bank holds an estimated 100 billion francs in German sovereign bonds and thus finances between 7% and 8% of the German federal debt. See H. Schöchli, 'Standfest hinter der Nationalbank', *Neue Zürcher Zeitung*, 18 July 2012, available at: <http://www.nzz.ch/aktuell/wirtschaft/wirtschaftsnachrichten/standfest-hinter-der-nationalbank-1.17368206>.

[52] See H.-W. Sinn, 'Ohne Wettbewerbsfähigkeit zerbricht der Euro', Interview by A. Trentin, *Finanz und Wirtschaft*, No. 47, 13 June 2012, p. 20, available at: <http://www.fuw.ch/article/ohne-wettbewerbsfahigkeit-zerbricht-der-euro/>.

How Target-Like Balances Are Settled in the United States

Another useful comparison for the Eurosystem is the monetary system of the US, called the US Federal Reserve or simply the Fed.[53] The Fed has a Board of Governors based in Washington, but it also has 12 Federal Reserve Banks—let us call them 'District Feds'—which implement monetary policy in compliance with Fed rules. This is similar to the Eurosystem, with its Governing Council and Board in Frankfurt, and an NCB in each of its 18 member states. However, despite this similarity, there are substantial differences between the two systems.

In the US, money comes predominantly into circulation through the Fed's purchase of federal public securities (Treasury bills as well as securities issued by federal agencies and government-sponsored enterprises) held by private banks. However, during the crisis, the Fed also bought asset-backed securities issued by the private sector. Most purchases are made by the New York Fed acting on behalf of the Federal Open Market Committee. The portfolio thus created, the so-called System Open Market Account (SOMA),[54] is owned by all District Feds. In addition to this centralized form of money creation, the District Feds provide local refinancing credit through the so-called discount window, as well as refinancing credit against collateral ('repos'), the latter being similar to the credit offered by the Eurozone's NCBs. A number of additional facilities were introduced during the crisis years to provide short-term credit to the banking sector, among them the Term Auction Facility and the Primary Dealer Credit Facility. The Term Securities Lending Facility, in turn, allows swapping private for government assets so as to endow the private sector with better collateral for credit from private sources as well as the Fed.

Unlike in Europe, the US central bank system is not a governmental institution. The District Feds belong to the private commercial banks that hold stock in them, and are at their service. The Fed is, however, under public control and has to deliver its seignorage profit to the Federal Government. Their district boundaries have little to do with federal state borders: in some cases, several states belong to one District Fed; conversely, there are states whose territory falls within two different District Feds' jurisdictions.

---

[53] For a comparative analysis of the US versus the EMU system, see also H. James, 'Designing a Federal Bank', *VoxEU*, February 2013, available at: <http://www.voxeu.org/article/designing-federal-bank>.

[54] The Federal Reserve System Open Market Account (SOMA) is a portfolio of US Treasury and Federal Agency securities, foreign currency investments and reciprocal currency arrangements. It is used for the open market operations of the Federal Reserve System. Detailed information on activities and composition can be found at the Federal Reserve Bank of New York website, available at: <http://www.newyorkfed.org/about-thefed/fedpoint/fed27.html>.

In the US system, payment orders between the commercial banks flow through the District Feds, each of which keeps an Interdistrict Settlement Account (ISA) with each of the eleven other District Feds. The balance on this account is, in principle, the same as the Target balance of an NCB in the Eurozone, since it shows the net volume of payment orders a District Fed has performed on account of the others; in other words, how much credit it has granted them by crediting the accounts of beneficiary commercial banks, fulfilling the payment orders.

Imbalances in the ISA cross-district payment orders resulting from asymmetric money creation cannot be carried forward as in Europe, but have to be settled mutually between the District Feds in April of every year by handing over a respective ownership right in the SOMA portfolio.

To understand the US system, it is useful to recall how it evolved over the course of its two-hundred-year history. Initially there were only dollar coins issued locally by official mints, abiding by the rules about exact gold and silver content set by Federal law. Paper money was first brought into circulation in 1861 to finance the American Civil War. The Federal Reserve was not established until 1913. To be sure, there were earlier attempts at setting up central banks, in 1791 and 1816, but they were only granted 20-year charters and were closed once the charters expired.

Before the Federal Reserve System existed, money transfers were already being made across the country, without cash having to be transported physically from one place to another. People would send checks as payment, and in order for them to be cashed, transfers had to be made between the commercial banks involved. The banks carried out the payment orders and provided temporary credit to each other if the orders did not net out to zero, but eventually the balances had to be settled physically, usually with gold, which then had to be transported between the banks involved. Any lover of cowboy movies will understand that this was a costly and cumbersome settlement procedure.

The new Federal Reserve System made the settling process easier in 1915 with the establishment of a so-called Gold Settlement Fund, which contained physical gold and gold certificates at the Fed, in which each District Fed owned proportional shares.[55] The balance-of-payments imbalances between the districts were settled on a weekly basis by transferring a respective ownership share to gold or gold certificates between the District Feds, rendering the physical transportation of gold unnecessary. In 1934 District Feds had to deliver all their gold to the Federal Reserve System, and henceforth the settlement only took

---

[55] See Federal Reserve, *Federal Reserve Bulletin*, 1 June 1915, available at: <http://fraser.stlouisfed.org/docs/publications/FRB/pages/1915-1919/19705_1915-1919.pdf>.

place by transferring ownership rights to gold certificates.[56] After the gold-based Bretton Woods system of international exchange rates broke down in 1973, gold certificates also lost their role for the intra-US settlement procedure. From 1975 onwards, the transfer of gold certificates was replaced by the transfer of ownership shares in the SOMA portfolio acquired in the process of money creation. This, however, did not alter the nature of the settlement procedure.

There are at least four aspects of the Federal Reserve which explain why the US's ISA balances did not reach similar levels as in the Eurozone, or why they cannot be interpreted as evidence of local printing presses underbidding the capital market, as is the case in the Eurozone.

1. The private nature and structural disentanglement between state and district Fed borders limits the political influence on local monetary policy. This alone makes the bailing out of states with local refinancing credit collateralized with non-investment-grade government bonds, which was an essential ingredient of the ECB's bailout policy (see Chapter 5), unthinkable in the US. The asset purchases, which are the major channel of money creation in the US, involve a regionally unbiased portfolio of mostly federal government bonds rather than bonds issued by single states, let alone those issued by profligate states such as California or Illinois.

2. In the US, money normally comes into circulation because the NY Fed distributes it on behalf of the Federal Reserve System, buying federal government bonds that formerly had been sold throughout the United States to finance the federal budget, a process which itself should be more or less neutral with regard to the ISA balances.[57] If the NY Fed buys such bonds, it induces a flow of bonds from all over the union to New York and corresponding payment orders to other District Feds, which results in an ISA liability for the NY Fed. This liability is not comparable to the Target liability of a Eurozone NCB, since it does not result from underbidding the local capital market with the printing press, but ultimately from financing the government of the federation whose outlays benefit all regions equally. While this was a dominant aspect before the crisis, after the crisis broke out other aspects became more important.

---

[56] The Gold Reserve Act of 30 January 1934 transferred the entire stock of monetary gold in the United States, including gold and gold certificates held by the Federal Reserve banks, to the US Treasury. See Federal Reserve, *Monthly Bulletin*, February 1934, p. 67, available at: <http://fraser.stlouisfed.org/docs/publications/FRB/1930s/frb_021934.pdf>, as well as United States, *Statutes at Large of the United States of America from March 1933 to June 1934*, Part 1, pp. 337–344, Government Printing Office, Washington 1934.

[57] The government sells its bonds to investors throughout the US territories and uses the proceeds for government expenditure, which is widely dispersed throughout the US territories, so that no ISA balances emerge in net terms. The reader may think of the metaphor of paying for the federal government's expenses throughout the country with government bonds rather than money, which also would leave no traces in the ISA balances.

3. Given that the US is a federal nation with a common banking law, there are nationwide banks that concentrate their demand for money from the printing press on particular districts, typically those where their headquarters are located. Thus, for example, the Bank of America's headquarters are located in the Richmond district and the Wells Fargo headquarters in the San Francisco district. This may explain why these two districts built up particularly large levels of ISA liabilities during the crisis, when the Fed carried out its special liquidity-creating programmes, as explained above. Since these programmes gave all District Feds better access to the Fed's printing press, money creation was temporarily relocated from the NY Fed to other District Feds.[58] Obviously, there is no analogy between this mechanism and the Eurozone, if only because most European banks are national, while the few that do operate internationally have legally independent subsidiaries rather than branches in other countries.

4. The settling of the ISA balances with marketable securities makes resorting to the local printing press not impossible, but less attractive, because imbalances have to be settled by handing over ownership shares in the SOMA portfolio. It is true that the disadvantage from settling liabilities is limited, given that the interest on the respective securities net of expenditures has to be handed over to the Federal Government. However, some of the local profit remains in the District Fed insofar as its own wages and other amenities can be deducted before the rest of the profit is transferred to the Federal Government, which opens up room for the employment of more staff and the payment of higher salaries. Indeed, salaries across the District Feds in the US are very uneven, with some District Fed presidents earning 50% more than others.[59]

The limited incentive and possibilities in the US to issue more than the fair share of money locally has in the history of the US, time and again, led to substantial differences in short-term federal funds rates, often of 100 basis points and more, as documented by the 2013 EEAG Report on the European Economy.[60] These

---

[58] Cf. European Economic Advisory Group (EEAG), *The EEAG Report on the European Economy: Rebalancing Europe*, chapter 4: *US Precedents for Europe*, CESifo, Munich 2013, figure 4.5, p. 105, available at: < http://www.cesifo-group.de/DocDL/ EEAG-2013.pdf >. For a different explanation in terms of providing weaker districts with particular help from the Federal Reserve System, drawing a parallel with the ECB's help to particular regions, see P. Cour-Thimann, 'Target Balances and the Crisis in the Euro Area', *CESifo Forum* 14, Special Issue, April 2013, figure 16, p. 30, available at: <http://www.cesifo-group.de/DocDL/Forum-Sonderheft-Apr-2013.pdf>.

[59] In 2009, the St. Louis District Fed President was paid $ 276,800, while the President of the San Francisco Fed received $ 410,800. See S. Reddy, 'Fed Salaries: It Pays to be Private', *Wall Street Journal Real Time Economics,* 24 May 2010, available at: <http:// blogs.wsj.com/economics/2010/05/24/fed-salaries-it-pays-to-be-private/>, and EEAG, *The EEAG Report on the European Economy: Rebalancing Europe,* 2013, p. 106.

[60] See EEAG, *The EEAG Report on the European Economy: Rebalancing Europe*, 2013, figure 4.3, p. 103.

differences triggered a similar adjustment process as in the Bretton Woods system. If a region was short of capital to finance its current account deficit, it could not resort to the printing press to close the gap, but had to offer higher interest rates to the market to induce a capital import from other regions. This mechanism kept the balance-of-payments imbalances in check.

What this all meant for the development of actual ISA balances during the crisis is shown in Figure 7.8. The two solid curves show the evolution of the gross Target balances and the gross ISA balances, both in relation to the size of the respective economy (Eurozone and US GDP). It can be seen that the volume of ISA balances before the financial crisis struck was around 0.2% to 0.3% of GDP, rising during the crisis to 2% and then to nearly 3%, only to sink thereafter to a level comparable to that of before the crisis.

It can also be seen that the volumes typically came down in or around April of each year, in those cases when they had grown previously. This is because April is the month when the settlement has to be performed.

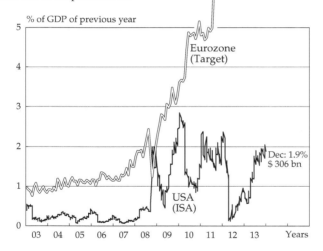

Figure 7.8 Target and ISA balances* as a share of GDP in the Eurozone and the USA, respectively (January 2003–December 2013)

* Sum of the gross Target claims and sum of the gross ISA claims, respectively, of the Eurosystem's central banks and the Federal Reserve System, respectively.

Source: H.-W. Sinn, 'Fed versus ECB: How Target Debts Can Be Repaid', *VoxEU*, 10 March 2012, available at: <http://www.voxeu.org/article/fed-versus-ecb-how-target-de bts-can-be-repaid>; H.-W. Sinn and T. Wollmershäuser, 'Target Loans, Current Account Balances and Capital Flows: The ECB's Rescue Facility', 2012, figure 9, updated.

Note: The chart is based on data up to December 2013.

The settlement is not for the full imbalance, but follows a specific formula that typically implies partial settlement only. What is actually calculated for settlement is the difference between the daily average of the balances over the previous twelve months and the unsettled remainder of the balances in April a year before. This is not entirely insignificant, since it means that, in the US, balances can also accumulate during a crisis. The balances, however, do not increase steadily and systematically, but are brought down on a regular basis through the settlement process, as the chart shows, and, to reiterate a point made above, unlike in the Eurozone, unsettled balances do not imply undercutting the market with the printing press to aid weaker regions.

In the Eurozone, the gross volume of Target balances amounted to around 1% of GDP until the financial crisis hit in 2007, rose steadily thereafter until it levelled off temporarily at about 5%, and rocketed afterwards to 11.4% of the Eurozone's GDP, or € 1.075 trillion, in August 2012. By December 2013, the Eurozone balances had come down to 7.3% of GDP, after the ECB's announcement of its readiness to make unlimited purchases of distressed-country government bonds in the secondary market, which induced new private capital flows to the crisis-stricken countries.

An interesting month showing how the American system works is April 2009. In the run-up to that month the balances decreased gradually, month by month, because the District Feds apparently took care, by granting less credit, to avoid the losses resulting from the reallocation of ownership shares in the Fed's clearing portfolio. The cutback in local credit from the printing press gave rise to an inflow of private credit from other districts. After the settlement deadline, the balances went up again. The downward-and-upward movement around April 2009 is evidence of the incentive effect mentioned above. In other years, the fear of a settlement as such reduced the balances. At the latest data point available as of this writing, December 2013, the gross volume of ISA balances amounted to merely 1.9% of US GDP, or $ 306 billion.

The comparison with the US starkly exposes a design flaw in the Eurosystem. If a monetary system offers the weaker economies unlimited amounts of money on a display window, confidence will be maximized, stabilizing the capital markets and minimizing interest rate differences across regions. But this is precisely what destabilizes the regions, since it encourages them to take on too much private credit in the first place. This, in turn, leads to inflationary overheating, huge trade imbalances and a loss of competitiveness until their external debt is so large that the markets begin to expect a breaching of the system ceilings and decide to withdraw, prompting the credit-dependent economies to start taking the money from the display window.

It is not sensible to induce absolute market confidence in the economy of a country or region through artificial protection mechanisms, such as unlimited amounts of funding on a display window or unlimited firepower of the central banks. The capitalist system thrives upon a healthy scepticism on the part of investors, i.e. upon the caution of those who fear losing their money. The possibility of losing the money invested should never be removed, because otherwise the markets run wild and control is lost, just like a car without brakes.

It has been argued that no measures can be instituted to put a brake on Target balances, since the Eurosystem would collapse as a result. The balances, it is said, are necessary for a smooth flow of transactions, and for this reason everything should stay as it is. If this were true, the US system would have collapsed long ago.

In reality, the US monetary system has persisted now for quite some time, because it does not offer the possibility of a self-service culture through its interdistrict settlement system and imposes tight constraints on local credit provision. Up to 1975, the US even required ISA balances to be settled with gold. The US system is not so strict as to demand a continuous flattening of balance-of-payments imbalances, and indeed the constraints were loosened after 1975 and during the crisis, as described above. Thus, as the chart shows, temporary balance-of-payments deficits did materialize. However, the mechanisms to limit the imbalances were still relatively strong before the crisis and have to some extent been maintained during the crisis. If private credit does not suffice to cover the balance-of-payments deficit, the District Fed in question may issue and lend out more money. But the resulting outflow of money must be swiftly compensated for by transferring ownership rights in the SOMA portfolio. The system thus has shock absorbers that are stiff enough to keep the wheels from bouncing about and to hold the economic vehicle on course.

After considering the evolution of the US system, the ECB's notion that it is unnecessary to settle the balances, but suffices just to chalk them up to a credit account as is done in Europe, is unconvincing.

A Fundamental Dichotomy in the Rescue Policies

Bankers, politicians, and quite a number of economists are satisfied with the way the Eurosystem functions. They argue that the crisis-stricken countries must carry out reforms to regain their competitiveness and the confidence of the markets and that, until that happens, ample liquidity should be provided.[61] Some observers even give the impression that the current account deficits and capital

---

[61] This view was, for instance, expressed by IMF Chief Economist Olivier Blanchard; see also I. Madár and K. Kovács, 'Blanchard: Eurozone Integration Needs to Go Forward or go Back, but it Can't Stay Here', *Portfolio.hu*, 3 October 2012, available at: <http://www.portfolio.hu/en/equity/blanchard_eurozone_integration_needs_to_go_forward_or_go_back_but_it_cant_stay_here.24931.html>; see also Z. Darvas, J.-P. Pisani-Ferry, and A. Sapir, 'A Comprehensive Solution for the Euro Crisis', *VoxEU*, 28 February 2011, available at: <http://www.voxeu.org/article/three-part-plan-tackle-eurozone-d

flight are exogenous occurrences to which the only sensible reaction is to provide generous amounts of ECB liquidity and public rescue packages.

This position is defensible from the perspective of money in the display window being the best deterrent against speculative attacks. It is also convenient for creditors and debtors alike, as it results in a bailout of over-indebted countries and their creditors with taxpayers' money. However, the accounting identities between the variables that play a role in a country's budget constraints mentioned at the outset of this chapter should not be overlooked. It is an irrefutable fact that a current account deficit and a private capital export can only occur simultaneously to the extent that central banks deliver fresh money, and hence public credit, to an economy, or to the extent that intergovernmental credit fills the funding gap. If public credit had not been available as an alternative, the crisis-hit countries couldn't have accumulated current account deficits and experienced capital flight simultaneously. That is the fundamental dichotomy in the rescue operations: they must either have made capital flight possible, which policymakers claimed to want to slow down,[62] or they must have sustained current account deficits, about which the policymakers complained.[63] Policymakers will have to concede the truth of at least one of these two uncomfortable conclusions.

In reality, the rescue operations probably did both. The ECB and the fiscal rescue funds slowed down the structural improvement of the current account deficits, as discussed in Chapter 4, because the alternative funding that they provided enabled the crisis-stricken countries to postpone reforms and continue business as usual. At the same time, the ECB credit and the rescue funds crowded out private international credit by providing funding at below-market conditions. Particularly egregious was the radical reduction of the ECB's collateral requirements, as described in Chapter 5, which effectively ditched the idea

ebt-crisis>; IMF, 'Greece. 2013 Article IV Consultation', *IMF Country Report No. 13/154*, June 2013, available at: <http://www.imf.org/external/pubs/ft/scr/2013/cr13154.pdf>; IMF, 'Spain. 2013 Article IV Consultation', *IMF Country Report No. 13/244*, August 2013, available at: <http://www.imf.org/external/pubs/ft/scr/2013/cr13244.pdf>; P. De Grauwe, 'In Search of Symmetry in the Eurozone', *CEPS Policy Brief*, No. 268, May 2012; Z. Darvas, J. Pisani-Ferry, and G. B. Wolff, 'Europe's Growth Problem (and What to Do About It)', *Bruegel Policy Brief*, No. 03/2013, April 2013.

[62] See M. Draghi, 'The Euro, Monetary Policy and the Design of a Fiscal Compact', *Ludwig Erhard Lecture*, Berlin, 15 December 2011, available at: <http://www.ecb.int/press/key/date/2011/html/sp111215.en.html>.

[63] See M. Draghi, 'Competitiveness of the Euro Area and within the Euro Area', *Le Monde,* and Association of Private French Companies (AFEP), *Les défis de la compétitivité*, Paris, 13 March 2012, available at: <http://www.ecb.int/press/key/date/2012/html/sp120313.en.html>.

of the singleness of monetary policy in the Eurozone and turned the ECB into a bailout institution.

Policymakers argued, not without reason, that their interventions were a necessary evil to give the crisis countries enough time to make the requisite adjustments. However, while the interventions were meant to be temporary and lead to a better equilibrium, they instead fuelled moral hazard and may have aggravated the problems that they intended to solve. It is symptomatic that, as Figure 4.8 showed, none of the crisis-stricken countries, except for Ireland, carried out a sizeable real depreciation, and some did not depreciate at all, during the first six years of the crisis. Ireland, whose bubble had burst two years before the Lehman debacle, initially had not been given the possibility of running Target deficits to solve its problems with the printing press. Only after the collapse of Lehman Brothers did the ECB hand over the keys to the local printing presses. In the initial years, Ireland had to fend for itself and accept the austerity imposed by the markets. The country started to cut its prices in response as early as 2007, a process that gradually made it competitive again.

By contrast, according to the data shown in Figure 4.9, Spain increased the wages of its public employees by 19% in the first three years, and Portugal by 10% in the first two years, after the start of the crisis in the summer of 2007, and Greek public sector wages even jumped by 28% in the first two years. Private wages rose somewhat more moderately, but they did rise despite the emergence of the crisis and only began to decline as of 2010, which in most cases only meant that this decline offset the wage increases seen during the first years of the crisis. To be sure, the real crisis intensified afterwards, and more recent data show that a moderate real depreciation is finally underway in Spain and Greece (though not in Portugal, see Figure 4.8); however, depreciation did not start to occur until a full five years after the crisis hit. The alternative credit provision by the ECB and the official rescue packages may have delayed the necessary structural improvements in competitiveness through real depreciation by half a decade.

The other crisis-stricken countries not only adjusted more slowly than Ireland, but also more slowly than comparable non-euro EU countries that were also tied to a fixed exchange rate regime. As indicated in Chapter 4, and as was also shown by Daniel Gros and Cinzia Alcidi, the so-called BELL countries in eastern Europe (Bulgaria, Estonia, Lithuania, and Latvia), whose exchange rate relative to the euro was fixed and which did not receive support from the ECB, adjusted much quicker than the southern euro countries.[64] The authors attribute

---

[64] See D. Gros and C. Alcidi, 'Country Adjustment to a Sudden Stop: Does the Euro Make a Difference?', *European Commission Economic Papers* 492, April 2013, available at: <http://ec.europa.eu/economy_finance/publications/economic_paper/2013/pdf/ecp492_en.pdf>.

this to the fact that the rescue operations 'created an environment in which the pressure for a quick adjustment was much weaker'.

This does not mean that the ECB should not have provided liquidity when the financial crisis broke out in Europe. The ECB's policy was probably the right one in the autumn of 2008, when the collapse of the Lehman Brothers investment bank threw the markets into a panic. In the opinion of many observers, a meltdown of the world economy was imminent and was averted at the last second by flooding the markets with freshly printed money.[65] But this justification faded away in the autumn of 2009, or by the spring of 2010 at the latest, when the world economy recovered with surprising vigour and it became clear that some European countries were not simply victims of a global crisis with temporary liquidity problems, but were also suffering from a fundamental lack of competitiveness, if not outright insolvency, as in the case of Greece. At that time, the markets charged significantly higher interest rates (refer also to Figure 2.2) or abstained entirely from financing some countries.

The rationale for the spring 2010 rescue decisions is disputable, because they delayed insolvency, bailed out the existing creditors, and helped countries to be spared the risk premia that the markets were charging, thus eroding new investors' returns on savings.

In the first instance, the rescue operations did not merely replace fleeing capital, but made the capital flight itself possible. If the ECB, applying a rigorous refinancing policy, had prevented excessive credit from being drawn from the local printing presses, and if no fiscal rescue credit had been available, private capital would hardly have been able to flee. The quantity of central bank money necessary to redeem the investors' credit claims by issuing international payment orders would simply not have been available, and investors would have been forced to accept the sort of haircuts that were eventually applied much later (in March 2012 to Greek debt and in March 2013 to Cypriot bank debt). By delaying bankruptcy, the ECB and the rescue funds helped Greece and Cyprus to delay the necessary reforms, and helped the banks and other investors to recoup their money, because the public credit provided the funds needed to redeem private credit. As Figure 5.1 showed, the great beneficiaries of the bailout policy were the banks of France, Germany, Great Britain, the Netherlands, Belgium, and Switzerland, in that order.

In the second instance, the rescue operations, in particular the ECB's loosening of collateral requirements and the granting of maturity extensions to facilitate access to refinancing credit, helped the borrowing countries, including those that did not apply for official rescue funds, by providing them with cheap finance under conditions at which they would not have been able to borrow in the

---

[65] See H.-W. Sinn, *Casino Capitalism*, 2010, p. 58.

market. The ECB's rescue policies helped both the debtors and their creditors, but inflicted losses on new savers by underbidding the capital market with the printing press and crowding private investors out of what otherwise could have been lucrative markets. Those who planned to entrust their savings to German life insurance companies, for example, in the hope of receiving a good pension later, definitely suffered from this, since the companies were forced to reduce the guaranteed minimum returns they had been offering. The observation reported in Figure 4.2 that the interest on net foreign debt paid by the GIPSIC countries *declined* during the crisis, despite the fact that both the stock of foreign debt and market interest rates increased dramatically, offers clear evidence of this effect.

The irony is that the ECB triggered even more capital flight when it tried to counteract it by making its own credit more affordable. Arguably, the events that occurred from summer 2011 to summer 2012, when huge amounts of capital fled Spain and Italy, can be interpreted in this way. The Big Bazooka, or the one-trillion-euro long-term refinancing credit decided upon by the ECB Governing Council in December 2011, was motivated by the attempt to fight capital flight.[66] However, as Figures 6.2 and 7.1 through 7.4 showed, this decision dramatically boosted the Target balances, which measure the capital flight, even further. The Big Bazooka was akin to attempting to extinguish a fire with gasoline.

The ECB and the community of states alleviated the immediate pain of market austerity, but at the same time they threw the usual self-equilibrating processes of market economies off kilter. For if capital begins to shy away from a country, the country's interest rates, net of risk premia, must go up in order to keep the capital from leaving as well as to reduce the demand for credit, thus equilibrating the local capital market. Alternatively, if the country has arrived at a Stiglitz-Weiss kind of scenario where it is unable to convince creditors to stay put by offering higher interest rates, it must declare insolvency, in line with one of the fundamental rules of the Maastricht Treaty (article 125 TFEU).[67] Obviously, the attempt to maintain the same nominal interest rates everywhere

---

[66] At his press conference ahead of the second tender of the Big Bazooka, on 9 February 2012, ECB President Draghi called the LTRO operations an 'unquestionable success' insofar as, among others, the 'money market funds, which were the first to take flight from the euro', came back on 8 March 2012. See also Introductory Statement to the Press Conference (with Q&A) by Mario Draghi, President of the ECB, and Vítor Constâncio, Vice-President of the ECB, 9 February 2012, available at: <http://www.ecb.int/press/pressconf/2012/html/is120209.en.html> and Introductory Statement to the Press Conference (with Q&A) by Mario Draghi, President of the ECB, and Vítor Constâncio, Vice-President of the ECB, 8 March 2012, available at: <http://www.ecb.int/press/pressconf/2012/html/is120308.en.html>.

[67] J. E. Stiglitz and A. Weiss, 'Credit Rationing in Markets with Imperfect Information', *American Economic Review* 71, 1981, pp. 393–410.

in the Eurozone by providing unlimited liquidity and undercutting the market rates sent huge waves of destabilizing private capital flows washing across the member states of the currency union. These capital flows would not have been possible had there been a settlement mechanism to keep local money supply tight and allow for equilibrating interest rate differentials.

The presence of such a settlement mechanism would certainly have led to a period of disinflation or outright deflation in the crisis countries, which would have brought about the necessary realignment of prices and wages earlier, paving the way for new growth and prosperity in those countries. Or it would have induced the countries, for which such a process would have been too painful, to leave the euro. But policymakers preferred to delay the costs of the necessary adjustments, prolonging the competitiveness crisis in the southern countries and turning their economic diseases into scleroses.

CHAPTER 8

Stumbling Along

*The Six Steps of the Crisis—Buying Government Bonds: The SMP—No Risk to
Taxpayers?—ESM & Co—Overview of Rescue Funds—The Liability Risk—The
OMT Controversy—The Statement of the German Constitutional Court—Banking
Union: Bail-in or Bailout?—The Plan—Bailing out the ECB—Undermining the
Market Economy and Democracy*

The Six Steps of the Crisis

The euro has turned into a trap for the European states that adopted it. The
southern states are trapped because the inflationary credit bubble brought about
by the euro deprived them of their competitiveness, and the northern states are
trapped in a liability spiral. The first of these traps was extensively analysed
in Chapters 2 and 4. This chapter studies the liability spiral resulting from a
sequence of public bailout operations, following the bailout with the printing
press discussed above.

Unfortunately, the sequence of measures to combat the crisis is not planned,
and no one has a notion of where this all will lead. Instead Europe is left stumbling from one crisis to the next. At each level of the crisis the idea to date has
been to find new sources of public funding to protect prior private and public debtors from defaulting. The new sources, however, only solve the financial
problems for a while, until they are exhausted and the loop of the crisis resumes.
Politicians always claim that the worst is now over, but this is their usual propa-
ganda. The truth is that the next crisis will again crop up in a corner of the
economy where it is not expected. Again, given prior policy decisions, new decisions are made to avoid another immediate collapse.

The political choices at each step are not irrational. There is always some compelling logic and urgency rationalizing the actual decisions taken. Nevertheless,
each step along this path dependency set by the immediate history may lead to

political structures in Europe that no one ever wanted and that undermine the basis of a free market economy, and even of democracy.

These are the six steps of the vicious spiral that have become apparent to date, some of which have already been discussed in this book. They are summarized here to give an overview of what happened. A more detailed analysis of the new steps will follow.

Step 1: The Implicit Bailout Promise (The Euro)

The announcement and introduction of the euro eliminated the exchange rate risk, but the risk of state bankruptcies that came in its stead was downplayed by EU institutions, even though the Maastricht Treaty's no-bailout clause (article 125 of the Treaty on the Functioning of the European Union, TFEU) clearly stated that investors would have to accept haircuts if a state could not repay its debt. As explained in Chapter 2, the EU's interpretation of the Basel regulation that treated all banks and all governments of the Eurozone alike, regardless of their credit ratings, requiring only minuscule or no equity holding as a counterpart buffer on the balance sheet, was a major mistake. It thoroughly contradicted the spirit of the no-bailout clause and had dramatic consequences for market behaviour, eliminating the care, caution, and scepticism that capital markets need to allocate scarce economic resources efficiently among competing uses and to avoid overheating.

In addition, the construction of the ECB system, with unlimited overdraft facilities for international payment orders, the extensive possibility for credit facilities in the form of Emerging Liquidity Assistance (ELA), and the pooling of profits and losses from refinancing credit that the NCBs provided to their local banking systems made it likely that, if worst came to worst, the ECB would be able to act as a lender of last resort, bailing out the debtors and their creditors. The almost unlimited firepower of the ECB was intended to create a maximum of financial stability and trust, but it induced opportunistic behaviour among both borrowers and lenders, causing the inflationary credit bubble that deprived the southern European countries of their competitiveness and drove them into intolerable mass unemployment.

Step 2: Lending of the Printing Press (Target)

The US subprime crisis swept over to Europe in 2007/2008. As investors shied away from financing over-indebted countries, the ECB allowed these countries to solve their problems with the printing press by dramatically reducing collateral requirements, extending the maturity for refinancing credit and allowing NCBs to provide extensive ELA credit to their national banking systems. This made it possible for the GIPSIC countries to issue net payment orders to other countries for the purpose of buying goods and assets, and for redeeming private debt. As discussed in Chapters 5–7, the credit strategy was a stealth bail-out that basically amounted to lending the printing press from the north to the south (and west) of the Eurozone. This satisfied the financial needs of stricken countries for a while, but pulled the ECB deeper and deeper into insufficiently covered risk positions.

Step 3: Buying Collateral (SMP)

When the spreads for some countries soared in the spring of 2010 and the market value of assets plummeted accordingly (refer also to Figures 2.2 and 2.3), the ECB had a problem, since the value of the collateral it had received for its generous provision of refinancing credit swiftly eroded. As the ECB could not react by withholding refinancing credit without risking a collapse of the southern banking systems, it decided to buy the collateral in order to preserve its market value. This can be seen as an important motivation for the ECB's Securities Markets Programme (SMP), which will be discussed below, even if the stated purpose was to preserve the transmission of the low policy interest rates to the wider economy. Another motivation was the attempt to help the distressed states by shielding the interest rates for government bonds from 'erroneous' market forces and improving the transmission of monetary policy signals. With the ECB buying their government bonds, the states could issue new ones without driving up the yields they had to offer.

Step 4: Change of Shift (ESM & Co)

The decision of the ECB Governing Council to buy government bonds appeared to conflict with article 123 of the TFEU, which forbids monetary state financing (in a direct form or in a way which circumvents such prohibition, as will be discussed below), and with the above-mentioned no-bailout article 125, both of which were Germany's essential conditions for signing the Maastricht Treaty and giving up the deutschmark. This prompted the president of the Bundesbank to object strongly to the SMP, ultimately leading to his resignation.

The Bundesbank's objection and the questionable legality of the ECB's rescue operations were a major reason for the uneasiness, at least among German politicians, in readily endorsing them. The general opinion was: yes, we accept the actions the ECB has taken, because no one else could have undertaken similar rescue operations fast enough to calm the markets, but now we have to shift gear. If someone must provide credit to other countries, it must be us! To this end, we need an institution that is democratically controlled, rather than having the ECB Governing Council making such decisions. This indeed was the compelling political logic that led to the intergovernmental rescue operations for Greece, the establishment of the European Financial Stability Facility (EFSF), the European Financial Stabilisation Mechanism (EFSM), IMF support, and, last but not least, the European Stability Mechanism (ESM), a permanent rescue fund.[1]

But there were other motives as well. The ECB also wanted to be relieved of the burden of rescuing states, and naturally the stricken countries and their creditors wanted to be bailed out. The latter actually saw the fiscal bailout activities as add-ons to, rather than substitutes for, the SMP.

And even without the SMP, the parliaments of the northern euro countries would have had to agree to the fiscal rescue activities in order to prevent a breakup of the Eurozone that would have cost them their Target claims, as will be explained in this chapter.

Step 5: Unlimited Promises (OMT)

One problem with relying exclusively on the fiscal rescue operations was, in the eyes of analysts, that the politicians were too parsimonious and imposed too many constraints on the use of potential funds to really impress the markets. As the capital flight from Spain and Italy continued despite the preparation of the ESM (see Figure 7.4), on 6 September 2012 the ECB promised unlimited government bond purchases for distressed countries that submitted themselves to the rules of the ESM, calling its promise Outright Monetary Transactions (OMT).

This programme generated fresh confidence and induced capital to return to the crisis countries, bringing about a further decline in the Target balances in addition to that directly induced by the fiscal rescue operations. The ECB President's promise to 'do whatever it takes' to save the euro, made concrete with the OMT announcement, has proven very effective in calming the markets, without the ECB having had to buy any additional government bonds to date.[2]

Step 6: Banking Union

While the OMT stabilized the market value of government bonds and hence the banks that held them, it made no contribution to stabilizing the value of the other assets in the banks' balance sheets that had come under pressure during the crisis. Mortgage claims in particular have often become toxic due to the collapse of the property markets in the crisis-stricken countries (see Figure 2.11). This posed a particular problem to the ECB, since it had provided an enormous

---

[1] The German Federal Constitutional Court declined appeals against the ESM on 12 September 2012, as will be explained below.

[2] See Introductory Statement to the Press Conference (with Q&A) by Mario Draghi, President of the ECB, and Vítor Constâncio, Vice-President of the ECB, 6 September 2012, available at: <http://www.ecb.int/press/pressconf/2012/html/is120906.en.html#qa>.

volume of additional funds to the banking sectors of the crisis countries against poor-quality collateral, as explained in Chapters 5 and 6, which by August 2012 led to € 1,002 billion in Target liabilities for these countries. Given that the entire Eurosystem, i.e. the ECB and the national central banks (NCBs) together, had an equity capital of only half of this sum (€ 496 billion by August 2012), the Eurosystem itself was at risk.

To help the banks and avoid the write-off losses for the central banks of the Eurozone, the EU Summit of 29 June 2012 in Brussels decided to make the ESM funds, which originally had been foreseen for the support of governments only, available for bank recapitalization as well.[3] As of this writing, this step is still in progress, and it is not clear what will be decided in the end. Two sections of this chapter will discuss the issue in more detail.

Other steps will certainly follow, when new problems emerge. For example, it is possible that Eurobonds will ultimately be introduced if the ECB keeps its promise to buy large amounts of government bonds. Alternatively, a recent statement of the German Constitutional Court that deems the OMT illegal might stop the drive towards debt mutualization. While the Court's statement has not yet been cast in the form of a binding ruling, it will probably terminate the OMT. The following sections will consider Steps 3–5 in more detail, before a final section discusses what all this might mean for the European future.

Buying Government Bonds: The SMP

The Securities Markets Programme (SMP) was announced on 10 May 2010 by the ECB, together with a voluminous fiscal rescue programme that will be discussed in the next section. The Greek interest spreads over German government bonds had increased sharply in the preceding months, while the market value of Greek government bonds had plummeted (see Figures 2.2 and 2.3). The yield for two-year Greek government bonds temporarily jumped to 38% on 28 April 2010. This pushed the Greek state to the brink of bankruptcy, and with it the Greek banking system, which had drawn much refinancing credit in exchange for government bonds.

Commercial banks holding Greek government bonds not only suffered huge write-off losses but the erosion of their collateral for refinancing credit as well. They faced both a solvency and a liquidity problem. When the rating agencies deprived Greek government bonds of their investment grade, the ECB tried to help by

---

[3] See Council of the European Union, *Euro Area Summit Statement*, 29 June 2012, available at: <http://www.consilium.europa.eu/uedocs/cms_data/docs/pressdata/en/ec/131359.pdf>.

waiving the requirement that government bonds possess an investment rating in order to preserve their eligibility as collateral (see Chapter 5). However, this could not stop the erosion of the value of collateral as such, since it depended on how the market assessed it.

At the time many experts thought that Greece should default, as contemplated in the Maastricht Treaty (article 125 TFEU), and even in the Eurosystem itself there were voices and vocating Greece's exit from the Eurozone. ECB President Jean-Claude Trichet, however, strongly objected to the idea of a default, as he feared contagion effects via the financial markets that could not be contained.[4] After all, the government bonds of Ireland, Portugal, Spain, and Italy were also in danger. France, whose banking system was heavily exposed to most of these countries, also vigorously objected to this idea.[5] Trichet successfully pushed for the SMP in the ECB Governing Council and had the Eurozone buy over € 200 billion worth of Greek, Irish, Portuguese, Spanish, and Italian government bonds.

The decisions regarding the SMP were taken against the votes of ECB Chief Economist Jürgen Stark and Bundesbank President Axel Weber. Both wanted to resign immediately but were convinced to stay on. They nevertheless resigned a year later in an open protest against the government bond purchases carried out by the Eurosystem.[6] Luxembourg and the Netherlands also voiced opposition against the Council's decision.[7] Trichet's opponents feared contagion via the political decision processes in Europe, arguing that a bailout of Greece was forbidden by the Maastricht Treaty and that it would send the wrong signals to

---

[4] See Introductory Statement to the Press Conference (with Q&A) by Jean-Claude Trichet, President of the ECB, and Lucas Papademos, Vice President of the ECB, 8 April 2010, available at: <http://www.ecb.int/press/pressconf/2010/html/is100408.en.html>.

[5] See M. Feldstein, 'Why France and Germany Try so Hard to Delay a Greek Default', *The National*, 29 September 2011, available at: <http://www.thenational.ae/business/industry-insights/economics/why-france-and-germany-try-so-hard-to-delay-a-greek-default>.

[6] As explained by Jürgen Stark on the occasion of a public lecture at Hanns-Seidel-Stiftung, 22 February 2013, in Munich. Weber immediately declared his opposition publicly on 11 May 2010; see A. Weber, 'Kaufprogramm birgt erhebliche Risiken', Interview with J. Schaaf, *Börsen-Zeitung*, 11 May 2010, available at: <http://www.bundesbank.de/Redaktion/DE/Downloads/Presse/Publikationen/interview_mit_bundesbankpraesident_axel_weber.pdf?__blob=publicationFile>; see also 'Brandbrief: Ex-Währungshüter Stark attackiert EZB-Kurs', *Der Spiegel*, No. 3, 14 January 2012, available at: <http://www.spiegel.de/wirtschaft/soziales/brandbrief-ex-waehrungshueter-stark-attackiert-ezb-kurs-a-809199.html>.

[7] See A. Kunz, 'EZB-Chefvolkswirt Stark tritt zurück', *Wirtschaftswoche*, 9 September 2011, available at: <http://www.wiwo.de/politik/ausland/europaeische-zentralbank-ezb-chefvolkswirt-stark-tritt-zurueck/5212924.html>.

other indebted countries, undermining the incentives to solve the problem by raising taxes.[8]

The purchases began in May 2010 with Greek and Irish government bonds. Portuguese bonds followed in June 2011. When the purchases stopped in February 2012, the Eurosystem had bought a total of about € 83 billion from these three countries. In August 2011, the central banks of the Eurosystem also began to buy huge quantities of Italian and Spanish government bonds to support their market price. By the end of the programme, € 94 billion had been spent on Italian and € 47 billion on Spanish government bonds, bringing the total of all government bond purchases to € 223 billion.[9] Figure 8.1 gives an overview of the evolution of such purchases over time. After that, the stocks held by the ECB gradually declined, presumably as some of the bonds purchased matured or were re-sold to the markets. By the end of 2012, the value of the stock of government bonds held by central banks had declined to € 209 billion, and by the end of 2013 to € 179 billion.[10]

Based on press reports, one might think that the ECB itself had purchased the bonds. But that is not quite right. The ECB's own purchases amounted to just € 13 billion.[11] The ECB primarily acted as a coordination centre that told the national central banks (NCBs) in the Eurosystem what they were to do. Ninety-three percent of the actual purchases were carried out by the NCBs in accordance with their corresponding shares in the ECB capital, and only 7% by the ECB itself. The NCBs, in turn, bought the government bonds in strict proportion to their capital keys. While these purchases were not perfectly

[8] See P. Bernholz, N. Berthold, C. B. Blankart, A. Börsch-Supan, F. Breyer, J. Eekhoff, C. Fuest, J. von Hagen, S. Homburg, K. Konrad, A. Ritschl, F. Schneider, H.-W. Sinn, V. Vanberg, R. Vaubel, C. C. von Weizsäcker, *Ökonomen-Erklärung*, 16 September 2011, and P. Plickert, 'Ökonomen unterstützen Wirtschaftsminister Rösler', *Frankfurter Allgemeine Zeitung*, 16 September 2011, available at: <http://www.faz.net/aktuell/wirtschaft/europas-schuldenkrise/insolvenz-griechenlands-in-betracht-ziehen-oekonomen-unterstuetzen-wirtschaftsminister-roesler-11228684.html>. W. Franz, C. Fuest, M. Hellwig, and H.-W. Sinn, 'Zehn Regeln zur Rettung des Euro', *Frankfurter Allgemeine Zeitung*, No. 138, 18 June 2010, p. 10, available at: <http://www.ifo.de/de/10_regeln/w/3rXTZnXx3>.

[9] See Barclays Capital, 'ECB SMP: Marking to Market', *Interest Rates Research*, 6 January 2012; and M. De Pooter, R. F. Martin, and S. Pruitt, 'The Liquidity Effects of Official Bond Market Intervention', *Discussion paper*, Federal Reserve Board of Governors, 2013.

[10] See European Central Bank, *Details on Securities Holdings Acquired under the Securities Markets Programme*, press release, 21 February 2013, and see also European Central Bank, *Annual Accounts of the ECB for 2013*, press release, 20 February 2014.

[11] See European Central Bank, *Annual Accounts of the ECB 2013*, 20 February 2014, p. 19.

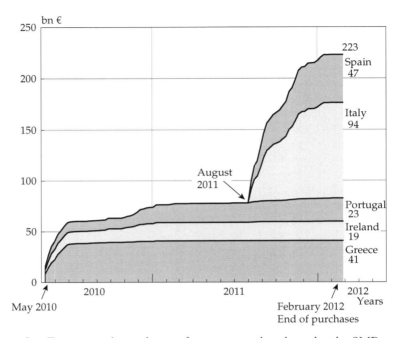

Figure 8.1 Eurosystem's purchases of government bonds under the SMP

Sources: Barclays Capital, 'ECB SMP: Marking to market', *Interest Rates Research*, 6 January 2012; M. De Pooter, R. F. Martin, and S. Pruitt, 'The Liquidity Effects of Official Bond Market Intervention', *Discussion paper*, Federal Reserve Board of Governors, 2013.

synchronized, as some NCBs went a bit ahead of others, the synchronization according to the capital keys took place within days or weeks. Thus, for example, the Bundesbank had participated in the purchases to the tune of € 48 billion, the Banca d'Italia of € 32 billion, and the Banque de France of € 36 billion.

While the purchases partially stabilized the interest rates, the NCBs in the Eurosystem took on high risks of default in the process, since if a country defaults, they would have to write off the associated claims, with the write-offs eating into the NCBs' capital. In the case of the Bundesbank, for instance, if the government bonds it has purchased were to lose their value, the Bundesbank would lose 52% of the € 93.1 billion in capital (including reserves) that it had at the end of December 2013.

There is a debate over whether or not the ECB should attempt to hold seniority claims over private investors. In the case of the Greek default of 2012, this was indeed the case. The bonds purchased by the ECB were first converted into new bonds, which were then exempted from the haircuts. However, this procedure was legally possible only because nearly all Greek bonds happened to be issued under Greek law. The extent to which this procedure can be generalized to other countries is unclear. In fact, as the haircut came along with a bond conversion under British law, a repetition of the trick will not be possible. This is why the ECB gave up its seniority claim when it announced its OMT programme, the successor of the SMP, as will be discussed below.

No Risk to Taxpayers?

Sometimes it is argued that losses of a central bank are virtual and of no real importance, given that a central bank can operate with negative equity capital. After all, according to the statutes of the Eurosystem, governments are not obliged to recapitalize their NCBs. The statutes just say that losses are deducted from retained earnings and current interest revenue, but they do not include an obligation for national governments to endow their NCBs with new equity if needed.[12] It would be nice if such a miracle were possible in a world of scarce resources, but of course it isn't.

While it is true that an NCB can operate with negative equity capital, it is certainly not true that the losses are virtual. Write-offs on assets always mean that the owner of these assets loses interest and principal repayments, whose present value is equal to the value of the assets. Thus the losses erode the normal equity and the seignorage wealth of the NCB resulting from credit provision to commercial banks, and as such they have to be borne entirely by the treasuries of the euro states that are entitled to receive the annual seignorage profit.[13] The reader may recall from Chapter 1 that the sum of normal equity and seignorage wealth in a dynamic calculation has been estimated to be € 3.4 trillion.

---

[12] See 'Protocol (No 4) on the Statute of the European System of Central Banks and of the European Central Bank', *Official Journal of the European Union*, C 83/230 EN, 30 March 2010, available at: <http://www.ecb.europa.eu/ecb/legal/pdf/c_08320100330en_ecb_statute.pdf>, in particular article 33 paragraph 2. Also, the related discussion of write-offs on ELA credit in Chapter 5.

[13] It is a bit surprising that the ECB on request informed the German Constitutional Court that a default of government bonds owned by the ECB would not incur any risk for national budgets on the grounds that it had enough risk provisions and could net the losses with its revenues in the years to come. See Federal Constitutional Court, *BVerfG, 2 BvR 2728/13*, 14 January 2014, Absatz-Nr. (1 - 105), Sachbericht, article 12, available at: <http://www.bverfg.de/entscheidungen/rs20140114_2bvr272813.html>.

A counter argument that could be raised is that no interest losses would arise if the SMP were financed by additional money creation by the purchasing central banks. However, such a policy would be inflationary and simply shift the losses to money holders, while the advantage would lie with those countries whose government bonds were bought and then written off. The ECB has, however, declared over and over again that it will not resort to inflationary measures and that it will sterilize the increase in the monetary base resulting from the SMP.[14] Moreover, the sterilization is more or less automatic in the full-allotment mode, as banks in the northern countries compensate for the extra liquidity by taking less refinancing credit from their central banks or lending them the funds they do not need. This was discussed in the section *Crowding out Refinancing Credit in the North* in Chapter 6. The government bond purchases, therefore, simply replace a corresponding amount of refinancing credit or asset purchases and reduce the interest income flow that would have resulted from them. If this interest flow is not replaced by the interest on government bonds because the issuers default, a permanent loss of seignorage would indeed occur for the finance ministries of the Eurozone countries and the taxpayers who stand behind them. This seignorage loss would equal the write-off losses. Not even central banks operate in a land of Cockaigne where resources can be created out of nothing.

Since all the NCBs in the Eurosystem must partake of such purchases in proportion to the allocation key of the ECB capital, the socialization of the Eurosystem's losses would be no help either. Each participating NCB, and with it its sovereign, would shoulder all of the losses from the bonds it purchased plus its share in the losses from bonds bought by the ECB. The effect would be identical if the respective sovereign itself had to write off assets it bought.

In Germany, in particular, the purchases are regarded with great scepticism because they resemble the monetizing of German sovereign debt that occurred during and after World War I, which gave rise to the hyperinflation that affected Germany during that period. Back then the Reichsbank financed the government by purchasing government bonds and paying for them with freshly printed money, with the consequence that the amount of money in circulation increased steadily. The currency lost so much value that by 1923 the banknotes were ultimately worth no more than the paper they were printed on. The petit bourgeois, people with too little wealth to invest in real assets, lost their savings and became radicalized, with dire consequences a decade later.

This is indeed a potential danger, but there is no need to think of such extremes. The default risk threatening the taxpayers of the still-solvent

---

[14] See European Central Bank, *Monetary Policy*, Instruments, Open Market Operations, 24 May 2010, available at: <http://www.ecb.europa.eu/mopo/implement/omo/html/index.en.html>.

European countries is reason enough to be concerned about this sort of monetary state financing.

ESM & Co

Supported by the urging of US President Barack Obama, ECB President Jean-Claude Trichet successfully convinced Europe's politicians in the spring of 2010 to come up with fiscal rescue programmes. On 2 May the governments of the euro countries, together with the IMF, agreed to establish a € 110 billion intergovernmental rescue programme for Greece (€ 80 billion from the Eurozone countries and € 30 billion from the IMF).[15]

Moreover, they agreed on 10 May to establish a separate rescue fund, the European Financial Stability Facility (EFSF) located in Luxembourg, that, with the guarantees of the community of euro states, was to issue bonds and lend out the revenue to needy countries that commit to undertaking reforms.[16] The EFSF had a maximum lending volume of € 440 billion and was limited to three years. The corresponding national laws implementing it were quickly adopted in the following weeks by the Eurozone members' parliaments.

Furthermore, the EU governments agreed on 11 May 2010 to set up the European Financial Stabilisation Mechanism (EFSM).[17] This agreement gave the EU the possibility to borrow and distribute up to € 60 billion in credit according to article 122 of the TFEU; this article actually refers explicitly to natural catastrophes beyond the control of individual countries.

The IMF was counted upon to be part of the rescue operations. It contributed funds and participated in defining the conditions that the recipient countries would have to satisfy.

But all this was insufficient to really calm the markets. For that reason, a permanent rescue fund under the name European Stability Mechanism (ESM) was agreed on at the EU Summit on 24/25 March 2011 in Brussels, and ratified by European parliaments in the following year. The ESM was to be endowed with

---

[15] See European Commission, 'The Economic Adjustment Programme for Greece', *Occasional Papers* 61, May 2010, available at: <http://ec.europa.eu/economy_finance/publications/occasional_paper/2010/pdf/ocp61_en.pdf>. Slovakia objected to these payments from the outset *and did not participate*. After the second tranche Ireland ceased its payment, with Portugal following suit after the fourth tranche.

[16] See EFSF Framework Agreement, available at: <http://www.efsf.europa.eu/attachments/20111019_efsf_framework_agreement_en.pdf>.

[17] See Council of the European Union, 'Council Regulation (EU) No 407/2010 of 11 May 2010 Establishing a European Financial Stabilisation Mechanism', *Official Journal* L 118/1, 12 May 2010, available at: <http://eur-lex.europa.eu/LexUriServ/LexUriServ.do?uri=OJ:L:2010:118:0001:0001:EN:PDF>.

a paid-in equity capital of € 80 billion, but the euro states were obliged to replenish any losses in equity capital of up to a total of € 700 billion if necessary. Up to this writing (February 2014), € 64.3 billion of the € 80 billion have been paid in. The ESM member states provide the paid-in capital in five instalments of € 16 billion each, of which the first four have been made. The final instalment is scheduled for April 2014.[18]

The ESM can borrow in the market by issuing bonds and lend the money to needy countries after they sign a memorandum of understanding about a reform agenda. The interest rate charged is above the rate at which the ESM can borrow, to cover administration costs, but below the market rate for the respective country. In the case of default, the ESM has a preferred creditor status over other creditors. The ESM's lending volume was limited to € 500 billion. However, it was agreed that the Governing Council can decide on extensions of the equity capital and the lending volume with a qualified majority of 85%, this majority being computed on the basis of the countries' shares in the ECB capital. Such a qualified majority is also necessary for other major decisions, such as acceptance of the memorandum of understanding.

Although the ESM was first announced as a replacement of the EFSF, it ultimately was decided as a complement, with both funds being able to operate simultaneously until the middle of 2013.

As a complement to the ESM, a Fiscal Compact was agreed by the EU countries that would impose more rigorous debt constraints on governments than the Stability and Growth Pact of 1996.[19] Basically, the Fiscal Compact required the countries to lift the fiscal rules of the Stability and Growth Pact to primary law at the country level. Moreover, the countries committed themselves to reducing their debt-to-GDP ratio at an average rate of 1/20 per annum of the difference between their initial ratio and the Maastricht ceiling of 60%, with somewhat more restrictive penalty rules being agreed upon. However, this compact has not really been taken seriously by anyone except Germany, which had demanded it as a quid pro quo to its agreeing to the ESM. Less than half a year after the Compact was ratified, France, Spain, Portugal, Slovenia, the Netherlands, and Poland asked for and were granted exceptions from its rules.[20]

---

[18] See Federal Ministry of Finance, *European Financial Assistance: ESM*, 10 July 2013, available at: <http://www.bundesfinanzministerium.de/Content/EN/Standardartikel/Topics/Europe/Articles/Stabilising_the_euro/Figures_Facts/european-financial-assistance-esm.html?view=renderPrint>.

[19] See also EU, 'Treaty on Stability, Coordination and Governance in the Economic and Monetary Union', (Fiscal Compact), 2 March 2012, available at: <http://www.consilium.europa.eu/media/1478399/07_-_tscg.en12.pdf>.

[20] See European Commission, *Commission Takes Steps under the Excessive Deficit Procedure*, MEMO/13/463, 29 May 2013, available at: <http://europa.eu/rapid/press-release_MEMO-13-463_en.htm>.

In addition to providing credit to the programme countries, the ESM can also buy their government bonds with funds borrowed in the market, for which purpose it set up the so-called Secondary Markets Support Facility (SMSF). While the € 500 billion limit on the lending volume neither applies to the SMSF nor to the volume of funds that the ESM borrows for the purpose of buying government bonds, the limited liability of the shareholders implicitly constrains the volume of the SMSF. For the countries to be rescued the SMSF is more attractive than direct ESM credit, since the SMSF does not have preferred creditor status. As of this writing, however, the SMSF has not yet been activated. Its parallels with the ECB's OMT programme will be explored below.

There was some uncertainty in Germany about the implementation of the ESM Treaty, with a number of appeals against the ESM at the Constitutional Court inducing the German President Joachim Gauck to postpone his signature. This uncertainty was removed on 12 September 2012 when the Court rejected such appeals in a preliminary ruling.[21] The plaintiffs were nonetheless successful inasmuch as the Court imposed a number of constraints on Germany's participation. It required the German representative to the ESM Governing Council to seek the agreement of the Bundestag before funding decisions are taken,[22] thus excluding the possibility of secret ESM decisions as foreseen in the Treaty,[23] and it asked the German government to demand a declaration from the other countries, binding under international law, that would exclude an interpretation of the ESM as involving joint and several liability that seemed to follow from certain ambiguities in its formulation.[24] After this declaration was given by all Eurozone countries with the exception of Estonia, by 27 September 2012, the ESM Treaty finally became effective on 1 October 2012.

---

[21] See Federal Constitutional Court, 2 *BvR 1390/12*, 2 *BvR 1421/12*, 2 *BvR 1438/12*, 2 *BvR 1439/12*, 2 *BvR 1440/12*, 2 *BvE 6/12*, 12 September 2012, available at: <http://www.bundesverfassungsgericht.de/entscheidungen/rs20120912_2bvr139012en.html>.

[22] See Federal Constitutional Court, *Headnotes to the Judgment of the Second Senate of 7 September 2011*, 2 *BvR 987/10*, 2 *BvR 1485/10*, 2 *BvR 1099/10*, 7 September 2011, available at: <http://www.bundesverfassungsgericht.de/entscheidungen/rs20110907_2bvr098710en.html>.

[23] See EU, 'Treaty Establishing the European Stability Mechanism (ESM)', article 10 paragraph 1.

[24] See Federal Constitutional Court, 2 *BvR 1390/12*, 2 *BvR 1421/12*, 2 *BvR 1438/12*, 2 *BvR 1439/12*, 2 *BvR 1440/12*, 2 *BvE 6/12*, 12 September 2012; S. Homburg, 'Retten ohne Ende', *Frankfurter Allgemeine Sonntagszeitung*, 29 July 2012, available at: <http://www.faz.net/aktuell/wirtschaft/europas-schuldenkrise/schuldenkrise-retten-ohne-ende-11832561.html>.

Overview of Rescue Funds

Figure 8.2 gives an overview of the entire public credit that flowed until end-2013 to the GIPSIC countries from the fiscal sources mentioned. It basically summarizes information about rescue measures as provided in the previous chapter, presenting it in a somewhat different way. Greece was the first country needing support. It received € 53 billion in intergovernmental rescue credit, based on an agreement that anticipated the formal rescue funds. Greece, Ireland, Portugal, Spain, and Cyprus together have received € 210 billion from the EFSF and ESM, of which Greece alone accounts for € 134 billion (EFSF). Furthermore, they received € 74 billion from the IMF and € 38 billion from the EU's natural catastrophe fund, EFSM. The graph shows how these fiscal rescue credits break down by country. As in the previous chapter, all figures are calculated net of the countries' explicit or implicit contributions to rescue activities such as contributions to the EU budget or mutual participation in the formal rescue funds. In all, Greece, Ireland, Portugal, Spain and Cyprus received € 367 billion net of their own contributions, while Italy contributed € 27 billion without receiving fiscal credit. Altogether, the GIPSIC countries (including Italy) received € 339 billion, or 11% of their 2013 GDP, with another € 41 billion earmarked in their favour. Excluding Italy, the other five crisis-stricken countries received € 367 billion, or 24% of their 2013 GDP, net of their own contributions.

In addition, the chart shows the credit provided to the GIPSIC countries by other countries' NCBs via the SMP (€ 113 billion) and via the local printing presses, as measured by the Target balances (€ 613 billion).[25] Italy is included in the list because it received the lion's share of the SMP, as shown in Figure 8.1, even though it received no fiscal rescue credit.

An item subtracted from the credit received is a € 61 billion intra-Eurosystem claim of the GIPSIC countries from their slightly under-proportionate issuance of banknotes. This is a topic similar to the Target balances. The money created in a country by way of asset purchases and refinancing operations may serve external financing needs not only by way of electronic payment orders, but also by being physically transported abroad. That is why an over-proportionate issuance of banknotes incurs an intra-Eurosystem liability, just like a Target liability, and an under-proportionate issuance of banknotes, an intra-Eurosystem claim. As this interpretation of over- and under-proportionate banknote issuance rivals other interpretations relating to different national payment habits, unlike the Target balances the intra-Eurosystem claims and liabilities related to banknotes are not recorded within the national balance-of-payments statistics and were therefore not

---

[25] For a detailed description, see Ifo Exposure Level, available at: <http://www.cesifo-group.de/ifoHome/policy/Haftungspegel.html>.

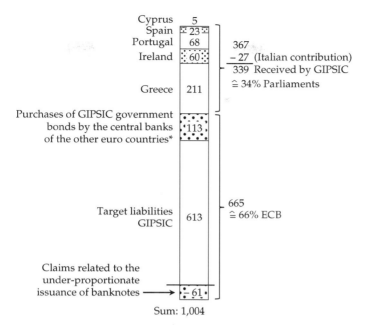

Figure 8.2 Public credit provided to the GIPSIC countries (December 2013, € billion)

* The sum includes a share of the € 13.0 billion in direct ECB purchases which have been allocated to the NCBs according to their respective capital keys.

Source: Ifo Institute calculations.

considered in last chapter's analysis. Nevertheless, they are reported in Figure 8.2 in order not to overstate the public credit received by the GIPSIC countries. Their claim from a slightly under-proportionate issuance of bank-notes is treated as a credit that they provided to other Eurosystem countries, and is thus subtracted from the ECB credit provided to them.

All told, the GIPSIC countries by the end of 2013 had received € 1,004 billion from the various sources, net of their banknote claims and net of their own contributions. At the peak of the crisis, in August 2012, they had received € 1.339 trillion, or € 10,000 per capita.

The figure does not show the credit potentially provided to the GIPSIC countries via the Covered Bonds Purchase Programmes (CBPP), as the details necessary to carry out a similar calculation have not been published. However, based on the considerations made in Chapter 7 in the context of Figure 7.1, it can be surmised that another € 36 billion might have to be added to the overall public credit figure of € 1,004 billion given in the diagram.

It is noteworthy that even without that qualification, the ECB's help is much larger than the help provided directly by the community of states, including the IMF. As depicted by the curly brackets central banks have provided 66% of the help given to the crisis countries, of which the lion's share corresponds to Target credit. Only the remaining 34% was subject to parliamentary approval. Considering that the ECB Council is not a democratic body (see Chapter 1, Figure 1.6), a legitimacy problem arises. While parliaments only agreed to these rescue measures with much trepidation, the ECB Governing Council, in which the creditor countries are in a minority, decides on such matters by a simple majority based on the one-country-one-vote principle, and in the case of ELA credit, even with a share of one-third of the votes (see Chapter 5).

Table 8.1 relates the rescue funds to the recipient countries' GDP levels and breaks down further the data shown in Figure 8.2. The second column in Table 8.1 shows the nominal Target-debt-to-GDP ratio, the third column the ratio of over-proportionate (or, if negative, under-proportionate) issuance of banknotes, the fourth the ratio of government bonds held by non-GIPSIC central banks and the ECB itself, the fifth the ratio of fiscal rescue credit provided by other states and international organizations, and the sixth the sum of all these

Table 8.1 International public credit relative to the recipient country's GDP (December 2013, %)

	Target debt	Over-pro-portionate banknote issues	Government bonds held by non-GIPSIC central banks	Fiscal rescue credit	Overall public credit	
Greece	27	6	9	115	157	(€ 288 bn)
Ireland	33	10	4	36	83	(€ 137 bn)
Portugal	35	− 17	7	41	67	(€ 111 bn)
Spain	21	− 5	2	2	21	(€ 214 bn)
Italy	15	− 1	4	− 2	16	(€ 244 bn)
Cyprus	44	0	0	28	72	(€ 12 bn)
GIPSIC	20	− 2	4	11	32	(€ 1,004 bn)

Sources: National central bank balance sheets according to H.-W. Sinn and T. Wollmershäuser, 'Target Loans, Current Account Balances and Capital Flows: The ECB's Rescue Facility,' *International Tax and Public Finance* 19, 2012, pp. 468–508, figure 1, updated; Eurostat, Database, *Economy and Finance*, Annual National Accounts; and Government Finance Statistics, Deficit and Debt; European Commission, *Economic and Financial Affairs*, Financial Assistance in EU Member States, Greece.

Note: For fiscal rescue credit see note to Figure 7.1.

items, i.e. the overall public credit provided to a country relative to its GDP. The numbers in brackets to the right of this column show the respective absolute values of the credit granted.

The results show that the GIPSIC countries together, by the end of 2013, received 32% of their joint GDP as public rescue credit from other countries. As Table 8.1 shows, the € 214 billion overall rescue credit provided by foreign countries to Spain, at 21% of GDP, is not too far from the GIPSIC average of 32% in relative terms. The rescue credit to Portugal and Ireland, by contrast, amounted to 67% and 83% of their respective GDP.

The outlier obviously is Greece. It received € 211 billion in terms of fiscal credit from abroad and € 77 billion from other central banks, which amounts to 157% of its GDP. If Greece also receives the € 32 billion already earmarked for it after approval by the Troika, this percentage will increase to 175% of 2013 Greek GDP.

All this money helped not only the recipient countries themselves, but to the extent it exceeded the cumulative current account deficit as shown in Figure 7.1, it also financed a capital flight, mostly a flight back home by investors from other countries. This was discussed in detail in the last chapter.

The rescue programmes were controversial because they contradicted the no-bailout clause of article 125 TFEU, as discussed in Chapter 1. The reader may recall the quote of Christine Lagarde, then Finance Minister of France, that it was clear to the European leaders that the ground-breaking decisions of May 2010 were in outright contradiction to the Maastricht Treaty. That explained the considerable opposition from experts in Germany. Not only Bundesbank President Axel Weber and ECB Chief Economist Jürgen Stark resigned, as mentioned earlier, but some suspect that even the resignation of German President Horst Köhler on 30 May 2010, submitted shortly after the Bundestag had passed the law accompanying the EFSF and for which no clear explanation was given, should be seen in this context.[26] Köhler, ex-IMF president and ex-state secretary in the Ministry of Finance under the Helmut Kohl government, had been one of the key figures in the Maastricht Treaty negotiations, insisting on the no-bailout clause and the exclusion of monetary state financing. The German government bypassed him when they prepared the EFSF and the rescue package for Greece.

---

[26] The Bundestag ratified the EFSF law on 21 May 2010, and Köhler signed it on 22 May 2010. For the relationship between this and the resignation, see P. Gauweiler, 'Erklären Sie sich!', open letter from CSU Bundestag member Peter Gauweiler to former German President Horst Köhler, *Der Spiegel*, No. 25, 21 June 2010, p. 27, available at: <http://www.spiegel.de/spiegel/print/d-71029975.html>.

The Liability Risk

The beneficiaries of the rescue policy were the crisis-stricken countries themselves, as well as those creditors who otherwise might not have got their money back, not least the powerful German and French banks and insurance companies. New creditors suffered because they now had to compete with the local printing presses and the rescue funds. Those likely to suffer most are the taxpayers of Europe's still-solvent countries. They will have to absorb all the risks and may, in the end, have to foot the bill. This is despite the fact that the Maastricht Treaty promised to protect them from this fate and that they never agreed by qualified majority, or even referenda, to the kind of constitutional change that the decisions of May 2010 implied, and particularly not to the voluminous rescue operations decided upon by the ECB Governing Council.

The reader may recall the quote from German Chancellor Helmut Kohl in 1998, cited in Chapter 1, in which he promised his fellow countrymen, repeating his words with gravitas, that the Maastricht Treaty protected them against liabilities from commitments of other euro countries and ruled out any financial transfers.

The taxpayers do not feel the burden imposed on them yet, because for the time being it is merely a liability. Since the losses have not yet materialized, will only occur in the future, and will fall on their victims in a diffuse and opaque way that is difficult to anticipate, the general public opposition has thus far been limited.[27] The political forces of governments and of financial institutions that needed the funds, because they would otherwise have faced immediate difficulties, prevailed in the political process, following Olson's theory that in a distributional conflict the smaller group tends to win out over the larger one because its gains and losses per capita are larger, which provides stronger incentives for collective lobbying action.[28]

Where the losses will occur depends, of course, on the circumstances. There will very probably be a flurry of camouflage activity by politicians when the losses become imminent. Clever accountants will shift them from one public institution to the next, and they will try to postpone the losses to future generations, by reducing and postponing the interest payments and extending the maturities of the liabilities instead of realizing the losses, which would have to be shown as write-offs in the accounts. As discussed in Chapter 5, this has been the

---

[27] The Taxpayers Association of Europe, however, has voiced its protest. See Taxpayers Association of Europe (TAE), *Stop the ESM! EU Citizens Have to Pay the Bill!*, 16 February 2012, available at: <http://english.taxpayers-europe.com/information/new/34-statements/150-stop-the-esm-eu-citizens-have-to-pay-the-bill.html>.

[28] See M. Olson, *The Logic of Collective Action: Public Goods and the Theory of Groups*, Harvard University Press, Cambridge 1965.

case with the Irish ELA credit, originally meant as short-term liquidity support that then was converted into Irish government bonds with an average maturity of 34 years. The trick was also used when Greece's public creditors accepted a rescheduling of their credit titles on 26 and 27 November 2012.[29] Among other things, the maturity of EFSF and intergovernmental credit was extended to the years 2041/2042, the interest payments on EFSF credit were waived for 10 years, the interest rates for the rest of the period were significantly reduced, and new EFSF credit was given to buy back old government debt from the market. Taken together, the measures were equivalent, in present value terms, to an immediate write off of public credit worth € 43 billion in favour of Greece.[30] None of this was booked in the public accounts of the countries that imposed the burden on their taxpayers.

Although it is not possible to predict the political camouflage that will follow, the public credit volumes shown in Figure 8.2, not counting the credit volumes earmarked (available if programme countries satisfy the conditions controlled by a troika of EU, IMF, and ECB) and the still-unused capacity of the rescue systems, represent a potential risk for the taxpayers. Table 8.2 gives an overview of the results of two calculations of the public losses in absolute and per capita terms for a selected number of euro countries, assuming two alternative worst-case scenarios:

  i) default and exit of the GIPSIC countries, and
  ii) default of the GIPSIC countries and dissolution of the euro.

These scenarios are not foreseen in any treaty, but they are not entirely implausible, as the lively public debate and various market indicators show. The two scenarios do not differ with regard to the fiscal credits provided, but they do differ concerning Target credit. The details of the calculations for the fiscal credit are spelled out in a note to the table. The role of Target credit is discussed below.

The Table shows the potential losses for the creditor countries from the fiscal aid programmes discussed above, from the SMP, and from Target credit, net of claims and liabilities from non-proportionate banknote issuance.

The last but one column gives the overall exposure showing, for example, that Germany faces a risk of € 401 billion, France of € 302 billion and the Netherlands of € 85 billion if the GIPSIC countries default and leave the Eurozone. Should

[29] See *Eurogroup Statement on Greece*, 27 November 2012, available at: <http://www.consilium.europa.eu/uedocs/cms_data/docs/pressdata/en/ecofin/133857.pdf>.

[30] The present value of the cost reductions for Greece was calculated at a rate of interest of 1.5% (interest rate on ten-year German government bonds in November 2012). The maturity extension by 15 years and the waiving of interest for 10 years results in a present value advantage of € 32 billion. The interest reduction by 100 basis points for the bilateral rescue credits accounts for an advantage of € 8 billion, and the reduction of EFSF credit fees of € 3 billion.

Table 8.2 Potential losses for selected euro countries after a GIPSIC default, two alternative worst-case scenarios (December 2013)

GIPSIC default and exit						
	Fiscal credit	SMP	Target claim	Bank-note claim[1]	Sum	Sum per capita
			€ billion			€ thousand
Austria	12	5	27	–3	41	4.9
Belgium	16	6	34	–3	53	4.8
Finland	8	3	17	–2	27	4.9
France	88	36	197	–20	302	4.6
Germany	116	48	263	–26	401	4.9
Netherlands	25	10	55	–6	85	5.1

GIPSIC default and dissolution of the euro						
	Fiscal credit	SMP	Target claim	Bank-note claim[1]	Sum	Sum per capita
			€ billion			€ thousand
Austria	12	5	–38	42	21	2.5
Belgium	16	6	–14	13	21	1.9
Finland	8	3	23	4	38	6.9
France	88	36	–8	77	193	2.9
Germany	116	48	510	–224	450	5.5
Netherlands	25	10	46	34	116	6.9

[1] Target-like claim on the Eurosystem from an underproportionate banknote issue.

Note: The potential losses for the individual countries were calculated as follows. Fiscal credit: country shares in the first intergovernmental package for Greece. EFSM credit according to the country shares in the revenue of the EU. EFSF credit according to ECB capital key shares, adjusted for the exclusion of the GIPSIC countries, which in the EFSF are treated as 'stepping out guarantors'. ESM credit according to ECB capital shares. IMF credit according to country shares in IMF capital. SMP according to ECB capital shares. The calculation of the Target and banknote losses and gains is explained in the text.

the euro itself be dissolved, Germany may even stand to lose € 450 billion, while the French potential loss would fall to € 193 billion. The reader should keep in mind that these calculations do not refer to expected or probable losses, but just show exposure levels in the sense of maxima of potential losses.

In the case of mere exits, all countries shown will suffer from similar potential per capita losses of around five thousand euros, the slight differences resulting primarily from the fact that the ECB capital shares, which are relevant for the distribution of losses, are not only determined by population shares in the euro area but also by GDP shares. If, on the other hand, the euro ceases to exist, Finns and Dutch will face the largest potential losses, with € 6,900 per capita, followed by the Germans, with € 5,500. The differences stem from the Target and banknote risks.

For many it is not at all obvious that a loss of Target claims is a real loss; indeed, the view is often voiced that Target balances are irrelevant statistical items that have no wealth implications whatsoever.[31] The key to understanding the Target losses is to recall, as shown in Chapters 5 and 6, that Target balances measure the relocation of refinancing credit (and similarly, funds provided by asset purchases) across borders. A country with a Target liability has issued more than its normal share of the Eurosystem's monetary base through the provision of credit by its NCB to the private banking sector. This extra credit enabled the emission of net payment orders to other countries, which had the effect of crowding out the respective refinancing credit being provided there, as shown in Chapter 6. With the relocation of refinancing credit, the source of the Eurosystem's seignorage, in terms of interest on this credit, was also being relocated between the countries. Since seignorage is pooled in the Eurosystem and redistributed according to country size (the ECB capital key), this relocation has no implications for the profit distribution of individual NCBs to their finance ministries if all banks service and repay their debts. However, if a country's banking sector defaults, which was an imminent risk for Greece, Ireland, and Cyprus (avoided and mitigated only by other rescue measures), the reallocation of the Eurosystem's seignorage revenue between countries can have severe consequences.

If banks default and cannot repay their refinancing credit, the permanent interest stream on such credit is no longer available for redistribution as seignorage, and the Eurosystem bears a loss whose present value is equal to the

---

[31] For a prominent voice arguing that the losses are non-existent due to the fact that in a modern economy money always is fiat money, see P. De Grauwe and Y. Ji, 'What Germany Should Fear Most is Its Own Fear', *VoxEU*, 18 September 2012, available at: <http://www.voxeu.org/article/how-germany-can-avoid-wealth-losses-if-eurozone-breaks-limit-conversion-german-residents>. The counterargument along the lines given here was provided in H.-W. Sinn, 'Target Losses in Case of a Euro Breakup', *VoxEU*, 22 October 2012, available at: <http://www.voxeu.org/article/target-losses-case-euro-breakup>.

write-offs on the refinancing credit itself. If all countries keep the euro, each one of them shares in this loss according to its share in the ECB capital. Unless the ECB wants to accept more inflation, this loss cannot be avoided by issuing new refinancing credit, since that would increase the monetary base. There is thus a loss of the permanent interest stream on the chain of short-term refinancing credit interrupted by a default.

In principle, the size of this loss is not limited to the Target balances, as it might also occur with normal refinancing credit within the scope of a country's provision of inside money. However, as shown in Chapter 5, the creation of extra refinancing credit, which led to Target balances and outside money in other countries, resulted from a rather extreme lowering in the ECB's collateral standards, which naturally entails a higher default risk. Thus, the Target balances are a rough indicator of the potential losses stemming from a lowering of the collateral standards.

They are an exact indicator of such losses if an NCB whose banking sector collapses defaults and leaves the Eurosystem, for then the legal relationship between the Eurosystem and the commercial banks of the exiting country is severed and only the Target claim on the respective NCB remains. This claim equals the credit the Eurosystem gave to the respective countries and thus the present value of the returns that this system would be entitled to receive. If the NCB defaults, then all or some of this return flow will never materialize.

To understand this better, it is useful to first think of a symmetrical situation where each country issued, by way of providing refinancing credit, an amount of money strictly in proportion to its size. In that case, the interest revenue collected by a particular NCB would flow into the Eurosystem pool and exactly the same amount would be returning from the pool to that NCB. If in such a situation an NCB defaults because of a collapse of the national banking system and the country exits the Eurozone, there would be no seignorage losses for the rest of the Eurozone, since all remaining Eurosystem NCBs would continue to collect seignorage from their own banks, pass it on to the remaining pool and receive it back from there. The finance ministry of the exiting NCB, however, would bear a loss, since it would no longer participate in the collection of the interest revenue earned by the Eurosystem.

This is actually one of the reasons why uncompetitive countries cling to the euro. If they stay in the Eurosystem after a collapse of their banking system, the seignorage losses will be shared by all other countries in proportion to their capital keys, while the country in question will continue to receive its share of the seignorage collected elsewhere.

Consider now a deviation from this symmetric case where one country issues and lends out more money at the expense of others, which brings about Target imbalances. This asymmetry implies that this country's banks will have to deliver a net flow of returns to the NCBs of other countries. If the NCB of this particular country and its banking system default and the country exits the euro, the rest of the Eurosystem will potentially lose the present value of this net flow of returns, which is measured by the country's Target liability. All remaining NCBs will now share this potential loss according to the capital allocation key. Since the allocation key is roughly in line with the relative population sizes,[32] the potential per capita losses of all countries are similar, as the upper right-hand columns of Table 8.2 shows.

Things are different when the Eurosystem as such breaks up, because this means that the pooling mechanism would no longer be available, a country's loss being then measured by its Target claim against the Eurosystem rather than by its share in another country's Target liability. The Target claim results from the shifting of this country's refinancing credit to other countries, and hence measures the present value of the return flow from this credit to which this country is entitled. However, after the breakdown of the euro this would be a claim against a system that no longer exists. The country would thus lose its Target claim. The second part of the Table refers to this case. As mentioned previously, Germany would be the biggest loser in absolute terms and Finland the biggest in per capita terms.

The fifth column takes account of the fact that a country's stock of refinancing credit may deviate from the level proportionate to its size, not because it made net payment orders to other countries, but also because it issued more or less than the normal quantity of banknotes, generating intra-Eurosystem claims or liabilities. This effect is particularly large in Germany. While Germany held a € 510 billion Target claim in December 2013, it incurred a € 224 billion liability from over-proportionate banknote issuance. Only the difference between these amounts, € 286 billion, can be interpreted as the present value of the interest return from other countries to which Germany is entitled, and only this difference would be potentially lost if the euro were dismantled.

Germany's over-proportionate banknote issuance largely results from the fact that the euro replaced the large, and growing, stock of deutschmark banknotes once circulating outside Germany, in particular in eastern Europe and Turkey.[33] The seignorage wealth resulting from the issuance of these banknotes was socialized upon the introduction of the euro and such issuance has since then been counted as a liability of the Bundesbank. It is unlikely that the Bundesbank would be able to reverse this socialization should the euro come to an end. It will be obliged to exchange the euro banknotes issued into deutschmark banknotes, while maintaining a latent liability with the Eurosystem. It will not be possible, however, to force the Bundesbank to honour this liability when the euro ceases to exist, since

---

[32] Strictly speaking, it is the average of a country's population and GDP shares.

[33] See H. Feist and H.-W. Sinn, 'Eurowinners and Eurolosers: The Distribution of Seignorage Wealth in the EMU', *European Journal of Political Economy* 13, 1997, pp. 665–689; E. Wenger, 'Nicht 90, sondern 150 Milliarden Verlust durch den Euro', *Frankfurter Allgemeine Zeitung*, No. 141, 21 July 1997, p. 12.

there is no clear legal base for it and since the Bundesbank holds the Target claims, the settlement of which would lack a legal base either if the euro is defunct. Thus, the Bundesbank's € 286-billion net claim will in all likelihood be lost.

The OMT Controversy

The fifth step of the crisis was the ECB's OMT programme, with OMT standing for 'Outright Monetary Transactions'. The term does not convey what this programme really is, namely the promise to infinitely extend the government bond purchases of the SMP type, limited to bonds which mature in one to three years. If a country needs help, submits itself to the rules of the ESM, and still has access to markets, the ECB may decide, and in fact promised, to buy its government bonds to preserve their market value and keep the interest rates low. President Draghi announced it with words that have become historical:[34]

> What I said exactly is that—and I repeat what I said in London the first time—we will do whatever it takes within our mandate—within our mandate—to have a single monetary policy in the euro area, to maintain price stability in the euro area, and to preserve the euro. And we say that the euro is irreversible.

He alluded with these words to a prior speech made on 26 July at an investors' conference at which, however, he did not mention the OMT.[35] In addition to the ESM, the OMT programme successfully calmed down the markets from September 2012 on and instilled fresh confidence among investors buying southern European bonds.

According to Figure 6.2, the Target balances did indeed decline. While it is true that, as shown in Figure 7.1 and the subsequent discussion in Chapter 7, 29% of the rapid decline in Target balances from summer 2012 to summer 2013 can be explained by additional fiscal rescue credit being disbursed, which reduced the Target balances on a one-to-one basis, 71% of the decline may be attributable to the OMT.

---

[34] See Introductory Statement to the Press Conference (with Q&A) by Mario Draghi, President of the ECB, and Vítor Constâncio, Vice-President of the ECB, 6 September 2012. For details on the OMT, see European Central Bank, *Technical Features of Outright Monetary Transactions*, press release, 6 September 2012, available at: <http://www.ecb. europa.eu/press/pr/date/2012/html/pr120906_1.en.html>.

[35] See also M. Draghi, *Speech at the Global Investment Conference in London*, 26 July 2012, available at: <http://www.ecb.europa.eu/press/key/date/2012/html/sp120726. en.html>. There he said: 'Within our mandate, the ECB is ready to do whatever it takes to preserve the euro. And believe me, it will be enough'.

It is worth noting in this context, however, that according to Figure 2.2 the decline in interest spreads actually began much earlier, in the winter of 2011/2012 (Spain: December 2011; Portugal: February 2012; Greece: March 2012). This points to the three-year Long-Term Refinancing Operations (LTROs) as well as to the ESM, rather than the OMT, as the major explanations for reduced tensions. After all, at the time there was no talk of the OMT. Meanwhile the three-year LTROs provided massive funds to banks, which in turn bought government bonds. Moreover, there were intense debates about the ESM throughout that winter, and the SMP was fully operative. Still, it cannot be denied that the OMT as of September 2012 also calmed the markets and helped convince investors to resume lending to the crisis-stricken countries. The President of the Swiss National Bank, Philipp Hildebrand, expressed this pointedly in the following statement:

> The ECB's OMT is a game changer. OMT's soothing power stems from the fact that market participants in effect see them as a commitment to the mutualisation of liabilities across the euro zone: countries standing together behind the debts of the vulnerable.[36]

From the viewpoint of the debtor countries and their creditors, a particular advantage of the OMT over the ESM's rescue credit was that the ECB explicitly declared that it would give up its preferred creditor status.[37] This is plausible insofar as its rank follows from the covenants attached to the respective government bonds, which are independent of who holds such bonds. Thus, it is understandable that the applause from international investors was deafening.

---

[36] P. Hildebrand, 'France's Economy Needs to Become more German', *Financial Times online*, 2 May 2013, available at: <http://blogs.ft.com/the-a-list/2013/05/02/frances-economy-needs-to-be-become-more-german/?#axzz2VLGgwKYo>.

[37] See European Central Bank, *Technical Features of Outright Monetary Transactions*, 6 September 2012, and Introductory Statement to the Press Conference (with Q&A) by Mario Draghi, President of the ECB, and Vítor Constâncio, Vice-President of the ECB, 6 September 2012. In the press conference, Draghi confirmed: '[...] we will accept pari passu treatment with the other creditors.' Cf. also D. Gros, C. Alcidi, and A. Giovanni, 'Central Banks in Times of Crisis: The FED vs. the ECB', *CEPS Policy Brief* 276, July 2012; S. Steinkamp and F. Westermann, 'On Creditor Seniority and Sovereign Bond Prices in Europe', *CESifo Working Paper* No. 3944, September 2012. C. Wyplosz, 'ECB's Outright Monetary Transactions' in: European Parliament, Directorate-General for Internal Policies, Policy Department A: Economic and Scientific Policy, *ECB Intervention in the Euro Area Sovereign Debt Markets*, Monetary Dialogue October 2012, Compilation of Notes, available at: <http://www.europarl.europa.eu/RegData/etudes/note/join/2012/492450/IPOL-ECON_NT(2012)492450_EN.pdf>.

Some economists who signed a public appeal even argued that the OMT was the 'most skilful and successful policy communication in decades'. What they liked in particular was the fact that 'without spending a single euro' it was possible to calm the markets and drive down the interest rates at which the debtor countries could continue to borrow. They maintained that, among multiple equilibria, the OMT produced the better one.[38]

However, things are not that simple.[39] Firstly, the OMT is the successor programme to the SMP and should be seen in this context. Secondly, in economic terms the OMT is tantamount to credit insurance provided free of charge by the ECB at the taxpayer's risks who, as explained above in the context of the SMP, would have to bear the cost of write-off losses. Thirdly, and most importantly, the Maastricht Treaty may not allow such credit insurance. The following sections will take a deeper look into these aspects.

As to the first issue, it is misleading to argue that no money has been spent, since the OMT is basically a continuation of the SMP. True, the differences are the changed conditionality, the announcement of unlimited purchases and the explicit relinquishment of seniority rights. However, purchases amounting to € 223 billion have been performed, as shown in Figure 8.1.

Secondly, it is certainly true that creditors and debtors like the free insurance that the OMT provides. It solves the creditors' problem that debtors may not be able to repay, and it helps debtors to continue borrowing. Creditors enjoy investment safety, and debtors can borrow at lower rates. The two parties can continue lending and borrowing as if the competitiveness and debt crisis resulting from the credit bubble had never occurred. There is indeed a different equilibrium than would have been reached if no such free credit insurance had been available. This does not necessarily mean, however, that the resulting equilibrium is 'better' in the sense of the economic theory of multiple equilibria, where

---

[38] See *A Call for Support for the European Central Bank's OMT Programme*, initiated by M. Fratzscher, F. Giavazzi, R. Portes, B. Weder di Mauro, and C. Wyplosz, 19 July 2013, available at: <https://berlinoeconomicus.diw.de/monetarypolicy/>. A worldwide collection of signatures from professors of economics, analysts and students had brought 211 signatures in three weeks. The response rate in Germany, where the appeal was launched with great effort by DIW, was meagre, except among DIW staff members. Of the sixty-one members associated with the Monetary Theory section of the German Economic Association (Verein für Socialpolitik), just four signed the appeal, and only one of the 113 economists assembled in the Public Finance section, even though they all had been asked to sign. These are the relevant sections of the Association.

[39] The following considerations draw on the author's expert testimony before the German Constitutional Court. See H.-W. Sinn, 'Responsibility of States and Central Banks in the Euro Crisis', *CESifo Forum* 15, 2014, special issue, pp. 3–36, available at: <http://www.cesifo-group.de/DocDL/forum1-14-1.pdf>.

anchoring expectations may prevent disastrous cumulative processes.[40] It just means another equilibrium, as there is always another equilibrium if a government institution intervenes in the market by subsidizing particular activities. This other equilibrium entails another distribution of income and wealth within the group of people living today, and between the present and future generations.

Given that a market for the kind of insurance that the OMT offers is already available, it could well be that the public intervention leads to a worse equilibrium. If creditors wished to have safer investments, they could buy CDS insurance in the market (credit default swaps). If they refrain because the ECB provides this insurance for free, they might lend excessively as they did in the years before the crisis, continuing the misallocation of resources that created Europe's mess in the first place.

It is a basic principle of a market economy that if someone uses a service, s/he has to pay for it. The payment ensures that the benefit to the user of the service is large enough to compensate the person who provides the service. This principle ensures allocative efficiency in the Pareto sense, and it explains the superiority of a market economy over a centrally planned one. The insurance market is no exception to this principle. Thus, government intervention in terms of providing credit insurance free of charge cannot be justified by simply pointing out that creditors and debtors like it, while the taxpayers, unaware of the risks imposed on them, remain calm.

Figure 8.3 shows how the premia for credit insurance of the GIPSIC countries, measured as a percentage of the capital insured, have developed in recent years. It demonstrates first of all that the insurance as such is a precious economic good with a sizeable market price. Thus the observation that 'not a single euro' was spent to achieve an economic effect is rather hollow. The protection of an insurance contract is a valuable economic good even if the damage does not occur and the insurance company does not spend a euro. Based on the logic of the OMT defenders, one could ask insurance companies to insure risks without receiving an insurance premium as long as the damage has not materialized, which obviously would be an absurd implication.

Had the taxpayers wished to absorb the risk imposed on them by the ECB decisions, they could have bought CDS contracts in the worldwide market for

[40] See P. De Grauwe, 'The Governance of a Fragile Eurozone', *CEPS Working Document* No. 346, May 2011, available at: <http://www.ceps.eu/book/governance-fragile-eurozone>; P. De Grauwe and Y. Ji, 'Mispricing of Sovereign Risk and Multiple Equilibria in the Eurozone', *CEPS Working Document* No. 361, January 2012, available at: <http://www.ceps.eu/book/mispricing-sovereign-risk-and-multiple-equilibria-eurozone>; G. A. Calvo, 'Servicing the Public Debt: The Role of Expectations', *American Economic Review* 78, 1988, pp. 647–661.

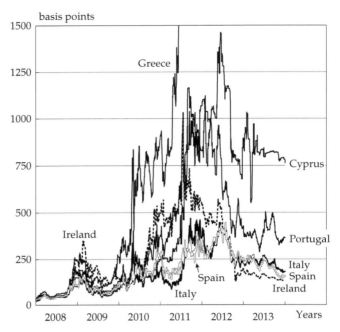

Figure 8.3 Trends in CDS premia for 10-year GIPSIC government bonds

Source: Datastream, Thomson Reuters CDS.

Note: the price of CDS protection against a Greek state bankruptcy increased until February 2012 to over 10,000 basis points (100%) and then ceased to be quoted on the market.

such contracts, which currently has a volume of about $ 27 trillion.[41] By doing so they probably could have earned an annual income of many dozens of billions of euros.

The chart, moreover, demonstrates that the calming of the markets through the fiscal rescue measures and the OMT announcement significantly reduced the CDS premia for most of the GIPSIC countries. Only Greek government bonds can no longer be meaningfully insured, because the default of Greece is no longer a random event. The decline of the CDS premia began in autumn 2011 and continued well into 2013. Based on the Q4 2011 premium, the insurance of, say, the 2013 'IPSIC' government debt (without Greece) would have cost 4.1%, or € 143 billion, at the rates reported in the chart. Two years later, by Q4 2013,

---

[41] See International Monetary Fund, *Global Financial Stability Report*, April 2013, p. 59.

the premium was only 1.9%, and the insurance for the same debt would have cost only € 68 billion. Thus, even if no rescue euro has actually been lost, the free insurance provided was worth € 75 billion a year, a bit more than 'a single euro'.[42]

The defenders of the OMT would probably argue that the situation in Europe was already too critical and close to collapse for such allocative considerations, and that without the free insurance provided by the OMT and other public rescue operations there might have been bank runs and bankruptcies creating contagion externalities that destabilize the markets. This, in principle, is a valid argument, but it is certainly not sufficient to make the case for the OMT.

For one thing, no one is able to prove how dangerous the situation really was. The financial industry always paints horror scenarios of contagion that would make the world fall apart unless investors are bailed out with public money. This, in a sense, is their business model. They undertake overly risky activities, collect the profits as long as things go well, and ask for the taxpayer to foot the bill when losses occur. This is the kind of artificial incentive to risk-taking and of artificial source of profits on which the capital market has nourished for so long.[43] Such apocalyptic stories were told before the Greek haircut of March 2012, the biggest in history, and before the haircut and bail-in of Laiki Bank in Cyprus, but catastrophic contagion effects failed to materialize in either case.

Cyprus has solved the problem with capital controls and limits on cash withdrawals from banks. Admittedly, these are measures one would have liked to avoid in a common currency area, but they nevertheless effectively prevented the bank-runs the defenders of the OMT are afraid of, and they were definitely cheaper for the taxpayers than bailing out the banking systems.

For another, there are political contagion and moral hazard effects that could be much more dangerous, in terms of increasing the incentive for states to over-borrow and of infecting the public budgets of the still-solvent states in the north, than a mere crisis of financial markets. Only a few of the states of Europe have sound finances, most have debt levels above the Maastricht line, and most suffer from a distorted age pyramid that, taken by itself, is enough to

---

[42] The government debt of the crisis countries, excluding Greece, totalled € 3,476 billion at the end of 2013.

[43] See H.-W. Sinn, *Casino Capitalism. How the Financial Crisis Came about and What Needs to Be Done Now*, Oxford University Press, Oxford 2010, chapter 4: Why Wall Street Became a Gambling Casino, p. 80; H.-W. Sinn, *Ökonomische Entscheidungen bei Ungewißheit*, Mohr Siebeck, Tübingen, 1980, especially pp. 172–192; English edition: *Economic Decisions under Uncertainty*, North-Holland, Amsterdam 1983, especially pp. 163–182; M. Dewatripont and J. Tirole, 'Efficient Governance Structure: Implications for Banking Regulation', in C. Mayer and X. Vives (eds), *Capital Markets and Financial Intermediation*, Cambridge University Press, Cambridge 1993, pp. 12–35; and M. Dewatripont and J. Tirole, *Prudential Regulation of Banks*, MIT Press, Cambridge 1994, pp. 97 and 113.

trigger budgetary crises around 2025 to 2030, when the baby boomers of major central European countries go into retirement. Adding to this the losses from rescue credits that will not be serviced would be a recipe for disaster. Thus, even with a substantial contagion risk concerning financial markets, the case for the OMT cannot be made unless it is shown that the political contagion weighs less than the financial one, that the damage done to financial institutions weighs more than the damage inflicted on fiscal systems, and, consequently, on entire societies.

Thirdly, whatever the truth about these economic considerations, the main problems are on the legal side. While many central banks around the world buy government bonds to finance states, with the attendant redistributive implications, the Eurosystem has been constructed around a more limited mandate for its central bank, because it is a common currency area without a common state, which is an unusual arrangement. Because a common state with redistributive functions has not been created and was, in part, vigorously rejected by those who pushed for a currency union (see Chapter 1), the Maastricht Treaty excludes the possibility of monetary state financing.

Apart from that, even with the central banks of federations like the USA or Switzerland, the kind of regional fiscal policy that the ECB developed during the crisis is unthinkable. While it is true that the US Federal Reserve buys federal government bonds, it would never act a lender of last resort for single states.[44] It would not even touch the bonds of near-insolvent states like California or Illinois. Equally, it is unthinkable that the Swiss National Bank would bail out single cantons. The liability principle has thus far been respected in the US and Switzerland. If states or cantons over-borrow, they are left to go bankrupt, and no central political institution, let alone the central bank, is going to help. This, in turn, prevents over-borrowing and reckless lending in the first place. This will be studied in more detail in Chapter 9.

If someone finds the present rule of law in the Eurosystem inappropriate, s/he should demand that it be changed by rewriting the Maastricht Treaty. It is not possible to have it changed by *force majeure* by technocratic institutions that take the liberty of self-defining the scope of their mandate. The ECB is independent within the set of rules granted to it by democratic institutions, but not in the sense that it can itself change these rules or redefine their limits. The ECB Governing Council was intentionally designed upon the basis of the one-country-one-vote principle regardless of country size because the scope of its mandate was limited to a narrowly defined monetary policy and the pursuit of price stability. It was not meant to carry out policies with serious fiscal implications. If the Governing

---

[44] See M. Feldstein, 'Dos and Don'ts for the European Central Bank', *Project Syndicate*, 29 July 2012, available at: <http://www.project-syndicate.org/commentary/dos-and-don-ts-for-the-european-central-bank>.

Council nevertheless makes such policy decisions, it subjects itself to what lawyers call the *ultra vires* offense, the offense of overstepping its mandate and misusing its power.

Even the Bank of England, which can pursue its monetary policy independently, always takes monetary policy decisions with fiscal implications to the Treasury to obtain democratic backing for them, as its ex-president Mervyn King emphasized in his farewell address.[45]

The two special rules that distinguish the Eurosystem from other monetary systems, and which were Germany's conditions for giving up the deutschmark, are laid down in articles 123 and 125 of the TFEU. The former excludes monetary state financing, the latter spells out the no-bailout clause, as discussed in Chapter 1.

In the meantime, article 125 of the TFEU has effectively been modified by political decisions of the EU parliaments when they set up the various fiscal rescue schemes discussed above. Lawyers are still debating intensely whether these decisions were compatible with the Maastricht Treaty or whether a revision of that Treaty would have been necessary.[46]

In the context of the SMP and OMT, article 123 of the TFEU is even more important, however, than article 125. It reads:[47]

> Overdraft facilities or any other type of credit facility with the European Central Bank or with the central banks of the Member States (hereinafter referred to as 'national central banks') in favour of Union institutions, bodies, offices or agencies, central governments, regional, local or other public authorities, other bodies governed by public law, or public undertakings of Member States shall be prohibited, as shall the purchase directly from them by the European Central Bank or national central banks of debt instruments.

[45] See M. King, 'Threats to Central Banks and their Independence', *Presentation at the conference Challenges to Central Banks in the 21st Century*, 25 March 2013, London School of Economics.

[46] See U. di Fabio, 'Finanzstabilität und Integration: Wege aus der Krise', Lecture given at *Munich Seminars*, CESifo and Süddeutsche Zeitung, 30 April 2012, available at: <http://www.ifo.de/w/3FaZQTUnS>; and U. di Fabio, 'Das europäische Schuldendilemma als Mentalitätskrise', *Frankfurter Allgemeine Zeitung*, No. 143, 22 June 2012, p. 9. See also M. Seidel, 'European Currency Union and Rule of Law', *CESifo DICE Report* 3, pp. 36–43, November 2012, available at: <http://www.cesifogroup.de/DocDL/dicereport312-rr1.pdf>; P. Kirchhof, *Deutschland im Schuldensog*, Beck, Munich 2012; G. Beck, 'EZB-Urteil: Londoner Jurist erwartet "Rechtsbeugung" durch Karlsruhe', *Deutsche Wirtschafts Nachrichten*, 6 June 2013, available at: <http://deutsche-wirtschafts-nachrichten.de/2013/06/06/ezb-urteil-londoner-jurist-erwartet-rechtsbeugung-durch-karlsruhe>.

[47] See EU, 'Treaty on the Functioning of the European Union (TFEU)', *Official Journal of the European Union* C 115/47, 9 May 2008, p. 99, available at: <http://eur-lex.europa.eu/LexUriServ/LexUriServ.do?uri=OJ:C:2008:115:0058:0199:en:PDF>.

The intention of this article is clearly the exclusion of monetary state financing. However, it does leave a small loophole with the word 'directly' in the last sentence. Strictly speaking, only direct purchases of government bonds from governments are forbidden, while indirect purchases are allowed. The ECB reads this as meaning that purchases in secondary markets are allowed.[48]

However, this interpretation is not convincing, because if it were true, the ECB and a member country could always circumvent it by first channelling government bonds through a commercial bank, perhaps even one that belongs to the government, before the ECB buys them. This risk was seen early enough by the European Council. It therefore ruled in a 1993 Council Regulation that 'purchases made on the secondary market must not be used to circumvent the objective of (...) article 104' of the Maastricht Treaty, which is now article 123 of the TFEU, and only secondary market purchases of government bonds of EU countries *not* belonging to the Eurosystem were allowed as exceptions.[49]

Instead of secondary market purchases, what might also and primarily have been meant by the indirect purchases allowed, are purchases through the banking system by providing banks with ECB's refinancing credit. After all, the ECB lends money to banks against collateral, and the latter use the money to buy government bonds that they then submit as collateral for their credit. As explained in Chapter 5, this sort of indirect monetary state finance has played a major role in the crisis. It is problematic enough in itself, given that banks bear the risk of state default and that the Eurosystem partakes of the risk of bank defaults. Nevertheless, banks can be expected to exhibit more care and caution in buying government bonds when they have to actually hold them than when they can sell them on to the Eurosystem after a waiting period of only a few days.[50] It is not at all plausible that the signatories of the Maastricht Treaty wanted to

---

[48] See European Central Bank, 'Decision ECB/2010/5', *Official Journal* L 124/8, 20 May 2010, available at: <http://www.ecb.europa.eu/ecb/legal/pdf/l_12420100520en00080009. pdf>. See also Introductory Statement to the Press Conference (with Q&A) by Mario Draghi, President of the ECB, and Vítor Constâncio, Vice-President of the ECB, 6 September 2012; as well as European Central Bank, *Monthly Bulletin*, October 2012, in particular 'Box 1: Compliance of Outright Monetary Transaction with the Prohibition on Monetary Financing', p. 7.

[49] See Council of the European Union, 'Council Regulation No. 3603/93', *Official Journal* L 332, 13 December 1993, Preamble and article 2, available at: <http://eur-lex. europa.eu/LexUriServ/LexUriServ.do?uri=CELEX:31993R3603:EN:HTML>; see also S. Homburg, 'Der neue Kurs der Europäischen Zentralbank', *Wirtschaftsdienst* 92, October 2012, pp. 673–677, available at: <http://link.springer.com/article/10.100 7%2Fs10273-012-1437-5>.

[50] The waiting period sometimes is only three days and often less than ten days. See Request for Information from the German Constitutional Court, 21 November 2012, and reply from the Bundesbank, 3 December 2012, Question 3. Internal documents of the Constitutional Court made available to the author in his function as an

ban monetary state financing with a meticulous description of all the variants being forbidden, and then using the one little and innocuously sounding adverb 'directly' to open up a giant loophole with obvious circumvention possibilities that allow for a reshuffling of financial risks on the order of hundreds of billions of euros among the nations of the Eurosystem.

To defend the ECB's interpretation, President Draghi pointed out that article 18 paragraph 1 of the Protocols of the Maastricht says that the ECB can operate in the financial markets by buying and selling 'marketable instruments', without there being a limitation to private assets.[51] However, this is just a general clause clarifying that the ECB can perform open market operations, which has never been disputed. The general clause is narrowed down and specified by article 125 TFEU, which for that purpose has been repeated with identical wording in article 21 of the Protocol of the Maastricht Treaty, which is one of the special articles of that protocol that cannot be changed by either the EU Commission or the EU parliament.[52]

A major legal problem of the OMT lies in its similarity with the Secondary Markets Support Facility (SMSF) of the ESM, as described above. The latter is an announcement to buy government bonds of a distressed country if necessary, without the ESM holding a seniority status, provided that the country submits itself to a formal reform programme agreed with the ESM. As explained, the ECB implicitly gave up its preferred creditor status when it announced the OMT but requires a beneficiary country to be part of an ESM programme. The OMT is therefore basically identical to the SMSF.

The only difference is that the supporting countries' liability is strictly limited by the ESM's equity capital of € 700 billion, while via the ECB, the countries' liability is unlimited or, to be precise, limited by the sum of the Eurosystem's equity capital and seignorage wealth, which is a much larger figure. As explained in Chapter 1, under static conditions the Eurosystem can absorb losses of up to € 1.615 trillion (€ 1.262 trillion monetary base and € 353 billion equity by 31 December 2013) and

expert for the Court. See also the ECB's testimony before the German Constitutional Court by its representative F. Schorkopf, *Stellungnahme der Europäischen Zentralbank, Verfassungsbeschwerden 2 BvR 1390/12, 2 BvR 1439/12 und 2 BvR 1827/12, Organstreitverfahren 2 BvE 6/12*, 16 January 2013, p. 32.

[51] See M. Draghi, 'Nichts tun wäre noch viel riskanter', *Süddeutsche Zeitung*, 14 September 2012, p. 19; and 'Protocol (No 4) on the Statute of the European System of Central Banks and of the European Central Bank', *Official Journal of the European Union*, C 115/230, 9 May 2008, available at: <http://www.ecb.int/ecb/legal/pdf/en_statute_from_c_11520080509en02010328.pdf>, in particular article 18 paragraph 1.

[52] While according to article 129 paragraph 3 of the Protocol quite a number of articles, including article 18, can be changed by the European Parliament and the Council, article 21 of the Protocol, and hence article 123 TFEU, is sacrosanct.

in a dynamic calculation, where future increases in the monetary base are taken into account, it might be able to absorb losses of up to € 3.4 trillion.[53]

It is not reasonable to allow the ECB Governing Council, a technocratic body of monetary specialists pursuing a limited mandate, to incur such enormous liability risks through simple majority voting while the ESM, controlled by parliaments and with 85% qualified majority voting, commands a much smaller sum to carry out exactly the same operations.

Apart from that, the parallelism between the OMT and the SMSF implies an *ultra vires* problem for at least one of the two institutions, the ESM or the ECB. If the government bond purchases are fiscal operations, the ECB is overstepping its mandate. If, on the other hand, they are monetary operations as the ECB claims, then the ESM is overstepping its mandate, since it is not allowed to carry out monetary policy. For logical reasons, at least one of the two institutions is operating *ultra vires*.

The ECB itself should have detected these problems and could therefore have been hesitant to announce the OMT programme. After all, its bylaws stipulate that the ECB's General Council must assess the compatibility of the ECB's policy with article 123 TFEU in an annual report to the Governing Council. The report is not published but is handed out to other EU institutions, among them the EU Commission. However, as always, the results of self-assessment are different from those of outside assessment.

The Statement of the German Constitutional Court

In February 2014, shortly before the final version of this manuscript went to print, the German Constitutional Court gave an outside assessment of the OMT in the context of its ruling over various appeals against the permanent rescue fund ESM, bundling tens of thousands of plaintiffs.[54] In its preliminary ruling of 12 September 2012,[55] the Court had rejected appeals for an injunction and allowed the German President Joachim Gauck to sign the ESM Treaty. However, at the time it also said that the cumulative effects of all rescue operations are to be seen

---

[53] See W. Buiter and E. Rahbari, 'Looking into the Deep Pockets of the ECB', Citi Economics, *Global Economics View*, 27 February 2012, available at: <http://blogs.r.ftdata. co.uk/money-supply/files/2012/02/citi-Looking-into-the-Deep-Pockets-of-the-ECB. pdf>.

[54] Federal Constitutional Court, *BVerfG*, *2 BvR 2728/13*, 14 January 2014, Absatz-Nr. (1–105), Sachbericht, article 12; see also Federal Constitutional Court, press release no. 9/2014, 7 February 2014.

[55] See also Federal Constitutional Court, *BVerfG*, *2 BvR 1390/12*, *2 BvR 1421/12*, *2 BvR 1438/12*, *2 BvR 1439/12*, *2 BvR 1440/12*, *2 BvE 6/12*, 12 September 2012.

as a whole, and that it will therefore also comment on the ECB's rescue policies in its main judgement, in particular on whether the ECB is overstepping its mandate when pursuing its OMT programme.

For the international press, the most important aspect of the German Constitutional Court's recent announcement was the Court's declaration that it would consult the European Court of Justice concerning the OMT. The press interpreted this as being good news for investors and the ECB. After all, the European Court of Justice is known for its proclivity towards European institutions so as to facilitate the European integration process. Thus, it is generally expected that it will wave the OMT through.

However, this is a misinterpretation of the situation, as the German Court did not hand over the case, but just asked the European Court for an opinion.[56] And it did not ask it whether or not the OMT is legal, but about what measures the European Court would suggest to make it legal, given that in its opinion this is not the case. In fact, the German Court has made it utterly clear that the ECB overstepped its mandate with the OMT programme, and that this programme violates EU primary law.

These are the Court's main views on the OMT:[57]

(1) The OMT programme may lead to a significant redistribution of wealth among the states of Europe if the bonds acquired are held until maturity. The ECB is not empowered to bring about such a redistribution of wealth.

(2) The selective purchase of the government bonds of crisis-afflicted countries is an economic policy measure. The ECB is not authorized to participate in economic policy measures.

(3) A procedure that differentiates between individual EU member states is fundamentally alien to the European Central Bank system.

(4) The OMT programme is the functional equivalent of the corresponding EFSF and ESM bailout programmes, but is not subject to any democratic controls.

---

[56] See H.-W. Sinn, 'Outright Monetary Infractions', *Project Syndicate*, 9 February 2014, available at: <http://www.project-syndicate.org/commentary/hans-werner-sinn-applauds-the-german-constitutional-court-s-ruling-on-the-ecb-s-bond-purchase-scheme>. See also W. Münchau, 'Germany's Constitutional Court Has Strengthened the Eurosceptics', *Financial Times*, 9 February 2014, available at: <http://www.ft.com/intl/cms/s/0/8a64e3ac-8f25-11e3-be85-00144feab7de.html#axzz2uEahyERf>.

[57] See also Ifo Institute, *Comments by the Ifo Institute and Prof. Hans-Werner Sinn on Today's Statement by Germany's Constitutional Court on the ECB's OMT Programme*, press release, 7 February 2014, available at: <http://www.ifo.de/w/3Sd4KMkse>.

(5) The ECB's intention to reduce differences in interest rates on government bonds supports the contention that the OMT constitutes monetary state financing, which is prohibited by article 123 of TFEU.

(6) Interest differentials are essential ingredients of a functioning capital market and should therefore not be mitigated by the ECB.

The German Court does make suggestions as to how the OMT could be modified in order to make it compatible with EU primary law. In particular, it suggests a capping of the programme's volume and, most importantly, an assurance that the ECB would not incur any losses on government bonds should the issuing state become insolvent. Thus, the ECB cannot promise to do 'whatever it takes', and it cannot hold government debt up to maturity and accept a *pari passu* position with private investors upon insolvency. Obviously, both of these provisions would kill the OMT, since the feature that made this programme so effective in terms of calming the market was precisely the implicit promise to buy the government bonds before maturity and unload the write-off losses onto the shoulders of taxpayers.

It remains to be seen how the European Court of Justice will respond. Rather than aiming for a showdown, it will probably try to find a compromise and negotiate with the German Constitutional Court. If not, a major constitutional conflict will erupt in Europe that could escalate in a way that could be detrimental to the euro. The German Court may then ask the Bundesbank not to participate in the OMT and the German government to renounce the EU Treaty.

Of course, it is more than understandable that other countries in Europe regard this possibility with concern. However, the European Court of Justice has no jurisdiction over whether or not European treaties are compatible with the constitutions of the member states. Should Germany have misinterpreted the Maastricht Treaty's no-bailout rule and the exclusion of monetary state financing because the European Court of Justice interprets it differently to the German Constitutional Court, the latter has the right to force the German government and parliament to take action.

In all likelihood, the German institutions are already being forced to change their attitudes. After all, the Court's opinion was revealed by the published statement, without having to wait until the final ruling out. The Court said very clearly, and with considerable emphasis, that the German parliament, the German government, and the Bundesbank are not only forbidden to participate in actions of European institutions that overstep their mandates, but must actively oppose the abuse of power by such institutions.[58] Moreover, it gave every

---

[58] Federal Constitutional Court, *BVerfG, 2 BvR 2728/13*, 14 January 2014, articles 45, 46 and 49.

German citizen the right to appeal to the Constitutional Court should these institutions not take the required actions.[59]

The Bundesbank therefore cannot be expected to participate in the OMT programme should the ECB Governing Council decide to activate it. It has been argued that this would not matter, as other central banks could in this case buy the government bonds, and the Bundesbank would still be participating in any write-off losses in the ECB system. This argument is valid if the euro survives the bankruptcies. However, if it doesn't, the risk-sharing will end, and it would be a matter of fierce negotiations whether or not the write-off losses on government bond purchases with dubious legal justification would be shared. The situation would be very similar to the negotiation about the sharing of Target risks. Apart from that, the political signal of the Bundesbank's not participating in the OMT programme would have its own implications for markets.

Optimistic investors and pessimistic taxpayers may think that all this is not very relevant as the German government, which holds a two-thirds majority in parliament, could amend the Maastricht Treaty in a way that makes the OMT and similar debt mutualization activities legal, even if they aren't under the current formulation. However, this may turn out not to be the case, since the Court declared that the German parliament does not have the right to make decisions that would empower European institutions to decide themselves about their mandate, barring it furthermore from agreeing to automatic decision procedures that would give European institutions access to the German budget, reducing the scope of discretion for future German parliaments.[60] Only case-by-case rescue decisions are possible for the German parliament, given the current legal architecture of the EU and given the German constitution. The implementation of redistribution mechanisms would call for a new German Constitution which, however, could only be based on the decisions of a new constitutional assembly or a referendum.[61]

---

[59] Federal Constitutional Court, *BVerfG, 2 BvR 2728/13*, 14 January 2014, article 51.

[60] Federal Constitutional Court, *BVerfG, 2 BvR 2728/13*, 14 January 2014, article 48. Cf. also Federal Constitutional Court, *BVerfG, 2 BvR 987/10*, 7 September 2011, article 126.

[61] The case for a referendum has been made by the Constitutional Court's Vice President Ferdinand Kirchhof, who, however, did not participate in the Court's ruling on the ESM; see J. Gaugele, T. Jungholt and C. C. Malzahn, 'Verfassungsrichter für Volksabstimmung über Euro', Interview with F. Kirchhof, *Die Welt*, 5 February 2012, available at: <http://www.welt.de/politik/deutschland/article13850704/Verfassungsrichter-fuer-Volksabstimmung-ueber-Euro.html>. Udo di Fabio, ex-Constitutional Court judge, argued that giving the ECB what it wants may require changing the German constitution, and if so, a referendum would be needed; see U. di Fabio, 'Die Zukunft einer stabilen Wirtschafts- und Währungsunion', *Stiftung Familienunternehmen*, May

Banking Union: Bail-in or Bailout?

The last step to be taken in the crisis so far is the creation of a banking union in the Eurozone. There is general agreement that the banking union needs a common banking supervision and common resolution rules to keep moral hazard incentives to national authorities in check. Indeed, it is not advisable to pool the risks from the ECB's refinancing credit and mutually stand in for additional bank risks through fiscal rescue funds, while leaving it to national authorities to regulate and supervise the banks on their territory.[62] Risk-sharing and redistribution necessarily require common behavioural constraints for the banks involved, as well as common supervision and resolution authorities.

The banking union was agreed upon at the EU Summit of 28 and 29 July 2012 with the following wording:[63]

> When an effective single supervisory mechanism is established, involving the ECB, for banks in the euro area the ESM could, following a regular decision, have the possibility to recapitalize banks directly.

Thus, first a common banking supervision under the control of the ECB is to be established and then community money is to be made available to the banks to cover their write-off losses from toxic investments.[64] The banking union with a central authority for recapitalizing banks with community funds is a quantum leap in the rescue philosophy, because not only are states to stand by each other, but private economic activity is to be mutually insured and subsidized through public channels.[65]

2013, especially p. 53; see also J. Jahn, 'Notfalls ist Deutschland zum Euro-Austritt verpflichtet', *Frankfurter Allgemeine Zeitung*, 2 June 2013, available at: <http://www.faz.net/aktuell/wirtschaft/europas-schuldenkrise/frueherer-verfassungsrichter-di-fabio-notfalls-ist-deutschland-zum-euro-austritt-verpflichtet-12205592.html>.

[62] For an in-depth discussion of the evolving European Banking Union, see also several articles in the *CESifo Forum* 13, No. 4, Winter 2012, 'European Banking Union', available at: <http://www.cesifo-group.de/DocDL/forum4-12-gesamt.pdf>. Cf. also S. Lautenschläger, T. Gstädtner, and S. Steffen, 'Wie ist das EU-Konzept zur Bankenunion zu bewerten?', *ifo Schnelldienst* 66, No. 1, 17 January 2013, pp. 3–13, available at: <http://www.cesifo-group.de/DocDL/ifosd_2013_01_1.pdf>.

[63] See Council of the European Union, *Euro Area Summit Statement*, 29 June 2012. See also W. Mussler, 'Krisenfonds soll Banken direkt kapitalisieren', *Frankfurter Allgemeine Zeitung*, No. 150, 30 June 2012, p. 11.

[64] The importance of a cross-border resolution regime and the cooperation between supervisory institutions at the national and EU level as a precondition for recapitalization of banks through the ESM was already pointed out by C. M. Buch, 'From the Stability Pact to ESM. What next?', *IAW Discussion Paper* No. 85, June 2012.

[65] See R. Vaubel, 'Probleme der Bankenunion: Falsche Lehren aus der Krise', *Credit and Capital Markets—Kredit und Kapital* 46, pp. 281–302.

While it is theoretically conceivable that the recapitalization of banks to which the governments agreed was meant to compensate for future write-off losses resulting under a new regulatory regime, the urgency of the calls for a banking union and the enormous political pressure imposed on Germany by the governments of France, Spain, and Italy as well as the ECB and the EU Commission makes it clear that another issue is at stake: sharing the legacy of the bursting asset bubble in terms of write-off losses on toxic assets accumulated in the banks' balance sheets in the years before the crisis.

Most of these write-off losses resulted from the banks' investing in very risky ventures during the credit bubble, ranging from overpriced real estate to overly indebted governments, and which now threaten the existence of these banks. Thus far, a significant proportion of the necessary write-off losses do not yet show up in the books, but as bonds and credit claims mature and debtors turn out not to be able to repay, the truth will gradually become visible in the balance sheets. Debtors who cannot repay include real-estate investors, normal business firms, private households, and states that are currently being kept afloat with community funds and which may need debt relief.

The causes of the misinvestment by banks were discussed in Chapters 4, 5, and 7. They include the political ties between national governments and national central banks, the excessively liberal interpretations of the Basel Accords that induced banks to load their balance sheets with government bonds, as well as the expectation of being bailed out with the local printing press, if necessary. All these factors stimulated the excessive foreign lending that induced the inflationary credit bubbles in the first place. In addition, there was much political arm-twisting during the crisis to have local banks, in particular in Spain and Italy, use the voluminous long-term refinancing credit the ECB offered in winter 2011/2012, which Mario Draghi called the 'Big Bazooka', to buy their governments' bonds to ensure the continuation of deficit financing.

There was also the problem of competition in laxity of local regulatory efforts that allowed banks to engage in overly risky activities.[66] A lax regulation attracts banking business and creates jobs in the financial industry. In addition, it opens

---

[66] See H.-W. Sinn, *The New Systems Competition,* Yrjö Jahnsson Lectures, Basil Blackwell, Oxford 2003, chapter 7: Limited Liability, Risk-Taking and the Competition of Bank Regulators. See also the debate with E. Baltensperger and P. Spencer on banking regulation, H.-W. Sinn, 'Risk-Taking, Limited Liability and the Competition of Bank Regulators', *Finanzarchiv* 59, 2003, pp. 305–329; E. Baltensperger, 'Competition of Bank Regulators: A More Optimistic View. A Comment on the Paper by Hans-Werner Sinn', *Finanzarchiv* 59, 2003, pp. 330–335; P. Spencer, 'Can National Banking Systems Compete? A Comment on the Paper by Hans-Werner Sinn', *Finanzarchiv* 59, 2003, pp. 336–339; and H.-W. Sinn, 'Asymmetric Information, Bank Failures, and the Rationale for Harmonizing Banking Regulation. A Rejoinder on Comments of Ernst Baltensperger and Peter Spencer', *Finanzarchiv* 59, 2003, pp. 340–346. In the Sinn paper in *Finanzarchiv,*

a channel for cheap credit for domestic uses. The possibility of reaping these benefits while shifting the risk of bankruptcy to other nations—or, even better, while others come to rescue to prevent the bankruptcy—is an irresistible temptation in particular for countries with their back against the wall, which see no chance of repaying their foreign debt anyway.

The distorted incentives on which the Eurosystem was built have melted the governments and banks of some European countries into an alloy of sorts, with dangerous implications for systemic stability. The vicious circle between hazardous state and bank finance created by the mutual interconnections between commercial banks, local central banks, and local governments has meanwhile backfired by increasing the financing costs of private business located in the GIPSIC countries, which in the end will have to foot at least some of the extra tax burden necessary to save the states in whose territories they reside. This has led to the demand to pool even more of the private investment risks through ECB actions.[67]

The EU Commission, the ECB, and the southern and western states of the Eurozone want to cut the toxic links between banks and their local governments

---

the externality that a lax regulation imposes results from the fact that bank failures would hurt creditors from other countries who, due to the opaqueness of regulatory systems, are unable to distinguish between good and bad regulators. Thus, regulatory competition settles to a 'lemon's equilibrium' with too-lax standards. The special aspect added by the Eurosystem is the institutionalized pooling of the returns from refinancing credit. See also R. S. Kroszner and R. J. Shiller, *Reforming U.S. Financial Markets*, MIT Press, Cambridge 2011; A. Admati and M. Hellwig, *The Bankers' New Clothes*, Princeton University Press, Princeton 2013; and A. Admati and M. Hellwig 'Does Debt Discipline Bankers? An Academic Myth about Bank Indebtedness', Rock Center for Corporate Governance at Stanford University Working Paper 132, February 2013; C. Goodhart, 'The Regulatory Response to the Financial Crisis', *CESifo Working Paper* No. 2257, March 2008, available at: <http://www.cesifo-group.de/DocDL/cesifo1_wp2257.pdf>, and C. Goodhart, *The Regulatory Response to the Financial Crisis*, Edward Elgar, Northampton 2010.

[67] For an appeal to ease funding of the private sector, thereby lowering the cost of borrowing, especially in the European periphery, see: ECB Executive Board member Benoît Coeuré in E. Kuehnen and G. Prodhan, 'Europe Must Do More on Small Business Loans', *Reuters*, 25 April 2013, available at: <http://www.reuters.com/article/2013/04/25/us-ecb-coeure-smallbiz-idUSBRE93O06420130425>; G. Soros, 'The Resistible Fall of Europe: An Interview with George Soros', *Project Syndicate*, 15 May 2013, available at: <http://www.project-syndicate.org/commentary/the-resistible-fall-of-europe--an-interview-with-george-soros>; and Spanish Prime Minister Mariano Rajoy in S. White, 'Spain's Rajoy Calls on ECB to Create Bank Lending Scheme for Smaller Companies', *Reuters*, 15 June 2013, available at: <http://www.reuters.com/article/2013/06/15/us-spain-smes-idUSBRE95E09Q20130615>; for claims to ease funding of the private sector, thereby lowering the cost of borrowing, especially in the European periphery.

by distributing the losses of banks among European taxpayers. However, this is certainly not the only possibility. An alternative is imposing the losses on the banks' creditors, which is often called a 'bail-in'. Given that the creditors made conscious investment decisions and enjoyed good returns for many years, they should stand up for the consequences of their decisions.

Understandably, this alternative has not been met with great enthusiasm by the financial industry. Thus, in the early stages of the European discussions about a banking union, a bail-in with haircuts for creditors was dismissed as too dangerous for the stability of capital markets and, if anything, left for the future. Accordingly, the European Commission in 2012 proposed protecting the banks' creditors from any haircuts until 2018.[68]

The argument for the bailout was that the fire is burning and needs to be extinguished. Yes, haircuts would punish those who made the decisions to invest and induce them to lend less recklessly in the future. But for the moment survival was more important than long-run efficiency. Without a bailout, the boat would sink with all passengers. As already explained, that is the usual knock-out argument used in every crisis by representatives of the financial industry to close the debate and open taxpayers' wallets. However, at a time when the crisis is completing its seventh year, this argument has lost the sense of urgency it had when the crisis began.

While applauded by the financial industry, the EU proposal hardly met with unanimous approval in Europe.[69] When two groups of German economists, 480

---

[68] See European Commission, *Proposal for a Directive of the European Parliament and of the Council Establishing a Framework for the Recovery and Resolution of Credit Institutions and Investment Firms*, COM(2012) 280 final, 6 June 2012, Preamble, article 52, available at: <http://eur-lex.europa.eu/LexUriServ/LexUriServ.do?uri=COM:2012:0280:FIN:EN:PDF>.

[69] See *Aufruf von 279 deutschsprachigen Wirtschaftsprofessoren,* 5 June 2012, available at: <http://www.statistik.tu-dortmund.de/kraemer.html> and *Stellungnahme zur Europäischen Bankenunion,* 12 June 2012, available at: <http://www.macroeconomics.tu-berlin.de/fileadmin/fg124/allgemein/Stellungnahme_zur_Europaeischen_Bankenunion.pdf>. See also H. Hau and H.-W. Sinn, 'The Eurozone's Banking Union is Deeply Flawed', *Financial Times*, 29 January 2013, p. 9, available at: <http://www.ft.com/intl/cms/s/0/47055db6-5b47-11e2-8ccc-00144feab49a.html#axzz2bjxANyUv>. These critics of the postponement of the bail-in rule were later joined by critical voices from Finland and the Netherlands; see J. Brunsden and R. Christie, 'German Push to Accelerate Bank Bail-Ins Joined by Dutch', *Bloomberg*, 5 February 2013, available at: <http://www.bloomberg.com/news/2013-02-04/german-push-to-accelerate-bank-bail-ins-joined-by-dutch-finns.html>. Ultimately, the ECB also warned that introducing the bail-in rules by 2018 would be too late and instead proposed the year 2015; see also Introductory Statement to the Press Conference (with Q&A) by Mario Draghi, President of the ECB, and Vítor Constâncio, Vice-President of the ECB, 4 April 2013, available at: <http://www.ecb.int/press/pressconf/2013/html/is130404.en.html>.

signatories in total, launched two separate but largely identical appeals, rejecting the idea of bailing out creditors on the grounds that this would distort future investment incentives and violate the liability principle, many politicians were alerted to the problem and pushed for a correction of the Commission's proposals. Interestingly enough, these were often politicians from the left. Solidarity made them agree to rescuing states with community funds, but not rich plutocrats who had misinvested their money.

The normal method of carrying out bail-ins is debt-equity swaps, i.e. the conversion of credit claims into bank shares. To be sure, banks have lost much equity capital during the crisis and now need to replenish it to be able to operate well. But instead of burdening the taxpayers, this equity capital could be supplied by the banks' creditors. Creditors could be asked to accept haircuts on their claims and receive shares in the bank instead. This would impose the losses first of all on the shareholders, who are actually supposed to bear the risk, and if the equity is not enough for that, on the creditors as well. Starting with hybrid capital earmarked for such losses and moving progressively from senior to junior credit claims, the creditors would have to accept the haircuts without any compensation.

A strong argument in favour of such a solution is the sheer size of the potential write-off losses and the large volume of bank debt which could be used as a buffer. Table 8.3 gives an overview of various estimates of the maximum potential write-off losses on toxic assets held by the banking sectors of the GIPSIC countries. Averaging the reports reviewed suggests that maximum write-offs on the order of around € 680 billion would have to be reckoned with, which is 65% of the € 1,035 billion aggregate stock of equity capital (including reserves) of the GIPSIC banking systems and many times more than the market value of this stock, which is only € 229 billion.[70] The range of the estimates is not very large. Adding the most pessimistic estimates yields a maximum joint write-off loss of € 735 billion, and adding the most optimistic estimates produces a sum of € 618 billion. The figures are truly alarming, as they reveal that in a worst-case scenario the write-off losses might wipe out over half the equity capital of the GIPSIC banks, and in Greece and Cyprus more or less all of it. Since banks tend to hold

---

[70] Capital and reserves of the banking systems as of March 2013 amounted to € 54.9 bn in Greece, € 131.9 bn in Ireland, € 50.8 bn in Portugal, € 395.3 bn in Spain, € 388 bn in Italy, and € 13.9 bn in Cyprus. Deutsche Bundesbank, *Time Series Database, Time series MFI*, Aggregated balance sheet of euro area monetary financial institutions, excluding the Eurosystem / Liabilities / Capital and reserves, available at: <http://www.bundesbank. de/Navigation/EN/Statistics/Time_series_databases/ESCB_Time_Series/eszb_details_ value_node.html?tsId=BSI.M.U2.N.A.L60.X.1.Z5.0000.Z01.E&listId=outstanding_ amounts_48>. See also V. V. Acharya and S. Steffen, 'Falling Short of Expectations? Stress-testing the European Banking System', *VoxEU*, 17 January 2014, especially table 3, available at: <http://www.voxeu.org/article/what-asset-quality-review-likely-f ind-independent-evidence>.

Table 8.3 Maximum potential write-off losses for GIPSIC banks

Country	Write-off losses banking sector (€ bn)	Average (€ bn)	Average/ (capital and reserves)	Date	Source
Greece	41.5			Q4 2012	Forbes
	49.4	57.1	103.9%	Q4 2012	J. P. Morgan
	64.0			May 2013	Handelsblatt
	73.3			Q3 2013	IMF
Ireland	98.6	98.6	74.8%	Q3 2013	IMF
Portugal	31.6	32.6	64.1%	Q4 2012	J. P. Morgan
	33.5			Q3 2013	IMF
Spain	242.6			Q4 2012	J. P. Morgan
	246.9	227.3	57.5%	Q4 2012	Ernst & Young
	192.5			Q2 2013	IMF
Italy	245.5			Q2 2012	Forbes
	253.0			Q2 2012	J. P. Morgan
	232.2	251.2	64.7%	Q4 2012	Ernst & Young
	250.0			March 2013	Banca d'Italia
	275.4			Q2 2013	IMF
Cyprus	15.0	12.8	91.7%	Q4 2012	Forbes
	10.5			Q2 2013	IMF
Total		679.5	65.7%		

Sources: M. Melchiorre, 'With Cyprus, The EU Needs To Urgently Erase Europe's 'Nobody Loses' Mentality', *Forbes Capital Flows*, 22 March 2013 (Greece, Italy, Cyprus), available at: <http://elibrary-data. imf.org/Report.aspx?Report=4160276> (accessed on 27 March 2014); International Monetary Fund, *FSIs and Underlying Series* (Greece, Ireland, Portugal, Spain, Italy, Cyprus); N. Panigirtzoglou, S. MacGorain, M. Lehmann, L. Evans and J. Vakharia, 'Flows & Liquidity. NPL Timebomb', J. P. Morgan, *Global Asset Allocation*, 10 May 2013 (Greece, Portugal, Spain, Italy); G. Höhler, 'Die Last der faulen Kredite', *Handelsblatt*, 27 May 2013, p. 31; Ernst & Young, 'Outlook for Financial Services', *Ernst & Young Eurozone Forecast*, Winter Edition 2012/13 (Spain, Italy); F. Goria, 'Sulle banche italiane un macigno da 250 miliardi', *Linkiesta*, 16 July 2013; Deutsche Bundesbank, *Time Series Database, Time series MFI* (Greece, Ireland, Portugal, Spain, Italy, Cyprus), available at: <http://www.bundesbank.de/Navigation/EN/ Statistics/Time_series_databases/time_series_databases.html>.

Note: The figures show non-performing loans as an estimate of maximum potential write-off losses.

only slightly more equity capital than is required by regulators, the write-off losses would drive the average bank into insolvency. Of course, individual banks can be perfectly safe despite the catastrophic averages, but the more such safe banks there are, the more devastating the situation for the others must be, given the average write-off figures.

The maximum potential write-off losses are not only large relative to bank equity but also relative to the equity of the ESM, which would be utterly insufficient to cover them. As explained above, the paid-in equity capital of the ESM as of this writing (February 2014) is € 64.3 billion of the € 80 billion contemplated if all countries pay in their shares. In addition, € 620 billion are to be paid in later on demand, such that a total equity stock of € 700 billion will theoretically be available. This would be enough to just cover the maximum potential write-off losses of the GIPSIC banks, but if the money were used for this purpose, little would be left for the principal function of the ESM, namely helping states rather than banks.

The debt of the banks themselves, on the other hand, would be more than sufficient, as it is more than ten times larger than the maximum potential write-off losses or than the ESM capacity, for that matter. This is shown in Figure 8.4, which provides an overview of the public and banking debt of the crisis countries. The upper left column depicts their public debt, which by the end of 2013 added up to € 3.798 trillion. The longer column on the right depicts the debt of the banking sector, i.e. the money that the banks have borrowed in the market to finance their own lending and other investment. The bank debt totals € 8.163 trillion.

The bank debt is divided into three categories, shown as a dotted area, in grey and in white. White represents sight deposits, immediately accessible. Grey is savings deposits. Dotted represents all other kinds of bank debt, including, for example, interbank credit and bank debentures. The refinancing credit that banks receive from their own NCBs is included here as well.

Given that the € 8.163 trillion of bank debt comes from the consolidated national bank accounts, the liabilities that a bank has vis-à-vis other domestic banks have already been deducted. This sum is thus the net debt of the respective national banking systems. The cross-linkages among the crisis countries, however, could not be disentangled. Therefore, the figure shown for the overall debt of the GIPSIC banking systems must be interpreted with some caution.

Part of the debt of the banking sector was used to finance the holding of government bonds. This part of the inter-linkages, € 1.160 trillion, has been accounted for and is represented by the overlap between both columns.[71] If it is subtracted, the sum of GIPSIC banking and public debts amounted to € 10.801 trillion by December 2013, as depicted by the figure above the dashed line. This

---

[71] Loans to general government and holding of securities other than shares of general government in the aggregated balance sheet of euro area monetary financial institutions, see: Deutsche Bundesbank, *Time Series Database*, Time series MFI (Monetary Financial Institutions).

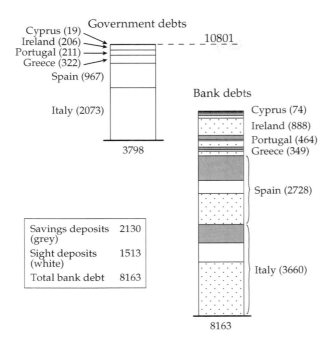

Figure 8.4 GIPSIC government and bank debt (December 2013, € billion)

Source: European Commission, Economic and Financial Affairs, Economic Databases and Indicators, AMECO – The annual macro-economic database; Deutsche Bundesbank, *Time Series Database*, Time series MFI (Monetary Financial Institutions); Ifo Institute calculations.

Note: The portion of the banks' deposits by Eurozone residents (excluding monetary financial institutions and governments) is depicted in white and grey, white standing for sight deposits and grey for savings deposits. Since the figures shown have been rounded, they do not add up to the round figure shown for the sum of the exact individual figures. Government debts 2013: European Commission forecast, November 2013.

represents 347% of the combined GDP of the crisis countries. In view of this truly staggering magnitude, it seems courageous to try to protect both the creditors of the GIPSIC governments and of their banks with taxpayer money from the still-solid economies of the Eurozone.

On the other hand, for exactly that reason, moderate haircuts to the debts of the banks of around 8.2% on average would be sufficient to cover the average of the maximum potential write-off losses. If sight deposits are to be excluded, 10.1% would be sufficient, and if savings deposits were also to be excluded, the necessary haircut would be 14.9%. These are certainly unpleasant figures for markets, but not exactly catastrophic. The situation is as it is. Shifting the losses to government budgets of the still-solvent countries in Europe would not make them smaller. Such a strategy would, for example, increase the average public debt-to-GDP ratio of the non-GIPSIC countries by ten percentage points, from 83% to 93%, if taxpayers were to be spared temporarily. (Later they will have to foot the bill anyway.) Alternatively, the maximum potential write-off losses would absorb one-seventh of today's VAT revenue of the non-GIPSIC countries for ten years (equivalent to increasing the public deficits by 1.0 % of GDP each year). The tax solutions would not only create wrong incentives for borrowers and lenders, they would also result in severe economic distortions due to tax avoidance and evasion activities, creating a considerable excess burden beyond the mere financial one.

These considerations have not remained hidden from the European Commission. After months of internal debates, the EC, on the occasion of the Cypriot crisis, changed the official strategy of postponing bail-ins until 2018 that it had proclaimed in June 2012. When the Cypriot banking system defaulted in March 2013, there was little political support for bailing out the Russian oligarchs and other rich investors who had parked their money there. The new head of the Eurogroup, Jeroen Dijsselbloem, and EU Commissioner Michel Barnier declared that henceforth there would be bail-ins following a clear pecking order for the losses to be allocated to different kinds of claimants.[72]

The Plan

Guidelines for the bail-in procedure and further details of the banking union were laid down by the EU Council and the EU Commission, serving as a basis for

---

[72] Directly after the bailout deal for Cypriot banks, Dijsselbloem suggested the Cyprus model and the involvement of creditors contained as a possible template for future cases, see also 'Cyprus Bailout: Dijsselbloem Remarks Alarm Markets', *BBC News*, 25 March 2013, available at: <http://www.bbc.co.uk/news/business-21920574>, or 'Bomb from Brussels: Cyprus Model May Guide Future Bank Bailouts', *Spiegel Online International*, 1 April 2013, available at: <http://www.spiegel.de/international/europe/cyprus-bank-bailout-model-has-increasing-numbers-of-adherents-in-eu-a-891849.html>. Barnier, who was responsible for drafting the proposal of the Single Resolution Mechanism, stated a similar opinion: 'I believe that [the public intervention] should happen only after shareholders, and all other creditors and uninsured depositors have been bailed in', see also N. Chrysoloras, 'Resolution Mechanism for Banking Union Can Be Created without Treaty Change, Says EU's Barnier', Interview with M. Barnier, *Ekathimerini*, 19 May 2013, available at: <http://www.ekathimerini.com/4dcgi/_w_articles_wsite2_1_19/05/2013_499678>. Barnier also indicated early on that his proposal included a pecking order for creditor participation; see also A. Roche, 'Europe Needs Clear Order for Loss Imposition in Bank Closures—ECB', *Reuters*, 12 April 2013, available at: <http://uk.reuters.com/article/2013/04/12/uk-eurozone-banks-asmussen-idUKBRE93B14S20130412>.

further negotiations with the European Parliament aimed at finalizing a regulation that is to be enacted before the end of the legislative period in May 2014, before this book is published.[73] The proposed legislation stipulates that shareholders and holders of convertible or junior bonds are to be bailed in first, up to 8% of a bank's (non-risk weighted) assets. Secondly, a Single Resolution Fund (SRF) to be endowed by the banks of the Eurozone is to be set up that would cover up to 5% of the bank's total assets should the 8% bail-in turn out to be insufficient.[74]

The 8% rule is proclaimed by politicians as a bail-in tool that protects taxpayers, but it is less protective than it sounds, as the 8% is to include the bank's equity.[75] Equity, whose normal function is to bear the losses, normally covers between 2% to 5% of a bank's total assets. Thus, the bail-in tool effectively means that creditor losses are limited to between 3% and 6% of a bank's balance sheet, not 8%.

Moreover, the priority of a bail-in is watered down because a surprisingly long list of exceptions is foreseen.[76] For example, deposits of up to € 100,000 are excluded, which is about the wealth of a median Dutch household or twice the wealth of a median German household.[77] The list of exceptions comprises pension claims, salaries of bank employees, liabilities from utility fees and taxes,

---

[73] See Council of the European Union, *Council Agrees General Approach on Single Resolution Mechanism*, press release 564, No. 17602/13, 18 December 2013, available at: <http://www.consilium.europa.eu/uedocs/cms_data/docs/pressdata/en/ecofin/140190.pdf>; European Commission, *Proposal for a Regulation Establishing Uniform Rules and a Uniform Procedure for the Resolution of Credit Institutions and Certain Investment Firms in the Framework of a Single Resolution Mechanism and a Single Bank Resolution Fund*, COM(2013) 520 final, 10 July 2013, esp. article 24, paragraph 3 and 7a, available at: <http://eur-lex.europa.eu/LexUriServ/LexUriServ.do?uri=COM:2013:0520:FIN:EN:PDF>; European Commission, *A Comprehensive EU Response to the Financial Crisis: Substantial Progress towards a Strong Financial Framework for Europe and a Banking Union for the Eurozone*, MEMO/14/57, 24 January 2014, available at: <http://europa.eu/rapid/press-release_MEMO-14-57_en.htm?locale=en>.

[74] See European Commission, *A Comprehensive EU Response to the Financial Crisis: Substantial Progress towards a Strong Financial Framework for Europe and a Banking Union for the Eurozone*, 24 January 2014, p. 5.

[75] See European Commission, *Proposal for a Regulation Establishing Uniform Rules and a Uniform Procedure for the Resolution of Credit Institutions and Certain Investment Firms in the Framework of a Single Resolution Mechanism and a Single Bank Resolution Fund*, 10 July 2013, article 24, paragraph 7.

[76] See European Commission, *Proposal for a Regulation Establishing Uniform Rules and a Uniform Procedure for the Resolution of Credit Institutions and Certain Investment Firms in the Framework of a Single Resolution Mechanism and a Single Bank Resolution Fund*, 10 July 2013, article 24, paragraph 3. See also Council of the European Union, *Council Agrees General Approach on Single Resolution Mechanism*, 18 December 2013.

[77] See Figure 2.12.

short-term interbank liabilities with a maturity of less than seven days, and a number of further items.

Next to the deposits, the most important item excepted from the bail-in is covered loans, i.e. loans collateralized with other assets, ranging from real estate (mortgage backed securities like the German Pfandbrief) to interbank credit claims.[78] While this exception looks quite natural at first glance, it is actually surprising, given that the collateral itself is already meant to secure the loans. The exception therefore provides a double security and is likely to bring in community funds if the collateral itself loses value. Thus, with this double security, EU institutions obviously want to create a class of super-safe assets ultimately protected by all participating countries.

Not much economic theory is necessary to predict that this would create grave moral hazard effects in the future. One such moral hazard effect would be circular trading among banks to artificially create collateral out of thin air. If people lend unsecured funds to their banks and the banks go bust, they would not normally get their money back. But suppose a number of banks had mutually exchanged debentures of equal value, which would make none of them richer or poorer and would not even result in net cash flows between them. Then each bank could give its outside creditors the debentures as collateral, and the creditors would then automatically be exempt from haircuts should these banks default. As explained in Chapter 5, banks used this trick to generate collateral for drawing refinancing credit from central banks. They could obviously also use it to protect their private creditors from bail-ins so as to be able to borrow at very low rates.

Apart from that, banks would be able to use mediocre collateral to borrow at artificially low rates to finance the inferior real investment projects as they did in the years before the crisis. This would help preserve the asset values and avoid losses, to the benefit of wealth owners in general, but it would also imply that the burning of capital that had characterized the pre-crisis period in southern Europe can continue. The inefficient use of scarce savings capital would result in many years of continued stagnation of the Eurozone.

German Landesbanks, state-owned investment banks that used to play an important role in the German capital market, show what kinds of inefficiencies can be expected. As the Landesbanks' creditors enjoyed unlimited state guarantees (*Gewährträgerhaftung*), they recklessly endowed the Landesbanks with low-interest funds which the Landesbanks then invested in often dubious assets throughout the world.[79] The EU Commission deprived these banks

---

[78] See European Commission, *Proposal for a Regulation Establishing Uniform Rules and a Uniform Procedure for the Resolution of Credit Institutions and Certain Investment Firms in the Framework of a Single Resolution Mechanism and a Single Bank Resolution Fund*, 10 July 2013, article 24, paragraph 3.

[79] For an early criticism and documentation of the Landesbanks' reckless investment behaviour see H.-W. Sinn, *The German State Banks. Global Players in the International Financial Markets*, Edward Elgar, Aldershot 1999.

of their privileges in a landmark decision in 2002,[80] forcing them to abandon their business model. This led to serious troubles for most of them. WestLB, Germany's third biggest Landesbank, had to be liquidated because the European Commission forbade the state of North Rhine-Westphalia to subsidize it. Given this justified and tough stance of the Commission, it is all the more surprising that this same institution now advocates similar kinds of guarantees for all banks of the Eurozone. North Rhine-Westphalian taxpayers are not allowed to bail out their own state bank, but they may have to participate in bailing out banks in other euro countries.

The big questions on the banking union are how to endow the SRF, and under what conditions it will help the banks' creditors. The Commission proposes a gradual transition to a common resolution system. It stipulates that each country is to establish a national resolution fund, and that the national funds will then gradually merge over a period of ten years. In the first year, the cost of resolving a bank—after the 8% bail-in and up to 5% of the balance sheet—is entirely borne by the national fund, but with each consecutive year an additional part of the cost is to be shared by all other funds in proportion to their size finally the cost of resolution would be fully shared by all national funds. The national funds, in turn, are to be set up with contributions by the banking industry and, if insufficient, by national governments. The target is to eventually endow the SRF with funds equivalent to 1% of deposits, a sum of around € 55 billion.[81]

There are many unresolved questions at this stage. One is what happens if a country's banks, or the country itself, are unable to endow the national resolution fund. There are plans to solve this problem by allowing the SRF to leverage its budget by borrowing funds in the market under the joint protection of taxpayers.[82] This could turn the SRF into a further community fund similar to the ESM.

The biggest problem is that the volume envisioned for the SRF is tiny relative to the maximum potential write-off losses of the GIPSIC banks, which could amount to up to € 680 billion, as reported in Table 8.3. If the write-off losses were spread equally across all GIPSIC banks, that would not be a problem,

---

[80] See European Commission, press release, *Understanding on Anstaltslast and Gewährträgerhaftung 07 17 2001*, available at: <http:// europa.eu/rapid/press-release_IP-02-343_en.doc >.

[81] See European Commission, *Proposal for a Regulation Establishing Uniform Rules and a Uniform Procedure for the Resolution of Credit Institutions and Certain Investment Firms in the Framework of a Single Resolution Mechanism and a Single Bank Resolution Fund*, 10 July 2013, chapter 4.3: *The Single Bank Resolution Fund*.

[82] Cf. P. Spiegel and A. Barker, 'ECB Blow to European Bank Backstop', *Financial Times*, 18 December 2013, available at: available at: <http://www.ft.com/intl/cms/s/o/64 49c452-678a-11e3-a5f9-00144feabdco.html#axzz2uRh2lasR >.

since these losses, as mentioned above, account for just 8.3% of the sum of all GIPSIC bank debt, which is equivalent to 7.4% of all GIPSIC bank assets (their aggregate balance sheet). Thus, the 8% bail-in rule could take care of all the losses in such a symmetric case. However, the write-off losses will certainly *not* be spread equally, but instead be concentrated on certain individual banks, where they may reach high percentages of these banks' balance sheets. Suppose, for example, that only five banks in the GIPSIC countries, with a joint balance sheet of € 1 trillion and an equity-asset ratio of 5%, lose half of their assets. Then the bail-in rule will yield a maximum of € 80 billion, of which creditors would bear € 30 billion in losses provided the exceptions from the bail-in are not binding, leaving an uncovered loss of at least € 420 billion, about eight times the entire SRF volume.

The European Commission has foreseen this difficulty and therefore advocates the build-up of a common backstop fund for the SRF, which it labels 'alternative financing sources'. This could be endowed by the ESM, bringing us back to the discussion of the last section. But it is entirely unclear, and still subject to negotiations at this writing, whether the ESM or a new kind of community fund will be brought into the mechanism.[83]

All in all, the impression from the preparations for the banking union is that, while nominally adhering to the principle of creditor bail-in, decisions are being prepared that would in fact bail them out at the expense of taxpayers. Given the long list of exemptions, the banks and their creditors will probably try to restructure the debt so that practically all creditors are protected. Taxpayers will then ultimately have no other choice but to foot most of the bill.

The community of states should protect itself against such a scenario by imposing rules on the minimum amount of liable equity and debt. First of all the equity-asset ratios should be significantly increased. The eight percent equity relative to risk-weighted assets—which typically is not more than two percent of total assets—that the Basel III agreement requires is definitely not enough.[84] It is also not enough to require in addition a minimum equity-asset ratio of three percent from 2018 onwards, as has been stipulated by the Basel III agreement.[85]

---

[83] See European Commission, *Proposal for a Regulation Establishing Uniform Rules and a Uniform Procedure for the Resolution of Credit Institutions and Certain Investment Firms in the Framework of a Single Resolution Mechanism and a Single Bank Resolution Fund*, 10 July 2013, article 24, paragraph 9.

[84] See Bank for International Settlements, *Basel III: A Global Regulatory Framework for More Resilient Banks and Banking Systems*, December 2010 (revised June 2011), p. 12; H.-W. Sinn, *Casino Capitalism*, 2010, chapter 7: *Policy Failure*, p. 141.

[85] See Bank for International Settlements, *Basel III: A Global Regulatory Framework for More Resilient Banks and Banking Systems*, December 2010 (revised June 2011), p. 61.

In reality, equity provisions that would avoid fiscal externalities being imposed on debtors and taxpayers would have to be a multiple of this.[86]

In addition, banks could be forced to attract hybrid capital endowed with a junior rank. The so-called CoCos (Contingent Convertible Bonds) would be ideal for that purpose. If a bank incurs losses that exceed certain threshold fractions of its equity, CoCos would automatically be converted into equity capital, according to pre-specified rules, to fill the gap.[87]

Unfortunately, however, no such rules beyond the overly weak Basel rules will be introduced, since some countries, notably France, have objected to a common minimum regulation for hybrid capital and insist that each country implement the necessary rules at its own discretion.[88] While there are strong economic reasons for a banking union in the sense of regulating the banks jointly, and weak reasons for pooling the losses, the political process seems to be moving exactly in the opposite direction, namely towards much pooling and weak regulation.

Bailing out the ECB

While there is broad agreement among economists that common banking supervision and resolution rules are necessary in the Eurozone, there is less agreement on the question of who should be responsible for these tasks.

This issue is important insofar as the ECB decisions on collateral and refinancing policy analysed in the previous chapters are evidence that collective decision-making is by no means sufficient to exclude moral hazard effects.

---

[86] This is, for instance, emphasized by Admati and Hellwig, who argue that banks need much more equity, at least on the order of 25% of their balance sheet total, which is about ten times as much as today; see A. Admati and M. Hellwig, *The Bankers' New Clothes*, 2013; and A. Admati and M. Hellwig, 'Does Debt Discipline Bankers? An Academic Myth about Bank Indebtedness', February 2013.

[87] See B. Rudolph, 'Die Einführung regulatorischen Krisenkapitals in Form von Contingent Convertible Bonds (CoCos)', *Zeitschrift für das gesamte Kreditwesen* 62, 2010, pp. 1152–1155, in particular p. 1153; as well as B. Albul, D. M. Jaffee, and A. Tchistyi, 'Contingent Convertible Bonds and Capital Structure Decisions', *Coleman Fung Risk Management Research Center Working Paper* No. 2010-01, available at: <http://escholar-ship.org/uc/item/95821712#page-2>.

[88] The national authorities are allowed to individually 'set minimum requirements for own funds and eligible liabilities (MREL) for each institution, based on its size, risk and business model', in order to ensure the capacity to absorb losses, until at least 2016, when a review clause 'would enable the Commission, based on recommendations by the European Banking Authority, to introduce a harmonised MREL applicable to all banks'; see Council of the European Union, *Council Agrees Position on Bank Resolution*, press release 270 No. 11228/13, 27 June 2013, available at: <http://www.consilium.europa.eu/uedocs/cms_data/docs/pressdata/en/ecofin/137627.pdf>, p. 4.

Majority decisions are no protection against the exploitation of minorities, and when the voting rights are unrelated to country size, they may not even be democratic. Care must thus be taken to endow the decision-making bodies with democratic representation and to agree to a sufficiently large quorum so as to protect minorities against exploitation by majorities.

According to a decision of the European Parliament and the European Commission of 19 March 2013, the supervisory function shall be given to an authority named the Single Supervisory Mechanism (SSM), led by the ECB.[89] Within the SSM, the ECB ensures the consistent application of uniform supervisory standards and is responsible for key tasks concerning the prudential supervision of banks. In principle, the ECB is to supervise all 6,000 banks in the Eurozone, but for the time being it will be responsible for the largest ones only, those with a balance sheet total of at least € 30 billion. The other banks would continue to be supervised nationally, but national supervision would be monitored by the ECB.

The ECB would also participate in deciding when a bank needs to be wound up by the so-called Single Resolution Mechanism (SRM). There is a very complex decision structure involving the Single Resolution Board (SRB), the ECB Governing Council, the European Commission, the EU Council, and national resolution authorities. While the SRB would have the leading voice, the ECB, as the supervisory authority, proposes initiating a resolution and also participates in the SRB together with the European Commission and the relevant national authority.[90]

Before the SSM and SRM initiate their activities, a stress test for European banks will be conducted to ensure, so its proponents say, that no banks will smuggle toxic legacy assets into the banking union, forcing national authorities

---

[89] See Council of the European Union, 'Council Regulation (EU) No 1024/2013 of 15 October 2013 conferring specific tasks on the European Central Bank concerning policies relating to the prudential supervision of credit institutions', *Official Journal* L 287/63, available at: < http://eur-lex.europa.eu/LexUriServ/LexUriServ.do?uri=OJ: L:2013:287:0063:0089:EN:PDF>. See also European Commission, *An Important Step Towards a Real Banking Union in Europe, Statement by Commissioner Michel Barnier Following the Trilogue Agreement on the Creation of the Single Supervisory Mechanism for the Eurozone*, MEMO/13/251, 19 March 2013, available at: <http://europa.eu/rapid/press-release_MEMO-13-251_en.htm?locale=en#PR_metaPressRelease_bottom>.

[90] See European Commission, *Proposal for a Regulation Establishing Uniform Rules and a Uniform Procedure for the Resolution of Credit Institutions and Certain Investment Firms in the Framework of a Single Resolution Mechanism and a Single Bank Resolution Fund*, 10 July 2013, chapter 4.1: *A Single Resolution Mechanism;* European Commission, *Commission Proposes Single Resolution Mechanism for the Banking Union*, press release IP/13/674, 10 July 2013, available at: <http://europa.eu/rapid/press-release_IP-13-674_en.htm?locale=en>.

or the ESM to bear more losses than they assumed. [91] The stress test will be carried out by the European Banking Authority (EBA), an independent EU institution that is part of the European System of Financial Supervision, based on a prior asset quality review by the ECB. The review, which has been conducted since November 2013, is expected to take a year.[92] Given that the ECB will need to hire about 1,000 personnel and mould it into an efficient organization to perform this task, the undertaking seems fairly challenging.[93]

The decision to involve the ECB is problematic insofar as the ECB Governing Council is not a democratically controlled institution and is the biggest creditor of the banks of the crisis-stricken countries, given that it bailed them out with the printing press against bad collateral. In fact, it must be feared that the ECB has only weak incentives to act against the smuggling of toxic assets into the banking union, given that write-off losses showing up before the establishment of the banking union might severely hit the ECB itself, and given that the occurrence of such losses inside the banking union could be cushioned with community funds. It must be feared, therefore, that the ECB will conduct a rather lax asset quality review, in particular with regard to the assets of the GIPSIC countries, because it is the banks of these countries to which it lent out three quarters of its monetary base (see Figure 6.7). It may let a few banks fail so as to preserve its credibility, but measures to thoroughly clean the balance sheets of banks cannot be expected. The incentives for truly cleaning the balance sheets could have been expected from an institution like the ESM, which would suffer from the asset smuggling, not from the ECB, which would benefit from it.

In this regard it is important to note that the covered loans protected from a bail-in described above include the ECB's refinancing credit, which was collateralized with increasingly bad assets during the crisis: as explained in Chapter 5, these were often non-investment grade assets. It will likely even include ELA credit that NCBs handed out, allegedly at their own risk, against self-defined collateral. The collateral and ELA policies resulted in the € 613 billion in GIPSIC Target liabilities by December 2013, which is quite a sizeable sum when compared to the € 353 billion overall equity capital of the central bank system available at that time. The reputation, if not the functioning, of the Eurosystem would be severely damaged if central banks had to bear their share in the write-off

---

[91] Cf. Eurogroup, *ESM Direct Bank Recapitalisation Instrument—Main Features of the Operational Framework and Way Forward*, p. 3, 'A Robust Valuation'.

[92] See European Central Bank, *ECB Starts Comprehensive Assessment in Advance of Supervisory Role*, press release, 23 October 2013 available at: <http://www.ecb.europa.eu/press/pr/date/2013/html/pr131023.en.html>.

[93] See N. Comfort, 'Draghi Raids Bankers in Rush to Hire 1,000 for Supervisor', *Bloomberg News*, 9 January 2014, available at: <http://www.bloomberg.com/news/2014-01-08/draghi-raids-bankers-in-rush-to-hire-1-000-for-supervisor.html>.

losses of the GIPSIC's banking system (see Table 8.3). This could explain why the ECB has insisted in the negotiations on the banking union that the ESM acts as a backstop for the losses. The ESM may then ultimately have to bear the cost of the ECB's overly lax collateral policy to maintain the illusion that the money on display is necessary to establish the right equilibrium without it ever being taken.

For the taxpayers of the still-sound euro economies, repackaging of write-off losses from the ECB to the ESM should not matter, since they would have to bear them anyway—through the ECB's reduction of seignorage distribution or through ESM equity losses. However, the ECB would keep its hands clean and feel justified to continue with its problematic refinancing strategy.

In well-intended speeches, politicians proclaimed that community funds are to come in only to protect against future bank losses occurring under the joint responsibility of a common Eurozone supervisory system. However, this would not solve the ECB's and the banks' immediate problems. Thus, the ESM in practice may also have to assume the losses stemming from the banks' legacy assets that accrued prior to the establishment of the banking union, when national authorities were responsible for regulating the banks and when the ECB helped out with hundreds of billions of euros in cheap refinancing credit. The new rules propounded by the Eurogroup might boil down to bailing out the ECB with ESM funds.

This bail out strategy complements the entire rescue architecture, as explained above. When private creditors shied away from financing southern European banks and sovereigns, the ECB provided the six crisis-stricken countries with about one trillion euros in extra credit from the local printing presses (see Figures 6.2 and 6.3) and asked non-GIPSIC NCBs to buy about € 100 billion worth of government bonds under its Securities Markets Programme (see Figure 8.1). The parliaments and other political institutions then had to bail out the ECB with the fiscal rescue packages EFSF, EFSM and ESM, as well as IMF money. However, while this help went to the sovereigns rather than the banks, the banking union is intended to bail out the ECB in an even more direct way, by bailing out the banks or by serving as a back-stop offering insurance to private investors brave enough to finance the banks under the protection of the ESM.

Undermining the Market Economy and Democracy

For more than half a decade now, the ECB and the fiscal rescue funds have been pumping fresh public capital and escorting private capital with the open or hidden protection of taxpayers to places where private investors, who realized that it was a mistake to follow the regulatory incentives, had no longer wanted to invest. This is probably the largest regional investment steering programme in history.

The very first steps of this programme have prevented the collapse of parts of the Eurozone and were therefore defensible. When the collapse of the global financial system at the time of the Lehman crisis was imminent, the rescue measures helped to avert disaster.

However, when the world economy recovered in 2009 and it became clear that southern Europe suffered from structural competitiveness problems and over-indebtedness rather than a mere temporary lack of market trust that caused liquidity problems, the European policies became objectionable. As the Irish and eastern European recovery stories showed, less public support would have meant more reforms, earlier wage cuts, and even some deflation, improving the competitiveness of such economies.[94] While Chapter 4 argued that an overly rigorous deflation strategy is dangerous because it would drive private and public debtors into bankruptcy, it was certainly not appropriate that all southern countries kept inflating for years after the outbreak of the crisis as if nothing had happened. Inflation of the GDP price level in Greece only stopped in Q3 2010, and then turned into a slight deflation. However, in Portugal and Italy inflation of GDP prices has not yet stopped up to this writing (Q3 2013). In fact, Portugal recently inflated even faster than the average of the Eurozone (see Figure 4.8). Only Cyprus and Spain entered a sizeable real devaluation after Q3 2012 (Cyprus), and Q1 2013 (Spain) respectively.[95]

The steering of capital flows is not generally appropriate for a capitalist market economy, because its allocative superiority over socialist systems results primarily from the fact that the allocation of the factors of production is determined by market forces rather than politics. Behind each unit of capital invested in the real economy, generating output and enhancing wage productivity, stands a wealth owner and financial investor who carefully tries to optimize his or her asset portfolio so as to keep risks small and earn a high rate of return. The caution and sleepless nights of this investor are the driving force of capitalism and a major reason for its allocative efficiency relative to other systems tried in history.

In view of this general presumption, interventions by public authorities that effectively change the spatial allocation of capital relative to what the market

---

[94] See also D. Gros and C. Alcidi, 'Country Adjustment to a Sudden Stop: Does the Euro Make a Difference?', *European Commission Economic Papers* 492, April 2013, available at: <http://ec.europa.eu/economy_finance/publications/economic_paper/2013/pdf/ecp492_en.pdf>.

[95] See Eurostat, Database, *Economy and Finance,* Quarterly National Accounts, GDP and Main Components, Price Indices, Gross Domestic Product, Seasonally Adjusted and Adjusted Data by Working Days. Note that inflation and deflation in this book refer to changes in the GDP deflator, as this is what matters for competitiveness. Consumer prices are less relevant, as they exclude investment goods and include imports.

would have chosen need very strong arguments that substantiate the existence of externalities or other market failures. And not only that. As Public Choice theory has convincingly demonstrated, policymakers also bear the burden of proving that the political distortions from which their interventions usually suffer weigh less than the market distortions they intend to correct.[96] The risk is too large that seemingly justified interventions may turn out to be rent-seeking machinery.[97]

The ECB does not deliver much in this respect. It defends its policies as being of a monetary nature, although the fiscal implications are obvious, arguing that they are necessary to maintain the monetary transmission process within the Eurozone.[98] Its basic premise is that the nominal short-term interest rates for collateralized credit should be equal everywhere in a common currency area, since the underlying collateral is perfectly safe. However, in view of the truly extreme lowering of collateral standards described in Chapter 5, in particular the scope given to individual NCBs in defining their own national standards, this is unconvincing. The banks of the GIPSIC countries definitely were more than satisfied with the combination of interest rates, maturities, and collateral standards that the ECB offered, since otherwise the Target balances could not have ballooned. The Target balances are proof of the ECB's systematic under-cutting of market conditions in some of the euro countries.

The ECB might even acknowledge that such was the case because, in its view, markets fail and need to be corrected. Since it maintains that the haircuts it applies daily to the collateral are sufficient to make the refinancing credit safe, the markets are at fault if they do not believe that this is the case and thus refrain from providing interbank credit under similar conditions.

This reasoning is also applied to government bonds. While the ECB accepts that there are risk premia for longer-term government bonds, it argues that the risk premia charged by markets are not justified to the extent that they stem from a redenomination risk (and other forms of over-pricing of risks by the markets). Markets are pricing in a redenomination risk related to a potential

---

[96] See W. A. Niskanen, *Bureaucracy and Representative Government*, Aldine-Atherton, New York 1971; H. Leibenstein, 'Allocative Efficiency and "X-Efficiency"', *American Economic Review* 56, 1966, pp. 392–415; G. Brennan and J. M. Buchanan, *The Power to Tax: Analytical Foundations of a Fiscal Constitution*, Cambridge University Press, Cambridge 1980.

[97] See G. Tullock, 'The Welfare Costs of Tariffs, Monopolies, and Theft', *Western Economic Journal* 5, 1967, pp. 224–232.

[98] See J. Asmussen, *Introductory Statement by the ECB in the Proceedings before the Federal Constitutional Court*, Karlsruhe, 11 June 2013, available at: <http://www.ecb.int/press/key/date/2013/html/sp130611.en.html>; for the detailed statement, see F. Schorkopf, *Stellungnahme der Europäischen Zentralbank*, 16 January 2013.

break-up of the euro which is not justified.[99] Thus, it intervenes with the OMT to keep the interest spreads low.

However, this argument is not convincing insofar as the risk of a euro break-up as such cannot explain differential risk premia between the euro countries; it can at best explain a risk premium of Eurozone assets relative to those of other currency areas with more inherent stability. Differential risk premia result from the expectation that some countries, after returning to their own currencies, would depreciate relative to others, but if so, this is because the price levels of these countries are too high, as discussed in Chapter 4, and need a realignment to regain competitiveness and debt-sustainability. Thus, the risk premia the ECB wants to eliminate are not the result of market failure but of rational and correct expectations on the part of investors. After all, investors will, with some probability, be repaid with a devalued currency, and the debtors' burden will be relieved insofar as their real repayment obligation in terms of internationally tradeable goods is reduced after a redenomination of their debt. They would be better off than in the case where their country had to undergo a real depreciation within the Eurozone by cutting wages and prices, because such a real depreciation would not reduce their debt burden. An outright currency depreciation after a euro break up that comes along with a conversion of debt into national currency means that both the creditor's interest return and the debtor's interest burden in real terms are reduced. It is therefore rational and efficient that both parties compensate for that possibility by settling for higher nominal interest rates.

This point touches on some of the first principles of economics, as it is one of the fundamental efficiency conditions of capital markets that capital be allocated among rival uses in a way that makes the sum of the marginal rate of return and the rate of expected price increase of an asset, measured in terms of a common numéraire, identical across all assets.[100] Following this rule ensures that a society's available stock of capital is allocated among competing uses in a Pareto-optimal way, i.e. in a way that maximizes present consumption without imposing a disadvantage on future generations. Thus, it is mandatory for the redenomination risk to be fully reflected in nominal interest rates, in the sense that the nominal rate minus the expected currency depreciation (minus a potential default probability) is equated across all countries and assets, in order to avoid wasting resources and to stimulate Eurozone growth. The ECB's interpretation of interest spreads resulting from redenomination risk as evidence market failure is simply wrongheaded.

[99] See F. Schorkopf, *Stellungnahme der Europäischen Zentralbank*, 16 January 2013, p. 20; and A. Di Cesare, G. Grande, M. Manna, and M. Taboga, 'Stime recenti dei premi per il rischio sovrano di alcuni paesi dell'area dell'euro' (Recent estimates of sovereign risk premia for euro-area countries), *Banca d'Italia Occasional Paper* 128, September 2012, available at: <http://www.bancaditalia.it/pubblicazioni/econo/quest_ecofin_2/qef128>.

[100] See R. Dorfman, R. M. Solow, and P. A. Samuelson, *Linear Programming and Economic Analysis*, McGraw-Hill, New York 1958.

For the same reason, there is nothing wrong with markets pricing the redenomination risk into the yields private companies have to pay. The considerations of the ECB to counteract such risk premia through the establishment of an actively managed ABS market for company risk are as flawed as the attempts to reduce the risk premia of states by way of its OMT programme.[101]

When the ECB advocates its policies in terms of easing monetary policy transmission it understandably tries to demonstrate that it remains within the tight legal mandate that it has been given. In fact, however, it is carrying out a regional fiscal policy that effectively subsidizes capital flows from northern to southern Europe by offering free-of-charge insurance for these flows. In the absence of a valid economic justification, this can be expected to distort the optimal allocation of resources and hamper growth in Europe, thus maintaining the Eurozone's laggard position relative to the rest of the world (see Figure 1.1).

The policy of forcing markets to compete with the printing press, also known as financial repression, can also be criticized because it deprives savers of some of the returns on their investment.[102] Rather than being able to earn risk-commensurate rates of return in countries that have over-borrowed, they have to content themselves with the conditions that the ECB Governing Council deems appropriate. Instead of lending directly, they offer their savings to their NCBs, which absorb the liquidity created by the corresponding Target balances. The Eurosystem thus effectively operates like a public purchasing organization that acquires savings from the north and determines the conditions under which these savings can be delivered to the south.

While this policy has helped the over-indebted states to reduce their budget deficits and the commercial banks of the crisis countries to recapitalize without having to hand over shares to those who provided the new capital, it has burdened the savers and their institutions. The capital-exporting banks of the

---

[101] ECB president M. Draghi announced on 2 May 2013 that the ECB had established a task force, together with the European Investment Bank (EIB), to assess ways to unblock lending to SMEs, for instance, by promoting a market for asset-backed securities (ABS) based on SME loans; see Introductory Statement to the Press Conference (with Q&A) by Mario Draghi, President of the ECB, and Vítor Constâncio, Vice-President of the ECB, 2 May 2013, available at: <http://www.ecb.int/press/pressconf/2013/html/is130502.en.html>. Whether this initiative implies that the ECB will itself buy ABS is unknown at present but, as M. Draghi has stated, the ECB 'is looking at all possible options'. So far, the ECB emphasizes that it does not have a precise position on what it will do and is 'far from reaching any conclusion'; see also Introductory Statement to the Press Conference (with Q&A) by Mario Draghi, President of the ECB, and Vítor Constâncio, Vice-President of the ECB, 2 May 2013.

[102] See S. Eijffinger, 'The Age of Financial Repression', *Project Syndicate*, 21 November 2012, available at: <http://www.project-syndicate.org/commentary/western-governments--increasing-use-of-financial-repression-by-sylvester-eijffinger-and-edin-mujagic>.

north have suffered from a severe profit squeeze; worker pension funds have run into difficulties; charitable foundations, which must live on interest income and cannot use their endowments, have had to cut their budgets; and life insurance companies have been forced to lower the guaranteed minimum interest. All of this has severely undermined trust in financial markets and supported a re-orientation towards the traditional pay-as-you-go pension system, which will be unable to cope with Europe's foreseeable demographic quagmire.

Europeans cannot live from hand to mouth for the simple reason that the ratio of mouths to hands will double in many countries by the middle of the century. Germany's baby boomers, for example, are about 50 years old as of this writing, but they have very few children. In fifteen to twenty years, when they realize that their private savings are insufficient, they will demand more from the next generation than it can fulfil. Ugly distributional clashes are all but preordained.

Figure 4.2 showed that the interest advantage that the GIPSIC countries enjoyed as a result of the rescue operations by the ECB and the community of states, as well as a profit squeeze on multinationals, amounted to € 209 billion in the five crisis years 2008–2012, of which the last year alone accounted for € 67 billion, or about 3% of GIPSIC net foreign debt. This sum was calculated by comparing the actual net investment income flowing from the GIPSIC countries to the rest of the world with a hypothetical income resulting from multiplying the net foreign debt position of these countries, as built up through current account deficits, with the average interest rate paid on net foreign debt in Q4 2007, before the explosion of market rates. Repeating a similar calculation for Germany, Europe's biggest creditor country, shows an investment income loss of € 197 billion in the five years from 2008 to 2012, and € 58 billion for the year 2012 alone. The latter sum amounts to about 5.3% of Germany's net foreign asset position, which itself shrank during the five years by € 336 billion euros due to write-off losses on foreign assets resulting from the dramatic increase in the market rates of interest, as discussed in Chapter 2 (Section *The Foreign Debt Problem*).

The path Europe has taken with the ESM and, in particular, the extensive ECB interventions, leads away from a market economy towards a system in which central planning authorities allocate funds across regions, using dubious ideological arguments when explaining their policies to the public. By doing so, these institutions behave like the typical bureaucratic organization, as described in the Public Choice textbooks, caught in rent-seeking activities.[103]

In Europe it is no longer the portfolio decisions of wealth owners but political forces that determine the spatial allocation of investment capital. This not only has grave negative implications for the dynamism and efficiency of the

---

[103] See G. Brennan and J. M. Buchanan, *The Power to Tax: Analytical Foundations of a Fiscal Constitution*, 1980, as well as M. Olson, *The Logic of Collective Action: Public Goods and the Theory of Groups*, 1965.

continent, but it is also creating political power centres that may undermine democracy. It is true that the ECB came into existence through democratic decisions. However, its current decisions are made by a technocratic body whose voting rules are not compatible with the idea of democracy, which gives every citizen the same weight in the decision-making process while protecting minority rights. A truly democratic decision-making process would need permanent democratic control over all decisions that have grave fiscal implications and are more than just narrowly defined monetary policies aimed at keeping the price level constant. To satisfy the rules of democracy, it is not sufficient for an institution to have once been established by a democratic decision.

The power wielded by the ECB is particularly problematic, since this institution is able to pre-determine future democratic decisions by limiting the scope of fiscal policy options available to parliaments. This is the path-dependence described in the introduction to this chapter which, parallel to the GIPSIC countries' competitiveness trap, leads to a liability trap for the other euro countries.

After the ECB allowed the GIPSIC countries to solve their financial needs with the printing press, turning the northern euro countries into Target creditors to the tune of € 1,002 billion in the summer of 2012, and after the Eurosystem had purchased over € 200 billion worth of government bonds through the SMP, democratically elected policymakers were no longer free to refrain from bailing out the GIPSIC countries and their banks with community funds, because this was effectively a policy of bailing out the ECB itself. Had they objected to doing so, the euro might have collapsed, the ECB would have been bankrupt, and the northern countries would have lost their Target claims. Obviously, the prior decisions of the ECB Governing Council forced the subsequent decision of European parliaments to set up the ESM to rescue the states and banks of the GIPSIC countries as well as their creditors, including the ECB. When parliaments were finally asked, no other alternative was left. They effectively bowed to the ECB Governing Council. The Governing Council put the gold credit card on the table, parliaments were annoyed to see that it was maxed out, and saw themselves forced to place the platinum card next to it to avoid surpassing the credit limit.

A similar risk will now occur with the OMT. Currently, the OMT is an insurance contract that has not yet paid out any indemnification, but the day will come when the ECB will have to keep its promise and buy huge quantities of GIPSIC government bonds to dampen the next wave of the crisis. When this happens, the Eurosystem's balance sheets will become loaded with government bonds, and the Eurosystem will have to reduce its refinancing credit to sterilize the impact on the money supply, possibly even to the negative range by borrowing funds from the banks in net terms. More and more NCBs will turn from net creditors to net debtors vis-à-vis their banking systems, following the example of Germany and Finland, whose central banks were pushed into this situation through the Target credit that they had to provide (see Figure 6.8). In this situation, it will be very tempting for the Eurosystem to stop the sterilization and resort to inflationary financing, and hard for the parliaments to say no to Eurobonds, which would allow the ECB to refrain from buying the government bonds.

Eurobonds are jointly guaranteed bonds that the individual states issue to finance their budgets and to redeem maturing old debt. Thanks to the joint guarantees, all states pay the same rate of interest, regardless of whether they will be able to redeem the bonds. Eurobonds will enable the ECB to get rid of the government bonds it holds on its books by reassuring investors who buy such bonds that they will get their money back.

The OMT insurance promise has effectively turned the government bonds of the Eurozone countries into a kind of Eurobond, since the repurchase promise involves the same kind of risk mutualization that Eurobonds offer. From a legal perspective, the step from the OMT to Eurobonds may be large, but from an economic perspective it is very small, and given that it is so small, it would not be a big deal for parliaments to sanction what has already become common practice.

While those who have always wanted Eurobonds might welcome this development, they must acknowledge that in this situation, too, parliaments will no longer be free to accept or decline their adoption. Today, there is strong opposition to Eurobonds in some Eurozone parliaments, and in Germany's in particular. This opposition will vaporize as soon as the ECB begins any large-scale purchases of government bonds of southern countries. Whether the outcome is eventually right or wrong, the decision procedure certainly is not right. Europe would move towards debt mutualization because a technocratic body, where Malta has the same voting power as Germany or France, foreordains the decision.

Unfortunately, things will not stop there, since Eurobonds will probably lead to even more borrowing, given that countries that over-borrow know that they can no longer be punished by capital markets demanding higher yields. The inability of certain parts of the European community to repay their debts will result in a situation whereby the compelling logic of stumbling from one wave of the crisis to the next by doing just enough to avoid disaster will ultimately require converting the Eurozone into a transfer union.

Again, the necessary steps will be decided democratically by the parliaments of the day, but the policymaking's path-dependency will already have severely reduced the scope for possible actions. What appears to be a democratic decision will, in fact, be a consequence of the prior decisions taken by the ECB Governing Council. Thus parliaments become vicarious agents of the ECB Governing Council, which is the true hegemon of the Eurozone.

The OMT has calmed down the situation by shifting the investment risk from investors to ordinary people: taxpayers, state pensioners, and other people whose livelihood depends on the state. Since investors are well-informed optimizers, who are always on guard and shy away after the slightest hint of trouble, while ordinary people tend to be slow to react, trust the state, and believe in the protection it offers, this redistribution has poured oil onto troubled waters for the time being. However, when ordinary people realize the burden imposed on the state that they have to finance and from which they receive their pensions and incomes, their mood may change and they may be spurred into taking action. That could be far more dangerous to the stability of the western world than a temporary financial crisis. To be specific: the foreseeable dangers of Europe's demography problem fifteen to twenty years from now are already immense. Adding the liability risk of avoiding a financial crisis with taxpayer money to this demographic problem is a recipe for potential political turmoil and disaster, which dwarfs the horrors of a mere financial crisis.

At best, Europe will turn into an economic system in which some countries and regions permanently rely on transfers from others, such as eastern Germany or the Italian Mezzogiorno today, and suffer from a permanent Dutch Disease, a situation where their goods are permanently overpriced, unemployment is high, and transfer dependence is perpetuated.[104]

This fate should be averted by rethinking the euro construct. Ferdinand Kirchhof, Vice President of the German Constitutional Court, expressed this with words to which little needs to be added:[105]

> We must not jump from this problem to that problem, but should, with prudence, rethink the overall concept of the euro and the European Union.... The union has to re-organize its inner structure, sharpen the relationship between itself and the member states and, above all, become more democratic.

---

[104] See also G. Sinn and H.-W. Sinn, *Jumpstart—The Economic Unification of Germany*, MIT Press, Cambridge 1992; H.-W. Sinn, *Can Germany Be Saved? The Malaise of the World's First Welfare State*, MIT Press, Cambridge 2007, chapter 5: *The Withering East*, especially pp. 163–169; H.-W. Sinn and F. Westermann, 'Due Mezzogiorni', *L'industria* 27, 2006, pp. 49–51, English version as H.-W. Sinn and F. Westermann, 'Two Mezzogiornos', *NBER Working Paper* No. 8125, February 2001. For the Dutch Disease, see N. M. Corden and J. P. Neary, 'Booming Sector and De-Industrialization in a Small Open Economy', *Economic Journal* 92, 1982, pp. 825–848.

[105] Interview with F. Kirchhof by J. Gaugele, T. Jungholt, and C. C. Malzahn (translated by the author).

CHAPTER 9

Rethinking the Eurosystem

Changing Course—Learning from the US—Hard Budget Constraints—Neutral Money—Unbearable Debt—Restructuring the Debt—A Breathing Currency Union: Between Bretton Woods and the Dollar—The Path towards Unity

Changing Course

There is no alternative to Europe. After centuries of war and tension, the further integration of Europe towards a stronger union is imperative. Winston Churchill's proposal to build 'a kind of United States of Europe' remains valid, despite the fact that public support for the EU has waned during the crisis.[1] The free movement of goods, capital and people, the harmonization of product standards and tax systems, as well as a common foreign policy and defence are important instruments in achieving the goal of securing peace and prosperity in Europe.

However, there are many potential roads that Europe could take towards achieving its goals.[2] The road via a common currency union was obviously

---

[1] See W. Churchill, *Speech at the University of Zurich*, 19 September 1946, Council of Europe, available at: <http://aei.pitt.edu/14362/1/S2-1.pdf>, and I. Traynor, 'Crisis for Europe as Trust Hits Record Low', *The Guardian*, 24 April 2013, available at: <http://www.theguardian.com/world/2013/apr/24/trust-eu-falls-record-low>.

[2] Some are presented by W. R. Cline, 'Alternative Strategies for Resolving the European Debt Crisis', in W. R. Cline and G. B. Wolff (eds), *Special Report 21: Resolving the European Debt Crisis*, Peterson Institute for International Economics, Bruegel, Washington 2012, pp. 197–234; by G. B. Wolff, 'The Euro Area Crisis: Policy Options Ahead', in W. R. Cline and G. B. Wolff (eds), *Special Report 21: Resolving the European Debt Crisis*, 2012, pp. 235–252; or by H. Uhlig, *Exiting the Eurozone Crisis*, Presentation Given at the Advantage Financial Conference in Milan, 13 May 2013, available at: <http://home.uchicago.edu/~huhlig/papers/uhlig.milan.2013.pdf>.

stonier than expected, and it is now doubtful whether it will actually lead towards Europe's goals at all. A currency union automatically gives rise to joint liabilities and is therefore prone to moral hazard effects that need to be contained by a strong political power centre. That a currency union without a centralization of power would not succeed has rightly been emphasized by many observers.

Joint liability for the ECB's refinancing credit, combined with local access to the money-printing press, created bigger wealth risks for the European tax-payers than all other rescue operations combined. It fostered an atmosphere of over-confidence among investors that induced reckless lending and borrowing decisions. An excessive amount of money was lying around in the shop window, too much liability could be shifted onto public shoulders, too many risks were taken, and too much capital was flowing across borders. All of this contributed to the inflationary bubbles that ultimately deprived the southern European countries of their competitiveness, and other countries of their growth dynamics.

The currency union nevertheless had a theoretical possibility of succeeding if those charged with steering it had abided by the stipulations of the Maastricht Treaty. But they obviously lost sight of their goal after succumbing to temptations encountered along the way. The no-bailout clause was undermined by overly loose and distorting banking regulations, the Stability and Growth Pact was simply disregarded, and when the first state bankruptcy occurred in May 2010, the Maastricht Treaty was reinterpreted, if not downright violated, by the rescue programmes. That seemed the easier choice at the time, but by throwing the roadmap overboard, those in the driving seat lost their bearings.

Economists call this *time inconsistency*. Firstly, behind the veil of ignorance, some general rules are specified and enshrined in a treaty, but then, along the way, decision-makers prefer to ignore the rules and make decisions at their discretion. Following the rule of law, as Edward Prescott emphasized in his Nobel Prize acceptance speech, may be inconvenient at a given time, but it is better in the long run, as it is the only way to overcome the problem of time inconsistency in policymaking.[3]

Stumbling along and optimizing anew from moment to moment has created a path dependency that the signatories of the Maastricht Treaty had tried to avoid. This path dependency is likely to bring us no closer to the aspired-for United States of Europe, or to the peace and prosperity that everyone yearns for.

The policy decisions taken while stumbling through the euro's dark spell have boiled down to attempts at mutualizing debt and opening taxpayers' wallets to

---

[3] E. C. Prescott, *The Transformation of Macroeconomic Policy and Research*, Nobel Prize Lecture delivered at Stockholm University, 8 December 2004, p. 374, available at: <http://www.nobelprize.org/nobel_prizes/economic-sciences/laureates/2004/prescott-lecture.pdf>; see also F. E. Kydland and E. C. Prescott, 'Rules rather than Discretion: The Inconsistency of Optimal Plans', *Journal of Political Economy* 85, 1977, pp. 473–492.

meet immediate or future needs, the decisions being taken or prepared by the ECB Governing Council with little scope left for parliamentary action. This is a perilous course, as the early decades of US history show.

Learning from the United States

In 1790, the first US Secretary of the Treasury, Alexander Hamilton, had the federal government assume the state debts incurred during the revolution. The debt assumption was partly compensated for with the cession of not-yet-settled territories to the federal government (west of the Appalachians), and was to be serviced with the revenues from the joint import duties that the country had decided thenceforth to impose.[4] Hamilton wanted the slate to be wiped clean after the new federal country was founded, and he argued that debt mutualization was the 'powerful cement of our union'.[5]

Many think that this would also be a good model for Europe (leaving aside the cession of territories), and, as argued above, the ECB's OMT programme can be seen as the first step towards a mutualization of public debt in the Eurozone.[6] However, closer inspection reveals that this positive evaluation is less compelling than at first glance.

For one thing, the US state debts had been incurred partly during the revolutionary war to gain independence from Great Britain (1775–1783). It therefore seemed logical to mutualize them. The euro countries' debts, in contrast, did not result from a common struggle, but from the consumption decisions of individual governments. As discussed in Chapter 2, the interest-rate advantage brought by the euro was squandered.

For another, Europe did not found a unitary state; it simply established a common accounting unit for transactions, a view that is starkly highlighted by the Maastricht Treaty's no-bailout clause (article 125 TFEU).[7] As discussed in Chapter 1, notions of turning the Eurozone into a federal system have been firmly rejected by France.

---

[4] A. Hamilton, J. Jay, and J. Madison, *The Federalist: A Commentary on the Constitution of the United States*, in J. and A. McLean (eds), *The Federalist: A Collection of Essays Written in Favour of the New Constitution*, New York 1788, reprinted in The Modern Library, New York 2001.

[5] R. E. Wright, 'Cementing the Union', *Financial History*, Spring 2008, pp.14–18, in particular p. 15.

[6] German Council of Economic Experts, *Stable Architecture for Europe—Need for Action in Germany*, Annual Report 2012/2013, pp. 111–113.

[7] See EU, 'Treaty on the Functioning of the European Union (TFEU)', *Official Journal of the European Union* C 115/47, 9 May 2008, article 125, available at: <http://eur-lex.europa.eu/LexUriServ/LexUriServ.do?uri=OJ:C:2008:115:0058:0199:en:PDF>.

The US experience with debt mutualization was not good.[8] Mutualization of the initial debt gave rise to the expectation among the federal states that they would also be able to unload their debt onto federal shoulders in the future, which dramatically increased their willingness to borrow—not least because in the years 1812 to 1814 state debts had once again been mutualized in connection with a second war against Great Britain.[9]

The mechanisms were similar to those observed in the late 1980s in Argentina and Brazil, with excessive borrowing by their regional administrations. The provinces or states, respectively, borrowed to finance major projects, pushing aside repayment considerations in the hope that, if things got tight, the debts would be mutualized.[10] In both countries, the result was debt restructuring approximating a sovereign default of regional entities.

What happened in the US was not much better. State debt remained low until the mid-1820s, but thereafter it started to rise, among other things, because the states had started to issue tradeable bonds which had the advantage of lowering interest rates. The rise in indebtedness resulted primarily from investments in infrastructure such as roads, canals and, later, railroads, that consumed huge resources. In the southern states, a great deal of debt resulted from credit given to the owners of new private banks in order for them to pay in the required capital.[11] While the state economies prospered, bubbles developed, becoming dangerously large in the 1830s, when the debts of individual states increased rapidly. The bubbles eventually burst in 1837. Panic erupted in the capital markets, coinciding with the outbreak of a deep economic crisis that also engulfed the US's

---

[8] See J. Rodden, *Hamilton's Paradox: The Promise and Peril of Fiscal Federalism*, Cambridge University Press, New York 2006; T. Sargent, *United States Then, Europe Now*, Nobel Prize Lecture delivered at Stockholm University, 8 December 2011, available as video: available at: <http://www.nobelprize.org/nobel_prizes/economic-sciences/laureates/2011/sargent-lecture.html>; H. James, 'Lessons for the Euro from History', *Julis-Rabinowitz Center for Public Policy and Finance*, 19 April 2012, available at: <http://www.princeton.edu/jrc/events_archive/repository/inaugural-conference/Harold_James.pdf>; H. James, 'Alexander Hamilton's Eurozone Tour', *Project Syndicate*, 5 March 2012, available at: <http://www.project-syndicate.org/commentary/alexander-hamilton-s-eurozone-tour>; EEAG, *The EEAG Report on the European Economy: Rebalancing Europe*, CESifo, Munich 2013, chapter 4: US Precedents for Europe, pp. 95–107, available at: <https://www.cesifo-group.de/DocDL/EEAG-2013.pdf>.

[9] See B. U. Ratchford, *American State Debts*, Duke University Press, Durham 1941, in particular p. 74f.

[10] J. Rodden, *Hamilton's Paradox*, 2006, in particular chapter 8; and A. Markiewicz, M. D. Bordo, and L. Jonung, 'A Fiscal Union for the Euro: Some Lessons from History', *CESifo Delphi Conference*, Hydra, 23–24 September 2012, *NBER Working Paper* No. 17380, September 2011.

[11] B. U. Ratchford, *American State Debts*, 1941, p. 89.

European trading partners, Britain in particular, forcing most states to stop salary payments to state employees and payments to suppliers. After the panic subsided the markets calmed down somewhat, but by 1839 borrowing in the open market had practically ground to a halt and the economy was in depression.[12]

In this situation, the federal government bought a great deal of bonds from the various states to keep them solvent, in view of their lack of access to the market. The general expectation that the federal government would prove generous towards the overly indebted states, and ultimately assume the debt itself, seemed to be fulfilled.[13]

But the support only lasted for a short time until the federal government lost patience.[14] In 1841, Florida, Mississippi, Arkansas, and Indiana formally filed for bankruptcy. They were followed in 1842 by Illinois, Maryland, Michigan, Pennsylvania, and Louisiana. Other states such as Alabama, New York, Ohio, and Tennessee faced enormous financial strain and came close to bankruptcy. In total, nine of the twenty-nine states and territories existing in 1842 had filed for bankruptcy and four at least were bankrupt or on the brink of bankruptcy.[15]

The hope that the federal government would bail out the states, so that they could forestall bankruptcy, remained unrealized. The capacity of the federal budget proved insufficient, and the imbalances reached unbearable proportions. Tensions and strife among the states were on the rise, which in turn reduced the willingness to provide further support.

US historian Harold James, of Princeton University, observes that what Hamilton meant to 'cement' the US fiscal union eventually turned out to be 'dynamite'. James argues that the unresolved debt problem created tensions among the federal states because the federal debt had to be serviced by means of a politically divisive tariff that harmed the South while benefiting northern manufacturers. Furthermore, he maintains that these tensions fuelled those that resulted from other reasons and ultimately led to the American Civil War from 1861 to 1865.[16]

---

[12] B. U. Ratchford, *American State Debts*, 1941, p. 80.

[13] B. U. Ratchford, *American State Debts*, 1941, p. 85, in particular footnote 22.

[14] B. U. Ratchford, *American State Debts*, 1941, pp. 98–100; see also A. Grinath, J. J. Wallis, and R. E. Sylla, 'Debt, Default and Revenue Structure: The American State Debt Crisis in the Early 1840s', *NBER Working Paper* No. 97, March 1997.

[15] See A. Grinath, J. J. Wallis, and R. E. Sylla, 'Debt, Default and Revenue Structure: The American State Debt Crisis in the Early 1840s', March 1997; and W. B. English, 'Understanding the Costs of Sovereign Default: American State Debts in the 1840's', *American Economic Review* 86, 1996, pp. 259–275.

[16] H. James, 'Lessons for the Euro from History', 19 April 2012; see also EEAG, *The EEAG Report of the European Economy: Rebalancing Europe*, 2013.

Hard Budget Constraints

The United States provides very useful lessons for Europe, since the problems with fiscal federalism that it had to solve are similar to those now faced by the Eurozone. The trials and tribulations of the young nation's early decades should serve as a warning to all those who want to reinvent the wheel of history. Europe does not have to invent fiscal federalism, since the USA already did so a long time ago. Through a sometimes painful iteration process that lasted for two centuries, a state has evolved that, apart from its currently high central government indebtedness, appears to function reasonably well. At the very least, it provides some pointers on how Europe could evolve. Before stumbling blindly and leaving things to chance or to the pressure of financial investors, the architects of the new Europe would do well to learn from the US experience.

After an episode in which the USA suffered the consequences of debt mutualization, it was clear once and for all that each state must pay its own debts. The no-bailout principle became the universally accepted pillar of US municipal and state finance. Many states also began to put caps on debt levels and constitutionally prohibited extensive debt issuance. The State of New York was the first to implement a debt ceiling (totalling $ 1 million) in 1846, with other states following suit by 1860.[17] The self-imposed constraints did not prevent another debt crisis in the 1870s, when the world economy again fell into a depression, but this only reinforced and confirmed the austerity attitude that the US state governments, unlike the federal government, have shown ever since.

California was recently on the brink of bankruptcy. The salaries of teachers and other state employees have been deferred on several occasions and state jobs are being given only on a time-limited basis, with a layoff announced from the outset. In summer 2009, the Californian government paid $ 2.6 billion worth of invoices and salaries with IOUs, because it had no funds and the banks were giving it no further credit. The IOUs were used for a while in place of money, since they could be endorsed to third parties.

Minnesota and Illinois are not doing much better. Their finances are in dire straits, affected by severe fiscal crises.[18] In July 2011, the government of

[17] See A. Grinath, J. J. Wallis, and R. E. Sylla, 'Debt, Default and Revenue Structure: The American State Debt Crisis in the Early 1840s', March 1997; see also J. von Hagen, 'Monetäre, fiskalische und politische Integration: Das Beispiel der USA', *Bankhistorisches Archiv* Beiheft 30, 1996, pp. 35–51; J. von Hagen, 'Monetary Union and Fiscal Union: A Perspective from Fiscal Federalism', in P. R. Masson and M. P. Taylor (eds), *Policy Issues in the Operation of Currency Unions*, Cambridge University Press, Cambridge 1993, pp. 264–296.

[18] For Minnesota, see K. Dolak, 'Minnesota Government Shuts Down Amid Debt Fallout', *abcNews*, 1 July 2012; and for Illinois, see State Budget Crisis Task

Minnesota halted infrastructure projects and closed state parks in the midst of the tourist season because there was no money for park rangers. Thousands of state employees waited for their salaries, which the state was unable to pay.[19] In Illinois, several public facilities were closed and thousands of state workers were laid off in September 2011.[20]

The situation in some US states is far less precarious than it is in Greece today. The reader may recall from Chapter 2 (Figure 2.7) that the Greek state in 2013 had a debt-to-GDP ratio of 176% (despite the fact that in 2012 it enjoyed € 105 billion in debt relief, equivalent to 58% of its 2013 GDP). By contrast, the no-bailout principle of the US kept even the debt-to-GDP ratios of California, Minnesota, and Illinois below 10% in 2013, because investors, who know that no one would help them in the case of bankruptcy, become jittery at much lower debt levels than in the European debt-friendly institutional environment.[21] At a debt level of 10%, a state insolvency is not a big issue and can be easily handled. However, when the debt has reached Greek dimensions, the burden imposed by capital markets is much bigger, and the situation for everyone is much more precarious. Given that the no-bailout principle is firmly anchored in the US, insolvency is possible and punitive for those who depend on government money. Still, no one in the US would ever light upon the idea of organizing a common programme to provide the crisis states with financial support or creating a system of collective bonds that would enable these states, under the shield of joint liability, to regain access to the markets.

A good lesson was provided by the near-bankruptcy of New York City in 1975. The city, due to its economic size, can almost be equated with the state of New York as a whole. In the late 1960s, then-Mayor John Lindsay had tried to set up a European-style welfare state in New York. The consequence was that the poor throughout the US came in droves to New York in order to profit from its social safety net. The city was pushed to the brink of insolvency. Lindsay had to terminate his programme, but the city continued to suffer from the debts that it had accrued. In 1975, New York was practically bankrupt and was saved at the last

Force, *Report of the State Budget Crisis Task Force. Illinois Report*, October 2012, available at: <http://www.statebudgetcrisis.org/wpcms/wp-content/images/2012-10-12-Illinois-Report-Final-2.pdf>.

[19] See K. Dolak, 'Minnesota Government Shuts Down Amid Debt Fallout', 1 July 2012.

[20] See also J. Erbentraut, 'Quinn to Announce Thousands of Layoffs, Facility Closures', *Huffington Post*, 6 September 2011, available at: <http://www.huffingtonpost.com/2011/09/06/quinn-to-announce-thousan_n_950654.html>.

[21] See also C. Chantrill, 'Comparison of State and Local Government Spending in the United States. Fiscal Year 2013', *US Government Spending*, available at: <http://www.usgovernmentspending.com/compare_state_spending_2013pH0D>.

minute only by a loan from the teacher union's pension fund. The US government refused to come to the rescue. The headline of the New York Daily News became legendary: 'Ford to City: Drop Dead'. It summarized the position of then-President Gerald R. Ford.[22] Ford could not quite hold his hard stance, and in the following year the Congress provided some support from federal funds, but that was vastly insufficient. New York managed to tap fresh money only through the issuance of bonds collateralized with senior claims on future tax revenue.[23]

Other subordinate administrative divisions in the US suffered the same fate as New York City over the years. Time and again some go bankrupt and suspend debt service. In 2012 alone, twelve municipalities filed for bankruptcy.[24] Since the introduction of Chapter 9 of the US Bankruptcy Code in 1937, which provides for the reorganization of municipalities under an ordinary insolvency procedure, there have been around 600 such filings.[25] Between 1980 and 2012, 272 filings were tallied; in 2013 there were nine filings.[26] This figure included the city of Detroit, which defaulted on 18 July 2013.[27] After an insolvency is declared, an agreement is sought with the creditors to waive some of the debt, and then the

---

[22] F. Van Riper, 'Ford to New York: Drop Dead. Vows He'll Veto Bail-Out in Speech Attacking City', *Daily News*, 30 October 1975.

[23] New York City tax revenue was declared state tax revenue for this purpose, and it was transferred to a special-purpose organization, the Municipal Assistance Corporation (MAC) as collateral for the emission of securities to provide financing for the city. See L. Capodilupo, 'Municipal Assistance Corporation for the City of New York (MAC)', *William and Anita Newman Library and Baruch College*, City University of New York, April 2002, available at: <http://newman.baruch.cuny.edu/digital/2003/amfl/mac/mac_finding_aid_index.htm> and R. Dunstan, 'Overview of New York City's Fiscal Crisis', *California Research Bureau Note 3*, No. 1, 1 March 1995, p. 4, available at: <http://www.library.ca.gov/crb/95/notes/V3N1.PDF>.

[24] T. Barghini and C. Parsons, 'Factbox: Recent U.S. Municipal Bankruptcies', *Reuters*, 18 July 2013, available at: <http://www.reuters.com/article/2013/07/18/us-usa-detroit-cities-factbox-idUSBRE96H1BR20130718>.

[25] M. De Angelis and X. Tian, 'United States: Chapter 9 Municipal Bankruptcy—Utilization, Avoidance and Impact', in O. Canuto and L. Liu (eds), *Until Debt Do Part Us: Subnational Debt, Insolvency and Markets*, World Bank Publications, Washington 2013, pp. 311–351, especially p. 312.

[26] American Bankruptcy Institute, Statistics from the Administrative Office of the U.S. Courts, *Chapter 9 Filings (1980-Current)*, available at: <http://news.abi.org/statistics>; and United States Courts, Statistics, *Bankruptcy Statistics*, 2013 Bankruptcy Filings, Filings by Chapter and Nature of Debt, by District (table F-2), available at: <http://www.uscourts.gov/Statistics/BankruptcyStatistics/2013-bankruptcy-filings.aspx>.

[27] M. Dolan, 'Record Bankruptcy for Detroit', *Wall Street Journal*, 19 July 2013, available at: <http://online.wsj.com/article/SB10001424127887323993804578614144173709204.html>.

cities can operate again. That raises no hackles, since it is just as common as a company bankruptcy.

Since resources are scarce, the US introduced a system of hard budget constraints, after the failures of the early system of soft budget constraints. It is, of course, painful in every individual case, as painful as economic reality can be in the world, but it works, and also instils debt discipline without leading to a catastrophe. No one in the USA wants to repeat the experiences of the first decades after Hamilton.

The disastrous consequences of soft budget constraints were also evident in the downfall of the Soviet Union. That the soft budget constraints would spell the demise of the URSS was predicted by Hungarian economist János Kornai as early as 1980.[28] If the government wanted something, it was done. Goods were produced without anyone paying attention to the damage caused by withdrawing the factors of production from other uses. Politics was believed to have primacy over the laws of economics, but in fact it was the other way round. The hard laws of economics ultimately made the Soviet System unsustainable.

Hard budget constraints are like the brakes of a car. Going downhill, it is tempting to let the car roll freely instead of moderating its speed, but the consequence can be a hard braking at the end, or even an accident. When the euro was announced and eventually introduced, the Eurozone went through a phase of soft budget constraints. The car hurtled along—and kept going. Even today the driver doesn't dare hit the brakes hard. Some even want the vehicle to keep rushing along. They are calling for Eurobonds, the mutualization of bank debts and other measures to take the pressure off the brakes. They are thereby risking the same type of accidents that the USA experienced in its early decades.

Neutral Money

The easy access to the local printing press, which channelled the up to one trillion euros in extra credit from the northern central banks to the GIPSIC countries, as measured by the Target balances, is arguably the key design flaw of the Eurosystem and the feature that most fundamentally sets it apart from the US monetary system. It fits the money-in-the-shop-window theory, which posits that the Eurosystem needs sufficient firing power to stabilize the system, but unfortunately, contradicting the theory's prediction, the money on display has, in fact, been taken. Some of it has been returned in the meantime, to a sizeable extent because public credit, which reduces the Target balances on a one-by-one basis, was provided as a replacement, but as of this writing the stock taken is still about € 600

---

[28] J. Kornai, ' "Hard" and "Soft" Budget Constraint', *Acta Oeconomica* 25, 1980, pp. 231–246.

billion (see Figures 6.2 and 7.1). A substantial part of the extra ECB credit will turn into losses for the taxpayers, given that the write-off losses of the GIPSIC banking systems could be hundreds of billions of euros (see Table 8.3), and because the bank resolution strategy defined by the European Parliament limits the creditor bail-in to a tiny fraction of the banks' balance sheets (see Chapter 8's section *Banking Union*).

The money in the shop window has helped to make creditors reckless, and played a key role in feeding the inflationary credit bubble that deprived the southern countries of their competitiveness and caused huge *structural* current account imbalances in the Eurozone (see Chapter 4). The sharing of losses arising from financing zombie banks created strong moral hazard incentives for NCBs to opt for lowering collateral standards in the ECB Governing Council, to individually stretch the limits set by such standards and, as shown in Chapter 5, to extend excessive amounts of ELA credit at their own discretion, given that ELA's exemption from joint liability is a myth. To counteract such incentives, binding rules and strong constraints are needed, but such constraints are missing in the Eurosystem. It is true that without such constraints bankruptcies can be delayed, as was the case in Greece and Cyprus (see Chapter 5), but that bloats the burden of debt even further and shifts even more credit titles from private to public hands, opening a fire bridge from the private to the public economy.

To avoid the crash, the logic of the liability spiral will force member NCBs to buy even more government bonds, bringing the ESM's bonds even closer to Eurobonds, and to press ahead with the mutualization of bank debts to avoid the emergence of new Target credit. This is like trying to stabilize a car without brakes by flooring the gas pedal.

To stop the vicious liability spiral, it is essential to correct its root cause by terminating the ECB's regional fiscal policy that predetermines subsequent parliamentary rescue decisions and undermines European democracy. To this end, it is crucial to keep the Target balances in check. There are four ways to do this.

The technically simplest option is for the ECB Governing Council to end its policy of allowing low-quality collateral for refinancing credit (see Chapter 5). If refinancing credit were only granted against solid collateral, the banks would see no advantage in drawing credit from the ECB, since with good collateral they can tap the interbank market for cheap credit at any time.

But the Bundesbank has long since pleaded for more stringent collateral standards and has always been outvoted in the ECB Council. It is clearly impossible to reach a solution as long as the countries that profit from Target credit hold a majority in the Council. The issue calls for a more fundamental approach.

In the opinion of former Bundesbank President Helmut Schlesinger, Target credit should bear a punitive interest rate charged to the corresponding NCB, which would, of course, be excluded from the Eurosystem's pooling operations, and which should be high enough to cajole the deficit generating NCBs into reining in the refinancing credit they grant, so that market interest rates rise and the credit that had wandered off to other countries returns.[29] This is tantamount to an attempt to reintroduce the idea of an equilibrium between supply and demand in the local credit markets, something that characterized the internal US system, the Bretton Woods system, and the gold standard systems, as shown in Chapter 7. It would indeed be a suitable means, even one that presumably can be carried out by the Eurosystem's NCBs without having to change EU treaties.

It would be even better, though, to amend the Maastricht Treaty by applying rules similar to those used in the US, particularly as regards the settlement of Target balances. The most natural means of payment between countries, and even states within a currency union, is gold. A country may run a Target deficit for a year or more, but then it should settle its debt with the Eurosystem by redeeming it with gold or tradeable gold-backed securities, to be handed out to the holders of Target claims. Gold has always been used for settling balance-of-payments imbalances between countries, and even between states within a currency union, as the history of the US Federal Reserve, summarized in Chapter 7, has shown, and gold has remained an international means of payment to this day.

It might be argued that some countries do not have enough gold to meet their obligations. However, this is like saying that someone who built a house does not have enough cash on hand to redeem his debt. Since gold is an internationally liquid asset and a globally accepted unit of account, the debtor country always has the possibility of selling some other assets, say covered bonds or state property, at market prices against gold to fulfil its obligations.

Of course, this may be difficult for a country that is close to insolvency. It would of course be much more convenient to hand over some sort of debentures or to leave the system as is, with credit slumbering on the books, if necessary forever. But that is what hard budget constraints mean. If a country wants to run current account deficits and temporarily absorb resources from the rest of the world, it has to borrow or sell some of its own assets in exchange, and the conditions at which it does so must be mutually agreeable to all parties involved.

That said, the near insolvency of some southern European countries is a fact, and something must be done to clear the air for a prosperous future in a common European house. A joint European debt conference might be needed to forgive part of the crisis-stricken countries' debt. This will be discussed in the next section.

The settlement of balance-of-payments imbalances constrains the possibilities of a country to have net payment orders carried out through the Eurosystem, but not in the sense that individual payments could not be carried out beyond a certain

---

[29] H. Schlesinger, 'Die Zahlungsbilanz sagt es uns', *ifo Schnelldienst* 64, No. 16, 31 August 2011, pp. 9–11, in particular p. 11; and for the English version, 'The Balance of Payments Tells us the Truth' in H.-W. Sinn (ed.), The European Balance of Payments Crisis, *CESifo Forum* 13, Special Issue, January 2012, pp. 11–13, in particular p. 13.

limit. No capital controls would need to be imposed, as was recently the case in Cyprus, and unlike today a euro would have the same value everywhere. The constraint operates only indirectly, in the sense that it becomes less attractive for a given NCB to issue more money than is needed for domestic circulation. If an NCB wants to issue more than this amount, leading to the accumulation of Target balances, it would have to sell marketable assets to buy the gold needed for settlement. Since such a step may prove unattractive, it would put a limit on the issuance of new refinancing credit, the local commercial banks then having no other option but to borrow in the European interbank market at mutually acceptable conditions.

This is not at all a radical or constraining step. It just means imposing budget constraints. Budget constraints do not imply that a market equilibrium with a common currency that has an equal value everywhere is unattainable. To the contrary, it is the prerequisite for such an equilibrium.

Softer budget constraints that allow public borrowing at below-market conditions are dangerous for the stability of an economy, as they are likely to lead to overspending, overheating, and inflationary credit bubbles that undermine the competitiveness of countries. It is remarkable that the USA kept the internal gold standard until 1975, even though the country was a solid political federation, while it is considered self-evident by European politicians that the Eurozone does not need such a standard, even though it is far from becoming anything close to a federal state in the foreseeable future.

Depending on Europe's progress in creating a common federal state with the corresponding enforcement authority, in the distant future the gold standard might be given up and a solution similar to the current US system, based on a mere settlement with marketable assets, could eventually be adopted. As explained in Chapter 7, in the US, settlement is performed by handing over ownership shares in the Federal Reserve System Open Market Account (SOMA). However, there are at least two caveats with such a solution. One is that the US system of public budget constraints may also have become too soft. History will tell whether moving away from the internal gold standard really was a good idea. The other is that the main channel of money provision in Europe is the granting of refinancing credit rather than open-market asset purchases. Thus, there isn't an analogue to the open market clearing portfolio that could be reshuffled for the purpose of settling Target balances.

A possibility would be that all euro countries issue super-safe treasury bills that are collateralized with gold or property, and that bear a market interest rate appropriate for such instruments. A proposal along these lines was made by the European Economic Advisory Group (EEAG) in its 2012 *Report on the European Economy*.[30] The participating countries would apply these bills to amortize the

---

[30] EEAG, *The EEAG Report on the European Economy: The Euro Crisis*, CESifo, Munich 2012, chapter 2: *The European Balance-of-Payments Problem*, in particular pp. 75–79, available at: <http://www.cesifo-group.de/DocDL/EEAG-2012.pdf>.

Target liabilities accumulated by their respective NCBs. The bills would have to be market-grade and actually traded, which presupposes that the countries do resort to these instruments in the course of their normal borrowing.

While such measures are indispensable, they would cover only one aspect of the US system. Another important characteristic of the US system is that the Federal Reserve, through the Reserve Bank of New York, buys securities issued by the federal government and federal agencies, but not those issued by individual states, let alone those of troubled ones. As shown in Chapter 7, this precludes the kind of regional fiscal policy that the ECB has been carrying out with its SMP and OMT programmes. Translated into the Eurosystem, the Fed's policy would mean providing all NCBs with fixed refinancing lots according to the size of their jurisdictions' economies and, if at all, buying any national government bonds always in proportion to the size of the economy of the issuing countries.[31] Furthermore, limited additional lots of refinancing credit through systems similar to those available in the US could be introduced to meet emergency liquidity needs. All of this would work to reduce the Target balances in the first place and reduce the amounts that need to be settled.

Unbearable Debt

While a hardening of budget constraints is indispensable for a well-functioning Eurosystem, the introduction of the new rules by themselves would hit the GIPSIC countries hard and exacerbate their economic malaise. Before the new rules for a viable system in the long run can be implemented, the European debt problem needs to be resolved in the short run.

Whether a country's debt is sustainable depends largely on its GDP growth rate. According to the Domar formula, once developed to legitimatize Keynesian deficit spending, a country's public debt-to-GDP ratio, in short its debt ratio, will converge in the long run to the ratio of its deficit share in GDP and the long-term nominal GDP growth rate.[32] Thus, with appropriate assumptions of this growth rate, which no one actually knows or can observe today, unsustainable debt situations can be made to look sustainable. In a remarkable document, the IMF recently acknowledged that it had used this approach to calm the markets and

---

[31] See M. Feldstein, 'Dos and Don'ts for the European Central Bank', *Project Syndicate*, 29 July 2012, available at: <http://www.project-syndicate.org/commentary/dos-and-don-ts-for-the-european-central-bank>.

[32] E. D. Domar, 'The "Burden of the Debt" and the National Income', *American Economic Review* 34, 1944, pp. 798–827.

avoid stating that Greek debt is unsustainable, which would have forced it to stop its rescue operations and might have triggered Greece's bankruptcy.[33]

Unfortunately, instead of growing, some of the crisis countries may stagnate in the years to come, or even shrink in nominal terms, because they need to realign their relative prices, as shown in Chapter 4. If realignment takes place rapidly, as could be achieved with courageous labour market reforms, it will involve outright deflation. That would minimize the duration of mass unemployment, but would also imply a period of falling nominal GDP levels. If, on the other hand, prices prove sticky downwards and the ECB is unable or unwilling to inflate the other euro countries, most of the GIPSIC countries will be forced to continue shrinking in real and nominal terms. Thus, whichever of these two scenarios materializes, some countries will experience rising debt ratios.

The truth about the debt problem is bitter, since the artificial and inflationary growth created by the credit bubbles in the GIPSIC countries before the crisis struck concealed the debt problem for many years. Because countries over-borrowed, their economies overheated, and because they overheated, their debt-to-GDP ratios remained modest or even fell for some years, as in Spain or Ireland. The overheating increased the denominator of the debt-to-GDP ratios and kept the increments of the numerators small, as it implied ample tax revenue that drove down budget deficits. Both of these effects created the illusion that the debt problem was under control and that the countries would be able to simply grow out of it. In fact, however, the process deprived the countries of their competitiveness and made the debt unsustainable in a number of cases.

To understand the real danger this has engendered, it is useful to correct this distortion by evaluating the countries' GDP levels at competitive prices. An attempt to do this is shown on Table 9.1. The second column gives the actual debt-to-GDP ratios by the end of 2013, as known from Figure 2.7. The third column gives the debt-to-GDP ratios that would have resulted if all countries' price levels (GDP deflators) had grown at the average actual rate since the Madrid Summit in 1995, which marked the beginning of the interest-rate convergence that triggered the credit boom (see Chapter 2). The fourth column gives the debt-to-GDP ratios that would result after the necessary realignment of relative prices, as calculated by the benchmark scenario of the Goldman Sachs study cited in Chapter 4, given the 2013 Eurozone average price level and

---

[33] International Monetary Fund, 'Greece: Ex Post Evaluation of Exceptional Access under the 2010 Stand-By Arrangement', *IMF Country Report* No. 13/156, June 2013, in particular pp. 2, 21 and 33, available at: <http://www.imf.org/external/pubs/ft/scr/2013/cr13156.pdf>; see also K. Schrader, D. Bencek and C.-F. Laaser, 'IfW-Krisencheck: Alles wieder gut in Griechenland?', *Kieler Diskussionsbeiträge* No. 522/523, June 2013, in particular figure 17, p. 31.

Table 9.1 Actual and hypothetical public debt-to-GDP ratios (December 2013, %)

	Actual	Hypothetical correction for deviation from average inflation*	Hypothetical after necessary realignments**
Greece	176	222	237
NB: without haircut	234	294	315
Ireland	124	139	122
Portugal	128	142	180
Spain	95	109	130
Italy	133	164	148
Cyprus	116	144	
NB: GIPSIC	122	145	
Belgium	100	99	
Germany	80	67	67
Estonia	10	21	
France	93	92	117
Luxembourg	25	29	
Netherlands	75	77	
Austria	75	68	
Slovenia	63	67	
Slovakia	54	99	
Finland	58	56	

* Actual public debt level in relation to GDP evaluated at prices that would have prevailed had the country's GDP inflation rate followed the average of the euro countries since 1995 (Madrid Summit).

** Actual debt level in relation to 2013 GDP evaluated at competitive prices according to the study by Goldman Sachs, baseline scenario, Q3 2010, keeping the 2013 average Eurozone price level (GDP deflator) constant. See Table 4.1.

Sources: European Commission, *Economic and Financial Affairs*, Financial Assistance in EU Member States, Greece; H. Pill, K. Daly, D. Schumacher, A. Benito, L. Holboell Nielsen, N. Valla, A. Demongeot, and S. Graves, Goldman Sachs Global Economics, External Rebalancing: Progress, but a Sizeable Challenge Remains, *European Economics Analyst*, Issue No. 13/03, January 17, 2013; Ifo Institute calculations.

Note: Actual public debt 2013: European Commission forecast, November 2013.

taking into account that a bit of the necessary price adjustment may already have taken place.[34]

While some countries such as Austria, Belgium, Finland, and Germany would have lower debt-to-GDP ratios today if their relative goods prices had not changed, the GIPSIC countries would have much higher ones. On average, their debt-to-GDP ratio would be 145%, instead of the 122% shown in the official statistics. Italy's would be 164% instead of 133%, Spain's 109% instead of 95%, Portugal's 142% instead of 128%, and Greece's 222% instead of 176%.

Without the haircut of March 2012, which gave the Greek state a debt relief of 54% of its 2012 GDP at the expense of foreign and domestic investors, but at today's prices, Greece's official debt ratio in 2013 would have been 234% of GDP. This is shown in the first field of the second row of the Table. And without both the haircut and the increase in Greek relative prices that took place since the Madrid Summit, the Greek debt-to-GDP ratio would have been 294%, as shown in the next field to the right.

Things look even more dramatic if GDP is evaluated at hypothetical prices after the realignment that would follow from the Goldman Sachs baseline scenario shown in Table 4.1. Without the haircut and after the required deflation, the Greek public debt ratio would have been a whopping 315%. Recall that the Goldman Sachs figures give a favourable impression of the need for a Greek realignment. If the Greek price level were at the level of Turkish prices of 2011–2013, for example, the Greek debt-to-GDP ratio in the absence of the haircut would be 363%, and with the haircut 273%. These figures show with utmost clarity how unbearable the Greek debt situation is.

Portugal's debt-to-GDP ratio would be 180%, and Spain's 130%, if the prices were reduced in line with the Goldman Sachs baseline scenario. For both of these countries the figures look grimmer than in the case where the price-level correction is only made for the actual relative price increase since 1995. Ireland and Italy, in contrast, with ratios of 122% and 148%, would look a little better.

The debt-to-GDP ratios recalculated in Table 9.1 for competitive prices refer to official public debt, which is held by domestic and foreign investors as well as public institutions that have provided rescue funds to the governments of the crisis-stricken countries. A similar calculation is presented in Table 9.2 for the public rescue funds themselves, as analysed in the previous chapter (see

---

[34] H. Pill, K. Daly, D. Schumacher, A. Benito, L. Holboell Nielsen, N. Valla, A. Demongeot, and A. Paul, Goldman Sachs Global Economics, 'Achieving Fiscal and External Balance (Part 1): The Price Adjustment Required for External Sustainability', *European Economics Analyst* No. 12/01, 15 March 2012; H. Pill, K. Daly, D. Schumacher, A. Benito, L. Holboell Nielsen, N. Valla, A. Demongeot, and S. Graves, Goldman Sachs Global Economics, 'External Rebalancing: Progress, but a Sizeable Challenge Remains', *European Economics Analyst* No. 13/03, 17 January 2013.

Figure 8.2 and Table 8.1), that were made available by foreign countries or multilateral institutions, including the ECB, to the crisis countries' governments and central banks, and via the latter to the respective local commercial banking systems.[35] As broken down in Table 8.1, the rescue funds include the Target debt, the potential debt from an over-proportionate issuance of banknotes (or the potential claim from an under-proportionate issuance), government bonds held by non-GIPSIC central banks and the ECB itself, as well as fiscal rescue credit provided by other countries and multilateral institutions. Note that these items could not reasonably be added to the government debt shown in Table 9.1, since for some countries, Greece in particular, a large fraction of the public debt is held by international public institutions, and because the credit provided to NCBs for distribution to commercial banks overlaps with sovereign debt in the same measure as banks use refinancing credit to buy local government bonds, and then submit these bonds as collateral for the refinancing credit.

While the second column of Table 9.2 simply repeats the figures relative to current GDP from Table 8.1, the third one provides a recalculation based on GDP evaluated at average Eurozone prices, or, to be more precise, at the prices that would have prevailed in 2013 if the countries' GDP deflators had increased in line with the average since the Madrid Summit in 1995. The fourth column, as in Table 9.1, shows the public credit-to-GDP ratios that would result if GDP were to be calculated at Goldman Sachs 'competitive' relative prices as specified above, keeping the Eurozone average GDP deflator constant at its 2013 level.

Consider Greece. Greece has thus far received public credit from abroad (multilateral, bilateral and ECB), net of its own contributions to international rescue activities, equal to 157% of its 2013 GDP evaluated at actual market prices. It would have a public credit-to-GDP ratio of 198% if its GDP in real terms were the same as in 2013, while its prices had only increased in line with the Eurozone average since 1995. If, on the other hand, Greece's 2013 GDP is evaluated at Goldman Sachs-type competitive prices, this ratio would even be 212%. Portugal would also look worse, albeit much less dramatically, if its GDP were to be evaluated at such prices.

For Ireland, in contrast, the price correction produces a somewhat less problematic result. While Ireland's actual public credit-to-GDP ratio was 83% in 2013 and would have been 92% had Irish prices not increased faster than the

---

[35] The percentages shown in Table 9.2 are partly included in the public debt figures of Table 9.1. However, the credit provided to national central banks for distribution to commercial banks, which resulted in Target debt and the debt from an over-proportionate banknote issuance, is not included. This credit established a liability of the respective national central bank and is therefore a sovereign debt. While not included in the official public debt figures, the Target debt (though not the banknote debt) is included in a country's official net foreign asset position (see Chapter 6).

Table 9.2 Public credit provided by other governments or multilateral institutions relative to the recipient country's actual or hypothetical GDP (December 2013, %)

	Actual public-credit-to-GDP ratio	Hypothetical correction for deviation from average inflation*	Hypothetical correction for necessary realignments**
Greece	157	198	212
Ireland	83	92	81
Portugal	67	74	94
Spain	21	24	29
Italy	16	19	17
Cyprus	72	90	–
GIPSIC	32	38	39

* Actual public credit level in relation to GDP, net of the countries' own contributions to collective rescue activities, evaluated at prices that would have prevailed had the countries' GDP inflation rate followed the average of the euro countries since 1995 (Madrid Summit).

** Actual public credit level in relation to GDP, net of the countries' own contributions to collective rescue activities, evaluated at competitive prices according to the study by Goldman Sachs, baseline scenario, Q3 2010, keeping the 2013 average Eurozone price level (GDP deflator) constant. See Table 4.1.

Sources: See Tables 8.1 and 9.1.

Note: For the interpretation and the decomposition of the first column of this table, see Table 8.1. The percentages shown give the sum of Target debt, debt from an over-proportional issue of banknotes, government bonds held by non-GIPSIC NCBs, and intergovernmental fiscal credit, net of own contributions and credit repayments.

Eurozone average since 1995, its public credit-to-GDP ratio would 'only' be 81% if Irish GDP were evaluated at Goldman Sachs competitive prices.

All in all, the calculations presented in this section have a somewhat ambiguous policy implication. On the one hand, they are based on the view that the path towards foreign debt sustainability goes through a temporary increase in debt-to-GDP ratios, because a realignment of prices is necessary to generate the structural current account surpluses that would enable the countries to service their foreign debt. On the other hand, some of the resulting figures are truly huge and obliterate the hope that the countries will be able to manage their debt problems without help in the foreseeable future.

Greece in particular may need another haircut, this time at the expense of its public creditors, to reduce its debt burden. The first Greek haircut of

March 2012 cost foreign and Greek private investors € 105 billion, and the restructuring of November 2012 meant wealth losses for other Eurozone states amounting to € 43 billion in present-value terms, as shown in Chapter 8,[36] and yet a further restructuring of Greek debt might be in order. Portugal's situation is not quite as bad, but, evaluated at non-distorted competitive prices, it has a public debt-to-GDP ratio of between 142% and 180%, and the public credit it received from other countries is between 74% and 94% of its GDP. Portugal might also be a candidate for debt restructuring.

Restructuring the Debt

Debt restructuring has by no means been unusual in history. Since the 1950s, a haircut forcing private creditors to accept the exchange of their government or bank bonds has been applied no less than 186 times by ninety-five countries.[37] Figure 9.1 provides an overview of haircuts and sovereign defaults since 1978. The vertical axis shows the portion of the claims that were lost as a result of the haircut, while the size of the circles shows the absolute volume of the haircut. The haircuts applied by many developing countries in the early 1980s are clearly evident, as well as the debt restructuring performed by Russia in 1997 and 2000 and the bankruptcies of Argentina in 1987, 1993, and 2005.

Argentina had also demanded debt restructurings in 1956, 1962, and 1965. Its post-war history has been characterized by a long series of similar events. The first Argentine debt restructuring was negotiated by the military dictatorship under Pedro Eugenio Aramburu Cilveti, as soon as the dictatorship came to power in 1956. While it did try to repay the debt, it negotiated better terms than originally agreed. The negotiations with the creditors at the time took place in

---

[36] See Section *The Liability Risk*.

[37] U. S. Das, M. G. Papaioannou, and C. Trebesch, 'Sovereign Debt Restructurings 1950–2010: Literature Survey, Data, and Stylized Facts', *IMF Working Paper* No. 203, August 2012. For an overview of sovereign defaults over the centuries, see E. Streissler, 'Honi soit qui mal y pense?', *Austrian Academy of Sciences*, Vienna, August 2011. Explicit lessons for the Euro Area from the numerous restructurings in the emerging market countries are drawn in J. Zettelmeyer, 'How to Do a Sovereign Debt Restructuring in the Euro Area: Lessons from Emerging-Market Debt Crisis', in W. R. Cline and G. B. Wolff (eds), *Special Report 21: Resolving the European Debt Crisis*, 2012, pp. 165–186. The legal details of a sovereign debt restructuring are covered in many articles by L. Buchheit. See for example L. Buchheit, 'Sovereign Debt Restructuring: The Legal Context', in W. R. Cline and G. B. Wolff (eds), *Special Report 21: Resolving the European Debt Crisis*, 2012, pp. 187–196.

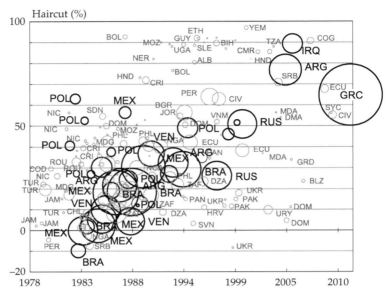

Figure 9.1 Full and partial sovereign defaults (1978–2010/2012)

Abbreviations: ALB: Albania, DZA: Algeria, ARG: Argentina, BLZ: Belize, BOL: Bolivia, BIH: Bosnia-Herzegovina, BRA: Brazil, BGR: Bulgaria, CMR: Cameroon, CHL: Chile, COG: Republic of Congo, CRI: Costa Rica, CIV: Ivory Coast, HRV: Croatia, COD: Democratic Republic of Congo, DOM: Dominican Republic, DMA: Dominica, ECU: Ecuador, ETH: Ethiopia, GRC: Greece, GRD: Grenada, GUY: Guyana, HND: Honduras, IRQ: Iraq, JAM: Jamaica, JOR: Jordan, MDG: Madagascar; MEX: Mexico, MDA: Moldavia, MOZ: Mozambique, NIC: Nicaragua, NER: Niger, NGA: Nigeria, PAK: Pakistan, PAN: Panama, PER: Peru, PHL: Philippines, POL: Poland, ROU: Romania, RUS: Russia, SRB: Serbia and Montenegro/Yugoslavia, SYC: Seychelles, SLE: Sierra Leone, SVN: Slovenia, ZAF: South Africa, SDN: Sudan, TZA: Tanzania, TUR: Turkey, UGA: Uganda, UKR: Ukraine, URY: Uruguay, VEN: Venezuela, VNM: Vietnam, YEM: Yemen,

Sources: J. Cruces and C. Trebesch, 'Sovereign Defaults: The Price of Haircuts', *CESifo Working Paper* No. 3604, October 2011; J. Zettelmeyer, C. Trebesch, and M. Gulati, 'The Greek Debt Restructuring: An Autopsy', *CESifo Working Paper* No. 4333, July 2013.

Note: The chart covers 181 sovereign haircuts over the 1978–2010 period, including the Greek partial bankruptcy of 2012. The vertical axis shows the percentage the haircut amounted to in relation to the market value of the government bonds in question, while the size of each circle denotes the absolute magnitude of each haircut.

Paris, and they led to the foundation of the Paris Club. The Paris Club is an informal group of nineteen official creditors that organizes debt restructuring according to a set of rules that have evolved from experience. The Club has since been often involved in renegotiations between debtors and creditors, the latest event being the debt relief negotiated in January 2013 for Myanmar after the fall of the military junta in 2011. Altogether, 400 debt agreements settled under the guidance of the Paris Club have been recorded.[38]

The Paris Club could also be involved in organizing a debt conference for joint negotiations between the GIPSIC countries and their creditor countries, along the lines of prior debt conferences in the 1920s, 1930s, and 1950s whose task was the settlement of war debt and reparation payments. The task of the new debt conference could be to reset the Eurozone's financial system by clearing the balance sheets and restoring the transparency and trust that the capital market needs to operate smoothly.[39] The debt conference would have to deal with three kinds of debt: state debt, bank debt, and Target debt, since they are all interrelated and have common origins.

Given the huge levels of interrelated debt, a solution that just prolongs maturities and reduces interest rates, as was chosen in the case of Greece and Ireland, is not advisable. That is not really a solution, but an attempt at camouflage that allows creditors to avoid write-off losses in their balance sheets and pretend to have more equity than they actually do. While it helps the banks and governments of the debtor countries, it makes the creditors vulnerable by allowing them to conduct their businesses with less capital than they show in their books. They should instead be forced to recapitalize by bringing in more equity capital from outside. The European financial industry could become a hollow shell with the camouflage strategy the EU has begun. It is much better for the long-run stability and prosperity of the European economy if the debt restructuring is honest, in the sense of going

---

[38] See U. S. Das, M. G. Papaioannou, and C. Trebesch, 'Sovereign Debt Restructurings 1950–2010', 2012, appendix.

[39] This proposal was made in H.-W. Sinn in his article, 'Rescuing Europe from the Ground Up', *Project Syndicate*, 21 December 2013, available at: <www.ifo.de/rescuing_europe/w/SvTE7mC2>. See also T. Beck and C. Trebesch, 'A Bank Restructuring Agency for the Eurozone – Cleaning Up the Legacy Losses' *VoxEU*, 18 November 2013, available at: <http://www.voxeu.org/article/eurozone-bank-restructuring-agency>. In the early stages of the crisis it had seemed that a gradual process of moving from liquidity help to piecemeal debt restructuring through maturity extensions would be effective, being expected to create proper incentives for governments to stop borrowing. See EEAG, *The EEAG Report of the European Economy*, CESifo, Munich 2011, chapter 2: *A New Crisis Mechanism for the Euro Area*, pp. 71–96. Time has moved beyond this proposal. Today, a more radical reset approach seems advisable.

for outright debt reductions and imposing a more parsimonious strategy on the economy, with more private savings and investment, and less consumption.

The public debt reductions will not only hit private investors but also creditor governments and their ESM and EFSF rescue funds, which will have to be recapitalized with more equity injections by governments. In the early stages of the crisis, governments could have avoided these losses, but now that they have bailed out private investors and taken over large parts of their portfolios, they will have to foot the bill. Nowadays, 80% of the Greek public debt is held by external public institutions and only 20% privately.[40] Moreover, the privately held debt is nearly exclusively located in the balance sheets of Greek commercial banks, which have used it as collateral for drawing refinancing credit from the Greek NCB.[41] This shows the nature of the problem. Taxpayers are already trapped. They should acknowledge this fate and write off their losses, rather than let their politicians continue along this path, which is merely dragging them ever deeper into the trap.

Private banks could be recapitalized by way of debt-equity swaps, along the lines discussed in Chapter 8. In principle, the EU proposals are on the right track by advocating a bail-in of shareholders and creditors to protect taxpayers, and by establishing a pecking order for how to allocate the losses. However, the list of exemptions is long. That, together with the cap set for the bail-in of shareholders and creditors combined at just 8% of a bank's balance sheet, and the proposal of using the resolution fund and/or the ESM as a public backstop, comes perilously close to a ruse. It is much more a recipe for a bailout rather than bail-in. To really protect taxpayers, the bail-in percentage should be much higher, and the list of exceptions much shorter.

For one thing, exempting deposits of € 100,000 each seems far too lenient, given that this is the median household wealth in the Netherlands and twice the median household wealth in Germany, for example. If there is to be such an exemption, it should be financed by the respective state and its national deposit insurance, so as to avoid the moral hazard effects that would necessarily result from international mutualization of responsibilities. Unfortunately, such restraint is not discernible in the European solutions, as the plans published at this writing anticipate a socialized solution with a gradual transition period.

---

[40] J. Zettelmeyer, C. Trebesch and M. Gulati, 'The Greek Debt Restructuring: An Autopsy', *CESifo Working Paper* No. 4333, available at: <http://www.cesifo-group.de/DocDL/cesifo-wp4333.pdf>.

[41] See European Banking Authority, EU-wide Transparency Exercise 2013 Summary Report, available at: <http://stress-test.eba.europa.eu/documents/10180/526027/20131216_EU-wide+Transparency+Summary+Report.pdf >, p. 13, and EEAG, *The EEAG Report on the European Economy: The Road Towards Cohesion*, CESifo, Munich 2014, available at: <http://www.cesifo-group.de/DocDL/EEAG-2014.pdf>, chapter 4: *Banking Union: Who Should Take Charge?*, figure 4.1, p. 93.

Moreover, some of the states that might wish to provide such a guarantee are themselves close to bankruptcy and would need community funds to do so. Thus, the exemption of deposits of this order of magnitude is hardly possible. Setting up a deposit insurance scheme in which one country guarantees another's deposits up to its own median wealth, or more, seems wholly out of proportion.

For another, there is no excuse for exempting covered loans from the liability hierarchy. To the extent that they are covered, such loans are protected by the respective collateral. If the collateral fails, be it a government bond, a private security or any other kind of private asset, the holders of covered bonds should bear the losses rather than ask community funds to step in, as the EU proposal envisages. Exempting covered loans from bail-ins would blow away creditors' caution when lending to zombie banks, prompting them to content themselves with low yields, as even bad collateral will probably be enough to enjoy the backup protection. Circular trading of bonds among banks to generate the necessary collateral out of nothing would also be a possibility, as it would provide the banks' creditors with common protection and would enable the banks to borrow at low interest rates. Moral hazard and the misallocation of resources are pre-programmed with this strategy.

Excluding covered loans from the bail-in exemption would, of course, hurt the ECB. After all, a rationale behind the exemption for covered bonds may have been the attempt to protect the ECB from the consequences of its overly lax collateral policy (see Chapter 5). But there is no point in protecting the ECB with the ESM or other community instruments, since it would just mean repackaging the potential write-off losses from one public budget to another, with no benefit to taxpayers. To the contrary, it would be in the interest of Europe's voters and taxpayers to avoid this ploy and show openly in the NCBs' balance sheets which risks have arisen from the problematic collateral policies adopted by the ECB Governing Council. This would put a stop to the reckless lending strategy out of local printing presses, which in effect is little more than a regional fiscal policy riddled with negative allocative implications and doubtful democratic legitimation.

Along with writing off some of the ECB's credit claims on banks, debt relief should naturally also be given for unrecoverable Target claims on indebted NCBs, as the Target debt resulted from the NCBs' excessive lending of freshly created money. The unavoidable write-off losses will have to be booked in the NCBs' balance sheets by shifting the Target claims from near-insolvent countries to the still-sound euro countries in proportion to their ECB capital keys. This relief should come together with the move to harder budget constraints in the Eurozone, in particular the move to the gold standard for future Target settlement proposed above.

Despite the need to forgive some of the debt, the countries themselves could make a significantly greater effort to redeem their debt. One possibility would be the sale of state property. Greece, for example, has state-owned property (excluding real-estate holdings) worth 85% of GDP in 2010, and additional real-estate holdings worth an estimated 87% to 130% of Greek GDP.[42] The Greek government had promised the Troika (ECB, IMF, EU), in a memorandum of understanding dated 2 July 2011, that it would privatize state property worth € 50 billion.[43] Its efforts have been rather scanty, however. By the end of 2012 its privatization receipts were only € 1.6 billion.[44] As of this writing, the Greek Finance Ministry's privatization website is still empty. Recall in this context that Alexander Hamilton's debt mutualization of 1790 came in exchange for handing over western territories. It is not plausible to solve all of Greece's debt problems without the country itself making a contribution.

Further measures that could be considered include wealth levies or mandatory government bond purchases by property owners.[45] After all, there is substantial private wealth in the crisis-hit countries, as revealed by a survey conducted by the ECB (see Figure 2.12). Even when differences in household size are taken into account, Italians and Spaniards, for instance, are on average 14% wealthier than Germans, 40% wealthier than Finns and 42% wealthier than Dutchmen. The wealth of Italians was emphasized by then-Prime Minister Silvio Berlusconi long before the ECB published its statistics.[46] Other troubled countries score similarly. There is much to be said for taking part of this wealth to help repay some of the debt, particularly in those countries whose debt also resulted from the fact that governments substituted debt financing for tax financing because a substantial fraction of private activities were carried out on the black market. Incidentally, the relative size of the black economy is strongly correlated with the debt-to-GDP ratio.[47]

[42] See International Monetary Fund, *Greece: Second Review Under the Stand-By Arrangement*, December 2010, p. 52.

[43] See European Commission, *The Economic Adjustment Programme for Greece: Fourth Review*, Spring 2011, p. 94.

[44] See European Commission, *The Second Economic Adjustment Programme for Greece: Third Review*, July 2013, p. 26.

[45] A similar proposal has been made by W. F. Richter, 'Zwangsanleihen—Ein Beitrag zur Konsolidierung', *Handelsblatt*, 25 November 2011, available at: <http://www.wiso.tu-dortmund.de/wiso/of/Medienpool/veroeffentlichungen_richter/WR_Veoeffentlichungen_Stand_Oktober_09/Zwangsanleihen.pdf>.

[46] Organisation for Economic Co-operation and Development, *Economic Outlook* No. 91, 2012, Statistical Annex, table 58; see 'Berlusconi: "Non facciamoci del male" / E sulla crisi: "Noi, i più ricchi d'Europa"' ['We, the richest in Europe'], *La Repubblica*, 20 June 2010, available at: <http://www.repubblica.it/politica/2010/06/20/news/berlusconi-popolarita-4996320/>.

[47] A. Prinz and H. Beck, 'In the Shadow of Public Debt: Are there Relations between Public Debt and the Shadow Economy?', *Economic Analysis & Policy* 42, 2012, pp. 221–236.

The right mixture of debt relief, privatization, and wealth levies could be jointly negotiated in a Paris Club debt conference convened to reset the Eurozone. The European debt crisis has many causes, and creditors and debtors alike share the responsibility. A way to distribute the burden fairly should thus be sought—and it is important that it be found soon. Speed has at least two advantages. One is that confidence would be quickly restored and the period of uncertainty for investors that is currently paralyzing economic activity would come to an end. The other is that it would keep the cost to taxpayers in check. Currently Europe is in a phase of substituting public creditors of southern countries for private ones, as the number cited for the Greek public debt showed. The more time elapses, the larger the portion of the portfolio of GIPSIC assets owned by governmental institutions, and the larger therefore the haircut loss affecting the taxpayers and the general population, who actually bear the least responsibility for the mess, and the larger the risk that investors would like to repeat the game after the haircut. Investors must learn their lesson, and to this end, it is essential to let them bear the losses arising from their poor investment decisions. There is no ethical or economic case for having investors protected by European states—the latter have enough on their plate as it is.

A Breathing Currency Union: Between Bretton Woods and the Dollar

In addition to the debt problem, the competitiveness problem also urgently needs to be tackled. Both problems are related, but not identical. Some countries, such as Italy, have a considerable public debt problem, but since the government debt is largely held by Italians, this is not a foreign debt problem. Italy may not need more than a 10% real devaluation to attain a situation in which its foreign debt is sustainable and the economy is competitive (see Table 4.1). On the other hand, it is difficult to imagine that Greece, Portugal, and Spain would be out of the woods if their public debt problem were resolved. As discussed in Chapter 4, Greece needs to depreciate by 36% to reach the Turkish price level and Portugal needs a depreciation of 29%. In various scenarios by Goldman Sachs, Spain, Greece and Portugal would have to devalue by 20% to 30% to achieve debt sustainability. Manufacturing wages in Spain are more than three times, and in Greece more than twice, as high as in Poland (Figure 4.12). Portugal's wages are about 60% higher. These countries will not be able to achieve sufficient degrees of depreciation in the foreseeable future, not least because only a very moderate realignment of their relative prices has taken place during the crisis (see Figure 4.8).

The spectrum of economists who consider it impossible to try to achieve a real depreciation of the required magnitude through a wage and price squeeze ranges from Friedman to Keynes. As explained in Chapter 4, one problem is that the labour unions are trying to block this development, since a symmetrical wage and price cut cannot convincingly be orchestrated, given that millions of contracts would have to be changed simultaneously. Another problem is the potential distortion of the balance sheets of the country's borrowers and lenders that could push many borrowers into bankruptcy.

Compliance with 'austerity conditions' attached to fresh public credit, which initially brings about a political lull, should not be confused with a real depreciation, which is the only mechanism that can reinstate competitiveness. Even now the supposed austerity programmes, which are nothing more than a restriction on new net borrowing, are deemed unbearable, and yet they haven't managed to bring about any sizeable reductions in relative price levels, as Figure 4.8 shows. To be sure, if one insists on hard expenditure cuts by not giving further credit and calling due old debts, it would be possible to induce a deflation, but the social systems of the affected countries would probably break under the strain and plunge the countries into chaos. Germany's experience at the time of the Weimar Republic, when prices sank by 23% from 1929 to 1933, because the Treaty of Versailles and the Dawes Plan tied it to the gold standard, should be warning enough, as discussed in Chapter 4.

The alternative solution, contemplated by many, is inflation in the core. To some extent that is indeed necessary. However, the ECB's primary mandate of ensuring price stability rules out this possibility. In addition, it would be difficult to overcome Germany's deep-seated trauma stemming from the hyperinflation from 1914 to 1923, which led to impoverishment and radicalization of the middle class. Only a small amount of extra inflation will be possible in the core, but that will be far from sufficient to allow for the necessary realignment of relative prices in a foreseeable time.

Apart from that, the Japanese example, mentioned in Chapter 4, has shown that it may not be easy to generate inflation. When the Japanese property bubble burst in 1990, the country's banks ran into serious difficulties. In the early years they were able to hide the write-off losses, but as loans matured and were not serviced, around 1997, the truth came out. About 40% of the banks were in trouble and had to be rescued or taken over by the state. Since 1998, at least prima facie, monetary policy has been extremely loose, with short-term rates hovering most of the time between zero and 0.5%.[48] Extreme Keynesian debt policies increased the debt-to-GDP ratio from 67% of GDP in 1990 to 244% of GDP in 2013. And yet, GDP prices

---

[48] It has been argued though that the policy was not as loose as it seemed, as the low interest rate was not accompanied by a large growth in monetary aggregates. See M. Friedman, 'Reviving Japan', *Hoover Digest* 2, 30 April 1998, available at: <http://www.hoover.org/publications/hoover-digest/article/6549>; A. H. Meltzer, 'Time for Japan to Print Money', *American Enterprise Institute Online*, 17 July 1998, available at: <http://www.aei.org/issue/foreign-and-defense-policy/regional/asia/time-for-

have fallen since 1998. The Japanese GDP deflator now stands at the same level as 1980. So even if the ECB wanted to trigger inflation, it is entirely unclear that it would ever succeed in doing so. A deflating economy has an unlimited appetite for liquidity, and it may prove impossible to get it going again by pumping even more money into it. The Japanese example proves that economists' age-old fear of deflation might be justified.[49]

So, the only options remaining are permanent transfers—or exits.[50] The perils of permanent transfers, which range from the Dutch Disease to the contagion effects upon other countries that want the same treatment, have already been mentioned in this book. The transfers make countries addicted, the wrong price vectors are cemented, and the countries never become competitive. The negative experiences with German reunification and the Italian Mezzogiorno, which despite huge, continuous transfers have not yet managed to develop competitive and self-sustaining economies, should serve as a warning.[51]

The catastrophic developments in the southern European labour markets depicted in Chapter 1 also show that such a strategy is a dead end. As was shown in Tables 8.1 and 9.2, Greece had received public credit of around € 288 billion, or 157% of 2013 GDP, by December 2013. Had Greek prices not increased faster than the Eurozone average since the Madrid Summit of 1995, that ratio would be 198% of GDP, given Greece's actual real 2013 GDP level. In relative terms, that sum is about forty times as large as the help the Marshall Plan provided to Germany after the war which, aggregated over the years, amounted to a credit equal to 5.2% of Germany's GDP for 1952.[52] In addition, Greece has benefited

japan-to-print-money/>; D. Laidler, 'Monetary Policy after Bubbles Burst: The Zero Lower Bound, the Liquidity Trap and the Credit Deadlock', *Canadian Public Policy* 30 (3), September 2004, pp. 333–340.

[49] See A. Hansen, *Full Recovery or Stagnation*, Norton, New York 1938. A. C. Pigou, *Employment and Equilibrium: A Theoretical Discussion*, Macmillan, London 1941. D. Patinkin, *Money, Interest, and Prices: An Integration of Monetary and Value Theory*, University of Chicago Press, Chicago 1956.

[50] Se also A. Hughes-Hallett and J. C. Martínez Oliva, 'The Importance of Trade and Capital Imbalances in the European Debt Crisis', *Peterson Institute for International Economics Working Paper* No. 13-01, January 2013.

[51] H.-W. Sinn and F. Westermann, 'Due "Mezzogiorni"', *L'industria* 27, 2006, pp. 49–51, and H.-W. Sinn and G. Sinn, *Jumpstart. The Economic Unification of Germany*, MIT Press: Cambridge, Mass., and London, England 1992.

[52] H. Berger and A. Ritschl, 'Die Rekonstruktion der Arbeitsteilung in Europa. Eine neue Sicht des Marshall-Plans in Deutschland 1947–1951', *Vierteljahreshefte für Zeitgeschichte* 43, 1995, pp. 473–519, table p. 479. Germany, in turn, was granted debt relief in the London Debt Agreement of 1953 of 30 billion deutschmarks (including forgiving the Marshall Plan credit), which was 22% of West German GDP for 1952. See

from an open haircut on public debt at the expense of private *foreign* investors of around € 65 billion, or 36% of its 2013 GDP (€ 105 billion including domestic investors). The implicit haircut represented by interest relief at the expense of other states, furthermore, benefited Greece to the tune of € 43 billion, or 24% of its 2013 GDP. A further € 32 billion in rescue credit, equivalent to 18% of Greece's 2013 GDP, has already been earmarked for the country and will be disbursed if Athens satisfies the Troika conditions. All of this has merely kept the patient alive, but has obviously not been able to cure it. Greek unemployment rates in 2013 were more than twice as high as those prevailing in May 2010, when the official rescue operations for Greece began. It is time to reconsider the therapy.

The only option that offers a faster way to regain competitiveness without riots and strife is an exit followed by devaluation of the new currency. On the basis of data made available by Reinhart and Rogoff, the Ifo Institute arrived at the conclusion, after studying 71 currency crises, that the current account balance of the countries that devalued their currency improved quite markedly within one or two years of devaluation, with their GDP rallying as well.[53] By the third year, their export growth already typically lay about two percentage points above the trend.

Three case studies conducted by the Ifo Institute, addressing the Argentine devaluation of 2002, its Thai counterpart of 1997, and the Italian devaluation of 1992, show the quick economic recovery that followed devaluation. In Argentina, the economy perked up as early as two quarters after devaluation, and in Thailand the upturn came six quarters later. Even Italy, where the devaluation process covered a longer period, quickly returned to growth. Indeed, all three countries had current account surpluses one year after starting their depreciation.

No member country, however, should be pressed into exiting the monetary union. The decision must be adopted by the corresponding governments and parliaments. Conversely, it cannot be accepted that countries that do not dare an exit, or that rule it out altogether, can assume as a matter of course that they will continue to be financed by other countries. Membership in the Eurozone

---

C. Buchheim, 'Das Londoner Schuldenabkommen', in L. Herbst (ed), *Westdeutschland 1945–1955. Unterwerfung, Kontrolle, Integration*, Oldenbourg, Munich 1986, pp. 219–229.

[53] B. Born, T. Buchen, K. Carstensen, C. Grimme, M. Kleemann, K. Wohlrabe, and T. Wollmershäuser, *Austritt Griechenlands aus der Europäischen Währungsunion: historische Erfahrungen, makroökonomische Konsequenzen und organisatorische Umsetzung*, Ifo Institute, Munich 2012; C. Reinhart, 'This Time is Different Chartbook: Country Histories on Debt, Default, and Financial Crises', *NBER Working Paper* No. 15815, 2010; and C. Reinhart and K. S. Rogoff, *This Time is Different: Eight Centuries of Financial Folly*, Princeton University Press, Princeton 2009.

does not include the right to be propped up with transfers from abroad when a country loses its competitiveness. The legal conditions for membership were laid out very clearly by the Maastricht Treaty.

Letting distressed countries remain members of the Eurozone on permanent life support does not really help them. While it protects the rich, who own government bonds and other assets, against wealth losses, and helps the government to finance its expenditure, the ordinary population gains very little from this strategy. The jobless young, in particular, stand to suffer from such a policy. If young people cannot enter the labour force and learn a trade, this will have strong negative implications for their entire life. One generation of Greeks and Spaniards may be lost by the countries' desperate attempt to stay in the Eurozone.

In view of the catastrophic situation that the euro has brought about in some countries and which drags on despite support from the community of nations, the question arises as to how much longer the respective populations of the countries affected can bear to follow this course. How long will the populations of Spain and Greece be willing to accept the bitter reality that one in two youths not in education is unemployed—one more year, two or three? Nobody knows. Tough political decisions must be made. Ultimately, no parliament will be able to avoid having to choose between radical social reforms that include wage cuts and an exit from the Eurozone.

If a country does decide to exit, the community of nations should make every attempt to ensure that this is an orderly process. It should support the process by helping to lessen the social burdens resulting from the recapitalization of banks, using debt-equity swaps. Moreover, an emergency programme with community funds should be instituted to secure basic services and energy provision to compensate for the expected increase in import prices.

Most of all, the stigma of a permanent separation should be removed. This can be accomplished by setting up a breathing currency union that recognizes the status of an associated member possessing a return option.[54] The associated member would have the advantage that it could adjust its exchange rate quickly to restore competitiveness, without having to fight for years with the unions and

---

[54] These passages are based on H.-W. Sinn, 'Die offene Währungsunion', *Wirtschaftswoche*, No. 29, 16 July 2012, p. 39, available at: <http://www.ifo.de/de/ Sinn_WiWo_2012/w/4FAADYipx>; H.-W. Sinn and F. L. Sell, 'Der neue Euro-Club', *Süddeutsche Zeitung*, No. 169, 24 July 2012, p. 19, available at: <http://www.ifo.de/de/ Sinn_Sell_SZ_2012/w/3qGgteRuJ>; and H.-W. Sinn and F. L. Sell, 'Our Opt-in Opt-out Solution for the Euro', *Financial Times*, 31 July 2012, available at: <http://www.ft.com/ intl/cms/s/o/b2c75538-da35-11e1-b03b-00144feab49a.html#axzz25VFx ZZXs>. A similar proposal was made in 2010 by Martin Feldstein. See M. Feldstein, 'Let Greece Take a Eurozone "Holiday"', *Financial Times*, 16 February 2010, available at: <http://www. ft.com/intl/cms/s/o/72214942-1b30-11df-953f-00144feab49a.html#axzz25VFxZZXs>.

other interest groups, sparing itself the attendant economic malaise and massive unemployment that could bring the entire country to the brink of collapse.

An existing arrangement, the longstanding European Exchange Rate Mechanism II, could provide the basis for such a currency 'association'. ERM II is the successor to ERM I, to which all EU currencies, with the exception of those of the new members from eastern Europe, formally belonged from 1979 to late 1998. It was replaced by ERM II on 1 January 1999, with the introduction of the euro. Conceived for EU member states that have not yet introduced the euro, ERM II at present includes Denmark and Lithuania. All countries that have adopted the euro since 2000 have done so on condition of spending a two-year period within ERM II without stress, staying within a range of ±15% with respect to a central rate against the euro. This mechanism could be expanded to allow it to also harbour, after a transition period, countries that left the Eurozone and plan to re-enter.

With such rules the Eurozone could become a breathing, open currency union, something between a currency union of the Bretton Woods type and a firm conglomerate like the US dollar zone. While the latter might in the end be desirable, as will be discussed in the last section of this book, the political will to form a federal state with a power centre that could enforce the rules needed to avoid the moral hazard problems associated with a common currency does not yet exist. Given this limitation, Europe needs a currency union that is more flexible than the dollar, allowing the necessary realignment of relative prices through exchange rate adjustments, and at the same time more rigid than a system of separate currencies with fixed exchange rates.

Exits from the euro would, of course, be a source of market irritation and turmoil. Every economist can spell out the contagion effects this might create. But the turmoil would be the result of the chaos created precisely by the fact that no orderly exit path has been defined; wild speculation about what might happen would trigger capital flight.

In practical terms, this is how an orderly exit could take place. The new currency would have to be prepared in secret and introduced as the new legal tender over a weekend, when the banks are closed. All deposits and all contracts between domestic partners denominated in euros, including wage contracts, loans, rental contracts, pensions, and even price lists, would be converted immediately, keeping the numerical values, into the new currency.

Naturally, the new currency will quickly come under devaluation pressure. The forecasts point to a devaluation for Greece of about a half to two-thirds.[55] But the exchange rate will eventually find its equilibrium. Once stable, the

---

[55] Citi Research, *Global Economic Outlook and Strategy*, 25 July 2012, p. 7, available at: <https://groups.google.com/forum/#!topic/brokeragesreport/WJWC3Wprr48>; M. Voss, 'Citigroup erwartet Griechenlands Euro-Austritt zum 1. Januar 2013', *Focus*,

country can formally join the ERM II. The exchange rate may oscillate thereafter, but only within the specified range. Since the ECB is obliged under the ERM II to help through interventions, the country will be able to fulfil this requirement. In addition, it must meet the other normal requirements for readmission to the monetary union, in particular the posting of sufficiently small deviations in yields and inflation compared to the Eurozone average, as well as meeting all indebtedness criteria.

Furthermore, it would be advisable to agree to a reform agenda with the country in question that would have to be fulfilled before a re-entry is possible. Nothing will convince the country's political forces of the necessity of reform more than the hope of their making possible a return to the euro.

There will, of course, be a host of technical problems. If the planned exit is leaked ahead of time, there will be bank runs, since depositors will try to withdraw all their money in order not to be affected by the currency conversion. In such a case, the conversion must proceed immediately and, if necessary, capital controls and a limitation of withdrawals from bank accounts have to be introduced, just as they were in 2013 in Cyprus. However, capital controls would not be necessary for long, for as soon as the conversion has taken place and the currency has depreciated, there would be no point in leaving the country, as the investors' wealth loss would have already occurred and could not be avoided by leaving. On the contrary, if the currency depreciation were to overshoot initially, as many believe it would, it would be attractive to bring funds whisked abroad back home to buy cheap domestic assets. If Cyprus exited the euro today, it could remove all of its capital controls tomorrow.

Fortunately, nowadays many if not most payments can be carried out electronically. Thus, the conversion of bank accounts, which can be carried out overnight, would achieve a fair amount of the necessary task. Nevertheless, bank notes are still of great importance to everyday life in most economies, especially in southern Europe. Their conversion is the most difficult part of the exit. Basically, there are three options for such a conversion:

The first option would be for the central bank to try to collect all the euro banknotes and exchange them for the new currency. But since the euro would continue to operate in the rest of the Eurozone, this option would necessitate permanent currency management, border controls, and a great deal of bureaucracy, since everyone would try to hoard euros and bring them out of the country. These problems mean that this option is not feasible.

26 July 2012, available at: <http://www.focus.de/finanzen/news/staatsverschuldung/90-prozent-wahrscheinlichkeit-fuer-grexit-citigroup-erwartet-griechen-austritt-am-1-januar-2013_aid_787927.html>; and D. Eckert, 'Was passiert, wenn die Troika den Stecker zieht', *Die Welt*, 27 July 2012, available at: <http://www.welt.de/finanzen/article108401579/Was-passiert-wenn-die-Troika-den-Stecker-zieht.html>.

The second option would be that all euro banknotes in the entire Eurozone, except for those of the exiting country, could be exchanged for new banknotes over a limited period. (Technically, old bank notes could be reused by being stamped accordingly.) Currency controls would only need to be in place by the end of the exchange period.

The third option would be to allow the euro as a parallel currency in the exiting country, in a similar fashion as is currently the case in eastern Europe or Turkey.[56] This would simplify the transition problem enormously. The new currency would be the only legal tender. All prices, wages, and debt contracts would be denominated in it, and it would be used for all electronic payment orders. However, cash transactions could still be conducted in euros, applying the new exchange rate. In this way, even if it proves infeasible to print all the necessary new-currency banknotes on time, cash transactions would still be possible.

One of the advantages of this solution would be that there would be no point in hoarding euros or even trying to bring them out of the country. Thus, no border controls and no capital controls like in Cyprus would be necessary. The danger of capital flight exists only before the conversion, but since this conversion is only virtual and does not affect the banknotes, it can be carried out over a weekend.

The new domestic banknotes, once printed, would in time crowd out most of the circulating euro banknotes, which would be used for purchases outside the new-currency country. The euros thus spent in the rest of the Eurozone would, in turn, crowd out the euros created there through refinancing credit and asset purchases. The economic effects would be very similar to those observed in the northern euro countries resulting from the extra refinancing credit that leads to net payment orders and Target debt, as discussed in Chapter 6. Thus, it would be appropriate to add the banknotes remaining in circulation after a currency conversion to a country's Target debt.

---

[56] There are numerous other proposals for parallel currencies. For example, the proposal to allow payment of all invoices in both the old and the new currency: B. Lucke and M. J. M. Neumann, 'Drachme als zweite Landeswährung einführen', *Handelsblatt*, 21 May 2012, available at: <http://www.handelsblatt.com/meinung/gastbeitraege/gastbeitrag-drachme-als-zweite-landeswaehrung-einfuehren/6656530.html>; and T. Mayer, 'Der Geuro', *DB Research*, 23 May 2012, available at: <http://www.dbresearch.de/PROD/DBR_INTERNET_DE-PROD/PROD0000000000288868.pdf>. Another example is the Matheo solution, according to which all Eurozone countries have a currency parallel to the euro in which domestic debt contracts and prices are denominated. See A. ten Dam, '"The Matheo Solution (TMS)" kann den Euro retten', *ifo Schnelldienst* 64, No. 23, 9 December 2011, pp. 22–25, available at: <http://www.cesifo-group.de/DocDL/ifosd_2011_23_2.pdf>.

Let us consider the case of a Greek exit. In December 2013, the Greek Target debt amounted to € 50.0 billion, while its monetary base was € 37.9 billion. The latter included € 25.4 billion in statutory banknotes and € 10.8 billion in over-proportionate banknote issuance, as measured by Greece's intra-Eurosystem liability. If Greece were to exit, with statutory banknotes being exchanged into drachma, assuming that the rest had already diffused to other countries, the Greek central bank would have a € 60.8 billion liability vis-à-vis the Eurozone (= € 50.0 billion + € 10.8 billion). If, on the other hand, Greece were to keep the statutory euro banknotes, which could be used for purchases in the rest of the Eurozone after the printing of drachmas, the Greek central bank's liability would increase by an additional € 25.4 billion. While this sum is not peanuts, it is small relative to the Target and intra-Eurosystem liabilities it has already incurred, and even smaller relative to all the funds lent to Greece so far, including the intergovernmental, IMF and EU funds which, as summarized in Table 8.1, amount to € 288 billion. If Greece defaults on its debt, the question of whether or not it also defaults on its statutory banknote liability is obviously of secondary importance.

A major issue is its foreign debt, since it is denominated in euros, but that is not something particular to an exit and an open depreciation. As discussed in Chapter 4, in terms of foreign debt there is no difference between an internal depreciation through price and wage cuts and an external depreciation after introducing a new currency. The increase in the debt-to-GDP ratio would be the same in either case. And it bears emphasizing once again: as difficult as the debt situation might appear after such a depreciation, it is the only possible way for the debtor country to develop a structural current account surplus and to pay back at least some of its debt. The road back to repaying foreign debt is always via a depreciation and, therefore, always via an initial rise in the debt ratio.

A plausible way to handle the debt of the exiting country would be to apply the *lex monetae,* according to which the country has the right to convert its foreign debt into domestic currency. While this is more difficult for Greece today than it was before, given that the haircut of 2012 implied a restructuring of Greek debt under English law, the new EU rules to be specified for this case would probably govern these agreements.

There is some concern regarding a surge of inflation after a devaluation that could wipe out the devaluation effect almost immediately. Some economists have argued that a depreciation for that reason is no help for the exiting country.[57] This

---

[57] See B. Eichengreen, 'The Euro: Love it or Leave it?', *VoxEU*, 4 May 2010, available at: <http://www.voxeu.org/article/eurozone-breakup-would-trigger-mother-all-financial-crises>; M. Jacobides, 'Greece could become "the North Korea of Europe"', *London Business School News*, 16 May 2012, available at: <http://www.london.edu/news-andevents/news/2012/05/Greece_could_become_%E2%80%9Cthe_North_Korea_of_Europe%E2%80%9D_1432.html>.

concern would be justified if the depreciation occurred in an initial situation of competitive goods prices, but such is not the case with the Eurozone's distressed countries. These countries, through the inflationary credit bubble brought about by the euro, actually became too expensive, and are now stuck in the Eurozone with downward-rigid prices that are far above the equilibrium prices. Since an open depreciation removes a locking bolt that prevents prices in euro terms from falling to their equilibrium values, a bouncing back of the drachma prices nullifying this effect is not to be feared. Open depreciation would lead to inflation only if this depreciation went too far, pushing prices below their equilibrium level. However, if there were to be some inflation of drachma prices correcting this, there still would be a depreciation in net terms, helping the exiting country's economy.

Once depreciation and the necessary reforms had been conducted, a return from the ERM II to full euro membership would be relatively easy, because the banknote-exchange problem would not occur in the same form. After all, nobody would want to hide the national currency if it could not be used anywhere else; instead, those holding national notes would head for the bank to exchange them for euros. New euros sufficient for serving domestic liquidity needs could therefore be given to the country without incurring a liability to the Eurosystem.

The possibility of conducting an open devaluation is of crucial importance to the functioning of the Eurozone. On the one hand, the Eurosystem needs firepower in order to tackle balance-of-payments problems with fresh liquidity from the printing press. On the other hand, however, it needs hard budget constraints and interest spreads commensurate with each member country's creditworthiness in order to prevent excessive public and private borrowing and the emergence of economic bubbles. Both objectives evidently cannot be mutually reconciled within the Eurozone, as presently structured.

The ECB has denied the dilemma to date by pursuing a corner solution. It has disregarded the perverse incentives to the real economy and has merely tried to calm the markets by granting the countries experiencing balance-of-payments problems credit at ever lower rates of interest and with ever lower-quality collateral using the printing press, a policy which has subsequently led to numerous other fiscal and quasi-fiscal rescue operations. The anticipation of this policy by market investors triggered excessive borrowing in both the private and the public sectors in the first place, which, in turn, led to a loss of competitiveness among a significant number of member countries, turning them into a bottomless pit·for the still-solid economies in the currency union.

Pursuing such a one-dimensional policy goal has been a serious policy error, because in the presence of rival objectives, but lacking separate policy instruments, a middle way would have been more sensible. This error can only be corrected if limits are set to financial support and if the possibility of self-help is opened through a temporary exit accompanied by devaluation. For this reason, it would be useful if the Eurozone became a more open currency union with an ordered procedure for temporary exits and subsequent readmission. This is the only way for the troubled countries to restore their economies to good health, and arguably the best way for the Eurozone as a whole to overcome its balance-of-payments crisis.

In addition to the economic advantages, there would be political advantages as well. No member country would be expelled or have to feel that its chances were slipping away for good. If the exit option were portrayed as a practical policy measure, rather than the end of the world, it could be managed and implemented in such a way so as to be advantageous for almost everyone concerned, with the possible exception of some financial investors. It would strengthen both cohesion in Europe and the peaceful coexistence of its peoples.

A building that can only be entered but not exited is a trap. The euro has turned out to be such a trap for southern European countries. They were lured in by low interest rates, enjoyed some growth, and then experienced the inflationary credit bubbles that deprived them of their competitiveness; now they are having great difficulties in bringing about the necessary real depreciation. A breathing currency union would open an escape route, providing a space where the dwellers live in peace with each other.

The Path towards Unity[58]

The motto of the United States of America is *'E pluribus unum'*: *'Out of many, one'*. Europe's motto is *'In varietate Concordia'*: *'Harmony in diversity'*, which is officially translated as *'United in diversity'*. It is hard to express the differences between the US and the European model any more clearly than this. The USA is a melting pot. Uncountable ethnic groups fused into a homogeneous American composite. Immigrants arrive and leave their nationality at the border, and metamorphose into a quintessential American. Europe, on the other hand, is a mosaic of different peoples and cultures that have developed over the course of its long, turbulent history, who strive for good neighbourly relations and share common traditions that range from science to religion. People tend to stay where they grew up, speak their own language, and cling to their birth place.

These differences raise the question of whether a United States of Europe is worth striving for. Many refuse to accept this concept because they do not believe in the possibility of a unified European identity. A single political system like the

---

[58] This text contains passages, with the authorization of the publisher, from: H.-W. Sinn, 'Die europäische Fiskalunion', *Perspektiven der Wirtschaftspolitik* 13, 2012, pp. 137–178.

USA's presupposes a common language and a single nationality. Europe, for that reason, could not be anything but a confederation for the foreseeable future.[59]

That view may be too pessimistic, though. After all, in the heart of Europe, the Swiss Confederation proves that different languages and cultures can live alongside peacefully and prosperously in a common nation.[60] Switzerland grew from a defence union into a decentralized state with strong cantons and limited fiscal power allocated to the centre, and of course it also has a common currency. Like the US, Switzerland is based on the no-bailout principle and has little redistribution between the regions. Up to this day, a common foreign policy and a common army are the central pillars of the Confederation.

The achievement of the EU itself should not be downplayed. It has allowed Europe to overcome its horrible past and has generated a long period of peace and prosperity that few people after the war would have dared dream of. The Common Market has brought about a better division of labour, with gains from trade for everyone. Small countries in particular have profited, as the market integration helped to overcome the disadvantages of smallness and allowed them to participate in the economies of large scale formerly reserved for the bigger countries. The common political system helped to establish the rule of law everywhere and brought many practical advantages for everyone despite the cultural diversity. These advantages include the right to move freely across borders, the free movement of goods and services, legal certainty for cross-border economic activities, an infrastructure that does not end at national borders, and, last but not least, common security interests. These advantages have attained such an overwhelming importance in the lives of many Europeans that there is no reason to call European integration as such into question. Incidentally, a good deal of European identity has emerged in the EU, coupled with respect for mutual cultural achievements, that should not be overlooked.

To be sure, the subsidiarity principle enshrined in the Maastricht Treaty[61] states that the economic decisions should be left to the lowest possible level,

---

[59] J. Limbach, 'Es gibt keine europäische Identität', *Frankfurter Allgemeine Zeitung*, 26 August 2012, available at: <http://www.faz.net/aktuell/feuilleton/debatten/europas-zukunft/jutta-limbach-ueber-europas-zukunft-es-gibt-keine-europaeische-identitaet-11868798.html>; R. Herzog, 'Die dürfen nur nicken', Interview by T. Hildebrandt and H. Wefing, *Die Zeit*, 25 September 2011, available at: <http://www.zeit.de/2011/39/Interview-Herzog/seite-2>; and R. Brüderle, 'BRÜDERLE-Interview für die Rheinische Post', Interview by M. Bröcker, *Rheinische Post*, 4 July 2012, available at: <http://www.liberale.de/content/bruederle-interview-fuer-die-rheinische-post-7>.

[60] EEAG, *The EEAG Report on the European Economy: The Road Towards Cohesion*, Munich 2014, chapter 2: *Switzerland: Relic of the Past, Model for the Future?*.

[61] See EU, 'Treaty on the Functioning of the European Union (TFEU)', 9 May 2008, article 5.

ideally even to the individual level. Only in justifiable cases may decisions be elevated to a collective level, but even then to the lowest possible level in that category. If the individual is not to decide, then the family; if not the family, the community; if not the community, the state or province; then the country; and at the very end, the European institutions. Only close to the grassroots is the knowledge available that is needed for a proper solution, and only when the decisions are made at that level is the individual right to freedom guaranteed.

However, there are many justifiable exceptions that call for collective action. Along with the provision of infrastructure, defence, and basic economic freedom, there is the regulation of economic activities—after all, there is not much reason to hope that the competition among regulatory systems will select the best. More likely, the laxest will prevail.

The field of banking regulation is the most topical example. It was addressed in Chapter 8 in the section on banking union. If the rules and restrictions that banks must abide by are set at a national level, but banking risks are partially pooled by sharing the profits and losses from refinancing credit and asset purchases in the Eurosystem, the national regulatory bodies and the NCBs will always have an incentive to establish loose standards and provide generous credit, thus inducing excessive risk-taking, because the potential benefits accrue at home, while some of the potential losses fall on other jurisdictions. Regulatory competition degenerates into a competition in laxity. There are many similar examples from the fields of norms, taxation or income redistribution policies that have been examined in the fiscal federalism literature.[62] Therefore, many fundamental considerations speak for a deepening of the European integration process all the way to the establishment of a European confederation like Switzerland.

The perils of such a path always lie in the fact that collective decision bodies not only provide collective services that are useful for everyone, but can also abuse their power to redistribute resources between the participating countries. Democratic decision-making bodies are not immune. On the contrary, they make it possible for minorities to be exploited by the majority. In order to tackle this problem, special rules are needed to protect the minorities, such as a requirement for qualified majority or unanimity in decision-making. The fiscal decisions of the ECB Council discussed in this book represent a particularly dramatic example of this problem, because they are adopted by simple majority—and in the case of ELA credit fewer—by a body that is not democratically structured. This has led to a massive redistribution among the countries of Europe and from non-involved taxpayers in the still-stable economies to creditors around the world.

---

[62] See H.-W. Sinn, *The New Systems Competition,* Yrjö Jahnsson Lectures, Basil Blackwell, Oxford 2003.

Redistribution can be understood as providing a collective benefit to all countries if it takes the form of protective insurance. After all, at its core every type of insurance is a redistribution system that transfers the resources of those who have been lucky so far to those suffering damages. But for this interpretation to hold, it is mandatory that the corresponding decision be adopted behind the veil of ignorance, i.e. *before* catastrophe strikes and *before* it is known who was lucky and who wasn't.

This is definitely not the case with the current redistribution decisions in the Eurozone, since they are being adopted after the damages have become apparent. In addition, such an insurance scheme was explicitly ruled out from the outset, in the Maastricht Treaty negotiations, by the no-bailout clause (article 125 of the TFEU).[63]

The Eurozone's course towards joint liability—which follows on from the ECB's prior decisions to extend generous refinancing credit to banks by dramatically reducing collateral standards and by deciding to buy government bonds through its SMP and OMT programmes—does not lead to the establishment of a federal state in the real sense of the word, i.e. to a union of equals who by their own will, decide to come together and provide mutual assistance. Instead it leads, if anywhere at all, to a unitary state that will come into being through a disregard of the wishes of the population and through the actions forced upon them by a technocratic body that acts wholly independently and that pre-determines parliaments' subsequent decisions.

This path cannot lead to the establishment of a United States of Europe because a large proportion of Europe's people do not agree to it. Both in the northwest and the east the largest countries do not want this, and it can be safely assumed that they will never voluntarily agree to the joint-liability union now in the making. In Denmark, the enthusiasm for joining has cooled just as much as it has in Poland, while in the Czech Republic and Sweden the dismissive attitude towards the Eurosystem has become even stronger. The assertion that the Eurosystem can lead to the establishment of the United States of Europe is unconvincing. The road towards a joint-liability union is more likely to lead to deep divisions in Europe.

That is the problem with the mutualization initiatives of the European institutions during this crisis. Insurance is demanded without having previously entered into an insurance contract, because, in denial of the Maastricht Treaty, it is assumed that the Eurosystem implicitly represents such a contract. In order to justify the sweeping collectivization measures that are currently being called for, a unitary political state would have had to have been established, one whose

---

[63] See EU, 'Treaty on the Functioning of the European Union (TFEU)', 9 May 2008, article 125.

cohesive power goes even beyond that of the United States or Switzerland, since these countries rule out the mutualization of state debts.[64]

Whoever cites Hamilton, and calls for Europe's still-solid economies to assume the debts of the crisis-hit countries, must perforce establish a European federal state with the full consent of its citizens first. At the very least, those footing the bill today must be able to assume that their children and grandchildren will be able to count on similar protection from the other member countries in a hundred years, when they themselves may be in need of support. Only a unitary state can credibly justify and guarantee such long-term commitments, ensuring that today's net recipients of help will not renege on granting their reciprocal support in future, when the need arises. The constitution of this state is the insurance contract.[65]

A federal state needs a common legal system, a common army to protect it from external threats, and a central power that ensures that the rules and obligations of the insurance contract are met. It needs a common government, a parliament built on the one-man-one-vote principle, and a second chamber representing the individual states. Fiscal equalization and interpersonal transfer systems can only be established once these conditions have been satisfied, because only then can they be perceived as mutual insurance. The greater the redistribution tasks, the higher the system's centrifugal forces and the stronger the central power needed to hold everything together. Learning from US and Swiss experience, debt mutualization should never be part of such a system.

There is absolutely no willingness to create such a federal state in Europe today. The common legal system and army, which are the first and foremost perquisites of such a state, will not be forthcoming as long as Europe is not threatened by external enemies who force it to unite. The French state would not agree to communitarizing its *Force de Frappe*. For the foreseeable future, the EU will remain an alliance of states devoid of a strong central power.

---

[64] Compared to other integrated economic areas, the Eurozone was designed as a confederation with little collective risk sharing and almost no delegation of sovereignty. Through the rescue measures it moved in the direction of collective risk sharing without increasing the delegation of sovereignty, leaving the path of stable degrees of integration because of the missing implementation of strong fiscal contracts and rules, as described in H. Berger, 'Die Logik der Währungsunion', in K. Konrad, R. Schön, M. Thum, and A. Weichenrieder (eds), *Die Zukunft der Wohlfahrtsgesellschaft—Festschrift für Hans-Werner Sinn*, Campus, Frankfurt 2013, pp. 57–76.

[65] An early proposal for such a constitution was made by A. Spinelli and E. Rossi, *The Ventotene Manifesto. For a Free and United Europe,* Milan 1943. For a more recent, explicit and restrictive draft of such a constitution, based on the EU's current decision-making structures, see European Constitutional Group, *A Proposal for a Revised Constitutional Treaty*, April 2006, available at: <http://www.freiheit.org/files/600/A_Proposal_for_a_Revised_Constitutional_Treaty_10.04.06.pdf>.

The EU has remained stable without a central power to date because no significant redistribution between the states has taken place. The entire EU budget amounts to just 1% of GDP, which was perceived as advantageous all round, making everyone happy to go along with it. This seems to have been forgotten by many of those who advocate a transfer union without first founding a national state.

Those who advocate redistribution through the introduction of a fiscal union should be warned by the fate of the Soviet Union. The Soviet Union needed force to ensure cohesion despite the redistribution, but, as history has shown, this force contained the seeds of its own destruction. The Soviet Union was no fair mutual insurance system, whereby each state could bank on enjoying transfers from other states at some point.[66]

The USA and Switzerland, and not the Soviet Union, should be regarded as models for Europe. The USA has spent over 200 years developing its present system, Switzerland over 500. After their difficult initial years, they have evolved into fair, functional systems that largely respect fundamental freedoms, dispense with a debt union, and therefore function without an excessively strict central authority.

Whoever wishes to develop the Eurozone into a transfer and debt union that is even in a position to prevent state insolvencies should know that this will require much more central power than is available in the USA or Switzerland. Under such a system there would not be much room for freedom and the free will of the federal states. In the USA and Switzerland, the central governments cannot effectively limit the budgets of individual states or cantons. Instead, the regional bodies are left to settle up with their creditors alone if they have overcommitted themselves, and are ultimately left to declare insolvency. As paradoxical as this may sound, the risk of insolvency in fact is the stabilizing principle that holds everything together, because it invokes sufficient debt discipline to avoid insolvency in the first place, or to keep the debt small enough to make it manageable should an insolvency nevertheless occur. If regional entities borrow too much, investors will ask for higher interest rates, putting a brake on further borrowing and avoiding the kind of inflationary credit bubble that wrecked the southern European and Irish economies. Without such a self-correcting mechanism to prevent excessive capital flows, the currency union will never be able to stabilize itself. Political agreements among independent states will not be able to exert a similar kind of discipline as markets are able to enforce. It is utopian to believe that opportunistic, abusive behaviour in a debt union can be avoided by establishing a mere fiscal union.

---

[66] See also F. Heisbourg, 'EU arbeitet hart daran zu verschwinden', Interview, *Der Standard*, 17 April 2012.

Those wishing to start the formation of a European central state with a transfer and debt union that is only limited by a fiscal compact are playing a dangerous game. This path conjures up the threat of major conflicts and brings peril, which is anything but a contribution to peaceful co-existence. It turns friendly neighbour nations into debtors and creditors. The conflict between debtors and creditors, which heretofore has always been solved in Europe at the private level using legal means, would be elevated to the level of states. This path does not lead to the wished-for United States of Europe, but to chaos, and brings enduring discredit to the European ideal. It would jeopardize the cooperation and integration achieved so far in Europe. The better Europeans are not the romantics, but those who seek realistic solutions that accord with the free will of the people, the laws of economics, and the free decisions of parliaments, without the latter being predetermined by technocratic bodies overstretching their mandate, and solutions that can be applied without a forced redistribution of wealth.

During its first few decades, the USA committed a number of dangerous errors that Europe would do well to avoid. Anybody who wants a United States of Europe should seek to replicate the economic principles of the United States of America as they are today, and not to repeat the errors of the past. Europeans should waste no time in setting off along this path.

NAME INDEX

SUBJECT INDEX

AUTHOR AND EDITOR INDEX